£29.95

STRATEGIC
RENAISSANCE
AND BUSINESS
TRANSFORMATION

THE STRATEGIC MANAGEMENT SERIES

Series Editor
HOWARD THOMAS

STRATEGIC THINKING
Leadership and the Management of Change
Edited by
JOHN HENDRY AND GERRY JOHNSON
WITH JULIA NEWTON

COMPETENCE BASED COMPETITION
Edited by
GARY HAMEL AND AIMÉ HEENE

BUILDING THE STRATEGICALLY-RESPONSIVE ORGANIZATION
Edited by
HOWARD THOMAS, DON O'NEAL, ROD WHITE AND DAVID HURST

STRATEGIC RENAISSANCE AND BUSINESS TRANSFORMATION
Edited by
HOWARD THOMAS, DON O'NEAL AND JAMES KELLY

Further titles in preparation

THE STRATEGIC MANAGEMENT SERIES

STRATEGIC RENAISSANCE AND BUSINESS TRANSFORMATION

Edited by

HOWARD THOMAS, DON O'NEAL AND JAMES KELLY

JOHN WILEY & SONS

Chichester · New York · Brisbane · Toronto · Singapore

Other Wiley Editorial Offices

John Wiley & Sons, Inc., 605 Third Avenue, New York, NY 10158-0012, USA

Jacaranda Wiley Ltd, 33 Park Road, Milton, Queensland 4064, Australia

John Wiley & Sons (Canada) Ltd, 22 Worcester Road, Rexdale, Ontario M9W 1L1, Canada

John Wiley & Sons (SEA) Pte Ltd, 37 Jalan Pemimpin #05-04, Block B, Union Industrial Building, Singapore 2057

Library of Congress Cataloging-in-Publication Data

International Strategic Management Society Conference (12th : 1992 :
   London, England)
      Strategic renaissance and business transformation / edited by
   Howard Thomas, Don O'Neal, and James Kelly.
         p.   cm. — (Strategic management series)
      Consists of papers presented at the 12th International Strategic
   Management Society Conference, entitled "Strategic renaissance, The
   Transformation of economic enterprise" ... held in London, October
   14–17, 1992.
      Includes bibliographical references (p.   ) and index.
      ISBN 0-471-95751-8 (cloth)
      1. Strategic planning—European Union countries—Congresses.
   2. Organizational change—European Union countries—Congresses.
   3. Corporate reorganizations—European Union countries—Congresses.
   4. Employees—Training of—European Union countries—Congresses.
   5. Competition—European Union countries—Congresses.   I. Thomas,
   Howard, 1943-   .   II. O'Neal, Don.   III. Kelly, James.   IV. Title.
   V. Series.
   HD30.28.I556   1992
   658—dc20   95–5190
                                                                     CIP

British Library Cataloguing in Publication Data

A catalogue record for this book is available from the British Library

ISBN 0-471-95751-8

Typeset in 10.5/12pt Palatino by Acorn Bookwork, Salisbury, Wiltshire
Printed and bound in Great Britain by Bookcraft (Bath) Ltd

This book is printed on acid-free paper responsibly manufactured from sustainable forestation, for which at least two trees are planted for each one used for paper production.

Contents

SECTION II: ISSUES AND PATTERNS IN GLOBAL COMPETITION

SECTION III: MANAGING ORGANIZATIONAL LEARNING

Contributors

Dr Barbara Blumenthal
Temple University, 239 Ridgeview Road, Princeton, NJ 08540, USA

William C. Bogner
Assistant Professor of Management, Georgia State University, Department of Management, PO Box 4014, Atlanta, GA 30302-4014, USA

Jordi Canals
Associate Dean, International Graduate School of Management, University of Navarra, Avda. Pearson 21, 08034, Barcelona, Spain

Dr Christopher Carr
Senior Fellow in Strategic Management, Manchester Business School, University of Manchester, Booth Street West, Manchester M15 6PB, UK

John Child
Tanners Green Lane, Solihull, West Midlands B94 5JT, UK

Peter B. Dixon
Braxton Associates, 90 Long Acre, London WC2E 9RA, UK

Michael J. Earl
London Business School, Sussex Place, Regent's Park, London NW1 4SA, UK

Colin Eden
Department of Management Science, Strathclyde Business School, 26 Richmond Street, Glasgow G1 1XH, UK

Dr David O. Faulkner
Lecturer, Strategic Management Group, Cranfield School of Management, Cranfield, Bedfordshire MK43 0AL, UK

David Feeny
Templeton College, Kennington, Oxford OX1 5NY, UK

Lynda Gratton
Assistant Professor, London Business School, Sussex Place, Regent's Park, London NW1 4SA, UK

Hugh P. Gunz
Associate Professor of Organizational Behaviour, Faculty of Management, University of Toronto, 246 Bloor Street West, Toronto, Ontario, Canada M5N 1JB

Taïeb Hafsi
Professor, Management and Organizations Department, Service ARH, HEC, Montréal 5255 avenue Decelles, Montréal, Québec, Canada H3T 1VH

Barry D. Hedley
Braxton Associates, 90 Long Acre, London WC2E 9RA, UK

R. Michael Jalland
University of Toronto, 246 Bloor Street West, Toronto, Ontario, Canada M5N 1JB

Jan J. Jörgensen
Faculty of Management, McGill University, 1001 Sherbrooke Street West, Montréal, Québec, Canada H3A 1G5

James Langenfeld
Director for Antitrust, Bureau of Economics, US Federal Trade Commission, Washington DC 20580, USA

Dr Martin Lockett
Senior Principal, AMS-UK, AMS Management Systems UK Ltd, 1 Angel Court, London EC2R 7HJ, UK

Peter Lorange
President, IMD International Institute for Management Development, Chemin de Bellerive 23, PO Box 915, CH-1001 Lausanne, Switzerland

BENTE R. LØWENDAHL
Associate Professor, Norwegian School of Management, PO Box 580, 1301 Sandvika, Norway

CONSTANTINOS C. MARKIDES
London Business School, Sussex Place, Regent's Park, London NW1 4SA, UK

LÍVIA MARKÓCZY
Business Economics Department, Budapest University of Economics, Veres Palne UTCA 36, Budapest 1053, Hungary

JOHN MCGEE
School of Industrial and Business Studies, University of Warwick, Coventry CV4 7AL, UK

TERRY MCNULTY
Senior Research Fellow, Centre for Corporate Strategy and Change, Warwick Business School, Warwick University, Coventry CV4 7AL, UK

WIM OVERMEER
Stern School of Business, Department of Management and Organizational Behavior, 44 West Fourth Street, New York, NY 10012, USA

ANDREW M. PETTIGREW
Director, Centre for Corporate Strategy and Change, Warwick Business School, Warwick University, Coventry CV4 7AL, UK

DR NOEL TICHY
University of Michigan, School of Business Administration, 701 Tappan, Ann Arbor, MI 48109-1234, USA

HOWARD THOMAS
Dean, College of Commerce and Business Administration, University of Illinois at Urbana-Champaign, 1206 South Sixth Street, Champaign, IL 61820, USA

KEES VAN DER HEIJDEN
Strathclyde Graduate Business School, 199 Cathedral Street, Glasgow G4 0QU, UK

RICHARD WHIPP
Cardiff Business School, Aberconisay Building, Colum Drive, Cardiff, CF1 3EU, UK

RICHARD WHITTINGTON
Senior Lecturer, Department of Marketing and Strategic Management, Warwick Business School, Warwick University, Coventry CV4 7AL, UK

DENNIS YAO
Commissioner, Federal Trade Commission, Washington DC 20580, USA

Series Preface

The Strategic Management Society was created to bring together, on a worldwide basis, academics, business practitioners and consultants interested in strategic management. The aim of the Society is the development and dissemination of information, achieved through its sponsorship of the annual international conference, special interest workshops, the *Strategic Management Journal* and other publications.

The Society's annual conference is a truly international meeting, held in recent years in Toronto, Stockholm, Barcelona and Singapore. Each conference deals with a broad, current theme, within which specific sub-themes are addressed through keynote speeches and discussion panels featuring leading experts from around the world.

This volume is the second in the series representing Strategic Management Society annual conferences. Papers presented at these conferences tend to address not just the conference theme but, more importantly, to discuss "live" issues—those that are currently confronting the Society and its members. In this context presenters feel more freedom to step outside the boilerplate-type issues and formats that sometimes tend to constrain discussion, and utilize these conferences as an opportunity to take chances—to address issues that are more "interesting", though perhaps less conventional.

This gives the editors a broader range of ideas, thoughts and themes from which to select papers, and the opportunity to make available an interesting and intriguing selection of conversations to anyone interested in joining the conversations or in just reading about them.

Attending a conference at which a number of presentations are occurring simultaneously requires attendees to make choices and, in the process, inevitably miss some sessions that they may have found interesting. This results in most conference presentations playing to audiences of only a few or, at most, a few dozen of those who might be interested. This volume, as will others in this series, offers the opportunity for hundreds of interested individuals to, in effect, attend several of the most interesting conference presentations, while giving much wider exposure to those papers deemed most likely to be of interest to a broader audience.

This conference,* entitled "Strategic Renaissance: The Transformation of Economic Enterprise", was centred on the view that major corporations worldwide are transforming themselves into post-industrial organizations, while being heavily influenced by the political, economic and social changes taking place around them. Since much of the learning is still at an early stage there are more questions than clear answers. Nonetheless, business leaders have to address the task of change armed with the tools and experience available. This volume is a contribution to their endeavours.

The theme of the conference was selected with recent events in Europe very much in mind, but also a wider perspective that takes account of the forces in play around us, that suggest we are all living through a major chapter of history. The "renaissance" that is now taking place is not confined to any single aspect of life—eastern Europe is in the throes of political, economic and social turmoil, the GATT negotiations progress toward free trade, and major corporations worldwide are transforming themselves into post-industrial organizations.

The Conference Steering Committee reviewed more than 500 papers, ultimately selecting some 180 for presentation at the conference. We believe that the wisdom contained in the rich body of research and experience benefited all of the participants, and will be a major contribution to better understanding of the issues being addressed during this period of strategic renaissance.

So many fine papers were presented that a decision was made, early on, not to attempt to select a set of "best" papers from the conference. Judging which papers are best is highly subjective and is, moreover, unlikely to provide the balance of content that will make the volume interesting and useful to a broad range of members.

---

*The 12th International Conference of the Society, held in London, 14–17 October 1992, was attended by more than 600 delegates from the academic and business world.

With that in mind, a theme was selected that is not only consistent with the thrust of the conference but also strikes at the heart of the Society's mission. Papers were then selected that seemed representative of some of the most significant issues currently facing business strategists. The result is, we feel, an interesting and effective integration of strategic perspectives that exemplifies many of the most important issues facing strategic management, both now and in the immediate future.

An eclectic ensemble of contributors, including academics, business executives and consultants, addresses one of the Society's primary concerns—building and maintaining bridges between management theory and business practice.

Editorial commentary provides integration among the papers included, resulting in not just a volume of currently-relevant papers, to be read once and set aside, but a collection of interesting thoughts and approaches to management issues that are timeless in their nature and importance.

HOWARD THOMAS
Series Editor

Introduction

Strategic Renaissance and Business Transformation

With major corporations worldwide attempting to transform themselves into post-industrial organizations while being heavily influenced by the political, economic and social changes taking place around them, business leaders find themselves facing the prospect of dramatic change armed with traditional tools and experience.

Although it is impossible to include in one volume the breadth of ideas under discussion in this important area, the editors have selected contributions that offer interesting food for thought in four currently crucial strategic conversations.

Section I	Restructuring and Reorganization in the Public and Private Sectors

Today's global community presents commercial and government organizations with a new range of opportunities. To exploit those opportunities to the fullest, there is a need to work effectively with recently transformed governments, such as those of eastern Europe, and with institutions previously held by governments that are now privatized or in new agency-style organizations, in many areas of the world. Other services still being developed by governments are undergoing fundamental change.

This section focuses on the process of passing responsibility out from the centre—from communism to capitalism in eastern Europe; from public to private sector in other parts of the world—and the consequent management challenges.

Section II   Issues and Patterns in Global Competition

As cross-border linkages increase, organizations need to combine global management with strategies tailored to regional or local conditions. The big question is what the exact relationship should be between global and regional strategy. The new art of "globalization" is the subject of this section, in themes dealing with developing and implementing, and at the business unit and activity levels.

Section III   Managing Organizational Learning

In recent years it has become apparent that organizations, like people, either learn or fall behind those that do. The idea that learning from our own experiences and from those of others can be one of the keys to attaining and sustaining a competitive advantage has become one of the most actively discussed management topics. But organizational learning is much more than experience-based, as the chapters in this section demonstrate.

Section IV   Managing the Processes of Strategic Change

This section looks at the whole spectrum of management issues that, in sum, make for a transformation of the way in which the enterprise plans, acts and relates—to itself, others and the outside world. To that end, it investigates the industry context of change, and the purpose and process of organizational transformations, dealing with such issues as strategic and cultural change, leadership and change agency.

Section I

Restructuring and Reorganization in the Public and Private Sectors

Organizational change is surely one of the most widely discussed topics in the field of business management. By whatever terminology—restructuring, reorganization, flattening, downsizing, right-sizing, horizontalizing—business formats are undergoing massive change, perhaps on a scale broader than ever before. This is exemplified by the transformation of governments in Europe, which presents organizations, both public and private, with a new range of opportunities. Much of the discussion in this section focuses on the process of passing responsibility out from the centre—from communism to capitalism in eastern Europe, from public to private sector in Malaysia, Canada and the United Kingdom—and the consequent management challenges.

Hafsi and Jørgensen use the experiences of Malaysia and Québec to demonstrate how privatization can, by freeing the government from managing activities that are better managed by the private sector, improve a company's ability to govern itself, strengthen the private sector and foster enthusiasm and private entrepreneurial initiative.

Langenfeld and Yao offer a relatively new slant on the classic management dilemma of attempting to manage strategies for achieving long-term goals while under strong pressure for immediate results. They submit that events associated with the transition to a market economy in central and eastern Europe, and policy makers' responses to these events, will have important effects on "permanent" policies regarding competition. They argue that transition problems are different from long-term problems, and choices made today should, to the extent possible, be made recognizing the problems that they may present for future choices.

Based on a study of 11 international mixed management organizations (IMMOs) between Hungarian and foreign partners, Marckóczy and Child argue that the IMMOs replaced a previous dependence on State authorities with control by foreign partners, but resulted in a "new" paternalism that is not unlike the previous dependence. This calls into question whether or not IMMOs can meet their original expectations where this phenomenon exists.

Whittington, McNulty and Whipp address the issue of marketing professional services by responding to the questions: "What are the organizational transformations necessary to learn how to market?" and "How do organizations manage these changes?" They examine case studies of marketing implementation from two sectors—industrial research and development laboratories, and the National Health Service.

Chapter 1	Privatization and National Renaissance: The Cases of Malaysia and Québec *Taïeb Hafsi, Jan J. Jørgensen*
Chapter 2	Competition Policy and Privatization during the Transition of Central and Eastern Europe to a Market Economy: An Organizational Perspective *James Langenfeld, Dennis Yao*
Chapter 3	International Mixed Management Organizations and Economic Liberalization in Hungary: From State Bureaucracy to New Paternalism *Lívia Markóczy, John Child*
Chapter 4	Market-Orientated Strategic Change: Managing Complexity and Context *Terry McNulty, Richard Whittington, Richard Whipp*

The business transformation we are undergoing can be accurately portrayed as a renaissance, in effect replacing the hierarchical organization that has been the primary means of organizing work since almost the beginning of the industrial age with information age technology, based more on knowledge and communication.

It is difficult, if not impossible, to imagine what this business "revolution" will ultimately bring in the way of change in how we organize businesses, governments or even our private lives. What we can predict, however, is that these unseen changes will engender uncertainty and risk, as well as threat and its mirror-image, opportunity.

Communication technology is liberating people at all levels in organizations, as well as organizational constituents, from their dependence on hierarchies for information that is important to decision making. Many types of information that could have previously been withheld from diffusion are now becoming more akin to public goods. This represents a shift in power, from top management to those lower in the organization, and from organizations to those they are supposed to represent. Information, in the case of customers, for instance, reduces their switching costs, making them less captive to brand loyalty—in effect, giving them more power. For the organizations competing for their business, it is no longer business as usual.

＊The opportunity-side of this equation is that the same technology that provides the information for increasing the power of customers also allows organizations to gather and process enormous databases of customer information, giving them the ability to respond more appropriately, individually and quickly to changing customer needs, demands and desires.＊

To eliminate corporate redundancies, to effectively cope with the challenges of a better-informed market, and to effectively utilize the dramatic increase in customer data available, corporate restructuring is likely to be essential and dramatic. Leavitt and Whistler, in a 1958 *Harvard Business Review* article entitled "Management in the 1980s" predicted that the computer would do to middle management what the Black Death did to Europeans in the 14th century. Charles Handy, in *The Age of Paradox* (1994), compares what is happening now to what happened with the invention of the printing press—the authority of the church declined, because people could now read the Bible themselves and make up their own minds about God.

Privatization and National Renaissance: The Cases of Malaysia and Québec

TAÏEB HAFSI, JAN J. JÖRGENSEN

INTRODUCTION

Ever since Lenin focused on the "commanding heights" of industry, state ownership has been viewed as government's ultimate form of economic intervention. The Soviet state ownership model influenced the early development plans of India after its independence. Even the United States government has used state ownership to tackle special problems, as exemplified by the Tennessee Valley Authority established under Franklin D. Roosevelt in 1933, NASA in 1958 under Dwight D. Eisenhower and the National Resolution Trust in the 1980s under Ronald Reagan.

In western Europe, state ownership of business firms grew between the two world wars, and more dramatically after World War II. By 1978, state-owned firms accounted for 22% of gross national product (GNP) in Austria, 26% in Italy, 11% in Great Britain, 12% in the Federal Republic of Germany and 13% in France (Hafsi, 1984). In 1981 the socialist government of France

Strategic Renaissance and Business Transformation. Edited by H. Thomas, D. O'Neal and J. Kelly.
Copyright © 1995 John Wiley & Sons Ltd.

increased the state-owned firms' share to 17% of GDP, 35% of national investment, 30% of exports and 23% of salaried employment (Hafsi, 1984).

More recent international business and economic studies, however, while recognizing government's key macro-economic role, suggest that state ownership may hinder growth and development (Doz, 1986; Ostry, 1990; Porter, 1990; Rugman, 1990). Moreover, ownership of large chunks of the economy can lead to managerial problems that defeat the state's ownership goals (Hafsi, 1984). Property rights theory (Aharoni, 1982) has shown that the principal–agent problems of state ownership lead to situations where the agent (the firm) serves interests other than those of the principal (the government or the public).

Studies of the decision-making process in state-owned firms (Hafsi, 1981; Hafsi, Kiggundu and Jörgensen, 1987; Ramamurthi, 1985) suggest that the relationship between government and the state-owned firm seems to follow a cycle. At the firm's creation, the relationship is cooperative, and the firm behaves in harmony with the government's objectives. Indeed, the firm's managers are often the designers of the government's policies in the particular sector, as in the case of the petroleum sector at the founding of Petro-Canada or Elf Aquitaine (France).

As the firm develops its operations, it seeks to protect its "technical core" from outside intervention (Thompson, 1967). Its relationship with government becomes more adversarial (Hafsi, 1981). As government shies away from costly, intense confrontations, the firm becomes autonomous.

There comes a time when government, even if nominally the owner, is no longer in charge. The firm's managers respond more to the firm's competitive needs within the industry than to government objectives. The government cannot get the firm to go in directions that conflict with the managers' perceptions of the firm's needs. The government's loss of control is not due to its lack of formal power to force the managers to act as directed; it is rather the government's inability to have managers cooperate effectively to pursue government goals. The government's formal powers may be strong but are destructive if used.

As a consequence, the obvious prescription is that government must recognize that it is likely to be only temporarily the owner of a business firm. There are, of course, exceptions. For example, managers of a firm that is financially or strategically vulnerable are less likely to seek autonomy than those of a firm that is self-sufficient and strategically strong (Hafsi, 1981). Indeed, managers of weak firms may even work to strengthen their relationship with government and campaign against government exit from the industry (Hafsi, Kiggundu and Jörgensen, 1987).

Based on this understanding of the forces acting on the relationship between the government and the state-owned firm, government divestment is not a result of an ideological choice, but rather a managerial necessity. A government that failed to divest businesses that resist its directions would be overwhelmed by the managerial demands of control, and would lose its ability to manage the country as a whole. The collapse of the Soviet economy is an extreme example.

Hence national renaissance may currently depend on the government's ability to get out of business, while in the past it was related to government's entry into business. More precisely, the government's economic role, including that of entry into strategically important businesses beset by market or entrepreneurial failure, depends on its ability to exit from businesses that can now be better managed by the private sector.

Privatization therefore takes on a new meaning. It may spark renewal in the governability of a nation. In addition to freeing the government from managing activities better managed by the private sector, it may strengthen the private sector and foster entrepreneurial initiative.

In this chapter, we take the examples of the province of Québec, in Canada, and of Malaysia to show how privatization has played precisely such a stimulating role. In the Malaysia case, the government policies and programmes have been built around privatization. Privatization was both a catalyst and an indication of how committed the government was to allowing active private sector involvement in the new national policy.

The Québec case suggests that privatization programmes are more likely to succeed and have a meaningful impact when they are not viewed as ideologically driven. Furthermore, the government's management of the privatization process can play a major role in signalling the non-ideological nature of the divestment decision, while demonstrating its desire to use privatization to address shared societal issues.

The remainder of the chapter is divided into three parts: (i) the case of Malaysia, (ii) the case of Québec, and (iii) conclusions and implications for both research and practice.

MALAYSIA

GENERAL BACKGROUND

Malaysia is a federation of 13 states on the Malaysian peninsula and the island of Borneo, with an ethnically and religiously diverse population of over 19 million in 1994. It achieved independence from Britain in 1957 and became the Federation of Malaysia, including Singapore in 1963. Due to ethnic tensions, however, Singapore was forced out of the federation in 1965.

The country's economy has grown at a very fast pace since the early 1980s, stimulated by the rich and varied natural resource endowments of the country. Malaysia is a world leading exporter of rubber, tin, palm oil, cocoa and natural gas. Industrial development has also been impressive since 1973, and Malaysia has textile, forest product and electrical/electronics sectors that are internationally competitive. In the world competitiveness reports of 1992 and 1993, Malaysia was ranked fourth behind Singapore, Taiwan and Hong Kong, but before South Korea. As a result, the country attracts large amounts of foreign direct investment.

THE SOCIO-POLITICAL DYNAMICS

After independence, tension among the various ethnic groups was heightened by the highly unequal distribution of wealth and by the domination of foreign capital. The Bumiputra (Malay) ethnic group, with 57% of the population, held only 10% of the wealth, while the non-Bumiputra, especially Chinese, held about 30% and foreigners held 60%. Traditionally, the Malays (Bumi) held key positions in government, while the Chinese, with 32% of the population, dominated the economy, and the Indians, with 9% of the population, were concentrated in small-scale commerce.

In 1969, riots and violent confrontations opposed Malays and Chinese over the wealth disparity. The national fabric was in danger. The three main parties, ethnically-based, decided to work for national unity by creating a national political front, *Nacional Barisan*, whose programme was to manage the relationship between groups, and work to eradicate poverty in all groups while improving the distribution of wealth.

The New Economic Policy (NEP) was designed to restructure society "to correct the identification of race with economic function". Its explicit objective was to modify the wealth distribution so that "the corporate sector was to have at least 30 per cent Bumiputra ownership, other Malaysians [Chinese, Indian and others] 40 per cent and foreign interests 30 per cent, by 1990" (Economic Planning Unit, 1985a).

The private sector was perceived to be unable to pursue both the distributional objective and the profit objective, so to achieve the NEP goals, the government had to be heavily involved in the economy. Public investment grew at 12.6% annually in real terms during the 1970s, with a special emphasis on creating public enterprises in industry and commerce. The public sector came to account for 30% of total national consumption. By 1987 there were 525 non-financial public enterprises (NFPEs).

Thus, slowly, the government was led into "areas which were traditionally the preserve of the private sector". More worrisome was the low private sector role in the fourth plan (1981–1985), dropping from 63% of total investment in 1980 to 50.4% in 1985. The size of government was becoming too great for a healthy market-orientated economy. In the fifth plan, the government decided to reverse the trend by offering more incentives to private sector investment and disengaging government from business management. In the new national development policy, privatization of a large number of NFPEs was a key ingredient.

DR MAHATHIR'S GOVERNMENT POLICIES FROM 1983 TO 1988

Soon after becoming Prime Minister in 1981, Dr Mahathir Muhammad developed a set of four policies that were to affect profoundly the future of Malaysia:

1. The Look East policy
2. The Malaysia Incorporated policy
3. The Privatization policy
4. The Leadership by Example policy

The privatization policy was essential to the programme's success. Developing Malaysia Incorporated required giving more power to the private sector and building a social–economic coalition modelled on countries with similar Asian cultural backgrounds. The public sector had to set an example by following clearly enunciated ethical and professional standards.

The Look East policy meant searching for models in the East rather than in the West. The success of Japan and Korea was believed to be related to the attitude of these countries' citizens and business managers toward work, wealth creation and distribution. Success was also related to loyalty to the nation and to the enterprise, yet Dr Mahathir had to avoid privatization being perceived as a sell-off to the Japanese (Jomo, 1988) in a period when federal government foreign debt rose from $M4.9 billion (1980) to $M24.9 billion (1986) (Saravanamuttu, 1988).

In the Malaysia Incorporated policy, government, business and the workforce were urged to cooperate as if in one corporation to increase the well-being of the country and everyone. Dr Mahathir cautioned (Abdul Ghani et al., 1984):

> A sovereign state cannot be a business company. It can only run like a corporation ... the private sector forms the commercial and economic arm of the national enterprise, while the government lays down the major policy framework, direction and provides the necessary backup services. Thus the government becomes more the service arm of the enterprise.

The private sector is, however, expected to invest and develop a longer run outlook, while the government bureaucracy is required to provide more responsive and more efficient services. The workers and their unions "should understand that the working arrangement is in their real long term interest".

The Privatization policy was meant to reduce government's direct role in business. At the time the government was involved in many activities—postal and telecommunication services, radio and television, railways, shipping and aviation, airports, hospitals and clinics, ports, educational institutions, roads and other public utilities—as well as undertakings in agriculture and industry that were in competition with the private sector.

In Malaysia, the public sector was developed primarily to correct distributional imbalances that were the source of major socio-political conflict. By 1983, however, the situation had changed significantly. The Bumiputras now controlled a number of funds that could be tapped as a source of capital for the private sector. Share issues in the 1980s that had been earmarked for

Bumiputra investors had been largely oversubscribed. Dr Mahathir could therefore maintain that privatization would not negate the NEP objectives, since "The Bumiputras will get their share, both in terms of equity and in employment". Furthermore, the public sector was losing money, and the government no longer had the funds required for large utility projects. Accordingly, said Dr Mahathir (Abdul Ghani et al., 1984):

> Private sector participation will lessen the burden of the Government with regard to funds. Hopefully, self-interest will ensure that the utilities and other government-owned corporations transferred to the private sector, either fully or partly, will be better run, more efficient and more profitable.

Without privatization, he warned, there was the risk that improvements in utilities would be halted, with consequent deterioration of services and stifling of growth. Such a downward spiral would undermine the poverty eradication goal of the NEP.

Privatization had a broader meaning in the Malaysian context than the transfer of ownership to the private sector. Tan Sri Sallehuddin Bin Mohamed, the chief secretary to the Malaysian government, proposed various forms of privatization (Economic Planning Unit, 1985a,b), all of which reduced the direct presence of government in the economy. These forms included the following (paraphrased from the original):

- Privatization through transfer of ownership and control from the government to the private sector.
- Partial privatization, where government retains some ownership interest.
- Selective privatization, where a government agency divests some of its activities while retaining others.
- Commercialization, where the government-owned unit adopts commercial business practices without change of ownership, although it could involve adoption of a commercial organizational form, such as a private or a public limited company, owned by government.
- Greater private sector participation through some form of contracting out of services or activities by a government unit.
- Participation by the private sector through management contracts or sale of other managerial services to the government.

Privatization was meant to strengthen the Malaysian social fabric, and the relationships among business, labour and government. The Prime Minister had therefore to ensure that the process would not generate strains that would adversely affect the desired balance. It was not to benefit a particular group or party: "Everyone should benefit from it, or at the very least should not lose by it". Specific assurances were given to employees:

> Privatization does not mean that the government and the bureaucracy washes its hands clean of any responsibility after it is taken over by the private sector. The accountability for any public service or functions transferred to the private sector remains with the government...
> ...The NEP will not be ignored. It is also wrong to assume that only Bumiputras are entitled to the benefits of privatization. Non-Bumiputras are equally eligible. Indeed the government favors Bumiputra/non-Bumiputra partnerships.

Finally, Leadership by Example meant that the public sector had to play a major role in the success of each policy because it was very important in size and in political clout. To show that government meant business, red tape should be chased away. This policy required that both politicians and civil servants set the example in the implementation of policies. To do so, they had to understand clearly the policies, and explain and implement them in accordance with stated objectives (Jomo, 1988).

Implementation of the Privatization Programme

The privatization programme was launched in March 1983, but it was not until late 1984 that the policy started being implemented. It was under the direct control of the Prime Minister's department. The whole programme included 246 state-owned enterprises valued at $16.3 billion (Zabid, Hafsi and Zaynal, 1990). In 1993, the Bank Negara Malaysia, the Central bank, in its annual report, listed only 42 "non-financial public enterprises" in which the government held shares.

Three major privatization processes were looked at in more detail (Hafsi, Zabid and Zaynal Abidin, 1989; Zabid, Zaynal and Hafsi, 1989): the privatizations of Syarikat Telekom Malaysia (STM), Malaysian Airline System (MAS) and the Malaysian International Shipping Corporation (MISC). All three were considered successes.

For STM, it was commercialization rather than privatization. STM was "created" in 1986/87 as a replacement for the government department responsible for telecommunications, Jabatan Telekom Malaysia (JTM), within the Ministry of Energy, Posts and Telecommunications. STM was set up as a corporation run according to business principles (Ambrose, Hennemeyer and Chapon, 1990). Shares were to be sold to the public later. MISC and MAS were privatized through public offerings of shares on the Kuala Lumpur stock market. Both offerings were major successes despite bearish market conditions.

In all three cases, the main issues had to do with employee relations. Employees felt highly insecure in the case of STM. The government seemed to proceed in a hurry, without much consultation, thus creating much anxiety among employees and managers (Ambrose, Hennemeyer and Chapon, 1990). Later, it yielded to pressures and offered acceptable conditions and job security guarantees. Still, the situation was in 1988 perceived to be volatile, with serious resistance to the completion of the privatization process expected. In September 1990 the government announced its intention to sell 25% or 470.5 million shares in STM at $M5 per share, of which 50 million shares could be purchased by foreign investors (Ambrose, Hennemeyer and Chapon, 1990).

In the MISC and MAS cases, the government was not involved in managing the process: managers were in charge. However, government officials were closely associated in the process. The employees were consulted and their fears were allayed. They appeared to be satisfied with the way in which the whole operation had been managed.

Outcomes

These three privatizations had to be successes, firstly because they were the initial showcase of the privatization programme, and secondly because the three companies were essential for the development of the private sector. STM was to become the centre of an important electronics and telecommunications sector. Malaysia was already a major producer of telecommunications equipment and components, with exports totalling $500 million in 1988, but the industry was dominated by large foreign companies. There was a need for a significant national player that would provide the sophistication and the organization to the numerous small firms that were thriving in the industry.

MAS was the most visible company of the country. Everyone knew the rivalry between MAS and Singapore Airlines, and the great successes of the latter. Like Singapore Airlines, MAS had to be more aggressive and closer to the business community. It had to become the most important partner of small businesses in their export endeavour. In a sense, MAS needed the agility to become for the business community a source of market information and of transportation solutions.

MISC was in an interesting situation. The huge development of the gas field of Malaysia was a major growth opportunity for the company. In addition, sea transportation was critical to the development of domestic exports. The Malaysian government believed that a private company would be better able to develop relationships and partnerships with the multitude of sea transportation systems all over the world. It could also be a hotbed for the development of many small or medium-sized companies, needed for a well-organized sea transportation system.

DISCUSSION

During the early 1980s, the public sector of Malaysia played a significant role in the economy. However, financially strained— even strapped—the government was unable to provide the funding necessary to support the development of such important businesses as the airlines, telecommunications or shipping, to mention but a few.

At about the same time, business opportunities were numerous. Firstly, there was the development of the energy industry, which attracted significant investment, both local and foreign. Secondly, there were important regional investors willing to locate production plants in Malaysia, because of quota or manpower saturation in other countries of South East Asia.

To benefit from these important changes, the country was in need of clear direction. Direction meant not only major policy statements, but, more importantly, deeds: significant action that would confirm the government commitment to change. Of all the policies adopted by government, Look East, Malaysia Incorporated, Leadership by Example and Privatization, only the latter involved visible actions to signal commitment.

⟨ Privatization meant reducing the scope of government direct involvement in business. It was to be a major signal to the bureaucracy that a change in outlook was needed, that becoming a service organization for private business was essential for its own future. As a consequence, it provided flesh to the commitment to the Malaysia Incorporated policy and teeth to the Look East policy. The Leadership by Example policy was simply the confirmation of the new behaviour that was expected of government officials and public servants.⟩

⟨Privatization naturally became the key element of government policy. Economic renaissance, with new private business commitment and behaviour, within a new business environment favourable to local and foreign investment, depended greatly on its success.⟩

In 1988 the test was passed. Several important privatizations had taken place. But there were still some public sector firms for sale: the railways and the electric power company were perceived to be too big and inefficient to seem attractive to private buyers.

QUÉBEC

GENERAL BACKGROUND

Québec is the largest province in area, second largest in population, within the Canadian federation. In the 17th century, French colonists pioneered European settlement in lands along the St Lawrence River inhabited by the Huron, Iroquois, and Algonquian peoples. The colony of New France was proclaimed in 1663. In 1759, British forces seized Québec city, and New France was ceded to Britain in 1763. While the settlers retained linguistic and religious freedoms, French civil law and a seigneurial system, Catholics were largely barred from administrative positions after "the Conquest" (Latouche, 1988).

During and after the American Revolution, some 10 000 British loyalists fled the colonies into Québec, creating tensions between English and French speaking settlers that led to the 1791 division of Québec into Upper Canada (now Ontario) and Lower Canada (now Québec). Another 30 000 loyalists fled the American colonies into Acadia. Following the 1837 rebellions in Upper and Lower Canada, Lord Durham recommended a union of the two colonies and massive immigration to create an English majority. The 1841 Act of Union made English the only official language. The union lasted until 1867, when the colonies of Nova Scotia and New Brunswick joined Ontario and Québec in the Dominion of Canada under the British North America Act (Latouche, 1988; Levey and Greenhall, 1983).

Over time, two divergent views of Canada have emerged. Francophones see Canada as a product of two equal founding nations, while anglophones see Canada as a nation of what is now ten provinces and two territories. This division was underscored by the Québec government's refusal to sign the 1982 document that repatriated Canada's constitution from Britain. Constitutional accords negotiations in 1987 and 1992 to recognize Québec's unique status have failed to win approval.

By 1990, Québec had a population of about 7 million, or 26% of Canada's total population. Formerly Québec had the highest birth rate in Canada; now it has the lowest, leading to fears that its place in Canada and the status of the French language with Québec may be diminished by demography as well as by external influences.

THE SOCIO-POLITICAL DYNAMICS

Throughout the 1950s, the Catholic church controlled education and health in the largely rural Québec society. Those with ambition aspired to professions: the clergy, law and medicine. Business was not a valued profession: it was linked to amoral cities, where large-scale commerce was dominated by anglophones.

By forcing an unlikely alliance of rural traditionalists, the Catholic hierarchy, and anglophone business elites, the Union Nationale Party led by Maurice Duplessis dominated Québec politics for most of the period from 1936 to 1960, defending Québec's status by emphasizing rural Catholic values and refusing to participate in federal economic programmes. One consequence was that Québec's social, economic and educational development lagged behind that of Ontario. Eventually urban intellectuals, university graduates and trade unionists began to question the Québec government's aloofness from major economic and social spheres (Latouche, 1988, p. 1802).

Already in 1920 half of the population lived in urban areas, and the structure of the economy shifted dramatically between 1920 and 1940. Agriculture's share of the economy declined from 37% to 10%, while manufacturing's share grew from 38% to 64% (Latouche, 1988, pp. 1796 and 1801). Urbanization, education and a better material life eroded the power of the clerical hierarchy and traditional elites. Among the forces slowly changing this pattern was the Mouvement Desjardins, itself a credit union movement initially linked with the church to offer rural parishioners a savings bank alternative to the large anglophone urban banks (Giroux, 1990). The Caisses Populaires became business incubators for a future managerial class.

The 1960 provincial elections marked the start of a new era as the Liberal Party defeated the Union Nationale government.

GOVERNMENT POLICIES IN THE QUIET REVOLUTION

During the subsequent "Quiet Revolution", government leaders and intellectuals promoted the idea that the time had come for Québecers to become "masters in our own house". The *maîtres chez-nous* concept had several components (Ministère des Finances, 1986):

- to repatriate internal decision making centres into the French-speaking community;
- to enable Québec society to control, plan and orientate its expansion and development;
- to establish large-scale institutions to accelerate the development or processing of natural resources;
- to promote the cultural heritage of Québecers.

The Québec government owned few Crown corporations prior to the 1960s. Moral as well as fiscal concerns led to government control of wine and liquor sales in 1921. During World War II, the government established a sugar beet refinery and, more significantly, a small Hydro-Québec to produce and distribute electricity.

Expanding the state's role in society and economy was the key to becoming "masters in our own house". Following the Parent Commission of enquiry, the Ministry of Education took over an educational administration that had been dominated by the Church. A system of state-supported higher education, including junior colleges, was also established (Latouche, 1988, p. 1802).

An important symbolic act was the Liberal government's 1963 nationalization of most hydro-electric enterprises, which were incorporated into Hydro-Québec, with an expanded mandate that included research, exploitation and conservation. The nationalization was guided by René Lévesque, then in the Liberal Party.

Crown corporations proliferated during the "Quiet Revolution" of the 1960s and 1970s. Apart from nationalizing electricity, the government created the Société générale de financement du Québec (SGF) as its industrial development and finance corporation. The Economic Development Council (Conseil d'expansion économique) was set up as an economic planning commission. The Liberal government also established new public enterprises in key sectors:

- integrated iron and steel complex (SIDBEC, 1964)
- pension funds (Caisse de dépôt et placement du Québec, 1969)
- mining (SOQUEM, 1969); petroleum (SOQUIP, 1969)
- forestry (REXFOR, 1969)
- industrial development financing (SDI, 1971; SGF, 1973)
- housing (SHQ, 1971)
- broadcasting (Radio-Québec, 1969)

More Crown corporations were created in the 1970s for energy exploitation, housing, lotteries, industrial parks, agri-business, asbestos mining and fishing, and in the 1980s in air transport, water treatment, public works and recreation.

A key government economic tool was the pension fund for all private and public employees in the province, the Caisse de dépôt et placement du Québec. Unlike the Canada Pension Plan or Social Security in the United States, the funds in the Québec plan are invested in shares of private firms as well as in conventional treasury bills and interest bearing deposits. Hence, the Caisse de dépôt operates like a private pension fund, with two major differences. Firstly, it has aggressively used its status as government-owned enterprise to bypass security exchange regulations on trading and ownership. This led to conflict with the Ontario securities regulatory body, when the Québec fund acquired a large stake in firms listed on the Toronto Stock Exchange without notifying Ontario regulatory authorities. Secondly, although it seeks to maximize returns and enjoys operational autonomy from government intervention, it pursues socio-political as well as financial goals in its private investments, often in collaboration with SGF, the government's industrial holding group.

The Caisse de dépôt had a stake in 42 private and public firms in 1984, and 53 firms in 1990, while SGF had a stake in 11 firms in both 1984 and 1990.

While public enterprises accounted for a larger share of the economy in another province (Saskatchewan), Québec led all 10 Canadian provinces in the total number of public enterprises: 49. Moreover, Québec's public enterprises with total assets of $52 billion in 1983 rivalled the asset size of federal public enterprises ($60 billion in 1983). For Québec's public enterprises, the overall return on assets was 3.9%, thanks largely to positive returns in electricity and high profits for alcoholic beverage and lottery monopolies (TABLE 1.1), while the federal government's enterprises showed a 1.4% return on assets, largely due to losses by firms in transportation and communications.

The provincial government accounted for 25.9% of Québec's GDP in 1985; adding in other levels of government raised the percentage over 50% (Ministère des Finances, 1986). The 15 largest public enterprises employed 26 000 persons directly, or 64 000 indirectly, including subsidiaries and associate firms in which the state had at least 20% control.

Under the Parti Québécois (PQ), Crown corporation investment accounted for as much as a quarter of total investment in the province (1978), but well over 90% of this was concentrated in the hydro-electric sector for the James Bay project.

Of growing concern were the losses incurred by a number of government enterprises, including massive cumulative losses totalling more than a billion dollars by the asbestos mining firm (SNA), the steel firm (SIDBEC), and the development enterprise for the James Bay region (SDBJ) (Ministère des Finances, 1986).

Near the end of its mandate, the PQ government became involved in several public sector divestment initiatives on an *ad hoc* basis: Sidbec Normines, SAQ, Québecair, plus a strategic retrenchment at Hydro-Québec (Hafsi and Demers, 1989, 1990). As Premier René Lévesque (1981) stated:

TABLE 1.1 Sectorial distribution of Québec provincial public enterprises, 1983

Québec provincial government public enterprises	Number of firms	Firms with full data	Adjusted assets (000s)	Assets by sector (%)	Return on assets (%)	Debt ($C, 000s)
Agriculture, fishing, forestry	6	3	256 152	0.5	-1.6	103 535
Mining, petroleum, energy	5	5	26 020 796	49.8	2.8	17 785 099
Manufacturing	5	2	1 076 657	2.1	-13.7	594 544
Transport and communications	6	4	174 375	0.3	-33.5	93 630
Commerce	2	1	154 593	0.3	167.2	24 887
Banking, insurance, etc.	10	9	21 592 991	41.3	6.5	12 560 670
Construction, real estate, land	3	3	2 685 288	5.1	-10.9	2 125 453
Other services	12	11	266 237	0.5	49.9	138 532
Total	49	38	52 227 089	100.0	3.9	33 426 350

Source: Calculated from data in Economic Council of Canada (1986), Table B-1, Statistical Summary, pp. 157–164.

The state apparatus' legitimacy is now based on its ability to abstain, to disengage itself from social responsibilities, to reduce its "non productive" expenses, to model its operations on private sector practices, to renew with the principles of productivity, profitability and competitiveness, to prefer market mechanisms for a more automatic regulation of social exchanges.

GOVERNMENT POLICIES FROM 1985 TO 1988

Changing Goals and Mounting Losses

The 1985 return of a Liberal provincial government signalled that the nationalists' success in commerce momentarily overshadowed the political dream of sovereignty for Québec. The new government outlined its motives for privatization in 1986 (Ministère des Finances, 1986). Firstly, the original need for state firms to fill an entrepreneurial void had been met. Québec had developed a dynamic managerial class, many of whom first served in the Crown corporations. Secondly, increasing global competition weakened some Crown corporations, and the government could no longer afford to sustain their losses. Thus privatization by the Québec government was linked to mounting losses of some Crown corporations and the desire of private entrepreneurs for new areas of investment (Ministère des Finances, 1986, p. 11):

A new, Francophone managerial class has taken over in many sectors of the economy, and a record number of dynamic business firms have been established, as the new registrations with the Montréal Stock Exchange show. It is therefore becoming increasingly difficult to justify government intervention on the grounds of entrepreneurial shortcomings in Québec.

The government cited the new international economic order's demand that economic growth be linked to efficiency as further evidence of the need to rebalance the portfolio of state enterprises.

IMPLEMENTATION OF THE PRIVATIZATION PROGRAMME

Privatization Strategy and Structure: Learning from Others

To determine a method for privatization, the Québec government compared the British and Canadian experiences, concluding that public support was a key element for success and that the public was more interested in the "why" of the process and the consequences of privatization than in technical and financial details. In its policy statement, the government stressed that privatization was not an end in itself, and that it would be carried out pragmatically on a case by case basis.

The structural objectives of strengthening the economy and ensuring a continued Québec presence in key sectors would take precedence over maximizing financial returns from sale of Crown corporations.

Management of the privatization process was entrusted to a ministry for privatization within the Ministry of Finance. The ministry reviewed the role of Crown corporations within a socio-political climate where the state sought a reduced economic role because of deficits and general confidence in a viable Francophone private sector.

The new formal process was structured as follows:

1. Review of the Crown corporation's dossier by the Standing Cabinet Committee on Economic Development (CMPDE).
2. Analysis of four options for the firm:
   i.   total or partial privatization;
   ii. reorganization followed by later privatization;
   iii. reorientation or turn-around;
   iv. the status quo.

   The analysis would be carried out by a joint committee consisting of the minister responsible for the firm, the minister of state for privatization, one or more representatives from the firm, and representatives from other departments.
3. Development of a consensus and plan for realization of the chosen alternative.
4. Joint submission of the plan by the minister for privatization and the responsible minister for the firm to the CMPDE and then to the whole Cabinet for review and approval.
5. Implementation by the ministry for privatization assisted by an operational task force, with legislative scrutiny and approval where needed.
6. Formal review of the programme as a whole by the minister for privatization.

In most cases, privatization proceeded quickly and relatively smoothly with little public controversy, other than charges by the opposition that the sale price of some firms was too low. The exceptions were the abortive SAQ outlet sale and the turbulent Québecair saga. Some firms, such as Domtar (construction materials) and SNA (asbestos), failed to attract buyers. The government finally found a buyer for SNA in 1992, at a substantial discount from the initial purchase price.

OUTCOMES

In its published assessment of the privatization programme, the Québec government emphasized cuts in losses by state corporations, retention of control of divested units in Québec, the use of proceeds to reduce debts of parent enterprises, and the restored ability of slimmed-down parent Crown corporations to undertake new socio-economic initiatives (Ministre délégué, 1988).

Québec completely divested its holdings in Québecair (airline), la Raffinerie du sucre du Québec (sugar refining) and Madelipêche (fisheries). It sold off three subsidiaries of SOQUEM, four holdings of SOQUIA in food processing and distribution, three of REXFOR in forestry, four of SNA in asbestos, and one each of SGF and SOQUIP (TABLE 1.2). The proceeds were largely used to reduce the debt of parent corporations. SAQ, Loto-Québec and Hydro-Québec were explicitly excluded from the privatization exercise.

To assuage concerns that privatization might extend to key assets such as Hydro-Québec, the government announced in October 1988 that the main goals in privatization had been attained and that the future pace would be slower. The minister in charge of privatization did suggest that there might be some privatization within government services such as health.

Despite privatization and claims that the new managerial class has tilted the state–market boundaries to the private sector, the Québec government continues to have a major indirect role in key economic sectors through the Caisse de dépôt et placement du Québec (Brooks, 1987) and SGF, its own alternative policy instruments. The Québec government privatized in order to intervene more effectively and at a lower cost. Slimmed-down Crown corporations have been given redefined mandates, as illustrated by SOQUEM, which was to foster mineral exploration in remote, undeveloped areas while leaving development to the private sector.

TABLE 1.2 Québec provincial government: public sector divestment, 1984–1988

Crown corporation or holding	Governance status	Employees	Transfer date	Buyer or divestment mode	Proceeds ($ million)
Cambior Inc.	SOQUEM*	412	14/8/86	Public share offering (69%)	170.0†
Crustacés-des-Îles Inc.	Madelipêche*	1045	31/12/87	Groupe Delaney	3.1
Distex-SNA	SNA (50%)*	470	17/7/86	Echlin Inc.	3.2†
Donohue	SGF	2025	7/7/87	Mircor (51%)	320.0
Filaq-SNA	SNA (66.7%)	n.a.	10/2/88	Industries 3-R Inc.	0.1†
Grande-Entrée	Madelipêche*	320	14/8/87	Groupe Hubert	0.5
Industries 3-R Inc.	SNA (30%)	n.a.	10/2/88	Industries 3-R share repurchase	0.1†
J.E. Landry Inc.	SOQUIA (42%)	n.a.	19/1/87	Provigo	2.9†
La société minière Louvem	SOQUEM (22%)	110	5/11/87	Ressources Sainte-Geneviève	8.4†
Lupel-SNA	SNA*	n.a.	30/7/86	Cascades Inc.	5.6†
Madelipêche Inc.	Québec*	1000	19/11/87	Groupe Delaney	1.1
Mines Seleine Inc.	SOQUEM*	200	29/4/88	Société canadienne de sel Ltée	35.0
Ministry of Public Works	Govt. Department	n.a.	1/10/84	Transformed into Crown corporation	
Panofor Inc.	Rexfor (33%)	n.a.	29/10/87	Normick-Perron (assets only)	14.0†
Papier Cascades Cabano	Rexfor (30%)	n.a.	31/8/87	Cascades Inc.	11.0†
Pêches Nordiques Inc.	SOQUIA (92%)	n.a.	4/3/87	Fruits de mer d l'Est du Québec	2.5†
Provigo	SOQUIA (6.7%)	23 000	17/3/86	Unigesco (26%)	48.4
Québecair	Québec	827	1/8/86	Nordair-Metro (CP Air 35%)	21.0
Raffinerie du sucre	Québec*	94	18/9/86	Sucre Lantic Ltée	43.2
Scierie des Outardes Enr.	Rexfor (60%)	n.a.	31/3/88	Cie. de papier Québec & Ontario	11.0†
Sidbec-Normines	Sidbec-Dosco (50.1%)	940	31/12/84	Mine closed; pellet plant leased to QC	–67.5
Soc. des Alcools du Québec	Québec*	(2459)	1985	Privatization of outlets aborted	
Soc. des pêches de Newport	SOQUIA (39%)	600	8/2/88	Fishermen	3.5†
SOQUIP-Alberta	SOQUIP*	n.a.	23/12/87	Sceptre Resources Ltd.	188.8
Total (excludes SAQ and double counting)		31 043		Total proceeds	825.9
				Of which provincial treasury	102.9

*Crown corporation or wholly-owned subsidiary.
†All or majority of proceeds kept by Crown corporation.
n.a. Not available.
Source: Ministre délégue (1988).

DISCUSSION AND CONCLUSIONS

Two troublesome cases, SAQ and Québecair, occurred at the start of a programme of multiple public sector divestments. Apart from the SAQ false start and the Québecair saga, the Québec government's experience with privatization has gone relatively smoothly. Facing overextended resources, the province divested or slimmed-down key Crown corporations. In the privatization process it included representatives from the privatization candidate, espoused clearly understood goals, and kept socio-political goals in the forefront.

In the Québecair and Cambior cases, privatization was not the first solution proposed. The government had no pre-conceived solution or at least did not push for privatization at the outset. Generally, it identified the key stakeholders, and pushed them to find a solution. Their solution finally became the government's. The political process and proposal formation processes were intertwined. Similarly, for SIDBEC the problem-solving process was lengthy and open.

The political process involved significant negotiation and commitment-building in all cases except SAQ. In most cases commitment-building was linked to shared recognition of the problem and how privatization could help. In the SIDBEC, Cambior and Québecair cases, consensus emerged from the problem recognition process: (i) the need to stop SIDBEC's financial losses, (ii) the need to reduce the firm's debt burden in the case of Cambior, and (iii) the eventual recognition that fleet renewal was not enough to solve Québecair's competitive problems.

The Québec privatization programme has been characterized by consensus on what to do supplemented by individual case by case consideration of how to do it. The programme has emphasized continuing government policy goals for each sector rather than maximizing the number of firms to be divested. The Québec government retains an economic role even as it divests.

CONCLUDING COMMENTS AND IMPLICATIONS

The cases of Malaysia and Québec are interesting because of the clear government willingness to intervene for the achievement of

socio-economic goals. The recent history of both of these governments highlights the particular role that privatization has taken in
the process of industrial renewal and national development.

In both cases, privatization was presented as an instrument of
national development rather than as a political or an ideological
goal. Probably aware of the divisive power of ideologies, governments steered away from them. Both governments had, however,
important and explicit socio-economic goals; in Malaysia, increasing Bumiputra share of national wealth, and in Québec developing a francophone business class.

These goals had in the past been pursued with some degree of
success through the creation of public sector firms. Most of the
Malaysian Bumiputra and the Québec francophone managerial
class were reared in the public sector. A reasonable next step was
to open the game and avoid a split within society along the
private–public divide. In Malaysia, the Bumiputra were back in
the saddle, even though still economically dominated by the
Chinese business community. In Québec, the francophones were
now a dominant business group.

In addition, the managerial challenges of the public sector in
both countries were too big for a government involved in many
other pursuits. Most of the key public sector firms were already
autonomous and difficult to direct. At the same time governments all over the world were under fire. They were perceived
to be too big and inefficient. Public sector firms' deficits were
frequently cited as a measure of government management shortcomings.

Privatization was therefore a natural response to such concerns.
Malaysia and Québec are typical responses. They happen to highlight two significantly distinct approaches to privatization. The
Malaysian experience emphasized the formulation of the privatization strategy. Privatization was seen as the instrument of
national redeployment, and a mechanism by which private sector
investors were encouraged to take a more active part in national
development.

The actual process of privatization was mostly left to the firms'
managers. The only exception was STM, but that involved commercialization in preparation for privatization rather than privatization itself, and it was the learning ground for government. In
the STM case, the lack of involvement of key stakeholders was
clearly problematic, and government officials learned important
lessons for subsequent privatizations.

In Malaysia, renaissance meant new government practices after the heavy-handed policies of the previous years. A new partnership between the private and the public sectors was needed in order to attract foreign investors. A combination of policies highlighting government's objectives had to be supported by deeds. The privatization policy was the proof needed to convince everybody.

In Québec, privatization was mostly part of a strategic process, by which the management of government was adapted to the needs of an increasingly complex economy. In a sense, privatization was not seen as a stimulant for the economy, but rather as a signal of new government practices in managing the economy. It was the recognition that government's role was not managing business, but rather helping the private sector to do so.

The Québec government has even rejected the suggestion that the privatization policy was designed to provide it with fresh financial resources. Actually, the proceeds from the sale of firms were used to strengthen the firms' competitive positions rather than to finance government programmes or reduce government's own deficit. As in the Malaysian case, privatization was not an end in itself, but a way of showing government's willingness to change the nature of its involvement in stimulating and directing the economy.

Thus, the Malaysia and the Québec cases are both different and similar. They are different, because the emphasis was on formulation in the first case and on implementation in the second. The difference is probably a reflection of the different stages in which the economies were. The more complex Québec economy, with sophisticated telecommunications, aerospace and pharmaceutical sectors as well as traditional resource-based sectors in forest products, minerals and fisheries, cannot be directed easily by broad strategic statements, even though a sense of direction is also needed.

The two situations were nevertheless similar, because privatization was in both intended to signal new government practices. In Malaysia, privatization was the start of a new societal deal. In Québec, it was the start of new managerial practices, with the disengagement of government from direct business management and more systematic support to business competitiveness.

The two cases suggest that:

1. It is important to steer away from divisive ideological stands.
2. Privatization is more readily accepted if it appears to be a solution to a widely accepted problem. Managerial concerns are good justification for the decision to privatize.
3. Managers are important for the conduct of the privatization process. Their involvement and motivation are frequently required for the operation's success.
4. The process of privatization could easily be divided into two important sub-processes, one that takes place within government (or, better said, outside of the firm targeted and its task environment), and one that takes place within the firm and its task environment.
5. Clear government strategy statements are helpful for a smooth privatization programme.
6. Privatization is such a dramatic move on the part of government that it attracts attention and may be a powerful signalling mechanism for major changes in government practices.
7. The detailed qualitative and historical study of major decisions, such as privatization, provides a unique perspective on the processes by which strategic changes are initiated and conducted at the government level.
8. Patterns, on the processes by which such decisions are formulated and implemented, require rich qualitative data, but many more cases are needed to help to generalize the findings.

ACKNOWLEDGEMENTS

This work has received support from the Canadian Social Sciences and Humanities Research Council and the Canadian Centre for Management Development. The authors gratefully acknowledge the research contributions of Zabid Abdul Rashid and Zayual Abidin of the University Pertanian Malyasia (Selangor) and Christiane Demers and Ameur Boujenoui of École des Hautes Études Commerciales to this chapter. This work is part of a comparative study of managing divestment in Canada (federal and Québec), France, Malaysia, the Netherlands, the United Kingdom, the United States and Sénégal. Earlier findings from the research were presented in Hafsi and Jörgensen (1992a, 1992b) and Hafsi, Jörgensen and Koenig (1993). Thanks are due to other current and former members of the HEC–McGill Public Sector Divestment Research Project: Joëlle Piffault, Pascal Beaudoin, Fang He, Roch Ouellet, Roberto Fachin, Michel Labelle, Loralie Barker and Abdoukhadire Sall, for their assistance and intellectual support.

REFERENCES

Abdul Ghani et al. (Eds) (1984). *Malaysia Incorporated and Privatisation*. Petaling Jaya, Selangor, Malaysia: Pelanduk Publications.

Aharoni, Y. (1982). State-owned enterprise: An agent without a principal. In L.P. Jones et al. (Eds) *Public Enterprise in Less-Developed Countries* (pp. 67–76). New York: Cambridge University Press.

Ambrose, W.W., Hennemeyer, P.R. and Chapon, J.-P. (1990). *Privatizing Telecommunications Systems: Business Opportunities in Developing Countries*, Discussion Paper 10. Washington, DC: International Finance Corporation.

Brooks, S. (1987). The mixed ownership corporation. In *Who's in Charge? The Mixed Ownership Corporation in Canada* (pp. 84–102). Halifax: Institute for Research on Public Policy.

Doz, Y. (1986). *Strategic Management in Multinational Companies*. Oxford: Pergamon Press.

Economic Council of Canada (1986). *Minding the Public's Business*. Ottawa: Minister of Supply and Services.

Economic Planning Unit, Prime Minister's Department, Malaysia (1985a). *Guidelines on Privatization; For Use by Government Agencies*. Kuala Lumpur.

Economic Planning Unit, Prime Minister's Department, Malaysia (1985b). *Guidelines on Privatization; For Use by the Private Sector*. Kuala Lumpur.

Giroux, N. (1990). Le retournement stratégique: Le cas de la carte Visa-Desjardins. Doctoral thesis, Université de Québec à Montréal.

Hafsi, T. (1981). The strategic decision-making process in state-owned enterprises. Doctoral dissertation, Harvard University, Boston, MA.

Hafsi, T. (1984). *Enterprise Publique et Politique Industrielle*. Paris: McGraw-Hill.

Hafsi, T. and Demers, C. (1989). *Le Changement Radical dans les Organisations Complexes: Le Cas d'Hydro-Québec*. Montreal: Gaëtan Morin.

Hafsi, T. and Demers, C. (1990). Strategic divestments by government; a management process perspective. *Canadian Journal of Administrative Sciences* 7(3), 37–46.

Hafsi, T. and Jörgensen, J.J. (1992a). *Managing Public Sector Divestment*. Ottawa: Canadian Centre for Management Development.

Hafsi, T. and Jörgensen, J.J. (1992b). Privatization and national renaissance: The cases of Malaysia and Quebec. Presented at the 12th Annual International Strategic Management Society Conference, London, September.

Hafsi, T., Jörgensen, J.J. and Koenig, C. (1993). Strategic divestment in the public sector; patterns from France and Great Britain. In L. Zan, S. Zambon and A.M. Pettigrew (Eds) *Perspectives on Strategic Change* (pp. 277–306). Boston: Kluwer Academic Publishers.

Hafsi, T., Kiggundu, M.N. and Jörgensen, J.J. (1987). Structural configurations in the strategic apex of SOEs. *Academy of Management Review* 12(4), 714–729.

Hafsi, T., Zabid, M.A.R. and Zaynal Abidin, M. (1989). Managing the divestment process in government: The privatization of Syarikat Telekom Malaysia. Working paper, École des Hautes études commerciales, Montreal.

Jomo (Ed.) (1988). *Mahathir's Economic Policies*. Petaling Jaya, Selangor, Malaysia: Institute of Social Analysis.

Latouche, D. (1988). Québec. In *The Canadian Encyclopedia*, 2nd edn (pp. 1793–1802). Edmonton: Hurtig Publishers.

Lévesque, R. (1981). Le Québec economique dans un deuxième mandat. Presented at Colloque 1981, l'École des Hautes études Commercials, 31 October.

Levey, J. and Greenhall, A. (Eds) (1983). Canada. In *The Concise Columbia Encyclopedia* (pp. 132–135). New York: Columbia University Press.

Ministre délégué aux Finances et à la Privatisation (1988). *Privatisation des sociétés d'etat; rapport d'étape, 1986–88*. Québec: Cabinet du Ministre délégué aux Finances et à la Privatisation, October.

Ministère des Finances (1986). *Privatization of Crown Corporations' Orientation and Prospects*. Québec: Ministre délégué à la Privatisation, February.

Ostry, S. (1990). *Governments and Corporations in a Shrinking World*. New York: Council on Foreign Relations.

Porter, M.E. (1990). *The Competitive Advantage of Nations*. New York: Free Press.

Ramamurthi, R. (1985). Performance evaluation of state-owned enterprise in theory and practice. Working paper No. 85-31, College of Business Administration, Northeastern University, Boston, MA.

Rugman, A. (Ed.) (1990). *Research in Global Strategic Management*. Greenwich, CT: JAI Press.

Saravanamuttu, J. (1988). The Look East policy and Japanese economic penetration in Malaysia. In Jomo (Ed.) *Mahathir's Economic Policies*. Petaling Jaya, Selangor, Malaysia: Institute of Social Analysis.

Thompson, J.D. (1967). *Organizations in Action*. New York: McGraw-Hill.

Zabid, M.A.R., Hafsi, T. and Zayual, Z.A. (1990). The privatisation of Malaysian international shipping company (MISC). Research paper, UPM, Malaysia.

Zabid, M.A.R., Zayual, Z.A. and Hafsi, T. (1989). The privatisation of Malaysian airline system (MAS). Research paper, UPM, Malaysia.

2

Competition Policy and Privatization during the Transition of Central and Eastern Europe to a Market Economy: An Organizational Perspective

JAMES LANGENFELD, DENNIS YAO

INTRODUCTION

Competition (antitrust) policies in Central and Eastern Europe need to address short-term problems associated with the transition to a market economy as well as develop institutions suitable for a mature market economy. In this chapter we employ an organizational perspective to explain some of the decisions taken in the short run and to examine how those decisions may affect

Strategic Renaissance and Business Transformation. Edited by H. Thomas, D. O'Neal and J. Kelly.
Published 1995 John Wiley & Sons Ltd.

competition agencies' abilities to carry out their longer term missions. The theme of the chapter is that events and responses during transition will have important effects on "permanent" policy, that the transition period problems are different from the long-term problems, and that choices made today should, to the extent possible, be cognizant of the problems such choices might present for future choices.

We begin with a brief introduction to the goals and nature of competition policy, then discuss competition policy as an "organizational/legal technology" through which antitrust policy is implemented and note that, while there is a relatively limited amount of controversy over whether the technology works in mature economies, the same technology may not work for transitioning economies. This discussion is followed by a brief review of privatization and its relationship to competition policy. We then address some of the transition issues faced by these emerging institutions, and from a Selznickian (Selznick, 1957) perspective argue that many of these issues are critical events that will shape the long-term goals and capabilities of the agencies.

THE WESTERN VIEW OF COMPETITION AND THE TECHNOLOGY OF COMPETITION POLICY

While western economies differ somewhat in their approaches to competition policy, the bulk of the analysis and its implementation is relatively similar. There is a reasonably well-established economic and legal basis for antitrust analysis that is largely shared by enforcers in mature market economies. They seek to protect consumers and promote the free flow of goods and services in a competitive market economy (Langenfeld and Blitzer, 1991, p. 354).

In general, these laws seek to present buyers with a free choice of goods and services from independently acting suppliers. Monopolists can restrict output and raise prices above cost if buyers have no alternative choices. However, if sufficient choice is available to buyers, they can choose the most desirable products at the most attractive prices, forcing the suppliers to reduce their prices to their costs (including a return on capital invested) and also inducing suppliers to further reduce costs.

Anticompetitive behavior can take place when a dominant firm undertakes actions that prevent entry by new firms or raises the costs of its competitors without offering a better or cheaper product. Similarly, if competitors agree to raise price and restrict output, buyers do not have adequate choice because they are not being presented with independently offered products and prices. This result is an outcome much like buyers facing a single monopoly supplier.

The specific business practices challengeable under most western laws are similar, if not identical. Most western laws condemn the abuse of dominant positions in a market to establish or maintain supracompetitive pricing,[1] establish some form of merger review,[2] and condemn price fixing and territorial allocations among competitors as illegal unless some overwhelming efficiency justification can be shown. Additional goals of European integration and realization of economies of scale, plus the legal construction of the Treaty of Rome and continental law systems, have led to some differences across western enforcement policies.[3] However, these differences have narrowed over time, and indications are that this process of convergence will continue.

Most countries of eastern and central Europe have passed competition laws and have operating antimonopoly offices. These laws are often modeled on competition laws of the western European community, in particular focusing on Articles 85 and 86 of the Treaty of Rome, but are also influenced by US antitrust laws and are crafted to meet the locally perceived needs of each country.

In central and eastern Europe, including Russia and the former Soviet Republics, additional policy goals may lead to differences in enforcement of competition policy from that of the US and western Europe. One important difference between eastern Europe and the West is that in the East competitive markets did not already exist when a competition law was adopted. An end to central planning does not create real markets or the benefits from these markets until competition is allowed to develop. This is particularly true in the former Soviet bloc, where state-owned enterprises were either monopolies or organized into cartels by government ministries. One goal of competition law in these countries is therefore to nurture the development of competitive markets.

In addition, the prevention of monopoly pricing through competition policy may be particularly important in former centrally planned economies, since only a portion of the benefits of a market economy will be passed on to the population if the transformation to the market merely creates privately-owned monopolies. Accordingly, eastern and central European competition policy may be proactive in the sense that it encourages the restructuring of industries and helps introduce firms to competition.[4]

Moreover, certain buyer and seller arrangements (such as exclusive contracts or refusals to deal) may be more problematic than in the US because of scarce capital and other impediments to entry. The breaking of old links that reflect inefficient business relationships may be needed.

Finally, monopoly pricing and output reduction are illegal in virtually all of the laws, as in western Europe. Remedies such as price controls are available, and antimonopoly agencies, such as the Polish Antimonopoly Office (PAO), have attempted to use them.[5] If competition will take a long time to develop, it has been argued that interim price limits could be the best way to prevent incumbent monopoly abuses.

Western competition analysis of many central and eastern European situations often consists of projecting experiences in relatively mature market economies onto an economic setting with which the world has had little experience. Overlay the political issues and the prospects that any one government will stay in power long enough to exert a consistent economic policy, and it becomes difficult to argue that the exact technology for competition policy in a transition economy is truly known.

Despite these concerns, there are at least three reasons for thinking that the western models of competition policy may be desirable and useful. Firstly, the western approach is likely to be economically sensible since western laws and institutions appear to function reasonably well in achieving the common goals of competition policy.

Secondly, most central and eastern European countries wish to become part of the EC (EU), so it may be politically practical for these countries to adopt laws and organizations based at least loosely on western models. Harmonious laws, if not an actual condition, will help to facilitate that goal.

Thirdly, adoption of western models can legitimate both the eastern and central European competition agencies as well as portions of the overall economic policy. Given the uncertainty associated with the applicability of the western "technology" of antitrust to transition economies it seems plausible that the mirroring of western institutions may serve the purpose of providing external (and internal) legitimacy to these institutions. In these circumstances it is difficult to assess the effectiveness of antitrust policy because the outcomes that occur from these policies (if you can observe them accurately) cannot be compared with outcomes that would have occurred had a different enforcement decision been reached. The inability for assessments based on outcomes leads, as suggested by Meyer and Rowan's (1977) institutionalization theory of organizations, to evaluations that are based on visible manifestations of the organizations, such as the type of laws, procedures, personnel, or organizational structure associated with the agency.

All of these countries depend heavily on the West for financial support, sources of investment capital or investment, and other resources. Thus it matters for the central and eastern European countries that outsiders such as the World Bank, the International Monetary Fund (IMF), and western businessmen believe that these countries have an appropriate competition policy. While such entities in the short run cannot easily evaluate outcomes other than by comparison with western solutions to (possibly) similar problems, these entities can observe and be troubled with laws, structures, or procedures that appear unorthodox. Thus, even if a central and eastern European competition agency knew that adopting a western form might be inappropriate, it might still adopt such a form to legitimate itself with critical outside sources of resources. Such inappropriate forms could be decoupled in practice from the actual operations of the organization.

THE CONTRASTING DEVELOPMENT OF PRIVATIZATION GOALS AND LAWS

The development of the privatization agencies provides an interesting contrast to that of the competition agencies. Privatization is an essential aspect of the transition to a free market economy, together with such steps as the adoption of a transparent and just legal system, price liberalization, open trade and convertible currencies. Privatization creates a set of incentives for investors and workers to develop products that they can sell to reap the rewards of their efforts and investments.

Not only does privatization develop investment and more

responsive management within a country, it can also stimulate foreign investment and reduce a government's budget deficit during the transition.

The goals of the privatization process, however, usually contain elements other than creating a well-functioning market system. Privatization can also be used to redistribute wealth. There is the question of how to deal with the claims of those from whom state-owned property may have been confiscated, handle the sale of privatized enterprises to people who may have benefitted "unfairly" under the previous regime, and handle workers' and managers' claims on the business. Most efforts at privatization have some element of income redistribution, if only to prevent government employees from disposing of government assets at low prices in order to receive a "kick-back" from private purchasers of assets. Accordingly, the goals of privatization are often more diverse than those of competition agencies.

Privatization agencies also differ from competition agencies because of the absence of a "correct" or consensus western model for privatization. The technology of privatization is relatively unknown and the goals of privatization agencies differ. Thus, we see a number of different types of privatizations and structures for privatization agencies. In most of the countries there has been massive "spontaneous" privatization, where managers have taken control of their enterprises. In the case of small retail and distribution enterprises, many have been subsequently sold to managers or in auctions without excessive interference of the privatization agencies (Johnson and Kroll, 1991; Sachs and Lipton, 1990). This process led to complaints that the *nomenclatura*—the former communist elite—and black marketeers were the only ones who could afford to buy state property (Hare, Canning and Ash, 1995). Concerns of impropriety resulted in the creation of the State Property Agency (SPA) in Hungary, slowed the speed of privatization in Poland, and resulted in a careful auction process in the Czech and Slovak Republics.

In the Czech lands and Slovakia, the process involves development of a privatization plan, transfer of the assets to the Fund for National Property; a decision concerning the disposition of the property, and, if voucher privatization is chosen, an auction.[6]

The Privatization Ministry's main task is to approve a privatization plan, subject to concurrence and review by other government bodies. Management and other groups usually initiate the plans, and the Fund for National Property decides the form of ownership and control.

Poland's system is similar, except that the Ministry of Ownership Transformation and the Parliament appear to be much more involved in determining which enterprises should be allowed to go private. Despite starting their reform process earlier, Poland has not made as significant strides as the Czech and Slovak Republics.[7]

Hungary is so far the leading example of a privatization system that does not use any voucher system.[8] The process was primarily designed to prevent spontaneous privatizations, where the state did not get adequate compensation from the purchasers of the assets.

The politics of privatization appears to have created these idiosyncratic organizational responses, not only because of the diversity of goals and the lack of a clear model from the West, but because privatization may be more salient in the short run than competition policy to both the citizenry and to interested (and important) foreign parties. Privatization approaches also may be more idiosyncratic because they are transitory processes that demand some haste. The institutions created to effect privatization, at least in theory, should fade away, and do not need to be viable beyond the transition period. Agencies, such as those responsible for competition policy, are being created during the transition period and presumably will last into the indefinite future. Accordingly, idiosyncratic forms of (say) competition policy and institutions could present long-run problems if such policies and institutions are not effective beyond the transition and if such institutions become entrenched.

Beyond the long-run nature of competition policy, competition policy would seem to have at least four advantages compared to privatization and many other newly created institutions in eastern Europe. The consensus on the relatively narrowly focused goals of competition policy and potentially anticompetitive acts has led to relatively consistent policies to date, whereas agencies such as those responsible for privatization appear to have diffuse goals. Secondly, there has been a great deal of management turnover in other types of agencies. The management and general direction of many competition agencies have been very stable.[9] This is particularly true in Poland, which has seen several governments come and go, but whose competition office has not been significantly affected by the changes. Thirdly, the competition agencies do not appear to have been subject to as much special interest pressure as many other government agencies. Fourthly, competition agencies have a clear counterpart in developed market economies, whereas organizations such as privatization agencies either do not exist or have had relatively short tenures in the West.

TRANSITION PROBLEMS AND ORGANIZATIONAL DEVELOPMENT

We now look directly at some transition problems that are faced by the central and eastern European competition agencies. The perspective that we adopt is one which suggests that organizational change is not easy, that organizations become institutionalized as discussed by Selznick (1957), and therefore that early decisions will indirectly affect later decisions. This approach contrasts with a more "economic" approach that starts from a premise that organizations can be continually optimized to fit changing conditions.

Selznick describes organizations as developing distinctive characteristics and competencies over time in response to critical challenges posed to the organization from within and from without. These characteristics and competencies, as imbued in the structure, procedures, and personnel of the organization, can be both benefits and liabilities; while well tailored to some needs, they may restrict an organization's ability to meet other needs. Not only are organizational capabilities developed over the natural history of the organization, so too are the goals.

Selznick's classic study of the US Tennessee Valley Authority (TVA) (1949) illustrates these ideas. President Roosevelt pushed for the TVA as "a corporation clothed with the power of government but possessed of the flexibility and initiative of private enterprise. It should be charged with the broadest duty of planning for the proper use, conservation, and development of the natural resources of the Tennessee River drainage basin" (quoted in Selznick, 1949, p. 5). After the TVA was created by Congress in the early 1930s, it faced the difficult challenge of developing and administering a whole-scale federal program to a region suspicious of the federal government. To do this, the TVA coopted a number of local leaders, trading broader participation in decision making for local political support. The result was that the TVA pursued a number of goals that were goals of the coopted local officials and not of the program as originally designed. For example, the Agricultural Relations Department within the TVA became a proponent of the land-grant college system and "under the pressure of its [coopted] agriculturists, the Authority did not recognize Farm Security Administration and sought to exclude Soil Conservation Service from operation within the Valley area. This resulted in the politically paradoxical situation that the eminently New Deal TVA failed to support agencies with which it shared a political communion, and aligned itself with the enemies of those agencies" (Selznick, 1949, p. 263).

While the TVA experience may be an extreme example of what Selznick calls institutionalization, some of the broad themes of his argument seem relevant to understanding the development of the competition agencies in central and eastern Europe. In what follows we will sketch some possibilities suggested by the theory and what we know about competition agencies and their relationships to privatization agencies and other parts of the government.

A basic premise of this approach is that an organization's ability to change its policies and its underlying capabilities diminishes over time: organizations become rigid. Among other causes, rigidity may result from development of distinctive competencies that are "more efficient" to pursue than developing new competencies, changes in organizational goals, and information production systems that are geared to traditional needs.[10] To the extent that development of rigidity occurs, it poses a severe management challenge to agency administrators, especially if the organization's environment is expected to undergo substantial but unpredictable change.

Competition agencies in central and eastern Europe are new organizations existing in rapidly changing economic and political systems. An important question in this regard is whether responses to current external considerations and constraints will create structures and procedures that may prove somewhat unfortunate in the intermediate future.

In what follows we look at five transition problems that the competition offices have faced, their solutions to the problems, and how those solutions may create problems for the future. We focus on "transition" problems: currently salient problems that will become considerably less salient in 10 or so years, because transition problems are more likely to introduce organizational institutions that are ill suited to the agencies' long-term missions.

These problems are: finding appropriately trained management and staff (the human resource problem), the interrelationship between privatization goals and competition goals (the privatization emphasis problem), the lack of a full set of regulatory laws and institutions (the incomplete institutions problem), the lack of a culture of competition within the economy (the non-market culture problem), and the lack of available economic information about firms and industries (the information availability problem).

THE HUMAN RESOURCE PROBLEM

One of the most difficult problems for the young enforcement agencies is absence of a pool of potential hires trained in the law or in western economics. This shortage has a direct effect on the nature of analysis done in the agencies, and also an indirect effect in that the agencies lose trained personnel to the private sector. In addition, there may be an equally powerful, but more invidious, effect on organizational structure and decision making. We focus primarily on the latter concern.

The importance of the background of the staff and leadership on organizational structures and on organizational development has been noted by observers studying western agencies. For example, with respect to staffing issues in the US antitrust agencies, Katzmann (1980) and Weaver (1980) note that professional training has an influence on the types of cases that are supported. Antitrust lawyers are seen as preferring simpler cases involving conduct explicitly prohibited by law, whereas economists prefer complex structural cases based on arguably shakier legal precedent.

The implications for central and eastern European enforcement agencies of staffing are likely to be more severe. There, not only is professional training an issue; so is the problem that many individuals' experiences with a central planning perspective may frame their view on enforcement and potential remedies.

Staffing considerations can also impact the organizational structure chosen by the agency. For example, agencies whose staff have more "generalist" professional training such as from law and economics may find generalist departments such as merger shops or investigation departments more congenial, whereas agencies employing industry specialists (engineers or production managers) are more likely to have departments based on industry type.

Staffing by types of background varies widely across agencies. This outcome is a partial reflection of the talent available and, where less-constrained choices can be made, of the preferences of the initial leadership group. We have been told by officials from almost all of the competition offices in central and eastern Europe that there is a shortage of trained attorneys, in part because the former Communist system usually did not use a transparent court system to resolve disputes. Moreover, most economists trained under the Communist system studied Marxist rather than market economics. We have also been told that the emerging private sector has been able to pay two or three times the existing government wage to attract the best individuals out of government service.

The result of these shortages, and the relative abundance of "engineers" (technically trained industry specialists) has led to a mix of staff at these agencies that differs from that of most western competition agencies. For example, the former CSFR Federal Competition Office had more engineers than lawyers and economists and had departments based on industry groups. In contrast, the Bulgarian Committee for the Protection of Competition is composed largely of lawyers, and has a structure built around data collection and investigation groups and *ad hoc* case investigation teams drawn from the departments.

The nucleus of the Hungarian Economic Competition Office (GVH) was composed of socialist-trained economics and industry experts but, to its credit, it now has a number of new employees with experience in business enterprises. It is divided into a Competition Council (a group that acts as judges of competition and consumer protection cases) and a Directorate of Experts (staff who investigate and prosecute cases). The Directorate is divided into offices that concentrate on different areas of the economy—industrial, commercial, services, and food processing—which takes advantage of the areas of expertise of its staff (Hungarian GVH, 1991/2).

The Polish Antimonopoly Office, which has a plurality of economists and engineers, has been organized around two major departments, one that examines the structure of industries (unlike other agencies, the PAO can order divestitures) and a legal department. Monopolistic practices cases are developed and prosecuted by the legal department, composed primarily of lawyers and some industry experts, and the regional offices. The other major enforcement department deals with industry structure. Although headed by an attorney, that department is made up of industry experts and economists.

The heads of these offices have varied backgrounds as well. Some of them have professional training in economics or law, some are politicians, others have been judges. The president of the PAO and her vice president were formerly academic economists (another possible reason why the PAO has so many economists). In Hungary the president is an economist, but his vice president is a lawyer. In Bulgaria, the committee is composed largely of politicians and judges. In the Czech Republic, the head is a politician and a former enterprise manager.[11]

There are some potential problems that could arise from the current mix of experience of these staffs. For example, engineers with pre-transition period industry expertise could be expected to focus their analysis on production cost considerations and to weigh heavily arguments that duplication of facilities would raise costs. This type of duplication (e.g. two firms have two presidents, but one firm need employ only one president, etc.) always exists in competitive markets. However, competition induces efficiencies on firms that usually outweigh these additional costs. If too much weight is given to technical efficiency arguments and too little given to competitive concerns, then these agencies may not be sufficiently aggressive in pursuing cases that facilitate market development.

Although reorganizations can fix transitional staffing problems, it is unlikely that this will be easy to accomplish. Firstly, those currently in management and in staff will become interest groups that are likely to resist shifts reducing their influence (Pfeffer, 1978). Secondly, the organization will develop "knowledge" through operating procedures and culture that will be built around the existing human resources, and these elements of organizations generally persist through reorganizations (Cyert and March, 1963). Thirdly, although the legal systems in these countries are based on a civil system of laws, past cases cannot but influence how these agencies analyze future cases. Thus, we would expect that each competition agency will, on the basis of their initial staffing alone, develop in different directions than their sister agencies. Because these agencies were formed in 1990 or later, it is too early to be sure what directions are being taken.

The type of previous professional experience that leadership and staff has had can also make a difference. The Hungarian GVH was formed out of the former Hungarian Price Office. While that office did oversee price liberalization, it will be interesting to see if that background influences the degree to which the office is willing to engage in regulatory (price or quality) approaches. To date, the policy of the GVH has been to avoid price regulation, although it has the ability to force prices it believes to be monopolistic down to lower levels. The temptation of using explicit "command-and-control" regulation, however, is likely to pervade almost all of the competition agencies because staff and management experience has been that of central planning.

The use of outside technical assistance by these countries may also influence their early development. These agencies have received help from the EC, OECD, the German Cartel Office, the US antitrust agencies, and others.[12] In general, this advice has stressed the importance of focusing on anticompetitive behavior and structural relief (e.g. facilitating new entry), rather than on price and output controls.

THE PRIVATIZATION EMPHASIS PROBLEM

Privatization has progressed at different rates and in different directions in each central and eastern European country. The extent and nature of privatization has a direct effect on the types of cases that will be faced by competition agencies. For example, where the privatization agencies are not concerned with competition issues, many state monopolies could become private monopolies. Such a policy, if accompanied by a protectionist trade policy, would present numerous monopoly pricing problems for the competition agency. Privatization plans that encourage foreign investment lead to different issues than privatizations that are focused on internal investment or voucher programs.

Poland, for example, plans to have some 20 investment funds own the shares of 600 large privatized firms. Such a scheme could introduce politically explosive issues relating to potential antitrust problems caused by the investment fund managers. One fund might own large blocks of shares in competing companies. Such issues may also prove troublesome in the Czech Republic, where investment funds have obtained (through market means) a substantial fraction of ownership vouchers to be used in privatization.

Competition policy concerns may not be welcomed by heads of privatization agencies because such concerns are likely to interfere in the attainment of a swift and profitable sale: the goal of most privatization agencies.

> To put it simply, the (mostly) foreign buyers want to purchase good market positions ... and the Hungarian companies themselves are also interested in selling themselves in one unit, because a strong market position ensures their future prosperity. Caught in the middle the AVU [State Property Agency] is unable to overcome these interests ... The concrete dilemma quite often looks like this: the AVU has an immediately realizable and financially promising business deal on its hands, but it is expected to opt for a financially worse, lengthy and perhaps also divided privatization deal which promises to create competition.
>
> (Hungarian GVH, 1991/2, pp. 16–17)

This statement captures the feelings that were expressed in our own conversations with officials of the privatization agencies in Bulgaria and Hungary, where competition considerations seem secondary to other goals. In addition, privatizations may sometime be negotiated under conditions that reduce competition. This presents interesting policy dilemmas for the competition agency.

One would suspect that large privatizations will occur in industries where anticompetitive concerns are most likely to surface. This being the case, the possibility of conflict is clear. However, given the political salience of privatizations and the greater importance given to privatization over competition issues, competition agencies may well be faced with cases that are resolved with politics playing an important, if not dominant, role.

The situation appears to be different in Poland and the former CSFR, where the competition agencies have had a "veto" over privatization plans. Because of the high political profile of privatization efforts, however, agencies in these countries have been reluctant to exercise this veto, causing one to wonder about the ultimate effect this formal power gives to the competition agencies. Poland, for example, has only vetoed two privatizations directly; the primary influence the agency has had is through the clever use of conditional approvals (60 during this time) that force later actions on the part of the privatized firm to accommodate some competition concerns. Confrontations between privatization agencies and competition agencies can affect more than just the outcome of a case. For example, the head of the Slovak Antimonopoly Office resigned after a battle over a privatization that led to the former CSFR parliament siding with the privatization agency.[13] However, even in Poland, the Czech lands, and Slovakia the impact of the competition offices is limited, because privatization is the responsibility of a "ministry" and the competition agencies are "offices" with organizationally less clout.

Because of privatization's effect on the structure of domestic industry, privatization choices by the government (as well as foreign trade choices) will determine to a great extent the types of anticompetitive conduct most likely to emerge. Thus, to the extent that the competition agencies are able to influence the privatization process, they have an opportunity to change their long-run environment, or conversely, if they are unable to influence privatization, their environment will be given to them.

If, for example, competitive concerns result in privatization into smaller units, less antimonopoly (but possibly more merger) oriented enforcement actions would occur relative to a policy of privatizing large multiplant enterprises as single dominant firms. In addition, if privatization does not include restructuring of enterprises that takes into account competitive concerns, then subsequent antimonopoly cases against these firms could inhibit further privatization attempts. Unless purchasers clearly understand the future policies of a competition office, the purchasers could perceive that the "rules of the game" changed after the purchase, reducing expected profits, increasing business uncertainty in an already somewhat uncertain economy, and thus discouraging future investors.[14] Moreover, purchasers of privatized companies may believe that they have an implicit understanding with the government regarding competition constraints and could bring to bear political pressure to prevent competition agencies from taking actions against these companies. Accordingly, it appears critically important for competition agencies to work closely with the privatization ministries, either to fix potential competitive problems during the process or (at least) to make investors aware of the future constraints to which these companies may be subject.

THE INCOMPLETE INSTITUTIONS PROBLEM

In countries such as Bulgaria and Poland, the lack of pre-existing regulatory agencies creates a vacuum for competition agencies to get into the regulatory (or sometimes consumer protection) game. Such a mix of functions could be problematic. Antitrust regulation begins with the premise that markets work. The job of antitrust officials is to ensure conditions under which this will happen, for example, by preventing mergers that would reduce the number of competitors in an industry. Price regulation (in its most polar form), especially with respect to natural monopolies, begins with the opposite premise: markets do not work and the market mechanism needs to be replaced with government regulation of prices. Because of the differences in starting points, these approaches are not fully compatible, and an antitrust organization that also does price regulation may be inclined to interfere in the workings of the market more than it should.

Because of the size of the national economies, the state monopoly starting point, and the slowness of privatization efforts, a primary area of enforcement activity for these agencies is policing abuse of dominant position. Often, this abuse amounts to an evaluation of whether the offered price is a competitive price. For example, in 1991, 48 of the 114 cases investigated in Hungary involved abuse of dominant power. While most of these cases were found to be unsubstantiated, in many the office was forced to "judge prices by the terms of the competition law," and the office in some rare cases was able to determine "which part of a concrete price increase was justified and which was not" (Hungarian GVH, 1991/2, p. 12), despite the concern that "the Competition Law must not be allowed to reintroduce the quasi-official pricing of goods."[15]

While competition agencies may rightfully feel compelled to engage in some price regulation because of the lack of other institutions, such actions are, by western standards, more interventionist than is considered to be appropriate for a competition agency. Intervention (in terms of prices or standards) can lead the agency to treat anticompetitive problems at least in part as a price-oriented (or quality-oriented) regulatory agency would do—assessing what the proper level is—arguably undermining the underpinnings of the antitrust approach to correcting potential market problems. Such interventions will also create some bureaucratic inertia favoring future interventions that may potentially be counterproductive to ensuring a freely operating market economy.

THE NON-MARKET CULTURE PROBLEM

A primary concern of the competition agencies is the extent to which the managers and consumers in the transitional economies understand how to compete (Fornakzyk, 1992). While it may be true in the long run that those who do not will either learn or be driven from the market, in the short run non-market behavior can lead to problems.[16] A common anecdote told about competition is that managers of recently demonopolized industries are often at a loss in deciding what price to charge, and so call the other competitors and determine the market price. Such a mentality could mean that many price-fixing cases will occur during the transition.

One bureaucratic tendency is for organizations to "find" and "solve" the same kinds of problems that they have previously encountered (Cohen, March and Olsen, 1972). If this tendency persists and the types of cases that emerge as a result of non-market culture are cases less likely to be a problem within a market culture, there may be undue emphasis on "non-market" culture types of cases such as monopolistic practices, buyer and seller agreements cases, and perhaps explicit price-fixing cases.[17] Of course, one expects that the market culture is likely to change gradually, so that agencies may be able to adapt successfully as their environment changes.

THE INFORMATION AVAILABILITY PROBLEM

Enforcement agencies depend heavily on information provided by the subjects of their investigations and by other parties. Without relevant information the analytical basis (especially that of the western agencies) for enforcement decisions is greatly weakened. The agencies have two major problems with information. Firstly, the information they desire may not exist, partly because firms may not have developed market-competition-oriented cost accounting data that they need for their own internal purposes.

Secondly, much general industry information is not collected.[18] Agencies, such as the PAO, have attempted to collect economy-wide data on industries that better reflect relevant antitrust markets, and the GVH has a separate division of data collection. However, for relatively small agencies to gather this information can be difficult, especially when so much of the historic information is now completely outdated and based primarily on supply-side production considerations. Moreover, even in an investigation, the agencies appear to lack the legal power to obtain as much information as western agencies can from the enterprises that are the target of an inquiry (e.g. the CSFR Volkswagen–Skoda joint venture investigation, where the agency stated that it did not receive sufficient information from the parties and was considering challenging the joint venture to block it until sufficient information was received).

Lacking information, heuristics and short cuts may be necessary. For example, the agencies may rely heavily on documents of intent and testimony, eschewing more sophisticated economic analyses, and may also rely heavily on rough industry concentration statistics. A question in this regard is whether such transitional short cuts will become longer term policy. For example, many observers believe that the past heavy reliance on concentration numbers for US antitrust decisions[19] has continued to greatly influence antitrust analysis, despite a changed understanding of the importance of such numbers and the existence of additional relevant information (Easterbrook, 1984). To the extent that the system can evolve to reflect information availability, more sophisticated analysis, etc., the initial responses to a general dearth of information will not pose a long-term problem. But such responses could still pose a management challenge in the future.

CONCLUSION

Competition agencies in central and eastern Europe are new organizations that are in the process of developing their structures, policies, and procedures. They also face a rapidly changing environment. To the extent that organizations do become constrained in their capabilities and goals as a result of their responses to critical events during their history, the types of responses developed in response to a transitioning economy may limit these agencies when they face a more mature economy.

The short-run environment has put considerable pressure on these agencies to prevent "high" prices that fall under the competition laws as possible abuses of dominant power. Lacking full trade liberalization and agencies that are developed specifically for regulatory purposes, competition offices have been forced (or have chosen voluntarily) to solve these problems. We believe that cultivation of this regulatory approach to competition may cause these agencies difficulty as they attempt to meet the needs of a mature market economy.

Despite these pressures, the normal work of an antitrust agency leads to an agency whose staff and management are firm believers in market solutions to economic problems. As a result such agencies (e.g. the US Federal Trade Commission and the US Department of Justice) have been primary advocates within the government of market-based approaches to policy problems. The PAO has served this role already and we suspect that the other agencies will do so also.

Finally, one interesting prediction that comes of this analysis is that if functions that are not normally the province of competition agencies (e.g. consumer protection) are placed within these agencies, the implementation of these functions is likely to be different than the implementation had the functions been located in a non-competition agency. It could be argued, for example, that the consumer protection functions of the US Federal Trade Commission might have been more interventionist (e.g. quality standard setting) if the functions had not been placed within an agency that also had a competition mission.[20] Many of the offices in eastern and central Europe have (Hungary, Bulgaria) or may acquire (Poland) such consumer protection responsibilities. We expect that these dual responsibilities will have a long-term impact on the evolution of competition and consumer protection in the respective countries. A consumer protection agency that mandated minimum quality standards could actually defeat the market, because it could mandate rigid standards that would prevent innovative new firms from entering the market and could facilitate collusion among competitors. Accordingly, both the short- and long-term evolution toward a market economy can be shaped by the breadth of responsibilities of a competition institution.

NOTES

1. Such practices may include, under certain circumstances, exclusive distributorships or tying arrangements that force the purchase of certain unwanted goods from the same supplier.
2. Mergers are reviewed and prohibited to prevent a competitor from buying its chief rivals when the merger would create a dominant firm or significantly enhance the ability of the remaining firms in the market to collude.
3. Traditionally, the EC's competition policy has also been used to help create a single market within the Community. Similarly, EC merger policy has tended to favor larger firms that supposedly could compete more effectively in international markets, allowing European firms to overcome a loss in economies of scale that could result from firms limited to relatively small home markets. Competition policies in countries such as Germany and France have tended more to encourage larger, more internationally competitive firms at the expense of domestic competition, with an antitrust emphasis on preventing dominant firms from engaging in monopolistic practices designed to eliminate actual and smaller potential competitors (Fox, 1986).
4. Such a goal may be tempered, however, with other concerns usually not under the direct purview of the competition agencies, such as allowing arrangements that foster exports.
5. US competition policy has tended to stay away from such determinations because it is difficult to know when a price or output has been set at the monopoly level, and US antitrust law does not permit competition agencies to fix prices.
6. Information from Andre Juris, official in the Slovak Antimonopoly Office. This system was established by the former Czechoslovakian government. At the time of writing (May 1993), the Czechs were proceeding with the program as planned. The direction and speed of the Slovak privatization program was somewhat less certain.
7. On 30 April 1993 the Polish Parliament approved a long-awaited plan for mass privatization of 600 large enterprises after defeating an earlier version in March (Slay, 1993).
8. At the time of writing (May 1993), the Hungarian government has indicated that it may introduce a voucher-type privatization program to supplement the existing system. The program will give citizens access to long-term, low interest-rate credit to purchase equity in privatizing enterprises (Okolicsanyi, 1993).
9. The Hungarian competition law went into effect on 1 January 1991, with the creation of the Economic Competition Office. The former head of the Price Control Board, Dr Vissi, and a significant portion of his old staff comprised the initial staff. He continues as the president of the competition office. Dr Anna Fornalczyk, a professor at the University of Łódź, has headed the Polish Antimonopoly Office since it became an independent agency under a new competition law in April 1990. However, the Federal Competition Office in Czechoslovakia was abolished on 15 October 1992, and the existing Czech and Slovak competition offices will

replace its functions. Such changes reflect the potential for politically motivated changes.

10. To the extent that organizations compete against each other, poorer performers can be expected to be replaced by better performers. Focus on the current environment—the selection mechanism—would appear to be very important in the analysis of organizations facing competitive pressure. Where organizations face very weak competitive pressure, such as is usually the case with respect to governmental organizations, focus on the historical relationship between the organization and its environment may well be of greater value for understanding the current organization than would focus on the current environment.

11. It is also possible that the leadership in these organizations may weigh the maintenance of the ruling group's power in decisions that affect the organization. See, for example, Michels' (1949) discussion of the "iron law of oligarchy."

12. Interaction with these groups can also be a source of legitimacy both inside and outside the country. The fact that similar cases were brought by western agencies is an important argument used to justify an agency's enforcement decisions. The eastern and central European agencies also interact with sister agencies in other eastern and central European countries.

13. Ironically, he (Dolgos) later emerged as the new head of the Slovak privatization agency.

14. That is, the sale price of a company reflects the purchaser's belief about government's future interference in the industry and about the constraints the government will place on a privatized company. If the purchaser believes he is buying a monopoly position in the domestic market for some period of time, but the competition agency prevents this from happening, then the investor will not get his anticipated returns. Future investors will be discouraged because, once some investors have been "fooled," others will fear further unanticipated government actions that would reduce anticipated profits.

15. There is also the problem of the general court system, capital market infrastructure, property rights, and other such issues that fall broadly under unfair competition statutes.

16. As a pragmatic response along related lines, President Fornalczyk of the Polish Antimonopoly Office has suggested that an appropriate industry structure in a transition economy might be less concentrated than in a mature economy because of the potential benefits that a transition economy would get from putting more managers "on line." Any problem posed by this approach could be remedied later through an appropriate merger policy.

17. Of 158 cases that were resolved by the Slovak Antimonopoly Office in 1991, 79 involved abuse of market dominance. Most of the abuse of dominance cases involved tying, which in the transforming Slovak economy is used as a means of rationing scarce commodities and of evading price regulation. These types of cases are rare in the US, where few products are price regulated.

18. In addition, because these agencies will often need to determine information from foreign sources (to determine potential entrants, the extent of a

market, etc.), this information is also difficult to obtain across borders. Western agencies face similar problems in this regard.

19. United States *vs.* Philadelphia National Bank, 374 U.S. 321. (1963).
20. The US Federal Trade Commission, for example, focuses its consumer protection responsibilities on making sure consumers are adequately informed, without requiring minimum product quality standards. The belief is that fully informed consumers can best make the decision about the quality of products they desire, and that a competition market will then respond by providing those products. In this way, the approach of the agency in these two areas of law enforcement complement one another.

ACKNOWLEDGMENTS

This chapter is an abridged version of a chapter in H.J. Blommestein and B. Steunenberg (Eds) (1994). *Government and Markets: Establishing a Democratic Order and a Market Economy in Former Socialist Countries.* Dordrecht: Kluwer.

The authors wish to thank Phyllis Altrogge for her comments and contributions, and participants at the 1992 Strategic Management Society Conference for their comments.

The opinions expressed here are those of the authors and do not necessarily reflect the views of the Federal Trade Commission.

REFERENCES

Cohen, M.D., March, J.G. and Olgen, J.P. (1972). A garbage can model of organizational choice. *Administrative Science Quarterly* **17**, 1–25.

Cyert, R.M. and March, J.G. (1963). *A Behavioral Theory of the Firm.* Englewood Cliffs, NJ: Prentice Hall.

Easterbrook, F. (1984). Limits of antitrust. *Texas Law Review* **63**(1), 1–40.

Fornalczyk, A. (1992). Competition law and policy in Poland. Speech before the International Bar Association, Budapest, Hungary, 21 June.

Fox, E. (1986). Monopolization and dominance in the United States and the European Community: Efficiency, opportunity and fairness, *Notre Dame L. Rev.* **61**, 984–1020.

Hare, G.P., Canning, A. and Ash, T. (1995). The role of government institutions in the process of privatization. In H.J. Blommestein and B. Steunenberg (Eds.) *Government and Markets: Establishing a Democratic Order and a Market Economy in Former Socialist Countries.* Dordrecht: Kluwer.

Hungarian GVH (1991/2). Report to parliament.

Johnson, S. and Kroll, H. (1991). Managerial strategies for spontaneous privatization. *Soviet Economy* **7**(4), 281–314.

Katzmann, R.A. (1980). In J.Q. Wilson (Ed.) *The Politics of Regulation* (pp. 152–187). Basic Books, New York.

Langenfeld, J. and Blitzer, M.W. (1991). Is competition policy the last thing Central and Eastern Europe need? *The American University Journal of International Law and Policy* 6(3), 347–398.

Meyer, J.W. and Rowan, B. (1977). Institutionalized organizations: Formal structure as myth and ceremony. *American Journal of Sociology* 83, 340–363.

Michels, R. (1949). *Political Parties* (translated from 1915 by E. and C. Paul). Glencoe, IL: Free Press.

Okolicsanyi, K. (1993). Hungary plans to introduce voucher-type privatization. *RFE/RL Research Report*, 2, 17 (23 April), pp. 37–40.

Pfeffer, J. (1978). The micropolitics of organizations. In J.W. Meyer (Ed.) *Environments and Organizations*. San Francisco, CA: Jossey-Bass.

Sachs, J. and Lipton, D. (1990). Privatization in eastern Europe: The case of Poland. *Brookings Papers on Economic Activity* 2, 293–333.

Selznick, P. (1949). *TVA and the Grass Roots*. Berkeley, CA: University of California Press.

Selznick, P. (1957). *Leadership in Administration*. Evanston, IL: Row, Peterson.

Slay, B. (1993). Poland: The role of managers in privatization. *RFE/RL Research Report*, 2, 15 (19 March).

Weaver, S. (1980). In J.Q. Wilson (Ed.) *The Politics of Regulation* (pp. 123–151). Basic Books, New York.

3

International Mixed Management Organizations and Economic Liberalization in Hungary: From State Bureaucracy to New Paternalism

Lívia Markóczy, John Child

INTRODUCTION

The privatization process in the eastern European countries, including Hungary, is regarded as having a prominent role in transforming these economies into more efficient market ones. One of the aims of the process is to "liberalize" the economy by releasing many enterprises from their dependence on and protection by the state. It aims to make the judgements of customers

Strategic Renaissance and Business Transformation. Edited by H. Thomas, D. O'Neal and J. Kelly.
Copyright © 1995 John Wiley & Sons Ltd.

and financial investors the criteria for managerial and organizational performance and the measure of how well managerial actions fit the new context.

One form of privatization is the establishment of *hybrids* between existing Hungarian companies and foreign (mostly western and Japanese) partners. Borys and Jemison (1989) use the term "hybrids" to describe arrangements that use resources and/ or organizational and governance structures from more than one existing organization. Hybrids that were formed between previously existing Hungarian firms (or their branches) and western firms are widely seen not only as a means for "liberalization" but also as a way of ensuring that these organizations adjust rapidly to the competitive conditions. Hybrids are expected to introduce market orientated managerial practices, technologies, organizational structures, procedures and financial resources into these organizations (Csáth, 1991; Denton, 1991; *Economist*, 1991; Robinson, 1991). The increasing importance of hybrids in the Hungarian economy is indicated by the rapid increase in their numbers and the scale of foreign capital investment (TABLE 3.1).

Those hybrids in which foreign managers work together with host country managers seem particularly conducive to the process of transferring western managerial know-how to existing organizations. We call these organizations international mixed management organizations (IMMOs) to differentiate them from other types of hybrids (Markóczy, 1993).

The general aim of this chapter is to investigate whether IMMOs are effective tools for fulfilling the expectations many have of them, including: (i) decreasing existing dependencies on the state; (ii) transferring western managerial know-how along

TABLE 3.1   Cumulative foreign investment in Hungary (1000 million HUF)

Year	Companies	Starting capital	Foreign investment	Total foreign investment (new and existing)
1989	1350	124.4	30.0	50
1990	5693	274.1	93.2	140
1991	9117	476.6	215.0	310
1992	13218	546.0	257.9	480
1993*	15311	569.1	275.0	700

Sources: Cégvezetés (1994); Hungarian Central Statistical Office.
*Six months.

with other resources; and (iii) assisting the adjustment of organizations to emerging market conditions. If IMMOs are indeed effective instruments for meeting these expectations, they are likely to develop organizational structures, procedures and managerial behaviours that support their implementation. Based on structural contingency theory (Lawrence and Lorsch, 1967; Pugh et al., 1969) and certain approaches towards managerial learning pursued by the foreign partners (Fiol and Lyles, 1985) predictions can therefore be made about what organizational structures and procedures should result:

1. Contingency theory suggests that decreasing dependence on the state is likely to result in decentralization of authority and control within organizations (Donaldson, 1985; Hickson and McMillan, 1981; Pugh, 1981; Pugh et al., 1969). Therefore, a decrease in dependence on the state should lead to decentralization within IMMOs unless this dependence is replaced by new dependencies on one or more of the parent companies (Killing, 1983) or still requires more time to be implemented.

2. Learning may happen at two levels (Fiol and Lyles, 1985). Transfer of knowledge at the lower level would mean introducing western managerial techniques in areas such as marketing or accounting without making an effort to change the understanding of business held by Hungarian managers. Effective knowledge transfer, however, requires learning at the higher levels, otherwise the new techniques will be applied according to the old logic. Higher-level learning means shifting the thinking of Hungarian managers towards a market and strategic orientation, which most of them lacked previously. In order to have a chance to learn at the higher level, Hungarian managers need to participate in the processes through which decisions of strategic significance are made.

3. According to contingency theory, those organizations with flexible organizational structures and procedures are better adapted to a highly turbulent environment, and should be able to handle the accompanying uncertainty better than those with bureaucratized, highly inflexible characteristics (Lawrence and Lorsch, 1967; Thompson, 1967). Since the Hungarian environment has become highly turbulent and generates considerable uncertainty, IMMOs with flexible organizational structures are expected to adapt better than those with inflexible and bureaucratic structures.

In eleven IMMOs described later we investigated whether the emerging organizational structures, procedures and participation of Hungarian managers in strategic decisions accorded with these predictions. This was found to be only partially so, especially in the large IMMOs. In half of the IMMOs authority remained centralized through the concentration of strategically important decisions into the hands of the foreign partners. Moreover, the procedures and practices that were introduced in all of the IMMOs investigated were simply the standard operational procedures of the foreign partners rather than flexible forms designed to suit Hungarian conditions. These outcomes imply the emergence of a new dependence within IMMOs on the foreign parent companies. This should account for the centralization of power in the hands of foreigners and for the introduction of their standardized procedures.

This chapter discusses possible explanations for the emerging dependence of Hungarian hybrid organizations on their foreign partners and explores whether this dependence has similar reasons and consequences as the previous regime of state paternalism. In order to identify similarities with this regime, the next section describes the sources and consequences of the previous paternalistic relationship between the state and the state-owned organizations. Changes in this relationship are discussed, and their effect on the starting positions of the partners in IMMOs are described.

THE PREVIOUS HUNGARIAN ENVIRONMENT

The "socialist history" of the Hungarian economy can be characterized by different stages of paternalistic relationship between the state and large, state-owned companies. Kornai described paternalism as a "material relationship between parents and their children" (1980, p. 575), where the power position of the state rested on allocating resources and on appointing managers to top positions. This resource and personal dependence extended from providing natural resources and directly appointing managers to providing legal exemptions, tax benefits and a helping hand to the "children in need", and having indirect influence on the appointment of top managers. Paternalism based on the allocation of natural resources characterized Hungary in the 1950s and early

1960s. The subsequent, though not unbroken, history of reforms transformed this paternalism into a milder form by the end of the 1980s. Dependence on the state for resources and personal advancement had a major influence on who was chosen to occupy top positions, the organizational structures and procedures that were formed, and the informal rules and values that directed managerial decisions and behaviours.

Thus, high positions were occupied by managers who were "politically reliable"—members of the Hungarian Socialist Workers Party (the communist party)—and who had sufficiently good connections with the Party and the government to bargain for additional resources. Those managers who were able to raise investment resources and pay higher wages to their employees gained the image of being successful managers, both in the judgement of the authorities and in the eyes of the public (Markóczy, 1991). Managers were judged more in terms of their ability to lobby the authorities effectively than in terms of their ability to make rational decisions or satisfy market needs. It did not, therefore require western managerial skills to be a successful state enterprise manager.

Dependence on the state favoured large, monopolistic companies which were closely connected to the state authorities and could readily lobby for preferential treatment and investment resources (Kornai, 1990; Révész, 1990; Schweitzer, 1982). These large, state owned firms were virtually extensions of the authorities (Kornai, 1990), and were highly bureaucratic, with formalized procedures and standardized task descriptions. They produced a large volume of reports according to the requirements of the central authorities. These reports, however, were often "massaged" and served to hide information rather than to provide it. Having valid information was considered a source of power in bargaining for resources (Szalai, 1989).

Lobbying for additional resources and benefits was part of the game at the macro level. In addition, building on personal connections was an important means of gaining personal preference and rewards within organizations (Pearce, Branyiczki and Bakacsi, 1994). One of the ways of lobbying for additional resources both outside and within organizations was to find excuses as to why requirements could not be satisfied with the resources provided. With this practice, additional resources could be gained to overcome unfavourable circumstances. These characteristics applied much less to small organizations, which did not enjoy sufficient influence to lobby for resources and which were also able to a large extent to avoid attention of the central authorities (Markóczy, 1990).

CHANGES IN THE HUNGARIAN ENVIRONMENT

The paternalistic relationship between the state and companies began to weaken with the significant economic reforms initiated in 1985. These reforms not only shook the old system but started to build market-related institutions and increase the role of the market in resource allocation. They included reform of the banking and legal systems, permission for companies to sell bonds and the start of privatization. Companies could no longer be certain that the helping hand of the state would be given in time although there were still several cases when companies in trouble were bailed out.

By 1989, deepening economic problems made it clear that economic reforms within the existing system could not provide adequate solutions. Changing the system itself seemed to be the only possible solution to the crisis. The process of replacement started with an agreement to hold free elections in spring 1990. As a result of these elections the Hungarian Socialist Workers Party, which by that time had divided into a conservative wing and a reform wing (this later became the Hungarian Socialist Party), handed over power to the Hungarian Democratic Forum (conservative party), which had achieved a simple majority.

After the election, economic changes continued and were aimed at transforming the economy into a western market type. These changes included the opening of a stock market, import liberalization, antitrust and fair competition laws and further steps towards privatizing state-owned companies. All of these measures, however, had been initiated by the previous government (reform communists) in the run-up to the elections.

The marketization process reduced the favourable treatment given to many of the large enterprises. It consequently exposed their inefficiencies and left them in bad economic shape. One of the possible ways out of the problems for these organizations was to try to find foreign partners who were ready to form hybrids with them. In this situation they searched for foreign partners to replace the previously paternalistic state by providing resources, technology and strategic direction for the "abandoned children". Since this often placed foreign partners in the role of saviours rather than equal partners, it was likely to influence both the initial power position of the partners and their future relationship.

THE MIXED MANAGEMENT ORGANIZATIONS INVESTIGATED

This chapter draws upon two studies conducted in 1990 and 1991. The first study, conducted in the summer of 1991 with the participation of colleagues from the Budapest University of Economics, produced case studies of four IMMOs that reported the difficulties of transferring western operational management, technology and know-how (Markóczy, 1993).

Three of the cases are manufacturing companies and one is a bank. Two of the manufacturing companies are large, while the other and the bank are relatively small. Two of the companies have Italian partners, one has a British partner and one has a French partner. At least 10 interviews were conducted in each company with managers at department head level or higher. Since there were normally no more than two or three senior foreign managers in each company, all of the foreign managers and seven or eight of the Hungarian managers were interviewed. In one company, however, only five interviews were conducted because top managers were unwilling to have more of their subordinates' time taken up. The case studies were based on open-ended, unstructured interviews, although the interviewers were given a written checklist for their own guidance. The interviews lasted between two and three hours.

The case study writers were instructed to ask the western managers what practices had to be changed within the companies and what difficulties they had experienced in making these changes. The Hungarian managers were also asked what had changed with the setting up of the IMMOs compared to the earlier practices of the companies or the parent companies. The interviewers were told to concentrate on exploring the changes instead of following the checklist in a mechanical way. The completed case studies were sent back to a selection of the interviewed managers for their comments.

The second study, which built on the experiences of the first study and another investigation that had been conducted in China (China–EC Management Institute, 1990), focused on the issue of organizational learning and change. It was carried out in the autumn of 1991 by the authors and other colleagues at the Budapest University of Economics. It included interviews with senior managers on the Hungarian and foreign side in 15 IMMOs. The interviewers followed an open-ended, structured questionnaire. Interviews lasted between one-and-a-half and two hours. Of the companies investigated, only seven are included in the present analysis; these are the ones where foreign partners had formed hybrids with existing Hungarian companies. The other eight organizations were newly established IMMOs, so they are not of interest here. Five of the seven companies are manufacturing companies, one service and one construction. Two of them are relatively large (one, in fact, very large), while the other five are small. There were two cases with Japanese partners, two with partners from the UK, and one each with partners from Germany, Austria and the United States. The foreign partners fall into three broadly-defined cultural regions, which were identified by Hofstede (1991): Anglo-Saxon (American and British), Germanic (German and Austrian) and Japanese. The sample had been drawn up so that any effect of national cultural differences on managerial learning and autonomy should become apparent.

The nationality of the foreign partner, the size of the IMMOs and the industry of the companies in both studies are listed in TABLE 3.2.

NEW DEPENDENCIES ON THE FOREIGNERS

For reasons discussed in the introductory section, a reduction in dependence on the state is expected to result in both decentralization and a decrease in bureaucratic formalized procedures, unless the former dependency is replaced with a new one. The following sections will examine whether these changes occurred.

BALANCE OF CONTROL AND DECENTRALIZATION

In most of the IMMOs the number of foreign managers did not exceed two or three. So for decentralization to happen, sharing or

TABLE 3.2 The IMMOS investigated

Nationality of partner	Size (employees)	Industry
Study 1		
French	1850	Electric
UK	1500	Engines
Italian	120	Banking
Italian	50	Machinery
Study 2		
American	13000	Lighting
Austrian	650	Construction
Japanese	160	Agricultural supply
Japanese	115	Glass-wool
Austral./UK	44	Transport
UK	32	Machinery
German	21	Chemical

delegating decisions to the Hungarian managers is a necessary, but not a sufficient, condition. A method for assessing the formal balance of control suggested by Child, Markóczy and Cheung (1995) implies that the power between Hungarian and foreign managers was relatively balanced. The measure suggests that Hungarians had the power of control in four of the IMMOs, that control was shared by Hungarian and foreign partners in another four and that the foreign partners had control in only three. The balance of control was assessed on the basis of three criteria:

1. the percentage equity held by the Hungarian and foreign partners
2. the division between partners of positions on the Board of Directors
3. occupancy of the CEO position.

If at least two of these indicators point to one partner, then control is judged to lie with that partner. If any two of the indicators show equal sharing between the partners, then the control is said to be balanced. (Control through the CEO position was taken to be balanced when there were joint CEOs.)

However, when we look at the participation in actual decision making, the power structure no longer appears balanced. A somewhat different picture emerges if we consider the participation of Hungarian managers in strategic decision making, in decisions about introducing new products or in those about changes to operational schedules. Hungarian managers participated in making strategic decisions and on the introduction of new products in only six out of eleven companies and in only two of the six large organizations. Hungarians made decisions about operational changes in five out of eleven companies and in two of the four large organizations.

Exclusion from the strategic decision making process reduces the possibility that Hungarian managers will develop a new strategic orientation, which many of them lacked beforehand for reasons discussed earlier. Only slight differences could be found in this respect based on the different national cultural backgrounds of the foreign partners. The Anglo-Saxon, Italian and Germanic partners, taken as a group, included the Hungarian members in strategic decision making in only half of the companies (in two of the four companies with the Anglo-Saxon partners and one of the two with Germanic and Italian partners). The French partner excluded Hungarian managers entirely. At first sight, the Japanese partners were the most participative since in both cases they included Hungarian managers in strategic decision making. However, although the Japanese managers did not formally retain strategic decisions in their hands, they made serious efforts to introduce strong collectivist cultural norms and values, which placed significant limits as to which decisions were acceptable. They emphasized that the Hungarian members had to develop absolute loyalty towards the IMMO, while they themselves preserved their strong loyalty towards their Japanese parents, which had to be informed in every detail about the activity of the IMMOs.

INTRODUCTION OF FOREIGN PROCEDURES

Foreign managerial procedures were introduced in all of the organizations investigated. Those most often mentioned were new financial information and reporting systems (10 IMMOs) and new decision making systems (10 IMMOs). Other new procedures were in the areas of marketing and market research (8 IMMOs), control (such as quality control and budgetary control) (6 IMMOs), production planning (3 IMMOs), new technology (6 IMMOs) and computerized information system (3 IMMOs).

Interviews with Hungarian managers suggest that these procedures were not always introduced after consideration of how best to suit the context, but were, rather, standardized bureaucratic procedures developed by the foreign parent in a different context.

For example, in one of the large manufacturing organizations with an American partner, marketing techniques were introduced that were not appropriate to the conditions of the European market. As the Hungarian chairman commented in an interview:

> Their trade policy is different. It does not work here. Europe requires another method. One big advertisement campaign is not enough. Here continuous contact with the customers is necessary. A more personal relationship is required, and they could not get accustomed to this.

The managing director of a large manufacturing company also complained about the unsuitable marketing approach introduced by the Japanese partner:

> In terms of marketing the Japanese approach has negative consequences. It took the Japanese managers a long time to understand that the Hungarian market requires the introduction of products which have already been forgotten because they are out of date in Japan. Similarly, they did not recognize the importance of TV commercials. They also found it difficult to understand that in Hungary there are only two TV channels.

There were, moreover, complaints about the bureaucratic nature of the foreign procedures that were introduced:

> The most serious problem is the clumsiness of decision-making. As we have to get approval for important decisions [from the foreign parent organization], we cannot take advantage of the situation, although after import liberalization the situation improved and the administration became quicker. At the same time the foreign managers do not understand a lot of things, such as the rapid change of regulations, or the characteristics of the Hungarian market.

Other Hungarian managers also complained about the bureaucratic nature of many of the new procedures. As the managing director of a constructing company with Austrian partners said, "The introduction of the accounting system was difficult and it sometimes seems to be a little bureaucratic".

A number of explanations could be offered for the introduction of standard foreign practices that left differences in the Hungarian context out of consideration. It could be the case, for instance, that foreign partners are relatively inflexible or strongly believe that what works in other contexts must work in Hungary as well. Another explanation would refer to Schaan's (1988) argument that, in addition to the formal means of control, the introduction of a parent company's policies and procedures can serve to place control in its hands. Since in each of the IMMOs foreign parents were even expected to introduce western managerial techniques and procedures, this itself supplied them with the potential to secure control in two ways. Firstly, foreign managers are familiar with these procedures and their potential limitations, which places the Hungarians, who do not have this experience, at a disadvantage. Secondly, the procedures and practices that are transferred from the foreign parent are likely to serve the interest of that parent through supplying information or imposing a framework of decision making.

The next section considers those procedures that had major significance for access to information and for possibilities of participation in the decision making.

INFORMATION COLLECTION AND CIRCULATION

New accounting and reporting systems were introduced in most of the IMMOs (10 out of 11). These were intended to overcome the differences between the Hungarian and foreign approaches to accounting and to build reporting systems that were effective according to the standards and purposes of the foreign parents. Since there was a requirement to satisfy both Hungarian and foreign accounting standards, the introduction of foreign accounting systems increased rather than decreased the number of bureaucratic procedures that were used. For example, in one of the organizations five kinds of balance sheets had to be prepared each month.

Some of the foreign partners reported that horizontal communication had been ineffective in the former Hungarian organizations. To redress this problem, formal systems for circulating information were introduced in five of the eleven IMMOs, and these were among the larger organizations studied. The new systems all employed standard forms of written communication.

In several cases, Hungarian managers expressed their concern that the newly introduced information systems served as a means of control for the foreign partner. As one manager in a large, manufacturing company which had a British partner said:

> The British are professional in dealing with information. They give people only exactly as much information as necessary. But on the other hand they know about everything, which substantially increases their power position.
>
> (Szabó, 1990, p. 25)

In another IMMO with American partners, the Hungarian chairman expressed the same view:

> Many of the Hungarian managers feel that the Americans retain certain information, so the Hungarians are handicapped because the possession of information means knowledge, and greater influence and power.

Although these views expressed by Hungarian managers might reflect certain biases and fears about foreign control, standardized information systems did in practice provide effective control mechanisms in the hands of the foreign partners who introduced them. There appeared to be no substantial differences among IMMOs in this respect according to the national culture of the foreign partners, although the picture is not clear since the number of cases is limited and larger size also appears to promote the use of standard information systems.

DECISION MAKING

There was a clear tendency among the IMMOs to introduce a well-defined responsibility system, which designated the framework of managerial authority and responsibility. These responsibility systems had been implemented in nine out of eleven cases. The new responsibility systems clarified the responsibility and authority of the managers concerned and in this way contributed to the delegation of decision making on operational issues. The delegation was, however, limited in scope. It was intended to motivate managers to make decisions within their designated areas of discretion and, by defining their responsibilities, to make them accountable for those decisions. It did not extend to decisions on changes to operating rules or procedures.

The introduction of decision responsibility systems had both a control and a motivational function. The clarification of responsibilities enhanced the ability to control managers' decisions because it both set limits to their discretion and made them accountable for the use of whatever discretion they were afforded. These new systems were, however, also a response to the inherited problem that stood in the way of delegation, namely the tendency of Hungarian managers to avoid responsibility by not taking decisions (Child and Markóczy, 1993; Markóczy, 1994/5). The new systems were intended to encourage Hungarian managers to make decisions within the framework of accountability.

POSSIBLE EXPLANATIONS

The limited participation of Hungarian managers in strategic decision making and the nature of newly-introduced organizational procedures implies that in many organizations the foreign partners have replaced the previous system of state paternalism with a new form that continues to leave the Hungarians in a condition of dependency. Foreign partners now establish strategic priorities and provide investment, technology and know-how, rather as government organs did under the former regime. This puts them into favourable position to fill key managerial positions, shape organizational structures and determine what organizational procedures are introduced. In this way, foreign partners are carrying forward the previous paternalistic role of the state into what may reasonably be called a "new paternalism" (Markóczy, 1993). There are several reasons why foreign investors are motivated to pursue this policy.

One explanation relates to the special characteristics of hybrids. Hybrids are special organizations in the sense that it is difficult to draw boundaries between them and their parent organizations (Borys and Jemison, 1989). Hybrids are often the focus of power struggles between the parents, as well as between the parents and the hybrid itself, which is likely to be seeking greater autonomy and to establish its own identity.

The concern of foreign investing companies to exert sufficient control to ensure a return on their outlays is therefore likely to be enhanced in the case of hybrids set up in transforming and risky environments. It is not surprising that foreign partners should use their power as resource providers to take control of IMMOs into their own hands. Their desire to exercise control, particularly in the formative years, will be strengthened in cases where foreign partners seek to fit their Hungarian affiliates into wider networks of international operations.

A further explanation relates to the efficient running of the IMMOs. Killing (1983) concluded that those organizations that are dominated by only one partner tend to be more effective than those with shared control, a view supported by a more recent study of hybrid firms in East Asia (*Business Asia*, 1992). In a highly turbulent environment it might be more effective if foreign partners dominate in firms since this way they can make market-orientated decisions more quickly than if they had to negotiate every issue with the Hungarian parents or managers.

The emergence of new paternalism could also be explained as a natural consequence of change in ownership. The setting up of IMMOs was in itself an instrument to switch ownership from the state to private parent organizations. It would be natural that the foreigners as the new owners should want to establish control of their organizations. Ownership, however, does not explain *per se* the new paternalism introduced by the foreign partners. Among the organizations investigated, six had majority Hungarian ownership and five had majority foreign ownership. If ownership were of crucial importance, then one would expect Hungarians to be in control of Hungarian-owned companies, which is not the case.

Another possible explanation for new paternalism would be the lack of long-term commitment by the foreign party towards the hybrids (Markóczy, 1993)—in other words, that the foreign side was not concerned to build up the local managerial competence of the hybrid. Many of the foreign investors were, at the beginning of 1990s, cautious not to invest more in an uncertain environment than they were willing to lose for the sake of getting a foot in the door of eastern Europe. In this case, the foreign partner is less interested in engaging in any activities that do not yield a short-term result, such as developing local managers through training and divesting real control to them.

On the other hand, new paternalism may itself be a short-term phenomenon. It might only be needed to overcome the more immediate need to place the hybrids on an effective footing by establishing foreign techniques and systems in the company, and by training Hungarian managers in their use. This has been the case, for example, in several IMMOs in China where, once Chinese managers had been trained, foreign managers and experts were withdrawn, leaving the company under local direction (Child, Markóczy and Cheung, 1995). During the interviews several western managers emphasized that their presence in Hungary could only be justified during the transformation period, after which they intended that the hybrid would be run by Hungarian managers. However, this expectation is not consistent with the frequent exclusion of Hungarian managers from decision making where they could acquire the necessary competence to run the hybrids in the future.

THE HUNGARIAN SIDE

The above explanations provide arguments for why foreign companies should use their powers to create dependence on the part of their Hungarian IMMO partners. However, it is not simply a foreign-induced phenomenon; the Hungarians, in many ways, contributed to the new paternalism as well. Their support for new paternalism appeared to reflect a view when the joint organizations were established that westerners were economic saviours rather than equal partners, and that in those circumstances Hungarian managers did not command authority. The routines and beliefs inherited by the Hungarians from the former system of paternalistic industrial governance were also likely to favour the emergence of new paternalism. Moreover, the Hungarians often lacked skills relating to marketing and finance, which obliged the foreign partner to fill key positions in that area with their own managers. These factors are now examined in turn.

IINITIAL EXPECTATIONS AND THE CRISIS OF HUNGARIAN AUTHORITY

As described earlier, Hungarian managers often expected the foreign partners to take charge of their organizations. They found it problematic and confusing if foreign managers did not fulfil these expectations.

One of the case studies, for example, describes how Hungarian managers in a large manufacturing IMMO with French partners expressed this problem (Kata and Szajkó, 1991, p. 19):

> They [Hungarian managers] feel that they do not get any support about what kind of expectations they have to satisfy ... The arising problems remain unsolved, there are no decisions made, there are no orders, there are no deadlines.

In other cases Hungarian managers had to rely on their foreign counterparts simply because their authority to take decisions was not accepted by their own Hungarian subordinates. In two cases the foreign management wanted to transfer its newly-gained authority to well-trained Hungarian managers, but found this impossible because Hungarian subordinates were only willing to accept the authority of the foreign managers. The result was that the foreign side chose the easy way out and filled the role of an external authority.

The CEO of a large manufacturing parent company described this situation in the following way (Markóczy, 1994/5, p. 26):

> The representative of company P [foreign partner] was here in our plant. He exercised constant control. It is a shame that his presence ensured that daily shortcomings were corrected on the spot and carried out properly. [For] the staff only accepted control from him and not from the Hungarian managers. This was the case with product R as well [in the other IMMO established by the company]. So I see a tendency that most of the employees are still more willing to accept instructions from outside authorities, even [Hungarian ones] such as KÖJÁL [authority for checking workplace hygiene], working safety instructors, fire authorities, and so on, though you could find these functions within the company as well. And they also carry out the task better if the instructions come from outside. This is unfortunate because I do not see any difference in the quality of know-how whether it comes from inside or outside the enterprise.

In the case of a large IMMO with British partners the case study writer presents the phenomenon in the following way (Szabó, 1990, p. 20):

> It was almost a uniform opinion among managers that "we Hungarians would have been able to [reconstruct the company] as well, perhaps only much slower". But most of the Hungarian staff believed that the foreigners would lead the company out of crisis. Some managers thought this belief was excessive and was just the manifestation of "Hungarians believe everything coming from a foreigner".

ADHERENCE TO OLD ROUTINES

Foreign partners mentioned several instances where they had tried to encourage their Hungarian colleagues to initiate and take decisions but had been confronted with resistance from them.

For example in a large manufacturing IMMO, an American manager complained about the unwillingness of Hungarian managers to take responsibility (Child and Markóczy, 1993):

> The Hungarians do not want to make decisions or take responsibility. If a problem was told to you [by a Hungarian] it becomes your problem.

In a small manufacturing IMMO, the British manufacturing director described the Hungarian reaction when something went wrong:

> The traditional Hungarian reaction is that someone is playing a nasty trick on me. They say: "It is not my fault that something goes wrong. It is because somebody tries to attack me." That is how Hungarians think. It is because Hungarian management is based very much on the punishment for mistakes, which encourages people not to take decisions.

The survival of servility was mentioned by an American manager in a large manufacturing company:

> We do not know whether the Hungarians agree with the decisions or are just good soldiers.

Foreign managers also described the tendency for older managers to be unwilling to pass on information that would present themselves in an unfavourable light to their partners:

> The older managers, especially those above forty, are accustomed to "whitewash" information which passes upwards.

LACK OF SKILLS

In some organizations, foreign staff had to occupy leading managerial positions simply because Hungarian managers lacked the skill to run the organization in a way that would satisfy the requirements of the foreign partners. This was the case in two IMMOs with Anglo-Saxon partners. As the foreign managing director of a medium sized manufacturing company said:

> I was sent here because the plant started a manufacturing operation and it was impossible to find a Hungarian senior manager with the necessary experience.

In the other one, a small service hybrid, the first CEO was a Hungarian who had to be replaced by a British manager because of his incompetence. The senior Hungarian manager described the previous CEO in the following way:

> The first Hungarian CEO was a complete "dead-end street". He hindered the introduction of T's [foreign partner] services. He was not abٍc to create a unified organization where all employees were thinking in the interest of the organization as a whole.

AN ALTERNATIVE EXPLANATION

The reasoning we have pursued up to this point makes considerable reference to the historical institutional context of Hungarian firms. It has emphasized, *inter alia*, the historical roots of why Hungarians support new paternalism. One could argue, however, that the behaviour we have described is primarily an expression of resistance on the part of Hungarian interest groups towards changes, bearing in mind the intrusion into their organizational life that the foreign presence represents. Examples of similar self-defensive behaviour can also be found in hybrids between western firms (Shenkar and Zeira, 1987), which suggests that it is not necessarily a product of the specific Hungarian situation.

Although it is quite possible that the conflicting interests and expectations held by Hungarians and foreigners have given rise to some resistance to change and increased the likelihood of the behaviour noted, the Hungarian context cannot be ignored. Other research has shown that the behavioural characteristics we have noted existed in Hungary prior to current changes. For example, Pearce (1991) discussed the problems of holding back information and avoiding decision making in organizations in the previous Hungarian context, while Hankiss (1983) identified servilism and a concentration on excuses rather than on action as a problem in Hungarian society as a whole. The question of whether these inherited behavioural tendencies are the product of the previous state socialist system of governance or of an intrinsic Hungarian culture has been the subject of another paper (Child and Markóczy, 1993). Either way, the Hungarian context is relevant.

CONCLUSION

This chapter has argued that in IMMOs between Hungarian and foreign partners the previous dependence on the state authorities has often been replaced by foreign control. Like the previous paternalism of the state, the new situation derives from resource dependency (Pfeffer and Salancik, 1978), now on the foreign partners, and it has similar structural and behavioural consequences. It is indeed sustained by behaviours and expectations that were formed under the previous regime. Following Markóczy (1993), we call this phenomena new paternalism.

The emergence of new paternalism in IMMOs puts into question whether the organizations where it occurs are able to meet the expectations that Hungarian policy makers and their advisers place upon them. In regard to the goal of liberalizing Hungarian industry, the establishment of hybrids has released firms from their dependence on the state, but at the same time foreign control has been introduced through the provision of investment resources, technology and know-how. This made it possible for the western parents to put their managers into key positions, often leaving out the Hungarian managers from strategically important decisions. Hungarian managers have been left without support or the direct means of learning how to run the company strategically. The lack of learning at this higher level helps to preserve the previous routines, attitudes and beliefs of the Hungarian managers, rather than forcing some changes in these.

A further goal is that of enhancing the competitive edge of Hungarian firms by introducing western managerial and operational practices. These practices were introduced into the IMMOs. They were, however, in many cases the standardized operational procedures of the foreign partners, which were not developed or modified to suit the Hungarian situation. This is likely to limit the contribution they make.

The emergent new paternalism in a number of Hungarian–foreign hybrid firms is likely to make them less effective instruments to fulfil the expectations that are placed on them. New paternalism is, nevertheless, not necessarily a negative phenomenon. It may simply be the price to pay for these organizations to be run more effectively, or even to survive in the short run, and, in this way, to ensure a smoother transformation of the formerly state-owned organizations into more competitive, market-oriented organizations in the long run.

ACKNOWLEDGEMENTS

The research reported here was supported by the International Management Center, Budapest, by the Milan Chamber of Commerce, and by an association of thirteen Hungarian corporations in association with the Department of Business Economics of Budapest University. Both authors would like to acknowledge Aston University where John Child was a professor and Lívia Markóczy was a visiting scholar supported by the British Council during the final stages of this study.

REFERENCES

Borys, B. and Jemison, D.B. (1989). Hybrid arrangements as strategic alliances: Theoretical issues in organizational combinations. *Academy of Management Review* 14, 234–249.

Business Asia (1992). Corporate structure: Stay single, stay wealthy. *Business Asia* 14, 234–249.

Cégvezetés (1994). Hová jön a pénz? (Where does the money come from?). *Cégvezetés* March, 76–78.

Child, J. and Markóczy, L. (1993). Host country managerial behaviour in Chinese and Hungarian joint ventures: Assessment of competing explanations. *Journal of Management Studies* 30, 611–632.

Child, J., Markóczy, L. and Cheung, T. (1995). Managerial adaptation in Chinese and Hungarian strategic alliances with culturally distinct foreign partners. In S. Stewart (Ed.) *Joint Ventures in the People's Republic of China: Advances in Chinese Industrial Studies* (Vol. 4). Greenwich, CT: Jai Press.

China–EC Management Institute (CEMI) (1990). *The Management of Equity Joint Ventures in China*. Beijing: China–EC Management Institute.

Csáth, M. (1991). Strategic alliances: Joint venturing in central and eastern Europe (problems and opportunities). The case of Hungary. In D.E.

Hussey (Ed.) *International Review of Strategic Management*. 2(2) Chichester: John Wiley.

Denton, N. (1991). Need for western capital: Special survey on Hungary. *Financial Times* 30 October, p. 7.

Donaldson, L. (1985). *In Defence of Organisation Theory: Reply to the Critics*. Cambridge: Cambridge University Press.

The Economist (1991). Special survey on eastern Europe. *The Economist* September.

Fiol, M.C. and Lyles, M.A. (1985). Organizational learning. *Academy of Management Review* **10**, 803–813.

Hankiss, E. (1983). *Diagnózisok (Diagnoses)*. Budapest: Magvetö Kiadó.

Hofstede, G. (1991). *Culture and Organizations: Software of the Mind*. Maidenhead: McGraw-Hill.

Hickson, D.J. and McMillan, C.J. (Eds) (1981). *Organization and Nation: The Aston Program IV*. Farnborough, Hants: Gower Press.

Kata, P. and Szajkó, L. (1991). Organizational culture in GA, case study, International Management Center, Budapest.

Killing, J.P. (1983). *Strategies for Joint Venture Success*. London: Croom Helm.

Kornai, J. (1980). *A hiány (Shortage)*. Budapest: Közgazdasági és Jogi Könyvkiadó (published in English as *The Economics of Shortage* (1980). Amsterdam: North-Holland).

Kornai, J. (1990). The Hungarian reform process: Visions, hopes and reality. In J. Kornai (Ed.) *Vision and Reality, Market and State*. Budapest: Corvina; New York: Harvester Wheatsheaf and Routledge.

Lawrence, P.R. and Lorsch, J.W. (1967). *Organization and Environment: Managing Differentiation and Integration*. Boston, MA: Harvard University Press.

Markóczy, L. (1990). Case-study of the IE Bank, case study, International Management Center, Budapest.

Markóczy, L. (1993). Managerial and organizational learning in Hungarian–western mixed management organizations. *International Journal of Human Resource Management* **2**, 277–304.

Markóczy, L. (1994/5). Modes of organizational learning: Institutional change and Hungarian joint-ventures. *International Studies of Management and Organization*, **24**, 5–30.

Pearce, J.L. (1991) From socialism to capitalism: The effects of Hungarian human resource practices. *The Academy of Management Executive* **5**(4), 75–88.

Pearce, J.L., Branyiczki, I. and Bakacsi, G. (1994). Person-based reward system: A theory of organizational reward practices in reform-communist organizations, *Journal of Organizational Behavior*, **15**, 261–282.

Pfeffer, J. and Salancik, G. (1978). *The External Control of Organizations. A Resource Dependence Perspective*. New York: Harper and Row.

Pugh, D.S. (1981). The Aston program of research: Retrospect and prospect. In A.H. Van de Ven and W.F. Joyce (Eds) *Perspectives on Organization Design and Behavior* (pp. 135–166). New York: John Wiley.

Pugh, D.S., Hickson, D.J., Hinings, C.R. and Turner C. (1969). The context of organization structures. *Administrative Science Quarterly* **14**, 91–114.

Révész, G. (1990). *Perestroika in Eastern Europe: Hungary's Economic Transformation 1945–1988*. San Francisco, CA: Westview Press.

Robinson, A. (1991). Row over plans for leading drug companies' privatisation program, Special Survey on Hungary. *Financial Times* 30 October, p. 6.

Schaan, J.-L. (1988). How to control a joint venture even as a minority partner. *Journal of General Management* **14**, 4–16.

Schweitzer, I. (1982). *A vállalatnagyságról* (On the size of companies). Budapest: Közgazdasági és Jogi Könyvkiadó.

Shenkar, O. and Zeira, Y. (1987). Human resources management in international joint ventures: Directions for research. *Academy of Management Review* **12**, 546–557.

Szabó, F. (1990). A G-H szervezeti kultúrája (The organizational culture of G-H), case study, International Management Center, Budapest.

Szalai, E. (1989). *Gazdasági Mechanizmus Reformtörekvések és Nagyvállalati érdekek* (*Economic Mechanism Reform Efforts and Interests of Large-Scale Companies*). Budapest: Közgazdasági és Jogi Könyvkiadó.

Thompson, J.D. (1967). *Organizations in Action*. New York: McGraw-Hill.

4

Market-Orientated Strategic Change: Managing Complexity and Context

TERRY McNULTY, RICHARD WHITTINGTON,
RICHARD WHIPP

INTRODUCTION

Over the past few years, managers have been coping with a
momentous shift in the organization of economic activity. Worldwide, markets are replacing bureaucracies. Halal (1993) and Ackoff
(1993) do not hesitate to compare the processes begun under
Perestroika in the former Soviet Union with the radical restructuring of corporate America since the 1980s. Just as the planned
economies of eastern Europe collapsed under the pressures of
political–economic competition, so have new models of competitive organization forced the huge bureaucracies of American big
business—General Motors, IBM and the like—into fundamental
processes of transformation. These new models of organization are
decentralized, self-organizing and inspired by the fluidity and
spontaneity of the market (Handy, 1990; Peters, 1992). Tom Peters
(1990) urges that the power and stimulus of the market should be
forced into every nook and cranny of the corporation.

Strategic Renaissance and Business Transformation. Edited by H. Thomas, D. O'Neal and J. Kelly.
Copyright © 1995 John Wiley & Sons Ltd.

Recent history gives strong grounds for accepting the potential economic advantages of the new market-inspired approach. The problem is getting there—as the case of eastern Europe amply demonstrates. This chapter focuses on the struggle of eight British organizations—four hospitals and four Research and Development laboratories—to move from their previously cushioned bureaucratic existence to new, more competitive forms of organization, as for the first time, they confronted the challenge of market forces. In their efforts to become more market orientated, all eight organizations undertook radical decentralizing organizational change. But the lesson of their experience is that this kind of market-orientated change is neither simple nor unambiguously rewarded. Internally, organizational changes were complex and multi-level, going far deeper than merely developing new marketing functions. Often these changes set off disruptive centrifugal forces. Externally, success in market-orientated change required a transition from exaggerated conceptions of market competition towards a view of the organization interacting within a complex context of both economic and non-economic relationships. This external context needed to be positively managed rather than ignored or caricatured. The checks and reverses that these organizations endured in the shift from their old bureaucratic ways stemmed often from a failure to control and manipulate the very market forces that market-orientated change is supposed to ride.

This chapter begins by introducing some recent theoretical insights from the marketing literature on the process of market-orientated change and the environment in which it takes place. It goes on to introduce the eight case organizations in more detail and the new market pressures that these hospitals and laboratories were now struggling to cope with. The next section presents a multi-level model of the shift from a bureaucratic to market-orientated regime in such professional services. This model highlights the repercussions of this change on staff throughout the organization, with new roles imposed at every level from top management down to support staff. Next, the chapter focuses on problems in the change process, tracing their roots to inadequate management of context, both market and non-market. It is contended that successful market-orientated change, especially within professional services, entails an almost paradoxical rejection of free market ideology: visions of atomistic competition and implacable market forces need to be replaced by more measured notions of collaboration and control/The conclusion develops the implications for top managers in the domains of organization, human resources and strategic management.

COMPLEXITY AND CONTEXT

A central theme is that it is easier to state the advantages of market-based forms of organization than actually to put them into practice. There exist very few studies of how the change from bureaucratic to market regimes is achieved, but what the few exceptions do tell us is that the process is complex and fraught with risk. Consider the following brief accounts. At a major Canadian accountancy practice, a programme of market-orientated change was found to entail such deep changes in role and status at every level that finally the initiative was revoked (Hinings, Brown and Greenwood, 1991). At American Blue Cross/ Blue Shield, the internal market launched at the beginning of the 1980s gradually degenerated into an incoherent entrepreneurism that left the organization nearly fatally exposed during the downturn of the early 1990s (Gamble, Sheehan and Shields, 1993). Also in the United States, Control Data's transfer of staff functions to an internal consultancy basis failed in the context of a strong, centralized and collaborative corporate culture (Noer, 1993). In Eriksson's (in press) Finnish confectionery firm, the marketing department did finally triumph, but only after a 15-year struggle punctuated by many reverses and forced departures.

These cases are more than salutary warnings. They confirm a consistent finding of recent research on strategic change: effective change management requires deep attention to complex processes over extended periods of time (Pettigrew, 1985), a constant struggle to sustain corporate coherence (Pettigrew and Whipp, 1991) and the sophisticated management of environmental context, sociological as well as just market (Whittington, 1990). It is these three general issues—managing complexity over time, the problem of coherence and the importance of context—that provide the underlying themes of our analysis of market-orientated change here. But in approaching the eight case studies, we can also draw from two emerging streams of work in marketing that have a more precise relevance: firstly, recent advances in the field of marketing implementation; and secondly, a new approach to markets that stresses the "embeddedness" of organizations in their contexts.

Marketers have long preached the superiority of what they have traditionally called a "marketing orientation" (Hooley, Lynch and Shepherd, 1990). Only recently have they begun to investigate what this orientation might really mean to practitioners and how it actually gets implemented. Kohli and Jaworski's (1990) field enquiry into how managers themselves conceived of marketing led them to a significant redefinition of the discipline's core concept. Their conclusion was that what matters for managers is "market orientation" rather than the traditional "marketing orientation". By shifting the focus to markets rather than marketing, they removed the orientation from the exclusive domain of a particular function. What the market orientation means in practice is an organization-wide commitment to three activities in particular: the generation of market intelligence pertaining to current and future customer needs; the dissemination of this intelligence throughout the organization; and a coherent, coordinated response to the identified market opportunities (Kohli and Jaworski, 1990, p. 6). The common theme of these three activities is the need for engagement by the organization as a whole. It is this concept of market orientation that the eight case study organizations were groping towards, mostly with considerable difficulty.

This organization-wide conception of the market orientation has clear implications for implementation. Implementation is seen as not just the creation of a powerful marketing department, customer sensitive and fully loaded with all of the best techniques. Rather, the market orientation involves pervasive changes in such areas as organizational structures, information systems, organizational culture, top management, human resources and inter-departmental cooperation (Piercey, 1991). These kinds of changes take time: Kohli and Jaworski (1990) admit that implementation of a market orientation is a long, hard process that might take up to four years. Our evidence suggests that it can take even longer.

Thus, the marketing literature itself has begun to set an agenda of organization-wide issues important to the achievement of market-orientated change. These issues all played their roles in the case histories analysed here, and are reflected in the multi-level model of market-orientated change that we present. However, in explaining the successes and failures of the eight organizations, we need to extend this organizational focus just one step further, to include the nature of organizational context (Pettigrew, 1985; Whittington and Whipp, 1992). At least two features of this context are important. The first—surprisingly absent in the models of the marketing literature (Kohli and Jaworski, 1990)—is the role of the market itself in stimulating implementation of market orientations. Here we propose an apparent paradox: that the relationship between market pressures and market orientation is not a simple linear function, but that beyond a certain point market pressures are actually destructive of market-orientated behaviour. The task for management, there-fore, is to keep exposure to market pressures in measured propor-tions.

The second important contextual element in market-orientated change is acknowledgement of the socially-embedded nature of organizations and their markets. Sociologists and economists are increasingly abandoning the notion of organizations as existing as detached atoms interacting at arm's length through fleeting and anonymous market transactions. Rather, organizations are recog-nized as frequently participating in densely interknit and con-tinuous relationships, in which trading is personal and governed by institutionalized norms of behaviour (Granovetter, 1985; Hodgson, 1988). In these conditions, market exchange is not the austerely economic interaction once supposed, but inescapably a sphere of social activity in which a host of non-economic factors—altruism, friendship and extra-organizational loyalties—are constantly involved. As marketing theorists of industrial networks (Axelsson and Easton, 1992; Easton and Araujo, 1993) increasingly recognize, this conception of the environment has fundamental implications for market strategy. Strategy is not a matter of atomistic competition between discrete, rivalrous orga-nizations, but takes place in a community of regularized relation-ships between people with a range of social functions and identities. Collaboration exists alongside competition; immediate advantage is balanced by mutual benefits in the long run; interac-tion involves the exchange of information as well as just money and goods.

This industrial network conception of the environment is parti-cularly relevant to professional services. Here the interaction with consumers is not anonymous and detached, but typically personal and responsible. As Yorke (1990) astutely observed, the profes-sional "has" clients, in an almost possessive relationship. Profes-sionals are also often committed to the reproduction of the particular institutionalized practices involved in their work (Keat, 1991). These practices put a high value on practitioners' own criteria of excellence, rather than on market-defined notions of performance. Moreover, these traditional practices promote both the free exchange of information among fellow practitioners and the collective advance of standards—of medicine or science— rather than individualistic competition for simple economic advantage. Practitioners identify with a community that extends far beyond the bounds of their particular organization: their loyalties and networks entail collaboration as well as competition.

Thus this section warns that market-orientated strategic change is not easily achieved, especially in professional services. Introducing the market orientation takes time and has repercussions throughout the organization. The development of an effective relationship with the external environment requires the management of a tightly knit context of economic and social relationships. The following sections analyse these problems as they occurred in our case studies, but first a few words about the research.

THE RESEARCH

The study is based on intensive comparative analysis of eight organizations, four in the British National Health Service (NHS), four in R&D. The research concentrated on laboratories or hospital departments where coping with increased market pressures had been identified by management as a critical issue. The cases were researched by means of both interviews and access to various public and internal documents; 158 interviews were undertaken, the vast majority tape-recorded. Interviews were carried out during 1991 and 1992 with both managers and professional staff (doctors in the NHS, scientists and engineers in R&D). Feedback sessions with senior managers took place in all eight organizations.

Of the four R&D laboratories, two (NRO and ERO) were independent research organizations and two (EngCo and ProcCo) were in-house central laboratories. TABLE 4.1 gives basic data on their size and sectors. All four laboratories faced intensifying market pressures. ERO was a former industrial research association, which since the mid-1970s had been coping with major reductions in its government subsidy and a decline in its mem-

TABLE 4.1 The case studies

Case	Sector	Status	Staff	Interviews
R&D laboratories				
ERO	Engineering	Independent	250	23
NRO	Natural resource	Independent	250	23
EngCo	Engineering	In-house	200	14
ProcCo	Process industry	In-house	1800	14
NHS hospitals				
Northtrust	NHS	Trust	2000	15
Southtrust	NHS	Trust	2000	18
EastDMU	NHS	Directly managed	1500	14
WestDMU	NHS	Directly managed	1500	37

Notes: Case names are pseudonyms.
Data are approximate for the sake of confidentiality.

bership fee income. NRO was a former government laboratory that had been privatized in the early 1980s. The EngCo laboratory was the central facility of a diversified engineering company, and had been facing declining corporate funding and increased reliance on the internal customer-contractor principle throughout the 1980s and early 1990s. A similar move to the customer-contractor principle was occurring at the ProcCo central laboratory, which was part of a process industry multinational.

During the early 1990s, the four hospitals were coping with the new "internal market", a government-imposed transition from the former bureaucratic allocation of work to a more competitive sourcing of activity. All four cases were urban public hospitals, with a full range of medical and surgical services and budgets of around 50 million ($75 million). In April 1972, Northtrust and Southtrust became "trusts", still publicly owned but with greater managerial independence. EastDMU and WestDMU were "directly managed units" at the time of the research, under the ultimate control of regional management but already preparing for trust status in 1993.

In sum, the sample provides eight professional service organizations, shifting from bureaucracy to increasing reliance on the market. In terms of size, ownership and sector, the sample is quite diverse. We can expect, therefore, that our findings in these two sectors will be fairly robust for other professional service organizations facing market-orientated change.

Managing Internal Complexity

We have argued that market-orientated change involves far more than simply introducing marketing techniques, grafting on a marketing department or loud exhortations to treat the customer as king. Market-orientated change is an organization-wide commitment. Following Pettigrew and Whipp (1991), this chapter presents the process of market-orientated change in our case organizations as proceeding at many levels and over an extended period of time.

FIGURE 4.1 captures key levels and changes shared by organizations in both sectors. The vertical axis distinguishes four chief organizational levels, from top and line management strata, through the service professionals themselves (e.g. researchers and doctors), and finally to the various support staff (professional and commercial). The horizontal axis measures the extent of market-driven change. As the figure indicates, market-driven change brings new roles at every level of the organization, with the balance between new and old shifting with the degree of change. This section draws on the experience of the eight cases to illustrate this complex ensemble of changes, taking the four levels in turn. As we shall see, among our case organizations, progress along the horizontal axis of market-orientated change was often uneven, and raised thorny issues at every level.

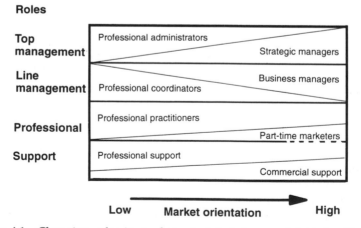

FIGURE 4.1   Changing roles in market-orientated change. Adapted with permission from Whittington, McNulty and Whipp (1994)

TOP MANAGEMENT

Under the bureaucratic regime, top management in hospitals and R&D was mainly routine, focused on control of budgets, the administration of stable programmes of work and the supervision of professional careers. By and large, professionals managed professionals. Among our R&D laboratories, top management had been exclusively made up of senior scientists and engineers. The hospitals differed in having a dual structure, with Medical Committees responsible for clinical staff, and nonmedical managers administering the rest.

However, market-orientated change soon overtakes such stable administrative patterns, challenging both the nature and the role of top management. Thus our laboratories began to admit financial and marketing specialists into their top teams, while the hospitals created single structures, unifying senior doctors and managers at the top. These new, more managerial, teams were having to think about what sort of business they were, and what sort of business they wanted to become. Organizations were being reconceptualized, not just as traditional agglomerations of scientific disciplines or medical specialities assembled according to professional logics, but as businesses whose activities were defined by market demand and organizational advantage.

At the early stages of market-orientated change, business portfolio concepts were widely used in our organizations. At ERO, for example, one manager commented:

> It is like a holding company, in that you are always in fear of asset-stripping—that companies buy you up because you are a good buy at the time and they get rid of you when it does not suit their portfolio any more. Now ... there are always discussions about dropping a particular discipline because it is no longer viable.

At EastDMU, the general manager recalled how he had drawn his hospital as a flower, with certain services at the core and others as petals around it, and told his senior medical staff that some of these petals might well drop off.

Most of the organizations we observed had begun the shift to the more dynamic, market-defined notion of the organization represented by portfolio management. This is an important first step. Less clear, however, was a movement further along the axis of FIGURE 4.1, to the definition of a coherent corporate strategy capable of coordinating organization-wide responses to market opportunities. This next stage in the development of top-level strategic management is an issue to which we shall return later.

LINE MANAGEMENT

A key part of developing a market-responsive organization is internalizing the market by the creation of decentralized business units (Peters, 1992). This decentralization of business responsibility, especially when reinforced by new portfolio concepts at the top, enforces a radical change in the role of line managers. Under the bureaucratic regime, the line management of professionals was typically restricted to the coordination of fellow professionals. In the R&D laboratories, line managers concerned themselves mainly with assembling the right combinations of skills for projects and monitoring progress and costs. Within the dual structure of the NHS, the heads of medical divisions had even less responsibility, negotiating collective facilities such as beds, operating theatres and support staff, but with little control over colleagues' outputs or expenditure.

Market-orientated change transforms these limited coordinating roles. As indicated in FIGURE 4.1, line managers become business managers, increasingly responsible for both the costs and revenues of their departments. In the hospitals, this new business management role was reflected in new titles, with "clinical directors" (appointed) replacing "heads of medical divisions" (elected). The effect on the clinical directors, according to one Southtrust manager, was to turn "poachers into gamekeepers". Clinical directors identified themselves increasingly as managers responsible for resources, rather than professionals caring only for their clinical practice. Similar changes were forced on line managers in R&D, where full profit centre responsibility was increasingly imposed on departments. Line management accountability was clear. At ERO:

> it is the departmental managers who will get kicked if there are bad results. They are the guys under pressure ... They are the line MDs of their business units.

As we shall see, however, this decentralized accountability could have dangerous side effects.

PROFESSIONALS

The decentralizing pressures of market-orientated change extend the roles of professional doctors, scientists and engineers as well. Whereas in the past professionals had worked simply as practitioners, concerned primarily with their scientific or medical tasks, they now had to take on new roles as what Gummesson (1991) calls "part-time marketers". As well as just satisfying the client needs presented to them, professionals had increasingly to ensure that clients came in the first place. As a consultant at Northtrust recognized:

> One is aware that we have to go out and push the market and try to claw in referrals from GPs and from other hospitals. Whereas we could rest on our laurels before, now we have to go out and positively advertise.

Professionals have a critical role in marketing professional services: typically, clients' problems are highly complex and often clients are themselves professionally qualified. In the NHS, clinicians were selling to medical general practitioners. As a Northtrust manager stressed, "GPs will not relate to an accountant or planning manager ... telling them what the business is about. They are going to relate to the people (i.e. doctors) they are going to refer to". The case in R&D was very similar. A NRO senior manager accepted that he could deal with "only the most superficial customers". As one of his engineers put it, "The technical experts are the people best placed to do the marketing ... We are the natural marketers".

But it is important to recognize that it was now relevant technical expertise, rather than simple professional status, that was important in the market-place. The satisfaction of client needs often demanded a team approach, bringing in professional support staff on a more equal basis with traditionally elitist professional groups. Thus, nurses played a central role in hospital quality initiatives. Often, too, the client demand was for a more accessible set of skills than those of the specialist professional. At

ProcCo, one highly successful technician described himself as "marketing the chip" to divisions, presenting his lack of "fancy" qualifications as a positive advantage to clients resentful of PhD-trained scientists from the central laboratory. The result was the market-driven osmosis between professional and support levels indicated by the dotted line in FIGURE 4.1.

SUPPORT STAFF

In addition to this levelling of traditional hierarchy between professionals and non-professionals, market-orientated change shifts the balance among support staff. In all eight of our organizations, the large nursing and technical staffs supporting the lead professional group were facing significant pressure for increased productivity and often cuts in absolute numbers. The main gainers from the more market-orientated regime were the commercial support staffs, especially in finance and accounting.

As they moved into the market-place, the starting point for these organizations was often not marketing but finance. Financial information was doubly vital: firstly, for effective pricing, and secondly for the operation of decentralized cost and profit centres. In both sectors, pricing was a critical but problematic issue. In both R&D and the NHS, costs were often difficult to predict, and would be attributable to the wide range of activities necessary to fulfil complex client needs. At Southtrust, the general manager had identified 427 basic cost codes, with a further 1000 derivatives. Without reliable cost information, marketing initiatives would be complete gambles: explosive sales of an underpriced service could bankrupt the whole organization. At the same time, motivation and control of the newly decentralized departments depended heavily on appropriate financial information. As a directorate manager at Northtrust protested:

> Our information systems are poor and that worries me because if I am going to be held accountable for something, I need good information. I will not have responsibility without control.

Thus it is the financial and accounting support staff who play the most important role in the early stages of market-orientated change. At NRO, it was a financial director who was first to penetrate the formerly exclusively scientific board of directors; the new marketing manager had to wait three more years before he could assist informally at executive board meetings. In the hospitals, indeed, most of the marketing has been done so far by "contracts managers", usually with financial backgrounds and reporting to finance heads. Specifically marketing professionals were far from central to the early stages of market-driven change that we observed. This absence may have been an important element in the failure to develop a more strategic approach, which we discuss in the following section.

MANAGING CONTEXT STRATEGICALLY

We have seen that market-orientated change is a complex, comprehensive process, involving new roles at every level of the organization. Many features of this change are common between even two such different sectors as industrial R&D and NHS hospitals. Up to here, however, the focus has largely been internal. In this section we want to recall our earlier discussion of the external context to insist on the importance of managing both market and non-market relationships. Our argument is twofold. On the one hand, if market forces are allowed to get out of hand, effective marketing is among the first things that suffer. On the other hand, if non-market relationships are too heavily handled, then management risks needlessly suppressing a valuable source of long-term advantage.

It is the curvilinear relationship between market pressure and marketing effectiveness that FIGURE 4.2 describes. Naturally, market pressures are an important stimulus to market-orientated behaviours. In the NHS, it was the government's internal markets initiative that pushed hospitals along the horizontal axis of market orientation. But market pressures were still uneven, and the absence of competitive pressures—either because of endless waiting lists or monopoly control over a particular local service—still left many hospital departments on the left-hand side of the axis. In the words of one WestDMU consultant, "we do not market our services particularly because we do not have to—we have a monopoly". The laboratories followed a similar pattern, market-orientated activity beginning to develop as they were increasingly exposed to market pressures (following cuts in

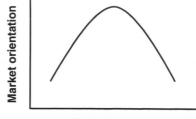

FIGURE 4.2   Market pressure and market orientation

subsidy or privatization). Over the past 10 years, laboratories had been advancing rightwards along the horizontal axis towards a greater market orientation, especially as decentralization internalized market pressures at departmental level. As a ProcCo middle manager put it, "most of our team are aware that the only way they will survive is by marketing their services".

However, market forces can drive organizations too far along the horizontal axis of FIGURE 4.2, with truly market-orientated activity suffering as a result. The organization-wide generation and dissemination of market intelligence and the coordination of response require the ability to raise heads above the short term and a readiness to cooperate as well as compete. In all of our organizations, there were signs that market pressures were damaging the long-term and promoting a dangerous internal competitiveness. We argue that these tendencies reflect a failure at the top management level to respond to the changing roles implied by the shift towards a market orientation, especially the need to manage strategically.

Under market pressure, decentralized departmental responsibilities easily degenerate into corporate incoherence. Among our case study organizations, fierce competition for customers often broke out even between fellow departments. As a manager at ERO observed:

> There is a danger with individual cost centres, to try to maximize the work you do yourself ... expanding in a big way and taking on jobs which should probably be done in other departments. This isn't good for ERO as a whole, particularly since you may end up doing something for which you don't have the expertise and you may do a bad job, and leave a bad taste in the client's mouth ... ERO isn't a single

entity; it is a collection of cottage industries competing against one another and the outside world.

It was not surprising in these conditions that at ERO—as at the other laboratories—the attempts by central marketing to collect and disseminate market intelligence organization-wide were rudimentary and often ignored. At ProcCo, the attitude was, "I want the job, and stuff everybody else". Coordinated responses to market needs were constantly undermined by short-term competitiveness, leaving customers ill served and management incapable of consolidating experience into organization-wide learning.

Nor was it easy to develop any sense of corporate strategy among decentralized units fighting for survival. At NRO, a senior manager cheerfully observed of the post-privatization years, "I managed by survival and that was an extremely good motivator. Everybody wanted to make a job of it and survive. Survival is a super motivator". But as the organization gradually reached a more assured position, this senior manager began to ask, "what do you replace survival with?". There was a vacuum in the place where strategy should have been. It took nearly a decade before NRO developed a cohesive strategic plan, significantly under the pressure of the marketing department. Likewise, after more than 10 years in the market-place, ERO's new managing director complained, "we are bottom-up led; we are survival led". As this research was finishing, the space in the laboratory's entrance hall where ERO's mission statement had once hung was left empty.

In terms of FIGURE 4.1, it seems that changes at the top management level often lag changes lower down the organization, with market-orientated change not being coordinated within an adequate framework of strategic management. The strategic task for top management is twofold. Firstly, it has to establish the markets in which the organization really has a significant competitive advantage. To continue in markets where there is no clear advantage leaves the organization fighting constantly for short-term survival, with centrifugal pressures internally and constant risk to long-term customer interests. The organization needs to dominate markets, not just be driven willy-nilly. The second task, then, is to transcend the conception of the organization as simply a portfolio of competing departments, and begin to knit together a more strategically coherent unit. Only thus can the organization as a whole develop the coordinated responses to market requirements that are the hallmark of true market orientation (Kohli and Jaworski, 1990).

In developing a strategic approach to markets, top managements should not neglect the non-market context in which they operate. Excessive market pressures can unleash disruptive forces among professionals, so crucial in their new role as part-time marketers (Gummesson, 1991). As our earlier discussion stressed, professional workers are embedded in a network of institutionalized relationships, the media for collaboration and knowledge building as much as for custom and competition. In this context, exaggerated importation of simple marketing approaches risks rupturing frail ties of trust and neglecting long-term sources of market advantage. Crude attempts to develop new markets, increase sales or promote competitiveness often result only in failure and cynicism.

In the R&D laboratories, new marketing or business development departments often launched initiatives to identify and secure new markets. For them, early success in bringing a big contract from a new customer appeared to be the speediest means to organizational legitimacy. By and large, these initiatives ended in failure, with the exception of a few overseas contracts. These big marketing pushes were based on a misconception of the nature of the markets in which the laboratories were operating. As the engineers and scientists repeatedly insisted, "cold calling" or "creative selling" does not work in R&D. What mattered was mutual trust and knowledge built up over many years between particular individuals on both sides of the customer–supplier divide. A manager at NRO reflected in hindsight, "we thought marketing was about finding new customers, whereas in fact you need to go on at the existing ones". Gung-ho prospecting for new markets was often a distraction from the ultimately more rewarding task of consolidating and extending established ones.

Here, it was the professionals themselves, as "part-time marketers", who were key. Just as the theorists of industrial networks argue (Axelsson and Easton, 1992), successful marketing in both hospitals and laboratories involved "old boys' networks", "chums" and "connections and connections of connections". However, professionals' ability to market through these networks was often squeezed out by exactly the controls that were supposed to enforce more customer contact. At ProcCo, an exaggerated desire to ensure that everyone paid their way led to a requirement that all professional staff charged out 100% of their available hours to a customer. With no official time allowed for the exploration of new opportunities, marketing quite literally became, in the words of one engineer, "a renegade system". Marketing was only possible if you "cooked the books": "you have to steal the time from somewhere", explained another ProcCo engineer. At NRO, the 90% target for chargeable hours so squeezed time for the informal contacts that engineers complained, "you need a job number just to talk to somebody" (recognizing this, management finally reduced the target to 82% chargeable hours). Such time pressures were not so bureaucratically crude in the NHS, but frequently there was still inadequate space for the investment in relationships and exchange of information required for effective marketing. At Southtrust, a harried doctor expostulated, "When I've dealt with one patient, there is another one pushed in front of me. ... We are spending so much time on our basic work that we don't do anything else. ... We can't just go on and sit in meetings".

Clearly, effective networking takes some organizational investment. Professional networks also entail some constraints. Following Keat (1991), professionals do not just identify with the individual advantage of their organization, but with the collective advance of their profession and its standards. Unless properly understood, these community loyalties could provoke significant frustrations and conflicts among managers and professionals alike. Thus, a senior manager at one of the trusts complained of his medical staff's reluctance to compete against colleagues in other hospitals: "... ultimately they are all gentlemen, hung up on the *National Health Service*. They feel guilty about taking work from colleagues; they back away when they've got the knife in their hands". On the other hand, professionals could be uncomfortably frank in communicating technical information to the customer. One EngCo engineer admitted:

> I am not too sure that I'm the right sort of person to talk with customers. I'm quite happy to divulge information that probably shouldn't be divulged ... [or to] say where I am surprised that some people are going ahead with certain systems, and where they are leaving certain loopholes and certain black areas. ... Unfortunately that makes me a bad person to go ahead and talk to customers, as far as EngCo sees itself.

The sense of professional community clearly entails risks and restraints for management. At EngCo, the response was in fact to rupture the possibility of relationships developing between professional engineers working on the same problems in both the client organization and the central laboratory: divisions typically acted as the intermediary. An equivalent break had occurred at ERO, where the demand for economies had reduced participation at professional seminars and conferences—important means for engineers to develop knowledge, build reputation and establish contacts with fellow professionals in client organizations. However, at least as great a danger is to view these professional relationships too one-sidedly. The professional exchanges and responsibilities of doctors and engineers might often jeopardize short-term opportunities, but they can also build advantage and consolidate relationships in the long run. Doctors in their regional medical committees can establish informally which hospitals are really best equipped to offer certain services in their local areas, regulating disruptive attempts by weaker units to compete by low price or poor quality. Research engineers can win long-term trust by informing client engineers of "black areas" before they are implemented, rather than waiting for the inevitable embarrassment afterwards.

In short, top management does not necessarily serve its strategic interests by attempting to force on its professionals an exaggerated competitiveness or focus on the bottom-line. Of course, professional networks are a source of risk, but they are costly to suppress and might as well be exploited. To turn these networks to advantage, however, requires that top management first makes a more concerted effort to engage their professionals positively, then that it trusts them to act in the long-term interest, accepting short-term embarrassments on the way. From the evidence of our case studies, the necessary policies of training, coordination and guidance for professionals are widely absent. Among the R&D laboratories, only EngCo had invested in a significant marketing training initiative, and this was confined to senior management in the faith that its good effects would trickle down. Elsewhere, as an engineer at ProcCo put it, marketing training was by "osmosis", by observation and experience. Attempts at coordinating and disseminating market intelligence were often rudimentary, with only NRO and ERO attempting systematic corporate recording of external contacts. As they engaged in everyday professional exchanges, professionals—doctors, scientists or engineers—were often at a loss for lack of an explicit strategic framework. A departmental manager at EngCo was most forceful:

> What I want—maybe I'm wrong, being parochial or bloody-minded—is some means of judging, a technology strategy which helps me prioritise what my people do, who I work with in the rest of the building, who I need resources off, my recruitment strategy. What I need to know is the direction EngCo intends to go. That's what I need to know.

Again, a strategic approach is required. Just as the development of corporate strategy is critical to managing the market context, so is the communication of a clear strategic framework important to inform the professional networking that makes up the non-market context. Effective strategic management should equally buffer decentralized departments from centrifugal, short-term pressures and provide a vision that allows professionals to interpret, flexibly and for themselves, their professional practice within an overall senses of corporate purpose. The experience of the eight professional service organizations is that these are lessons not easily learnt.

CONCLUSIONS

This chapter has addressed the challenge of market-orientated strategic change in professional services. The experience of our case organizations have been summarized in two figures, the first stressing the multi-level nature of the change process over time, the second the dangers of failing to master pressures from the market environment. Although these figures are essentially descriptive, they have clear implications for management action.

Clearly, market-orientated change has organization-wide repercussions. Organizational structures become increasingly decentralized, managed by financially-accountable business managers, and controlled through new systems of financial information. Professionals are plunged directly into the market-place, taking a front-line role in the marketing of services. Traditional status boundaries blur, with a more egalitarian involvement of supporting staff. At the same time, new categories of commercial support staff grow rapidly and claim increasing representation at top level. These are all changes that demand careful management from the top, setting a substantial agenda in terms of training, career structures, reward system and corporate culture. Line managers and professionals need to be trained to compete in the market-place and rewarded according to their success. Career structures should now acknowledge client-relevant criteria, abandoning the traditional rigidities of professional hierarchies. The corporate culture should become both more commercial and more inclusive—accepting commercial, technical and professional staffs as complementary components of competitive advantage and reinforcing identity with the success of the corporation as a whole.

Here, already, are plenty of issues, but the evidence of the cases suggests that the toughest challenge for top management is to change itself. A first uncomfortable requirement is for top management to open its doors to those from outside the profession, especially financial and marketing experts. This was something only slowly and grudgingly done in the R&D laboratories. The next task is to move beyond the role of professional administration towards strategic management. Here identifying strengths and weaknesses in the existing portfolio is clearly an important first stage, but the ability to offer a coordinated corporate response to market demands requires something more. Rather than simply cutting back those parts of the portfolio that seem individually to lack competitive advantage, top management needs to construct a positive, corporate-wide strategic competence and vision.

A coherent strategy should address both the market and non-market contexts. In the absence of clearly defined competitive advantage, and without an overall strategic framework, market pressures drive decentralized departments to compete internally in a destructive battle for short-term survival. A market-driven organization is not necessarily a market-orientated one. Top management needs to establish sufficient areas of market dominance to secure its decentralized units from short-term pressures and allow them to build long-term relationships with their clients. Here professional networks will be as important as formal marketing. If set within a clearly communicated strategic framework, the informal processes of professional networking can be mobilized for the acquisition of knowledge, the raising of standards, the development of trust and the partitioning of markets. In professional services, market-orientated strategy is not just about markets: it involves collaboration as well as competition, community as much as commerce.

ACKNOWLEDGEMENTS

This article draws partly on Whittington, McNulty and Whipp (1994), with permission. The research on which it is based was funded by the Economic and Social Research Council.

REFERENCES

Ackoff, R. (1993). Corporate Perestroika. In W.E. Halal, A. Geranmayeh and J. Pourdehnad (Eds) *Internal Markets*. New York: Wiley.

Axelsson, B. and Easton, G. (1992). *Industrial Networks: A New View of Reality*. London: Routledge.

Easton, G. and Araujo, L. (1993). Market exchange, time and industrial networks. In D. Brownlie, M. Saren, R. Wensley and R. Whittington (Eds) *Rethinking Marketing*. London: Sage.

Eriksson, P. (in press). The process of interprofessional competition: A case of expertise and politics. In D. Brownlie, M. Saren, R. Wensley and R. Whittington (Eds) *Rethinking Marketing*. London: Sage.

Gamble, J., Sheehan, M. and Shields, S. (1993). How independent subsidiaries tried to jump-start Blue Cross/Blue Shield. In W.E. Halal, A. Geranmayeh and J. Pourdehnad (Eds) *Internal Markets*. New York: Wiley.

Granovetter, M. (1985). Economic action and social structure: The problem of embeddedness. *American Journal of Sociology* **91**(3), 481–510.

Gummesson, E. (1991). Marketing-orientation revisited: The crucial role of the part-time marketer. *European Journal of Marketing* **25**(2), 60–75.

Halal, W.E. (1993). The transition from hierarchy to what? In W.E. Halal, A. Geranmayeh and J. Pourdehnad (Eds) *Internal Markets*. New York: Wiley.

Handy, C. (1990). *The Age of Unreason*. Boston, MA: Harvard University Press.

Hinings, C., Brown, J. and Greenwood, R. (1991). Change in an autonomous professional organisation. *Journal of Management Studies* **28**(4), 375–393.

Hodgson, G. (1988). *Economics and Institutions*. Cambridge: Polity.

Hooley, G.J., Lynch, J.E. and Shepherd, J. (1990). The marketing concept: Putting the theory into practice. *European Journal of Marketing* **24**(9), 7–23.

Keat, R. (1991). Consumer sovereignty and the integrity of professional practices. In R. Keat and N. Abercrombie (Eds) *Enterprise Culture*. London: Routledge.

Kohli, A.K. and Jaworski, B. (1990). Market orientation: The construct, research propositions and managerial implications. *Journal of Marketing* **54**, 1–18.

Noer, D. (1993). Lessons in converting staff units into profit centres. In W.E. Halal, A. Geranmayeh and J. Pourdehnad (Eds) *Internal Markets*. New York: Wiley.

Peters, T. (1990). Get innovative or get dead. *California Management Review* Fall **33**(1), 9–26.

Peters, T. (1992). *Liberation Management*. London: Macmillan.

Pettigrew, A. (1985). *The Awakening Giant*. Blackwell: Oxford.

Pettigrew, A. and Whipp, R. (1991). *Managing Change for Competitive Success*. Blackwell: Oxford.

Piercy, N. (1991). *Market-Led Strategic Change*. London: Thorsons/Harper Collins.

Whittington, R. (1990). Social structures and resistance to strategic change: British manufacturers in the 1980s. *British Journal of Management* **1**, 201–213.

Whittington, R., McNulty, T. and Whipp, R. (1994). Market-driven change in professional services: Problems and Processes. *Journal of Management Studies* **31**(6), 829–845.

Whittington, R. and Whipp, R. (1992). Professional ideology and marketing implementation. *European Journal of Marketing* **26**(1), 52–63.

Yorke, D.A. (1990). Interactive perceptions of suppliers and corporate clients in the marketing of professional services. *Journal of Marketing Management* **5**(3), 307–323.

Section II

Issues and Patterns in Global Competition

As cross-border linkages increase, organizations need to combine global management with strategies tailored to regional or local conditions. The big question is what the exact relationship should be between global and regional strategy. The new art of "globalization" is the subject of this section, in themes dealing with developing and implementing, and at the business unit and activity levels.

Canals looks at the process by which some firms emerge as global leaders, and what sort of competitive advantage they develop and sustain. He attempts to explain the combination of country-, industry- and firm-specific advantages in some industries, and how the mix changes over time.

Carr examines the question, "Faced with industry maturity and increasing international competition, should large nationally-based companies attempt to dominate their markets and, if so, should these markets be defined nationally or internationally?" He predicts outcomes based on competing theoretical arguments, then compares them with actual performance in one industry— vehicle components. He finds that Japanese successes have been most frequently based on something other than market domination (e.g. manufacturing or technological issues). Once successful, they have shifted to strategies for global dominance. British and US firms, on the other hand, have focused on domestic market dominance, with short-term successes, but long-term failures.

Dixon and Hedley provide a framework for determining what

drives competitiveness in the international environment, andwhat changes in strategy and behaviour are necessary. They suggest that competitiveness results from a firm performing better relative to its economy than an international competitor does relative to its economy. Success depends on managers understanding not only exchange rates and the effects of currency union, but particularly the "new" competitive dynamics (e.g. global pricing/marketing strategies, international sourcing/manufacturing, financial performance/resource allocation).

Earl and Feeny develop a global information technology applications framework, then use it to examine the information systems of four European businesses competing globally through different degrees of transnational form and in different stages of evolution. They conclude that although there may be some special difficulties in applying IT globally, they seem trivial compared with the management and organizational issues that arise.

Faulkner explores the progress of strategic alliance through the stages of formation, management and evolution. He offers Rover/Honda as an example of a successful alliance that survived and prospered over a long term (more than 10 years), and reviews its impact on company philosophy, particularly that of Rover. The results seem to provide evidence that strategic alliances can offer long-term advantages to both partners. Although Rover's hostile acquisition by BMW may not have been considered initially advantageous by Rover's management, the firm's attractiveness to BMW may offer evidence of the success of its alliance with Honda.

Chapter 8   Information   Systems   in   Global   Business:
             Evidence from European Multinationals
             Michael J. Earl, David Feeny

Chapter 9   Strategic Alliance Evolution through Learning:
             The Rover/Honda Alliance
             David O. Faulkner

The rapid advent of world markets, while offering seemingly endless opportunities for firms to expand and prosper, also represents a significant array of challenges, especially to companies that have been slow to take on a global perspective. One major challenge is changing the internal mindset of companies that have traditionally been national, rather than global, competitors. A global perspective requires a distinctively different way of thinking, strategizing and operating.

Globalization also carries increased risk, particularly when done in the context that is being pursued by some major companies. Ford, for example, is attempting to restructure itself to be able to offer global products, rather than the wide range of automobiles it now offers, which are tailored to individual national markets. Although dramatically increased economies of scale offer potential savings—through globalization of product development, purchasing and other activities—of billions of dollars per year, a problem or mistake, instead of being confined to a single country, region or production model, can now take on epic proportions.

Yet, considering the market potential of such untapped areas as the former Soviet Union, China and other regions formerly trapped behind the Iron Curtain or other political barriers, global competition offers potential that can justify substantially increased risk. *Billions* of potential customers may represent sufficient temptation to make the degree of perceived risk pale by comparison.

5

Country-, Industry- and Firm-Specific Factors in Global Competition

Jordi Canals

Introduction

Changes in leadership in global industries have been dramatic over the past 20 years. If one looks at the rankings of the largest firms in terms of turnover or performance in major world industries, the main players may or may not be different, but their relative positions in critical markets have radically changed. TABLES 5.1 and 5.2 offer some data on the changes in market share of different players in the car and banking industries in the past decade.

This observation seems to be irrespective of the nature of the industry: it happens in high-tech, low-tech or mature industries, and in services as well. Can it be considered a basic pattern in international business?

The explanations given for global competition and the ability of firms to compete internationally seem to focus on the possession of a basic advantage that gives a firm a leading edge in international markets. This advantage is firm-specific (Dunning, 1979; Kindle-

Strategic Renaissance and Business Transformation. Edited by H. Thomas, D. O'Neal and J. Kelly.
Copyright © 1995 John Wiley & Sons Ltd.

TABLE 5.1 World market share (%) of leading car makers, 1981 and 1990

	1981	1990
1. General Motors	20.9	17.5
2. Ford Motor Company	11.7	14.6
3. Toyota	8.2	9.4
4. Renault	6.8	4.2
5. Volkswagen	6.7	6.8
6. Nissan	6.5	6.8
7. PSA Group (Peugeot)	5.5	4.5
8. Fiat	4.9	5.3
9. Chrysler	3.6	5.4
10. Honda	3.1	4.0

Sources: *Ward's Automotive World* and EC.

TABLE 5.2 The world's largest banks in assets

Bank	Country	Assets ($m)
1991		
1. Sumitomo Bank	Japan	427 102
2. Dai-Ichi Kangyo Bank	Japan	445 707
3. Fuji Bank	Japan	418 956
4. Sanwa Bank	Japan	411 704
5. Crédit Agricole	France	307 203
6. Sakura Bank	Japan	420 348
7. Union Bank of Switzerland	Switzerland	183 911
8. Mitsubishi Bank	Japan	424 679
9. Barclays Bank	United Kingdom	258 339
10. Deutsche Bank	Germany	296 226
1975		
1. Bank America Corp.	USA	58 696
2. Citicorp	USA	55 538
3. Chase Manhattan Corp.	USA	41 143
4. Groupe BNP	France	34 728
5. Barclays Bank	United Kingdom	33 328
6. Crédit Lyonnais	France	32 837
7. Deutsche Bank	Germany	32 412
8. National Westminster Bank	United Kingdom	31 892
9. Dai-Ichi Kangyo Bank	Japan	28 910
10. Société Generale	France	27 651

Sources: *The Banker, Euromoney.*

berger, 1969), monopolistic (Hymer, 1960) and exploited better by the firm that possesses it across boundaries, rather than traded in the market (Casson, 1983; Caves, 1982; Williamson, 1975).

The origin and nature of this monopolistic advantage in international competition as opposed to domestic competition is discussed widely in the literature. Essentially, explanations hover around three basic dimensions. The first one is economics. This has been considered the basic dimension of global strategy: the interdependence between competitive positions of a single firm in different geographical markets and the potential advantages of coordination of activities (Porter, 1986). According to this assumption, a firm chooses a global strategy, in order to take advantage of some scale or scope economies in one or more functions of the business system: manufacturing, R&D, finance or marketing. Strategic moves and, particularly, first-mover advantages appear as important determinants of international success in several industries (Lieberman and Montgomery, 1988).

The second dimension of global competition is technology, not only in terms of scale or scope economies, but also as the ability to create, develop and market core technologies and competences from which new products will spring off (Cantwell, 1989; Prahalad and Hamel, 1990). Core competences are associated with the notion of resources that a firm possesses, and that are non-tradeable, unique and difficult to imitate (Barney, 1991; Dierickx and Cool, 1989).

Core competences are so critical that some authors argue that core technologies—and not basic manufacturing or marketing functions, as the economic dimension of global competition tends to highlight—determine the geographical breadth of an international firm and the optimal degree of integration among national units (Kobrin, 1991).

The third basic dimension of global competition is organizational design, or the ability of a global firm to localize and integrate different business units in different markets, managing such complexity effectively.

The organizational dimension of global competition links up with the importance of effective organizational forms in implementing successful strategies for international growth and development (Andrews, 1971; Chandler, 1962). More recently, Chandler (1990) pointed out that the success of large industrial firms in the United States and Germany—firms with global presence—is based upon three main factors: investment decisions, scale and scope economies, and effective organizations to manage the firms effectively.

Bartlett and Ghoshal (1989) also stress that the administrative heritage together with the ability of international firms to handle scale, local responsiveness and corporate learning across borders is critical in terms of understanding international success—or failure. The role of organizational design in international competition goes back to the work on transaction-cost economics (Casson, 1983; Caves, 1982; Hennart, 1982; Teece, 1980; Williamson, 1975). Decisions orientated towards economizing transaction costs by firms in different markets are considered decisive in explaining the emergence and growth of large corporations competing in international markets.

Lastly, a particular aspect of organizational design, institutional culture, has been mentioned as a potential factor explaining differences of performance in international competition (Kogut, 1990, 1991; Piore and Sabel, 1984). Specifically, the national organization of work, training and learning appear to be closely related with the ability to compete in the international arena (Kogut, 1991).

Although the arguments behind those dimensions might be compelling to better understand global competition and international success, they look from a single perspective at a rather complex phenomenon. Moreover, these arguments do not provide a coherent or a comprehensive framework to understand and predict the dynamics of global competition. For instance, authors emphasizing the critical role of core competences tend to overlook the importance of country-specific factors in creating these competences.

What should the basic features of such a framework be? Essentially, there are two: firstly, the framework should be comprehensive and integrative—that is to say, it should include, explain and integrate major factors observed in different industries—and secondly, it should try to explain coherently the recent evolution of competition in global industries and, at the same time, pose some major factors that will allow a better understanding of its future dynamics.

In this chapter, we try to sketch some aspects of a framework elaborated along these lines. Essentially, we try to address some basic questions, looking at several global industries:

• What are the basic sources of advantages for international firms?

- Is there any advantage that, under several conditions, is more critical and sustainable than others?
- Is there any relationship among the roles that the different levels of advantages play along the evolution of the industry?
- Is there any specific advantage that loses or gains importance when an industry matures?
- When a global firm loses global market share, is there any lever upon which the firm can build its renewal and regain edge in global markets?

The content of this chapter is based upon specific case studies of the major players in four industries: automobiles (capital intensive), VCR (technology intensive), watches (mature) and banking (a service industry). In studying these industries, we try to understand the different sources of the firm's competitive advantage and their relative importance over time. The information gathered comes from interviews with managers, information provided by companies and public data. The methodology followed has been historical and inductive, in order to generate new ideas stemming from the real world that pave the way for more quantitative analysis. The basic measure to explain global success used in this chapter is market share. This variable is not the only, nor the most important, performance indicator of a firm, but provides basic and useful information about the presence of global firms in different markets.

In the next section we describe the initial framework that we use to better understand global competition. This framework emerges from past contributions to the literature. We also pose some problems stemming from them. The third section formulates some basic propositions, based upon case studies, that provide a refinement of some of the previous arguments. Finally, we end up with some conclusions for scholars and managers and formulate some ideas for further research along this direction.

BASIC FRAMEWORKS TO UNDERSTAND GLOBAL COMPETITION

Classical and more recent models of international trade (Krugman, 1990) that try to explain the flows of trade and investment across countries have failed to offer a relevant and comprehensive framework to understand global competition (Yoffie, 1993). Comparative advantage, factor proportions, scale economies or monopolistic competition offer stylized, but rather partial views of a more complex phenomenon. Economic theory has been a fertile ground where new ideas have popped up, but barren in terms of a more global, integrative framework.

In the eclectic economics-management and organization theory literature we can observe more promising concepts. First, the so-called eclectic theory of international competition (Dunning, 1979, 1981): this theory provides a useful and provocative framework in which three dimensions appear to be critical:

- Ownership advantages (advantages related to specific firm competences and resources).
- Locational advantages (advantages derived from being in particular countries).
- Internalization advantages (related to the organizational design that economizes transaction costs and provides the right incentives to align different preferences of national subsidiaries).

The concept of ownership advantage links up with the ideas of firm-specific know-how (Hirsh, 1976), distinctive competence (Andrews, 1971) or, more recently, the concept of core competence (Prahalad and Hamel, 1990) or, in general, with unique assets and resources (Barney, 1991).

Porter (1990) provides an alternative vision of global competition. The purpose of his research is to better understand the role of nations as natural environments in which firms that compete internationally create and sustain competitive advantages in international markets. Porter does not try to answer the question of which firm-specific advantages are critical (Grant, 1991), but rather in which environments these advantages can be cultivated.

Although the "national diamond" presented by Porter is comprehensive and rich, with a dynamic nature, this framework does not delve into the waters of the activities of the firm. Specific advantages embedded in the way in which global firms organize and manage their business system seem to be less important in this framework.

By separating themselves from the role of the environment, Bartlett and Ghoshal (1989) offer a third framework to understand why some firms are more effective than others in global markets. Their work is based upon a more administrative tradition within management theory. This observation means that their focus is not the economics of global competition, but rather how to organize and manage the complexity in firms that compete in global markets with several business units.

Those authors distinguish three specific aspects that are inherent to the nature of global firms: scale, local responsiveness and transfer of knowledge across borders. It is interesting to note that Porter (1986) had already observed two of these three factors, scale and integration. Bartlett and Ghoshal get deeper in the analysis of the managerial implications of such concepts, by using cases of established global companies. The creation of new mind-frames seems critical to integrate these factors in order to manage the inherent complexity of such firms.

In a recent work (Canals, 1991), using both empirical evidence and previous scholarly contributions, we offered a synthesis of those paradigms. The framework that emerges distinguishes between three levels of analysis—country, industry and firm—to better understand global competition (see FIGURE 5.1). Dunning (1981) distinguished between firm-specific advantage (ownership) and country-specific advantage (location); our use of these concepts in this chapter is somewhat different.

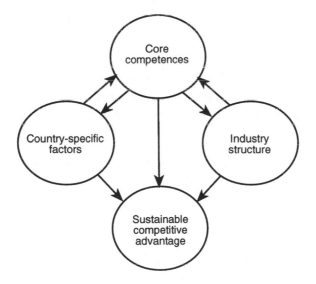

FIGURE 5.1 Categories of advantages in international competition: an integrative framework

The basic rationale behind this framework is that firms compete in specific industries and in specific national markets, and not only in countries. At the same time, their local platform is a combination of country- and industry-specific factors. In TABLE 5.3 we provide a synthesis of the mix of those advantages in the world watch industry.

Last, but not least, it is highly difficult to separate firm-specific advantages from country- or industry-specific advantages. In the end, how can we say that a well-trained technical force is a firm-specific advantage and not a country-specific advantage?

We attempt to address all of these questions in this and the next section, but we start by defining what we understand by country-, industry- and firm-specific advantages.

A country-specific advantage for a firm that competes internationally is one available to all firms operating in that country by the fact of being there. In this category of advantage, we include basic factors such as wages or the cost of capital; created, advanced factors such as the level of basic, secondary, university and technical education, the sophistication of the financial system, or the communications system; and policy factors such as tariff and non-tariff protection, or the structure of the tax system. Political, social and cultural factors play an important role in international competition (Lodge and Vogel, 1987), but in our framework they interact and have a final impact through the three factors mentioned above.

It is obvious that policy factors will, in the medium term, affect both basic factors and the creation or improvement of created factors. The difference between policy factors and the other two factors is that the first reflect the flow of different policies, while the other two are snapshots of certain factors at a specific moment.

The important feature of country-specific factors is that they reflect general conditions, stemming from the history of the country and the evolution of its social and economic structure, that affect all the companies operating in that country. As a result of these factors, a country or a region can become a unique geographical context that fosters innovation. This argument is used by Shan and Hamilton (1991) and Shan (1992) to explain basic patterns of foreign direct investment from a rather innovative perspective: these authors claim that foreign direct investment is motivated by country-specific advantages embedded in recipient firms.

TABLE 5.3 The world watch industry competitive advantages

	Country advantages	Industry advantages	Firm's competences
Swiss companies (up to 1960)	Low labour cost Government support Educational system	Relationships with suppliers Barriers to entry in distribution	Manufacturing quality Management of the network
Bulova, Timex (USA) (1960–1980)	Growing demand Distribution channels		Production automation New product Simple design at a low cost
Citizen, Seiko (Japan) (1980–1990)	Low salaries Government support	Intense rivalry	Process innovation Customer orientation International orientation
Swiss companies (1980s)	Educational system Basic infrastructure	Network of suppliers and distributors	Product innovation Process innovation Marketing capabilities

The economic structure of the industry in which a firm—or a particular single business unit of a firm—competes could also be a source of advantage. The existence of high barriers to entry in the industry, because of economies of scale or political protection at the national or international level—for instance, the EC or the North American Trade Agreement—are industry-specific and not firm-specific.

The same can be predicated of the position of a firm *vis-à-vis* its customers or suppliers and the way they interact, trade, learn and cooperate with one another. The nature of these relationships is basically industry-specific rather than country-specific. In fact, industries show very different patterns across countries in this respect. Of course, antitrust laws and national culture have an obvious influence in organizing such exchanges, but they are not the final, decisive driver of such advantages.

The nature of rivalry—based on cost or, rather, on offering higher value—and its intensity is also an industry-specific factor, although the influence of the national environment cannot be dismissed. In particular, the patterns of alliance formation among rivals within an industry, or between rivals, suppliers and customers, show elements that are inherent to the industry itself, not to the country or the firm.

In this respect, Noria and García-Pont (1991) observe the existence of networks of firms in which one can distinguish strategic groups and strategic blocks of producers and suppliers in the car industry. The opportunities of cooperating, learning and improving cost positions and the quality of products are industry-specific (Hamel, 1991).

The internationalization process of firms is also well explained, not only in terms of specific, monopolistic advantages of single firms, but in terms of networks of firms within industries. Mattson (1985), among others, develops some models of the internationalization process of firms in the context of an industry. As far as this process is a source of advantage for specific firms—for instance, in terms of expanding market share, gaining scale or scope economies or learning from other markets and customers—we can state the existence of advantages related to the industry.

This argument is coherent with the type of evidence on the geographical concentration of industries, recently presented by Piore and Sabel (1984), Krugman (1991) and Enright (1990). The importance of country-specific factors in this process of concentration is undoubtable, but most of the factors behind the success of these firms depend on features specifically related to the nature of the industry and critical relationships among its basic firms, customers and suppliers.

The third group of advantages observed in international competition is at the firm level. We can associate firm-specific advantages with monopolistic advantages defined by Hymer (1960), Kindleberger (1969) and Rugman (1981); ownership advantages, such as the ones described by Dunning (1979); core competences (Prahalad and Hamel, 1990); technological innovation (Cantwell, 1989; Grant, 1991); knowledge (Rugman and Verbeke, 1992); strategic assets and resources (Barney, 1991; Collis, 1991; Dierickx and Cool, 1989); organizational factors (Bartlett and Ghoshal, 1989; Chandler, 1962, 1990; Hamel, 1991); risk diversification and hedging (Lessard, 1986); or, simply, strategic decisions that create large, irreversible commitments (Ghemawat, 1991).

In general, we can define a firm-specific advantage as a particular resource or factor grounded at the firm level, either physically (people, physical assets, technology, patents) or tacitly (know-how, teamwork, informal organization, culture or management processes).

From a methodological viewpoint, it is important to distinguish between factors that, at some point, could be both country- and firm-specific; for instance, a well-trained workforce. In general, a country might offer an excellent educational system, with a highly educated and trained workforce. That is a general advantage related to country conditions.

Nevertheless, this advantage may be useless to a firm if it does not fit within the organization, culture and operations of that specific firm. Sometimes we observe in the same country and the same industry firms that thrive and firms that fail. Both are likely to have the same national advantages, but the way in which these advantages fuse and dissolve in single firms differs across firms. That, in turn, results in firms that carve out advantages from country factors and others that do not.

This framework, which we will try to refine in the next section, offers some answers to the questions posed earlier. Firstly, the relationship between country-, industry- and firm-specific advantages: since a firm operates in an industry in one or more countries, firm-specific advantages are influenced and moulded, to some extent, by country and industry factors available to all players. But, from the above discussion, the notion that the general factors impinge on specific firms depending upon those firms, emerges clearly. The level of education and training of people offer neat examples of that interaction.

Secondly, it is the combination of country-, industry- and firm-specific advantages that creates a unique lever for specific firms to compete successfully in international markets. Country factors can be important, but ineffective in high-tech industries evolving towards maturity. The VCR and the semiconductor industries provide good examples of this proposition.

As a radical contrast, firms with some unique core competences can be damaged in international competition by country factors, such as political protection or an uncompetitive, artificially appreciated exchange rate. The German car industry offers some evidence of this case.

The main conclusion is that firms create and sustain advantages based upon specific assets and resources which evolved along certain patterns, some of them intrinsic to the firm, others depending upon the country and the industry.

In terms of the income statement of a firm, country factors affect some of the items of revenues and expenses. But the explicit, final impact depends upon the combination of factors at the firm level, including the tacit knowledge accumulated across different departments and levels of management, and specific, largely irreversible, decisions taken by firms themselves. In short, it is the firm that, by using a nation as a platform and relationships specific to the industry in which it competes, creates and markets products with a good price–value combination for its customers.

The third factor that this framework tries to explain is that industry factors are not country factors. When Porter (1990) includes some industry-specific factors in his national diamond, he is considering that rivalry among competitors or cooperation between producers and suppliers or customers is bounded within countries. This contributes to the fusion between country- and industry-specific factors.

But this is only a special case in industries that do not have a high degree of internationalization. In global industries (automobiles, consumer electronics or banking), the impact of industry effects leaks across national boundaries. Hard-nosed rivalry among firms from different countries in the same national markets, or cooperative agreements among competitors, might or might not have a national basis. Moreover, cross-border alliances, especially in the banking and car industries, do not have this national context, but rather an international one.

Notwithstanding the progress that this three-level advantage framework offers, there are some basic questions that are still unresolved, which we try to address in the next section. Firstly, what role do the three levels of advantage play in real industries? Secondly, what is the dynamics of global competition and the evolution of these advantages? In other words, what are the factors behind the emergence of new industry leaders or the failure of previous leaders? Thirdly, is there any general pattern in explaining the new emergence of previously failed leaders?

THE DYNAMICS OF COMPETITION IN GLOBAL INDUSTRIES

CATEGORIES OF KEY ADVANTAGES IN INTERNATIONAL COMPETITION

Proposition 1

Country-, industry- and firm-specific factors are all important in explaining patterns of success and failure in global competition, although their relative importance may vary as industries evolve and mature. It is the unique combination of resources and assets by a specific firm—some of them directly related to the country and the industry in which the firm operates—that makes possible that firm's success in international markets.

This proposition has been sketched in the previous section, but we would like to show in detail the dynamic nature of that combination of advantages in some specific industries. Let us observe the global VCR industry.

This industry was born in the United States in the early 1950s, when RCA announced the coming development of a television picture recorder. The USA offered an incredible environment in which to nurture the VCR industry: a large pool of engineers, and the world's largest consumer market, with the highest penetration rate of TV sets, and sophisticated, closely related industries.

Rivalry within the industry was fierce. RCA started the race, but Ampex was the first firm to market the video-recording technology that rapidly became the standard of the industry. Other companies, such as CBS and CTI, jumped into the design and manufacturing of VCRs. Ampex technology was the industry standard until the early 1980s, but, paradoxically, Ampex had quit the VCR industry in 1972, allegedly because of financial distress. The same pattern was followed by RCA, which in 1984 announced that it would cease the production of its Selectavision VideoDisc (Rosenbloom and Freeze, 1985).

It is intriguing that the failure of the American firms in the increasingly global VCR market was due not only to external factors such as a growing competition abroad but also to factors specifically related to country-factors and to firm-specific factors.

The main country disadvantage for American firms was capital markets in the USA. Ampex suffered a great deal of pressure from capital markets to announce quarterly profits. This goal was incompatible at some point with developing a new technology whose profits would eventually arrive much later. Divestiture was the response.

This story shows clearly how country-specific advantages—or, in this case, disadvantages—can overcome and counter the weight of other country advantages and, even more important, the possession of the basic technology.

Together with this country disadvantage, a firm-specific factor should be considered. The cases of Ampex and RCA are, in many ways, parallel stories. Both companies achieved technological breakthroughs in the early stages of the VCR industry. They were successful, for instance, in developing high value, expensive video recorders for professionals, but not in manufacturing or marketing simple, cheap products to the mass market.

Ampex chose to form an alliance with Toshiba, Toamco, apparently with manufacturing capabilities more sophisticated than those of Ampex. The problem was that Toamco did not have previous experience in producing high volumes of a complex, cheap product. The election of the partner was a failure.

RCA products were the market leaders in the US—the world's largest market in consumer electronics—from 1974 to 1988, the year in which Panasonic took the lead (TABLE 5.4). The emergence of the Japanese VCR industry is illustrative of the way in which country, industry and firm advantages act in international competition.

The Japanese VCR industry had two broad, generic country advantages: a skilled population and pressure on manufacturers to fulfil special demands, such as the miniaturization required because of the small size of homes in that country. However,

TABLE 5.4   VCR industry: US market share (%)

	1980	1985	1988
Panasonic	15.0	12.1	13.1
RCA	27.5	13.8	11.3
Fisher	–	7.9	7.5
Sears	3.0	5.4	5.6
General Electric	3.1	5.2	5.0
Sharp	1.3	4.2	4.7
Sanyo	2.6	4.1	4.2
Magnavox	4.5	3.8	4.0
Mitsubishi	2.0	3.4	4.0
Zenith	6.1	3.6	3.8

Sources: Television Digest, Japan Electronics Almanac.

Japanese firms also had a big disadvantage: the technological level of the electronic industry in the early 1960s was far behind that of the United States. In particular, the first-mover advantages that Ampex and RCA possessed appeared to be unsurmountable by any latecomer to the industry.

How did Japanese firms such as Sony, JVC and Panasonic manage their country disadvantages, and how did they take over from the American firms? This is a long story, but the kernel of the argument boils down to a simple point: Japanese firms tried to compensate for relative country disadvantages with industry- and, mainly, firm-specific advantages.

Among the industry advantages, we should mention the intense internal rivalry among the main players, stimulated constantly by the MITI. The Japanese government also supported the industry in two ways: through generic subsidies to the consumer electronics industry, from which all of the main players in the VCR industry benefited, since they were large, integrated firms, such as Sony or Matsushita; and by helping Japanese firms to acquire the best available technology through licences.

The relationships among firms in the electronics industry were also a critical factor, because of the previous experience of the players in related industries, in terms of both developing the VCR and manufacturing cheap products in high volumes.

We can also distinguish several factors at the firm level. First and foremost is the ability of Japanese firms to improve their technology incrementally by introducing in each generation of

VCRs what they had learnt from the market responses to the previous one. This was a calculated way of decreasing the risk associated with a major technological venture.

On the other hand, Japanese producers were not interested in technological breakthroughs, but in manufacturing a very good and cheap product for the consumer market, at the lowest possible price, manufacturing and miniaturization capabilities were key. This pattern was quite different from the one followed by American firms.

Japanese firms realized their technological inferiority early and tried to offset that disadvantage by looking for convenient alliances with American firms. In the late 1960s and early 1970s, Sony and Toshiba, for instance, launched an alliance with Ampex, with the basic purpose of learning from the leader. In the late 1970s, when Japanese firms were already on the cutting edge of the industry in terms of technology, they established OEM agreements with American firms that were still unable to manufacture the right product for the American consumer market. By the late 1970s Japanese firms had gained access to that market with a consumer VCR.

The Japanese success in this industry shows how the interplay of industry and firm advantages was sufficient to overcome relative country disadvantages in relation to American firms. On the other hand, country advantages were critical in the beginning of the industry in the United States, but proved to be insufficient to maintain a pre-eminent position in the long term. Some firm-specific factors destroyed what country advantages had provided to this industry in its beginnings. This is a common lesson with other industries, which we will analyse later.

The automobile industry up to the late 1970s shows a rather different picture to the VCR industry, in terms of a slower globalization process, higher concentration in the industry, sharp fragmentation of national markets, high tariff and non-tariff barriers, and so on. Nevertheless, the pattern of advantages enjoyed by global competitors shows a curious similarity.

In this industry we have necessarily to refer to the fragmentation of the markets in three main regions: the United States, western Europe and Japan. Within western Europe, each one of the larger countries turns out to be an important unit of analysis. TABLE 5.5 shows the market shares of the larger players in western Europe, between 1981 and 1991. The differences in market share are striking. The loss of a clear pre-eminence by

TABLE 5.5   European car makers: market share (%)

Company	Market share (%)
1981	
1. Fiat	14.7
2. General Motors	14.5
3. Ford	13.5
4. VW Group	12.0
5. PSA Group	11.5
6. Renault	11.5
7. Others	23.3
1991	
1. VW Group	16.9
2. Fiat	12.9
3. General Motors	12.8
4. PSA Group	12.0
5. Ford	11.6
6. Renault	10.7
7. Others	23.1

Source: EC.

American firms, the emergence of Japanese firms as global competitors and changes in the European landscape were features of this industry in the 1980s.

The traditional dominance of American firms in the US and of European firms in western Europe traces back to a different set of arguments. In the case of the US the combination of country, industry and firm advantages is evident. The potential market was huge, the standards of living soaring year after year, the pool of engineers vast, and university and research centres were among the best of the world.

Those country advantages were combined with firm-specific advantages. American automobile firms were innovative, not only in terms of new technologies and products, but also in management (Chandler, 1962). These superior technological advantages and an important excess of financial resources led American firms into Europe, by building American transplants in some European countries.

European firms were dominant in their respective national markets: Fiat in Italy, Volkswagen in Germany and Peugeot and Renault in France. These firms had some technological expertise, but their main advantage for many years was an important domestic market protected by their governments. The car industry was considered to be of national interest.

Three main factors brought about an incredible revolution in the industry in the late 1970s and early 1980s. First, more expensive oil prices after the two oil shocks made consumers increasingly aware of the real costs of driving cars. Car makers had to change their designs in order to economize costs. Secondly, a free trade wave swept through Europe in the early 1980s, mainly as a result of the announcement of a single market by the end of 1992, with the abolishment of tariff, fiscal and technical trade barriers among European countries. Protection was bound to disappear in a few years. Thirdly, the Japanese revolution, which evolved through incremental approaches rather than in leaps and bounds, combined two engineering factors—inventory management and product development—to cause a revolution in the industry: a decrease in the market share held by American firms and the emergence in the early 1980s of Japanese firms as global players.

In the dominance of American firms up to the late 1970s, their failure in the 1980s and the emergence of Japanese players in the global scenario, we find some compelling arguments about the interplay of country-, industry- and firm-specific factors.

Nevertheless, a pattern seems to exist according to which country-specific factors *per se* tend to be more quickly perishable than firm-specific factors, as can be observed in the European car industry.

The world watch industry is also a good case (TABLE 5.6). This industry was born and developed mainly in Switzerland. Factors at the country level played an important role in the early Swiss dominance of the industry. Among others, we can cite the

TABLE 5.6   World watch industry

Country	World production (%)	
	1960	1990
Switzerland	72	45
Japan	8	32
United States	12	5
Others	8	18

Source: Federation of Swiss Watchmakers.

educated population through the apprenticeship system; low labour costs because of part-time workers; strong national commitment to the industry; and cultural factors and their implications for commerce.

Industry factors were also critical to the success of the industry: technology shared by the proximity of rival firms; cooperative marketing actions; proprietary technology; nationwide regulation of access to the industry and sale of components to other companies outside those officially established; lower vertical integration with an important division and specialization of activities and skills among firms; and, lastly, control of the distribution system.

Swiss watch makers were leaders, not only in Europe, but also in the United States, the largest market. But in the early 1950s the situation started to change, due to different new forces in the industry. We can single out at least three. Firstly, the rising standards of living converted watches from a luxury product into a mass consumer good. Large production volumes and lower costs started to be decisive.

Secondly, a revolution in merchandising swept across the US. Large supermarkets and malls spread around the country, and the opportunity to distribute products such as watches through these new channels was a real—not only a theoretical—threat for traditional channels, mainly, jewellers. In this context, some American firms, particularly Timex and Bulova, erupted in the market with a revolutionary technology, inherited from the old, decrepit Second World War defence industry. The outcome of this combination of country factors and new technology was radical. Timex and Bulova started to gain market share, first in the United States and later in Europe.

Swiss firms were slow in reacting to these marketing and technological changes, and their combination of country-, industry- and firm-specific advantages was incapable of deterring the rise of the American firms. Again, another combination of advantages was critical to becoming the leader in a global industry.

The pain inflicted by American firms on Swiss firms was similar to that suffered by the former in the 1970s, as a result of the emergence of Japanese players such as Hattori-Seiko and Citizen. Japanese firms found an important leverage in certain country factors, such as an important domestic market, dominance of distribution channels in Japan and an incipient but important consumer electronics industry.

The story of the Japanese watch makers shows that, having

important country factors, they became global players and provoked a significant erosion of the Swiss and American dominance through distinctive firm competences in technology. In trying to distinguish their products from those of their competitors, they invested heavily in the quartz technology, taking advantage of their past experiences in the consumer electronics industry in Japan.

In the mid-1980s, the re-emergence of the Swiss industry, with the Swatch and other stylish models, tells us an important lesson about the combination of the three levels of advantages described in this chapter, and the critical role played by firm-specific factors in taking over the leadership of the industry. This point leads to a second proposition.

The Evolution and Relative Weight of Advantages

Proposition 2

In the emergent stages of some industries (in particular, technology-intensive industries), country-specific factors seem to be important in combination with some firm-specific competences that give rise to new technology or products. Hence, in the emergent stages, countries offer natural environments leading to the creation and development of an industry. When the early technology of the industry matures, firm-specific factors appear to be more decisive than country factors.

These firm-specific factors have to do with how people and resources are managed to achieve a new breakthrough, rather than being general factors related to country characteristics, such as people or the cost of capital.

In the cases described briefly in the previous section we find some evidence in support of this proposition. The emergence of new leaders in the VCR, car and watch industries seems to match with that general observation. The same applies to other industries, such as fashion design, personal computers and semiconductors.

Nevertheless, at this point some caution is required. What Proposition 2 states seems to refer to industries intensive in technology. Can we proclaim the same of other industries? The commercial banking industry and a more profound analysis of the car and watch industries provide useful insights. In the case of banking, country factors appear to be particularly important in preventing a true globalization process. By country factors, we refer to the importance of domestic demand. Even if finance has become highly global in certain segments of the market—mainly capital markets—the financial services industry is still nation-driven. German banks have a certain market share in France not because they market sophisticated products in Germany, but because they are in France, close to French customers. The same applies to American banks, which are the most sophisticated in the world in terms of financial innovation, but desperately need to have a physical presence in every country where they want to sell their products.

The sad side of this story is that, since financial products tend quickly to become commodities, domestic firms have an important advantage: their national distribution network. This is the main reason behind the difficulty of foreign banks seizing important market shares in local markets. It also explains why, in general, foreign banks tend to accumulate more failures than local banks in foreign markets (Canals, 1993).

The banking industry tells us that, although innovation is important, country-specific factors tend to drive competition in local markets and prevent commercial banking from being a global industry.

Going back to the watch industry, we can distinguish three main segments: low price, disposable watches; traditional watches; and luxury watches. In the lowest segment of the industry, what drives competition is not technology, brand reputation or design, but cost. When technology or design is not key, it is the country that offers the cheapest costs—labour and capital—the most likely to succeed in the industry. The same observation can be stated of other industries, such as textiles or steel, in which cost, not quality, is the main driver.

As a result of those observations, we can state that in low technological-content industries, country-specific factors tend to be more important than technological or managerial break-throughs.

Finally, we will reconsider some features of the world car industry. What we said before about the emergence of new global players—Japanese firms—or the re-emergence of old players—Ford or Volkswagen—remains valid. But there is an important factor to bring in here: coalitions between national producers and governments.

Different forms of government support in the early 1950s and 1960s, not technology, was the critical factor behind the consolidation of national car makers in most of western Europe and in Japan. In the early 1990s, political competition (Yoffie, 1993) was still important in those countries.

Market leadership is not determined only by technological superiority, but by tariff and non-tariff protection of national industries. Even in EC markets, in which inter-Community trade has been completely liberalized, political competition hinders Japanese car makers from having a bigger say in the European industry.

What we observe in the car industry in terms of political competition seems to be common ground in other industries with considerable government intervention, such as the semiconductor and the telecommunications industries.

These cases shed enough light upon the importance of pervasive country-specific factors in certain industries with special characteristics, and lead us to another proposition.

Proposition 3

Country-specific factors such as the cost and supply of basic resources, domestic demand or government support are still drivers of competition in some industries (even mature ones), and temporarily invalidate the importance of other, superior, firm-specific factors.

PATTERN FORMATION OF NEW INDUSTRY LEADERS AND RE-EMERGENCE OF OLD INDUSTRY PLAYERS

In the evolution of several industries, discussed in the previous two sections, we observed some original ways followed by emerging leaders or re-emerging old players.

Some specific cases can be brought into the discussion: the emergence of Toyota and Nissan as global players in the car industry in the late 1970s has to do with strategic moves of critical importance. By strategic moves, we mean large commitments of resources to specific investment projects, mostly irreversible (Ghemawat, 1991) and orientated towards the development of new competences and capabilities.

In the case of Japanese firms, the basic move consisted of cooperative agreements with suppliers and huge investments in product development—from design to market—that changed the nature of the car industry and the way in which inventory and product design were managed. This is what we call a technological commitment.

This type of technological commitment was also critical in the re-emergence of Swiss watch markets in the early 1980s. New inventions such as the Swatch and new designs such as the ones created by luxury brand makers, with important commitment of resources to support new products, were decisive and highlight the importance of strategic decisions.

In the case of luxury brand makers, we can single out a third type of commitment—marketing commitment—related to the distribution of new products through revitalized channels and advertising them in a different way.

The re-emergence of Volkswagen in the mid-1980s had to do with different reasons. To become the biggest player in Europe meant, in the early 1980s, getting more access to other national markets. When Volkswagen announced in 1985 the acquisition of Seat, the Spanish state-owned car maker, to speed up the way towards leadership in Europe, it got involved in what we call a financial commitment. The acquisition involved many risks. Seat had been a big failure and its technological competences were scarce. The investments needed to revitalize the Spanish company were immense, despite financial support from the Spanish government. The return on investment was expected to be very low and, in the best scenario, the Spanish firm would pay out dividends as late as 1996. Nevertheless, with this acquisition, Volkswagen achieved several objectives. Firstly, it bought the biggest firm in the large Spanish market. Secondly, it acquired a firm in a country with much lower costs than Germany. Thirdly, Spain could be a successful platform from which to export in the future compact, cheap cars to other European countries and perhaps to eastern Europe. Finally, the management of the company convinced German unions that the traditional combination of low effort, complacency and high wages of the German car industry was no longer valid in the new Europe.

There is a final type of commitment also observed in some of the industries analysed mainly in the banking industry: the organizational commitment. By this concept we refer to major decisions about the way in which the company is organized and managed and, in particular, the integration and coordination with foreign subsidiaries. The nature of these decisions links up with the recent research conducted by Chandler (1990) on the success of large industrial firms and the contributions made by Bartlett and Ghoshal (1989) on the role of organizational design and administrative systems in global competition. Collis (1991) observes a similar pattern in the bearings industry.

Among the many cases we can observe in the banking industry, I will pick up only two. The first is Citibank, the largest global player in the 1970s, and now far behind some Japanese and European banks, but on the way to the recovery, at least in international markets. In Europe, Citibank changed the structure of its organization several times in the late 1970s and early 1980s, piling up failure after failure, not only because of tight competition in those markets, but also because of basic organizational mistakes (Canals, 1993). In an attempt to overcome the classical centralization/decentralization dilemma, Citibank Europe came up in 1989 with a new structure that combined a mix of business centralized in some European offices and other business decentralized, breaking away from old cultural patterns in the bank. Although the process is slow, in some European countries—France and Spain, for example—Citibank is again being considered an important player in certain segments of the industry.

Bank of America offers a similar case. After the decline of the bank in the early 1980s and the turnaround in the late 1980s, the bank is facing international operations in a pragmatic way. The major organizational thrust in this case has been moving away from centralization in San Francisco, giving more operational power to national subsidiaries and creating more accurate strategic control in San Francisco and London, the latter for European operations. As a result, Bank of America is a commercial bank in the United States, but operates as an investment bank in some European countries.

These observations lead us to another proposition.

Proposition 4

The pattern of emergence of new leaders or the re-emergence of old players in a certain industry seems to be associated with some strategic decisions that involve huge resources and are orientated towards the development of new competences and capabilities and commitment of resources. We can distinguish between technological, financial, marketing and organizational commitments.

FINAL COMMENTS

International competition and global strategies continue to be a puzzle in many industries. The patterns of emergence and decline of key players in major industries present different features, but in some cases it is possible to find some common points.

The observed patterns discussed in this chapter do not pose the question of determinism in the evolution of industries. Rather, we try to put forward a number of propositions, contingent upon certain characteristics of the industry under consideration, that may shed additional light upon the phenomenon of global competition.

Country-, industry- and firm-specific factors (core competences) are determinants of success (or failure) in global competition, but their relative importance changes as industries evolve. Any single internationally successful firm enjoys a unique combination of resources and capabilities, to the development of which country and industry factors may have contributed.

While stressing the importance of the national environment in global competition, in agreement with some recent studies, we argue that when an industry matures, firm-specific factors seem to gain increasingly more relevance, although domestic demand or government intervention may offset their importance.

Among firm-specific factors, decisions that imply large, irreversible commitments of resources of different nature (orientated towards developing new competences and capabilities) tend to be critical in explaining the emergence of new major industry players or the re-emergence of old players, climbing again to top positions in the industry.

REFERENCES

Andrews, K. (1971). *The Concept of Corporate Strategy*. Homewood, Il: Irwin.
Barney, J. (1991). Firm resources and sustained competitive advantage. *Journal of Management* **17**, 99–120.

Bartlett, C. and Ghoshal, S. (1989). *Managing Across Borders*. Boston, MA: Harvard Business School Press.

Canals, J. (1991). *Competitividad internacional y estrategia de la empresa*. Barcelona: Ariel.

Canals, J. (1993). *Competitive Strategies in European Banking*. Oxford: Oxford University Press.

Cantwell, J. (1989). *Technological Innovation and Multinational Corporations*. Oxford: Basil Blackwell.

Casson, M. (Ed.) (1983). *The Growth of International Business*. London: Allen & Unwin.

Caves, R. (1982). *Multinational Enterprise and Economic Analysis*. Cambridge: Cambridge University Press.

Chandler, A. (1962). *Strategy and Structure*. Cambridge, MA: MIT Press.

Chandler, A. (1990). *Scale and Scope*. Boston, MA: Harvard University Press.

Collis, D. (1991). A resource-based analysis of global competition: The case of the bearings industry. *Strategic Management Journal* 12, 49–68.

Dierickx, I. and Cool, K. (1989). Asset stock accumulation and sustainability of competitive advantage. *Management Science*, December, 1504–1514.

Dunning, J.H. (1979). Explaining changing patterns of international production: In defence of the eclectic theory. *Oxford Bulletin of Economics and Statistics* 41, 269–295.

Dunning, J.H. (1981). *International Production and the Multinational Enterprise*. London: Allen & Unwin.

Enright, M. (1990). Geographical concentration and industrial organization, doctoral dissertation, Harvard University, Cambridge, MA.

Ghemawat, P. (1991). *Commitment*. New York: Free Press.

Grant, R.M. (1991). Porter's competitive advantage of nations. *Strategic Management Journal* 12(7), 535–548.

Hamel, G. (1991). Competition for competence and inter-partner learning within international strategic alliances. *Strategic Management Journal* 12, 53–104.

Hennart, J.F. (1982). *A Theory of Multinational Enterprise*. Ann Arbor, MI: University of Michigan.

Hirsh, S. (1976). An international trade and investment theory of the firm. *Oxford Economic Papers* 28, 258–270.

Hymer, S. (1960). The international operations of national firms: A study of direct investment, doctoral dissertation, Cambridge, MA.

Kindleberger, C. (1969). *American Business Abroad*. New Haven, CT: Yale University Press.

Kobrin, S.J. (1991). An empirical analysis of the determinants of global integration. *Strategic Management Journal* 12, 17–33.

Kogut, B. (1990). The permeability of borders and the speed of learning among countries. In J. Dunning, B. Kogut and M. Blomstrom (Eds) *Globalization of Firms and the Competitiveness of Nations*. Lund.

Kogut, B. (1991). Country capabilities and the permeability of borders. *Strategic Management Journal* 12, 33–48.

Krugman, P. (1990). *Rethinking International Trade*. Cambridge, MA: MIT Press.

Krugman, P. (1991). *Geography and Trade*. Cambridge, MA: MIT Press.

Lessard, D.R. (1986). Finance and global competition: Exploiting financial scope and coping with volatile exchange rates. In M.E. Porter (Ed.) *Competition in Global Industries*. Boston, MA: Harvard Business School Press.

Lieberman, M.B. and Montgomery, D.B. (1988). First-mover advantages. *Strategic Management Journal* **9**, 41–58.

Lodge, G. and Vogel, E. (Eds) (1987). *Ideology and National Competitiveness*. Boston, MA: Harvard Business School Press.

Mattson, L.G. (1985). An application of a network approach to marketing. In N. Dholakia and J. Arndt (Eds) *Alternative Paradigms for Widening Marketing Theory*. Greenwich, CT: JAI Press.

Noria, N. and García-Pont, C. (1991). Global strategic linkages and industry structure. *Strategic Management Journal* **12**, 105–124.

Piore, M. and Sabel, C. (1984). *The Second Industrial Divide*. New York: Free Press.

Porter, M.E. (1986). Competition in global industries: A conceptual framework. In M.E. Porter (Ed.) *Competition in Global Industries*. Boston, MA: Harvard Business School Press.

Porter, M.E. (1990). *The Competitive Advantage of Nations*. New York: Free Press.

Prahalad, C.K. and Hamel, G. (1990). The core competence of the corporation. *Harvard Business Review*, May/June, 71–91.

Rosenbloom, R.S. and Freeze, K. (1985). Ampex Corporation and video innovation. In R.S. Rosenbloom (Ed.) *Research on Technological Innovation, Management and Policy* (Vol. 2). Greenwich, CT: JAI Press.

Rugman, A. (1981). *Inside the Multinationals*. London: Croom Helm.

Rugman, A.M. and Verbeke, A. (1992). Multinational enterprise and national economic policy. In P.J. Buckey and M. Lasson (Eds) *Multinational Enterprise in the World Economy*. Hants: Edward Elgar.

Shan, W. and Hamilton, W. (1991). Country-specific advantage and international cooperation. *Strategic Management Journal* **12**, 419–432.

Shan, W. (1992). Foreign direct investment and the sources of technological advantage. The Wharton School.

Teece, D. (1980). Economies of scope and the scope of enterprise. *Journal of Economic Behaviour and Organization* **22**, 3–17.

Williamson, O. (1975). *Markets and Hierarchies*. New York: Free Press.

Yoffie, D.B. (Ed.) (1993). *Beyond Free Trade*. Boston, MA: Harvard Business School Press.

6

The Demise of British National Market Leaders: An Examination of Strategic Choice and Performance in the Vehicle Components Industry

CHRISTOPHER CARR

INTRODUCTION AND LITERATURE REVIEW

Faced with the prospect of industry maturity and increasing international competition, large nationally-based companies need to decide whether to attempt to dominate their markets, and if so, how these should be defined geographically, or whether to seek success in some other way.

Market domination is frequently advocated, because of possible

Strategic Renaissance and Business Transformation. Edited by H. Thomas, D. O'Neal and J. Kelly.
Copyright © 1995 John Wiley & Sons Ltd.

experience benefits and also price advantages from greater market power (Buzzell and Gale, 1987; Haspeslaugh, 1982; Hedley, 1977; Levitt, 1965). Porter (1980) likewise stresses market power, advocating that this be determined by structural analysis. Strong market positions also depend on coherent, sensitive and sometimes creative policies throughout the value chain, designed to achieve either lower costs or differentiation (Porter, 1985). In the context of maturity, both entry and exit barriers may also require analysis (Harrigan, 1980; Porter, 1980).

Porter and colleagues (Hout, Porter and Rudden, 1982; Porter, 1980, 1986) suggest that more global (and not merely domestic) market dominance would be required where there are important interdependencies between competitive positions in different countries, and where structural characteristics are, on balance, favourable to a more global approach. Prahalad and Doz's (1987) research on multinationals provides a similar checklist of balancing considerations. A more global approach would be encouraged by the presence of multinational customers or multinational competitors, the intensity of capital or technology, pressure for cost reduction, universal versus heterogeneous customer needs, and sometimes access to raw materials and energy. Pressures for local responsiveness, on the other hand, depend on differences in customer needs, differences in distribution channels, the need to adapt products bearing in mind the availability of local substitutes, market structure, and demands by national governments such as those requiring local content. Other factors favourable to a more global approach might include global branding, and other more general strategic opportunities conferred by a multimarket presence (Ohmae, 1985).

Such market boundaries are difficult to resolve and may be controversial. In the case of washing machines, another mature industry, Baden-Fuller and Stopford (1991) argue that UK manufacturers have performed better as a result of pursuing national strategies, rather than defining the market as at least European, as might have been expected from cursory inspection of the issue of internationalization.

More global market domination may also depend upon being located in countries likely to win out in any particular industry. Porter's analysis (1990) of country competitiveness identifies traditional economic factors such as comparative advantage, but places greater emphasis on national demand characteristics (the presence of innovative buyers), supporting infrastructure (the fate of closely related sectors being highly interdependent), and the benefits arising from vigorous domestic rivalry. Companies achieving overbearing domestic market leadership, such as national champions, are viewed as likely to become complacent and, ultimately, uncompetitive—the car industry being a case in point.

Porter's warning on the dangers inherent in the possession of domestic market power (1990), however, runs counter to his central preoccupation with the acquisition of greater monopoly power (1980)—a theoretical paradox noted by Grant (1991). Nor is this contradiction between Porter's two books fully resolved by defining the locus of competition as global rather than national. If domestic market power entails the danger of complacency, so does global market power: and if such dangers are so important, does the issue of monopoly power really merit such a central place in strategic analysis? Since relatively few companies can hope to achieve dominant global market positions, would most companies not be better off down-playing market power altogether and seeking other routes to better performance?

Indeed, Collis' studies (1991a,b) of global competition in the bearings industry suggest that resource-based approaches may often be more appropriate. Rather than struggling to achieve market domination RHP, for example, would have fared better with a less ambitious strategy more attuned to its unique, if somewhat limited, resource base—a conclusion supported by Carr (1990, pp. 86–119).

One option, denigrated by Porter (1987), is to pursue the type of "financial control" (FC) style practised by conglomerates such as Hanson. This approach explicitly downgrades market share targets, with international operations often being divested, but frees business units to find other routes to good financial performance, and has often proved extremely successful in mature industries (Goold and Campbell, 1987a,b)—a graphic case study being provided by Roberts (1990). Many UK industrial companies are now controlled by such conglomerates and are potentially identifiable as adopting an FC style.

Another more positive resource-based option is suggested by the literature on manufacturing excellence (Hayes and Abernathy, 1980). Advocates of structural analysis (Ghemawat, 1986; Porter, 1980) see technological and manufacturing factors merely as part of an armoury designed primarily to shore some position of market power. Yet manufacturing operations can be formidable sources of competitive advantage in their own right (Garvin, 1983;

Hayes, Wheelwright and Clark, 1988; Skinner, 1978; Wheelwright, 1981). Also, in industrial markets, any attempt at gaining market power at the expense of customers risks counter measures (Baily and Farmer, 1981) and long-term cooperative relationships have underpinned the competitiveness of Japanese vehicle component suppliers (Carr, 1990; Carr and Truesdale, 1992; Lamming, 1989; Nishiguchi, 1989; Shimokawa, 1982).

Literature-based arguments can thus be found in support of each of the four following possible strategic choices open to major companies, faced with impending industry maturity and increasing international competition:

1. They can try to dominate domestic markets.
2. They can try to dominate European or even global markets.
3. They can eschew any attempt at dominating markets and seek to improve performance by the adoption of an FC style.
4. They can eschew any attempt at dominating markets and seek to improve performance in some other way (e.g. through greater emphasis on manufacturing or technological issues, based on closer and more collaborative relationships with customers).

The resource implications of such choices are so substantial that companies need to know which are likely to be most successful. This will now be examined.

METHODOLOGY

The question addressed involves so many highlighted variables as to be unanswerable in any general study pertaining to all industries. Even the PIMS database, arguably one of the most comprehensive general industry databases available (Buzzell and Gale, 1987), cannot discriminate between the first three options; and it contains no data on Japanese manufacturers, who have played such an important role in international competition. At the other extreme, the call for richer longitudinal studies (Pettigrew, Whipp and Rosenfeld, 1986) has been constrained by the practical difficulty of achieving such depth in more than one company (Pettigrew, 1985). The necessary compromise is to examine cases of mature industries subject to internationalization.

Baden-Fuller and Stopford (1991) have helped to rectify the lack of rich industry studies, but even their study of "globalization frustrated" in the mature domestic appliance industry lacks any research outside Europe.

This chapter examines another mature industry, vehicle components, where internationalization has already been well documented (Bertodo, 1991; Boston Consulting Group/PRS, 1991; Carr, 1985; Lamming, 1989; Nishiguchi, 1989). The sector's complexity allows examination of many rivals pursuing different strategies, in a variety of situations, while affording opportunities for international comparisons on a highly comparable, component by component basis.

Large British companies are of interest in having performed poorly in so many international markets (Carr, 1990), despite enjoying domestic markets among the most highly concentrated in the developed world (Davies et al., 1991, p. 1). British vehicle component companies have been particularly affected by internationalization and industry maturity. Since the early 1970s, their customer industry's output has grown modestly on a worldwide basis, and national output has fallen from a peak of 2 million cars in 1973 to 1.3 million in 1991, despite some recent recovery.

This investigation is based on a longitudinal study of the vehicle components industry. The author worked for GKN, one of Britain's largest vehicle component companies, between 1974 and 1980. This afforded access to GKN Forgings and GKN Hardy Spicer, discussed later. Since 1980, the industry has been studied continuously. To gain an adequate international perspective, 30 manufacturers in Britain were "matched" with 27 in Germany, the US and Japan on the basis of six specific components, with field research in all four countries (carried out between 1981 and 1983). Product sectors were chosen to cover a range of characteristics expected to influence competition (e.g. high versus low technology), further methodological details being provided by Carr (1990, pp. 49–59). Access to both top level management and the shop floor was achieved in all companies, and several UK companies allowed repeated visits. During the past three years, further field research has involved US, German and Japanese customers based in Europe, another 46 vehicle component companies in Britain and Germany, and another 6 suppliers serving UK-based Japanese customers; these studies have separate aims but were useful in clarifying the corporate management styles of a number of companies not visited during earlier field research, and for more recent developments. Secondary sources have been scanned continuously and comprehensively.

As in Baden-Fuller and Stopford (1991), one important performance measure has been return on capital employed (ROCE), averaged over several years, but this has not been used in international comparisons since German and Japanese companies have sustained strategies yielding ROCEs far lower than would be acceptable in Britain or the US (Carr, 1990, p. 108). Greater use has been made of productivity measures, and other measures to gauge quality and flexibility, these being considered as key purchasing criteria by customers (Womack, Jones and Roos, 1990). This allows supply-side issues to be addressed more adequately. Sales growth figures have been examined to check on "harvesting" and attention has been paid to exits, checking whether or not exits were likely to have been successful (Harrigan, 1980).

To achieve greater depth, meaningful international comparisons and a higher degree of explanation, this chapter again follows Baden-Fuller and Stopford (1991) in complementing examination of the industry as a whole with a more focused analysis of one fairly representative market segment, automotive forgings. This product segment is particularly advanced in terms of the product life cycle: the domestic market (in tonnage terms) has declined by two-thirds since 1965 (NADFS statistics). Product characteristics, though, have been less favourable to internationalization in this segment, as has been evident in the absence of multinationals and in the relatively low level of international trade. This is therefore one segment where market power might result from national as opposed to global market leadership.

Access in this segment was good. Employed as a development engineer with GKN Forgings between 1974 and 1978, the author had access to all sites and to long-serving staff, who, in turn, had detailed historical knowledge and access to performance records. This company has held a little under 50% of the domestic market, representing a dominant position. Subsequently, field research was carried out in ten other UK forging companies, three in Japan, one in the US and one in West Germany. The chapter will, however, return to the more general industry situation, again drawing on international comparisons, before reaching conclusions.

UK PERFORMANCE FINDINGS

UK SUPPLIER COMPANIES' COLLECTIVE PERFORMANCES

FIGURE 6.1 demonstrates the long-term declining profitability of UK supplier companies. Overall profitability has not correlated with trends in the domestic components market, which fell in line with the virtual halving of UK car production between 1973 and 1979. FIGURE 6.1 shows that suppliers' average ROCE remained stable at around 18%, never falling below 14.5% even during the first oil crisis. During the next few years UK car production remained stable at one million cars, yet profits plunged and remained low.

Imports of parts and accessories by 1988 were almost six times higher, in constant prices, than in 1970 (SMMT/Customs and Excise statistics). The import/export ratio rose from 0.24 in 1970 to 0.49 in 1980, to 0.97 in 1985, and to 1.30 in 1988. The steep decline in ROCE in the early 1980s was, nevertheless, traceable mainly to declining margins as a result of uncompetitiveness, rather than falling utilization in terms of sales/capital employed ratios. UK parts prices, which had been internationally competi-

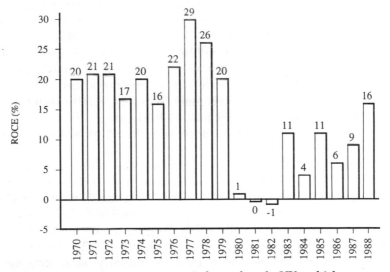

FIGURE 6.1 Average return on capital employed: UK vehicle component companies

tive in 1978 (Price Commission, 1979), became seriously uncompetitive after 1979 following a rise of some 40% in the inflation-adjusted exchange rate. Backed up by the threat of international procurement, customers succeeded in freezing component prices over the next four years (Bessant et al., 1984, p.61), thereby squeezing margins. Even Britain's largest engine reconditioner found any perception of market power to be illusory; holding out on price, its business was switched to another supplier and its plant was forced to close. The wholesale price index rose by 46% over the period, but suppliers were unable to pass on their own increased costs. Terms of trade improved after 1985, restoring the competitiveness of UK parts prices (House of Commons, 1987), improving margins.

UK car production rose from 1m to 1.4m in 1989 yet any resultant de-maturity in the domestic market has been associated with meagre overall profitability, compared with the earlier period of dramatic market decline. The stage of maturity appears to be an unreliable predictor of overall profitability.

PERFORMANCE DIFFERENCES BY TYPE OF COMPANY

Performance outcomes for 74 larger UK-based vehicle component companies, affording continuous accounts data, were analysed in terms of average ROCEs achieved between 1984 and 1988. Because of space constraints, TABLE 6.1 first details results for the top 10 performers, then focuses (for comparison) on the largest 15 companies, which in practice achieved strong domestic market positions. Size data in terms of sale turnover is included to facilitate examination of any size/performance relationships, and relative sales growth data as a check against "harvesting".

To help relate this data to the strategic choices identified earlier, national players are distinguished from companies achieving more global or at least regional (i.e. European) market positions, and subsidiaries of foreign multinationals (FMNCs) are identified separately. Twelve companies were classified following visits; others involved external sources and company accounts for data on overseas plants and export ratios. Secondly, companies were classified in terms of Goold and Campbell's (1987a,b) management styles. External sources were used for some well-documented companies; many were classified following visits but confidentiality arrangements preclude their separate identification.

GLOBAL MARKET STRATEGIES

Despite internationalization, only one British-owned company analysed in TABLE 6.1 has achieved a leading position in terms of global market share—GKN Hardy Spicer, in constant velocity joints. Its profitability has been excellent, though at the expense of static sales growth, which implies some "harvesting" since this world market segment is still growing. Such success attests to benefits hypothesized from proactive international market positioning, overseas plants having been established in Germany and the US. Notwithstanding Ghemawat's (1986) reservations, technological patents were critical in establishing this strategy. However, competition may now intensify following their expiry: NTN's constant velocity plant visited in Japan was modern and progressing rapidly, and mor recent discussions suggest that it is now challenging GKN's position more forcibly, particularly in the US.

Likewise supported by patents and substantial overseas production, Pilkington is the only other British-owned company to have approached global domination, having achieved the number two position in world automotive glass. Pilkington faces strong competition from US and French rivals, and is now being strongly challenged by Asahi Glass of Japan. Figures for its Triplex automotive glass subsidiary were incomplete, but were below those of other UK suppliers when averaged for the years where figures were available: some major development projects, such as "10/20" automotive glass, have proven commercially unsuccessful.

Alfred Teves, TRW United Carr and Eaton, all subsidiaries of German or US multinationals with significant world market positions, rank among the most profitable companies in TABLE 6.1. However, Cummins and Champion Spark Plugs, both US-based, global market leaders in engines and spark plugs respectively, have performed less well in recent years, having come under direct pressure from Japanese rivals.

These strategies appear globally integrated, exploiting know-

TABLE 6.1 Best performers of 74 vehicle component companies, 1984–1988

ROCE rank*	Company	Manu-facturing style†	Average ROCE, 1984–1988 (%)	Sales growth, 1984–1988 (% p.a.)	Size rank, 1984	Products	Type of player‡
1	BMAC	FC	75	12	73	Electric lighting accessories	National (small)
2	Hardy Spicer	SP	40	0	12	CV joints	Global
3	Alfred Teves	SP/FC	39	16	29	Brakes	Regional/global/ FMNC
4	TRW Untd	SP/FC	38	17	36	Sub-assemblies	Regional/global/ FMNC
5	Motaproducts	FC	34	24	41	Accessories	National (small)
6	Eaton	SP/FC	33	4	10	Axles, transmission	Global/regional/ FMNC
7	Albion Pressed Metal		31	21	48	Metal pressings	Regional/global (just acquired by Japanese FMNC)
8	Concentric Pressed Products		30	19	46	Pressings and fabrications	
9	Clearplast Vacumet		28	36	54	Plastic parts	Small national
10	International Radiators	FC	28	2	17	Radiators AM	Small national

Performance of largest companies (other than above)

38	SP	Lucas	11	7	1	Electrical	Regional/global
41	SP	Chloride	10	−4	2	Batteries	Regional/global
18	SP	Unipart	20	1	3		National/exporter
55	SP/FC	Automotive Products	6	6	4	Brakes	National/regional
63	SP	Cummins Engine	−4	11	5	Diesel engines	Global, FMNC
39	FC/SP	BBA	11	55	6	Brake linings	National/regional
59	SP	Dana	10	10	7	Truck parts/distribution	Global, FMNC
35	SP/FC	Armstrong	11	4	8	Steering wheels, silencers	National/regional
57		Quinton Hazell	6	−17	9		National
53	SP	GKN Sankey	7	20	11	Wheels, miscellaneous	National
44	SP	Jonas Woodhead	9	−4	13	Steering columns	National/export
67	SP/FC	TRW Cam Gears	−13	6	14		Regional/global/FMNC
27	SP	GKN Axles	16	8	15	Axles	National

Average UK non-global big players: 11% ROCE, 7.6% sales growth
Average 74 companies: 10.5% ROCE, 12.1% sales growth

*1, Largest; 74, smallest; 37.5, average.
†FC, financial control; SP, strategic planning.
‡Based on examination of overseas manufacturing plants and export ratio. FMNC, foreign multinational company.

how synergies and the ability to offer services in more than one country. The level of investments implied is huge: for example, each of GKN's constant velocity joints factories cost of the order of $100 m, even in 1979/80. Global market domination can be highly successful, but its attainment is rare, particularly for component companies not based in the US, Japan or Germany, which appear to be the most favoured countries.

STRATEGIES BASED ON NATIONAL MARKET LEADERSHIP

While global strategies were rare, many large British companies nevertheless historically invested heavily in acquisitions to achieve positions of national market dominance, thereby diverting resources from more basic manufacturing improvements. TABLE 6.1 demonstrates that (within this category) Lucas, Chloride, Automotive Products, BBA and Armstrong have sustained low profitability even relative to other UK-based suppliers; their growth performances, with the exception of BBA, were also unimpressive. Turner and Newall's Associated Engineering subsidiary could not be included in TABLE 6.1, because public data discontinued at the point of takeover; but earlier profitability was poor relative to the sector.

To examine how these larger, nationally dominant UK-based companies have performed over a longer period, companies were split into size categories, based on sales levels in 1975. The largest size classification was then dominated by such companies, but has performed poorly relative to the sector over 20 years, as demonstrated in TABLE 6.2.

TABLE 6.3 details many former UK market leaders forced into unprofitable exits: case study accounts are provided in Carr (1990, pp. 86–186) for RHP in automotive rolling bearings, Lucas/Smiths in automotive instrumentation, GKN Forgings in forgings and TI Cheswick in exhaust systems. In addition, between 1989 and May 1991, German vehicle companies acquired Camford Engineering, Jonas Woodhead and Birmid Qualcast, again all former domestic product market leaders. Strategies relying on national market leadership positions have proved remarkably successful, both in terms of profitability and in terms of sustaining strong long-term competitive positions.

TABLE 6.2 Profitability and sales growth performances by size classification

Profitability/sales growth	Size groups*					Average	Sample number
	1	2	3	4	5		
ROCE 1984–1988	11.1	10.1	12.4	9.5	9.2	10.5	74
ROCE 1979–1983	1.7	8.0	4.0	6.7	5.8	5.3	52
ROCE 1975–1979	16.6	20.8	24.8	19.0	20.7	20.4	81
ROCE 1970–1974	12.7	26.5	19.6	21.4	5.1	17.1	24
Growth 1984–1988	7.1	9.1	9.7	19.5	15.5	12.1	74
Growth 1979–1983	-0.0	-3.9	-2.7	6.2	3.4	0.8	52
Growth 1975–1979	15.9	7.6	23.8	22.1	25.4	25.4	81
Growth 1970–1974	3.4	0.1	2.6	-0.7	-3.2	0.4	24

Source: Inter Company Comparisons.
*Descending order.

TABLE 6.3   The fate of past national champions in the UK supplier industry, main areas of demise

Company	Product areas of former national leadership	Comments
Lucas	Electrical products	Divested to Magnetti Morelli of Italy following prolonged period of low profits
Smiths	Instrumentation	Divested via major joint-venture with Lucas in early 1980s; this subsequently failed commercially
GKN	Fasteners	ROCE ranking 1975–1978, 80th out of 81 companies, subsequently divested
	Forgings	Virtually divested after very poor profits in 1970s and early 1980s via joint-venture with BSC
	"Off road" wheels	GKN Sankey's ROCE averaged 1% over the past 15 years
Chloride	Batteries	Major investments commercially unsuccessful and divested to an Indonesian company, but its joint-venture with the Japanese remains
Dunlop	Tyres	European tyres divested to Sumitomo of Japan in early 1980s, following financial crisis
	Wheels	Divested to BRT following the same crisis
Wilmot Breedon	Wheels	Britain's other major national player in car wheels; closed this plant in early 1980s
Associated Engineering	Engine parts	Company absorbed by T&N in late 1980s
Automotive Products	Clutches	Company absorbed by BBA in late 1980s
Pilkingtons (Triplex)	Glass	Triplex not divested by Pilkington, but not highly profitable
Armstrong	Shock absorbers	Divested in May 1989 after poor profitability; company absorbed by Carclo in 1989
TI (Cheswick)	Silencers	Divested to Alvin of USA in 1989, after ROCE in one year fell back to minus 663%
Anonymous	Engine reconditioning	Britain's number one player, closed in late 1980s
RHP	Rolling bearings	Profit decline and major retrenchment activities in 1980s; acquired by Japan's NSK in 1990
Delanair	Air conditioners	Extremely profitable niche player; divested by Hanson, to Valeo of France
IMI	Radiators	Poor profitability and, like Unipart's Llenelli
Radiators		Radiators, divested in 1989/90 to Japanese

Strategies Not Based on Market Leadership

Three of the ten most profitable suppliers identified in Table 6.1—BMAC, Motaproducts and BRT's subsidiary International Radiators—are part of conglomerates that can reliably be classified as adopting FC styles. Before its disposal by Hanson, Delanair averaged the highest rate of return of all UK vehicle component companies between 1984 and 1986, and would have been similarly classified. BMAC and Motaproducts do not enjoy market dominance even in the UK. International Radiators and Delanair have little overseas presence, but have stronger domestic market niche positions. However, short-term profit objectives unambiguously take precedence over any market share considerations. Option 3 has proven a feasible route to high and fairly sustained levels of profitability.

Other companies in Table 6.1's list of the 10 most highly profitable companies lack substantial overseas positions and do not appear large enough to dominate domestic product markets. Companies choosing option 4, as opposed to option 3, could not be reliably distinguished. However, a separate group of companies have also been identified, serving UK-based Japanese car assemblers, conforming to this option (Carr and Truesdale, 1992). The longer term competitive prospects of such companies cannot be discounted in view of the loyalty of a customer base set to exceed 700 000 UK transplant cars by 1996 (DRI/McGraw-Hill, 1991): VW is now stepping up purchases from such suppliers in view of their "sharply increased competitiveness" (*Financial Times*, 3 July 1992, p. 19). Overall, concentrating on supply-side priorities can prove more attractive than any attempt at dominating markets.

Why Have British National Market Leaders Performed Badly?

The explanatory framework, developed in Table 6.4, highlights the effects of internationalization and of broad country factors as suggested by Porter's (1990) "diamond" framework, but also the impact of companies' more specific strategic choices. Such a complex framework is needed, not only because of the broad range of factors involved, but also to take account of earlier suc-

TABLE 6.4 Shifting sources of competitive advantage affecting UK national champions, 1930s–1990s

	1930–late 1960s, UK	1970s, UK/Europe	1980s, Europe	1990s, Global
UK factor endowments:	Low wage costs, but sharply increased cost of capital *after 1960s* and short-termism due to combination of continuing wage *pressure* and financial deregulation. Early skills base superseded due to developing German and Japanese production/technology skills.			
Demand	Strong, fast growing car producers/innovative buyers	UK car output declines, Japanese car assemblers most demanding on quality, cost and just-in-time	Japanese assemblers also most demanding on need to handle product variety and fast introductions. Benefits as multinational companies increase UK production	
Infrastructure	Strong support from assemblers and supporting industries	Car assemblers and supporting industries in declining positions; position further weakened by distant relationships between supplier and assembly sectors		UK increasingly dependent on multi-national car firms and overseas infrastructure
Pressures of vigorous competition	Still strong prior to domestic consolidation	Domestic champions cushioned by fairly monopolistic domestic positions	Hit hard by international competition	International rivals likely to absorb most remaining major sectors
Economics of scope and scale	Large and focused enough to gain some scope/scale advantages from growing home market	Larger companies' economies of scope (e.g. domestic market power) traded against focus and specialization	Domestic market power evaporates in face of international procurement	First-tier suppliers exploiting global positions to gain economies of specialization
Operational and technological advantages	R&D excellent, good quality and fairly good productivity	Complacent on quality, productivity, delivery flexibility/just-in-time	UK still complacent on handling product variety and fast introductions; Germans and Japanese able to devote more R&D to key areas such as electronics; UK suppliers responding in manufacturing issues but unable to bridge gap	

cesses. More comprehensive elaboration is provided by Carr (1990), but this explanatory framework will next be illustrated by focusing on one product sector, automotive forgings.

THE CASE OF AUTOMOTIVE FORGINGS

GKN Forgings (now part of United Engineering) became the dominant domestic market leader in forgings as a result of amalgamations, which gave it approximately half of a fragmented market. There were over 60 other British automotive forging companies. The company was commercially successful until well into the 1960s, supported by country-based advantages identified in Porter's (1990) "diamond": modest wage and capital costs; a strong, fast-growing, innovative UK customer base, disposed to outsourcing; competitive infrastructure, e.g. local engineering and steel into which GKN had backward integrated; and still vigorous domestic rivalry, until domestic consolidation and customer moves away from multi-sourcing began to take effect. Strategic choices were also adapted to this early situation:

- Appreciable economies of scope through ability to negotiate better margins with customers, assisted by full product line, and through advantages in steel procurement, which represented almost 50% of costs.
- Economies of scope through heavy R&D. This lead was still being maintained over German, US and even Japanese forges visited between 1982 and 1983.
- Several of GKN Forgings plants were re-equipped and re-laid out to meet the demand in the 1950s for volume automotive work: Garrington's plant was one of the largest, most modern automotive forgings plants in the world, enjoying substantial economies of specialization.
- "Hands on" management style of chief executives such as Lord Brookes, paying close attention to production issues, and resulting in good reputation for quality (then well ahead of Japanese) and relatively good productivity, assisted by a tough industrial relations approach and by high piecework incentives.

By the early 1970s, all four supporting conditions had become undermined and the company's competitive strategy was dangerously dependent on market power and economies of scope. Under less conducive investment conditions, the company failed to maintain its international lead in terms of modern, specialized plant. The style of the next generation of senior executives was less "hands on", with greater attention being placed instead on financial and other management control systems, and on handling immediate industrial relations problems. As quality and productivity slipped behind, car customers increasingly utilized international procurement (particularly in higher volume, higher technology forging market segments) to remove any element of monopolistic pricing.

A strategy of international dominance was ruled out when even one major overseas plant proved economically unjustifiable. In fact, *no* automotive forging company, in any country, has yet embarked on a global or even regional strategy because of a combination of low margins and high plant costs: only one substantial new forge has been built in western Europe since World War Two. There also proved to be negligible scope for re-asserting market power by offering customers "package" deals, involving other GKN automotive products. As opportunities for exerting market power waned, GKN Forgings paid dearly for slipping behind on basic manufacturing issues. Profitability remained low (both absolutely and relative to other UK automotive forgers) throughout the 1970s, and degenerated further in the early 1980s as the market declined and international competition increased.

From the late 1950s, major Japanese and German forgers pursued different priorities. Industrial consolidation was rarely feasible, reducing opportunities for exploiting market power or economies of scope. Forging companies remained smaller and commanded much lower domestic market shares than GKN Forgings in the UK. Cheap capital encouraged specialization, especially in Japan, where plants visited were notably modern. They benefited from rapidly growing, highly demanding customers, increasingly competitive, related supplier industries such as steel, which accounted for almost half their costs; while vigorous domestic rivalry precluded complacency. Both countries built up strong team skills in production areas, facilitating long-term improvement programmes such as "built-in" quality rather than *ex post* controls, then adopted in Britain and the USA. In Japan these same teams, with direct help from customers such as Toyota, assiduously improved productivity, yields and flexibility, seeking to achieve "just-in-time". UK and US forgers visited had ignored such initiatives, relying more heavily upon narrower skills bases in staff areas such as research and development. GKN Forgings led all three Japanese automotive forges visited in advanced technical developments, but such advances were infrequent and difficult to implement on any extensive basis.

Consequently by 1983, productivity in three Japanese automotive forges visited averaged 86 tons per manyear, even adjusting for outsourcing and on-site contract labour. Comparable figures for five UK companies visited averaged 24 tons per manyear, the highest figure being only 34 tons. In one very old West German automotive forge, productivity was 28 tons per manyear. Productivity at the US automotive forge visited was 86 tons per manyear, assisted by extremely long order runs. Exercising substantial market power, this company had felt able to turn away shorter orders, although this had sacrificed flexibility, increasingly demanded by customers seeking just-in-time delivery. Average US hammer change-over times had remained static at 2.6 hours, while those at comparable Japanese sites had fallen from about 40 minutes four years earlier, to some 17 minutes. UK forges had similarly made little progress by 1983 on either change-over times or on factory through times, both prerequisites in achieving manufacturing flexibility.

That scale advantages were limited is underlined by the superior performance of Japanese forging companies, which were smaller than GKN Forgings in terms of both plant size and the number of plants operated; yet, for organizational and internal political reasons by no means uncommon (Grinyer and Spender, 1979; Johnson, 1987), GKN Forgings found it difficult to shift from a success recipe founded on size. Investments in volume orientated presses continued. When rationalization became unavoidable in 1980, the company's more flexible and relatively better performing small plant was closed, to help prop up utilization of larger plants.

GKN Forgings' formal planning documents were sophisticated in terms of markets, competition, and financial and advanced technical developments, but operational performance parameters were treated more superficially. Inadequate projected results were sometimes boosted by projecting blanket productivity improvements, with capital budget provisions just being increased slightly to add credence. By contrast, Japanese business planning activities were crude in market and financial terms, but operational performance targets were highly detailed and closely monitored. One company's "business plan" comprised a single, large engineering drawing, divided into over 40 boxes. Two boxes in the top left corner contained small pie charts indicating present and projected domestic market share positions; but the remaining boxes were given over to operational parameters (such as yield rates, productivity, reject rates), with targets for specific production areas. No information was provided on financial matters and there was little supporting information on advanced technological developments, markets or competition. This Japanese company, like many others visited, expressed little interest in issues such as market positioning or market power; close, long-term customer relationships and the infeasibility of acquisitions rendered such considerations rare.

GKN Forgings' profitability remained poor and it has since been virtually divested by means of a joint-venture company, United Engineering, set up between GKN and British Steel. Its commercial outlook appears unpromising, although United Engineering's chief executive recognizes that "its future now depends on its competitiveness on a European, rather than a national scale" (*Financial Times*, 17 December 1991, p. 26). The US forge was closed down in 1987.

To interpret these findings, the absence of *any* strategies based on global or even regional market domination, suggests that option 2 is not yet feasible in this segment. GKN Forgings dominated its national market (option 1), to an extent unmatched by any other forging company in any other advanced country, but this has ultimately proved fruitless. While the US forger did not exercise such *overall* domestic market leadership, it nevertheless dominated the business of its major customer in a manner providing substantial market power over many years. Its closure likewise attests to the limitations of such approaches.

Other British automotive forgers visited are reliably classifiable as having pursued option 3 or 4. Most British forges visited were highly financially orientated, particularly compared to those in Japan, suggesting option 3, although the dividing line between options 3 and 4 proved difficult to determine reliably. Financial and sales performances of these companies were on average much better than those of GKN Forgings, but many may be forced to exit at some point.

Japanese and German forgers visited were classified as having pursued option 4. Although fairly large, the German forge was by no means a domestic leader, nor did it adopt an FC style. Profitability within a 5-year horizon was considered important, but not an overriding objective; as a long-established family firm, the company adopted a fairly long-term view and required modest returns. This company was revisited in 1990 and was still flourishing. Japanese forgers were able to take longer term views and placed even less stress on financial targets. The structure of the Japanese automotive industry and its supplier networks (Cusumano, 1989; Nishiguchi, 1989) appeared to have discouraged attempts at total market domination. Similarly, any attempt at improving negotiating power at the expense of customers (as suggested by Porter, 1980, and 1983) risked jeopardizing long-term collaborative relationships, perceived as highly important. Consequently, less emphasis was placed on financial and market positioning issues, and their almost obsessional operational concerns were spurred by vigorous domestic rivalry. Ultimately, as would be suggested by Porter (1990), Japanese automotive forgers have benefited. Operational advantages have proved more sustainable than those associated with market power. Their productivity lead, for example, is unlikely to have been eroded: even the German forge revisited in 1990 had only increased productivity to 30 thousand tons per manyear. Option 4 is soundly based.

SOURCES OF SUSTAINABLE COMPETITIVE ADVANTAGE IN THE VEHICLE COMPONENTS INDUSTRY MORE GENERALLY

While TABLE 6.5 demonstrates operational advantages *sustained* by Japanese suppliers for a wider range of products, most former UK market leaders (like GKN Forgings) gained only transitory benefits from scale and market power. (Carr (1992) provides more comprehensive details of international productivity comparisons.) Large companies created by amalgamations gained initially from better margins as smaller domestic rivals were eliminated. Product line offerings and production facilities could be rationalized, some products offering greater scale advantages, particularly while markets were still growing. Yet greater investment in acquisitions led to much lower organic investment than in German companies (SAC, 1991) and diverted managers from manufacturing issues. Waning market power, as international competition intensified, was insufficient to sustain comfortable profit margins.

TABLE 6.5   Supplier plants performance comparisons, 1983–1990

	Japan	US	Europe	Germany	UK
Productivity index, 1982/83*	308	312	n.a.	159	100
Number of machines per worker, 1987–1989†	7.4	2.5	2.7	n.a.	n.a.
Die change times (min), 1987–1989†	7.9	114.3	123.7	n.a.	n.a.
Productivity index, 1990‡	317	254	n.a.	203	100

*Unweighted averages of productivity indices, based on both physical and value measures, for several types of vehicle components, as detailed in Carr (1992).
†*Source*: Nishiguchi (1989, pp. 324–337), based on visits to 18 suppliers in Japan, 10 in the US and 18 in Europe.
‡Productivity indices based on a study of one type of component in a number of plants throughout the world, as further detailed in Carr (1992).

That scale economies were limited for most components is suggested by the absence of correlation between size and performance in TABLES 6.1 and 6.2. Regression analysis of ROCE against log(sales) between 1970 and 1988, carried out on the entire performance database, equally found no such correlation, a conclusion corroborated by Boston Consulting Group/PRS (1991).

For products offering greater scale economies, on the other hand, global rationalization has proceeded more rapidly, favouring foreign companies pursuing global strategies. Examples include SKF and Timken in automotive rolling bearings, Cummins in engines, Champion, Bridgestone and Michelin in tyres, and Bosch and Nippon Denso in automotive electronics. Following a shake-out the top four tyre companies now hold 70% of the world market (Slade and Fordham, 1990, 2.2, updated). Similarly, NGK's deputy managing director predicts that the future of spark plugs lies only with Champion, Bosch and NGK: "others will fade out or subcontract to the big players" (*Financial Times*, 19 September 1990, p. 9).

As TABLE 6.5 indicates, German and Japanese suppliers have increased R&D spending in such product areas: Asahi Glass' R&D/sales ratio, for example, has doubled. Japanese suppliers now have the largest shares of patents in the US, while Bosch of West Germany alone accounted for half of those obtained by European suppliers (Lamming, 1989). Many Japanese suppliers are also now internationalizing their operations, seeking benefits from "insider" operations across the "triad" of Europe, the US and Japan (Ohmae, 1985). Some 400 have followed Japanese vehicle assemblers by establishing operations in the US and several have begun establishing European operations (TABLE 6.3 contains some examples). A small group of companies pursuing option 2 may well increasingly dominate this type of "first tier", higher technology supply business. Against such competition, however, British national market leaders have performed poorly: a detailed case study of Lucas/Smiths' demise in the higher technology area of automotive instrumentation is provided in Carr (1990, pp. 150–168). Lucas is now reported (*Sunday Times*, 19 July 1992, p. 3.14) to be considering disposing of its brake activities (another area of domestic market leadership) to Bosch, after performing disappointingly in advanced brake systems.

CONCLUSION

This chapter has examined the prescription that companies anticipating the onset of industry maturity should aim to gain market domination, by studying empirically the outcomes of four types of strategic choices by major UK-based vehicle component companies.

Despite evidence of internalization, option 2, global market leadership, is rarely attainable, particularly for companies not based in most favoured nations (confirming the concerns of Porter (1990)). Many large British companies, in practice, defined their markets nationally, and achieved domestic market leadership positions (option 2), but outcomes have generally proved little short of disastrous, both commercially and in terms of competitive positions.

Other "resource-based" options, placing less emphasis on market power, have been associated with more favourable outcomes, supporting Collis' (1991a) call for a change of emphasis in approaches to strategic analysis. Suppliers pursuing an FC style approach (option 3) sustained the highest rates of profitability, although their longer term competitive prospects are open to question. Remaining British suppliers, pursuing option 4, sustained more modest levels of profitability, although still better than those of national market leaders, but a number, serving Japanese transplant operations, enjoy promising prospects.

Reviewing the worldwide position, the most successful competitive performances, in Japan, have most frequently reflected type 4 options. Vigorous domestic rivalry generally precluded domestic market domination, while operational priorities have paid off. Building on such firm foundations, several are now shifting to type 2 global strategies, particularly on products allowing greater scale economies. Some large US suppliers also opted for option 2, but most, having settled for national market leadership (option 1), now face savage competition from Japanese transplant suppliers, and are faring little better than their British counterparts.

Industries differ. Yet British national market leaders have performed equally dismally in other sectors subject to internationalization, often in spite of government support: Norton Villiers Triumph in motorcycles: Austin Rover in cars; ICL in computers. In these industries, domestic leaders in other countries have encountered similar difficulties (Bull and Olivetti in computers, in France and Italy, for example), while Japanese companies opting for other routes to competitive advantage still appear to be flourishing. Baden-Fuller and Stopford's (1991) findings in domestic appliances sound a warning that global strategies may not always result in better performances than nationally-based strategies, even in the context of apparent internationalization; but by neither distinguishing resource-based options, nor taking into account US or Japanese perspectives, their findings might offer misleading comfort to companies over-relying on national market positions.

REFERENCES

Baden-Fuller, C. and Stopford, J.M. (1991). Globalisation frustrated: The case of white goods. *Strategic Management Journal* **12**, 493–507.
Baily, P. and Farmer, D. (1981). *Purchasing Principles and Management*. London: Pitman.
Bertodo, R. (1991). The role of suppliers in implementing a strategic vision. *Long Range Planning* **24**(3), 40–48.
Bessant, J., Jones, D.T., Lamming, R.L. and Pollard, A. (1984). The West Midlands automobile components industry: Recent changes and future prospects, West Midlands County Council Economic and Development Unit Sector report no. 4, West Midlands County Council.
Boston Consulting Group/PRS (1991). The European vehicle components industry, report for the EEC Commission. London: Boston Consulting Group.
Buzzell, R.S. and Gale, B. (1987). *The PIMS Principles*. New York: Free Press.

Carr, C.H. (1985). The competitiveness of UK vehicle component manufacturers, doctoral dissertation, University of Warwick.

Carr, C.H. (1990). *Britain's Competitiveness: The Management of the Vehicle Component Industry*. London: Routledge.

Carr, C.H. (1992). Productivity and skills in vehicle component manufacturers in Britain, Germany, the USA and Japan. *National Institute Economic Review* February.

Carr, C.H. and Truesdale, A. (1992). Lessons from Nissan's British suppliers. *International Journal of Operations and Production Management* **12**(6), 49–57.

Collis, D.J. (1991a). A resource-based analysis of global competition: the case of the bearings industry. *Strategic Management Journal* **12**, 49–68.

Collis, D.J. (1991b). The visible hand of trade: The influence of firms on the pattern of trade in the global bearings industry, paper presented at the World Trade and Global Competition Conference, 3 December, Harvard Business School, Cambridge, MA.

Cusumano, M.A. (1989). *The Japanese Automobile Industry: Technology and Management at Nissan and Toyota*. Cambridge, MA: Harvard University Press.

Davies, S., Geroski, P.A., Lund, M. and Vlassopoulis, A. (1991). *The Dynamics of Market Leadership in the UK Manufacturing Industry 1979–1986*. London: Centre for Business Strategy, London Business School.

DRI/McGraw-Hill (1991). *World Automotive Forecast Report*, winter edition. Lexington, MA: DRI/McGraw-Hill.

Garvin, D.A. (1983). Quality on the line. *Harvard Business Review* **61**(5), 64–76.

Ghemawat, P. (1986). Sustainable advantage. *Harvard Business Review* September/October, 53–58.

Goold, M. and Campbell, A. (1987a). *Strategies and Styles. The Role of the Corporate Centre in Managing Diversified Companies*. Oxford: Basil Blackwell.

Goold, M. and Campbell, A. (1987b). Many best ways to make strategy. *Harvard Business Review* November/December, 70–76.

Grant, R. (1991). Porter's *Competitive Advantage of Nations*: An assessment. *Strategic Management Journal* **12**, 535–548.

Grinyer, P. and Spender, J.C. (1979). Recipes, crises and adaptions in mature business. *International Studies of Management and Organisation* **9**, 113–123.

Harrigan, K.R. (1980). *Strategies for Declining Businesses*. Lexington, MA: Lexington Books.

Haspeslaugh, P. (1982). Portfolio planning: Uses and limits. *Harvard Business Review* **60**(3), 70–80.

Hayes, R.H. and Abernathy, W.J. (1980). Managing our way to economic decline. *Harvard Business Review* July, **58**(4), 67–77.

Hayes, R., Wheelwright, S. and Clark, K. (1988). *Dynamic Manufacturing: Creating the Learning Organization*. New York: Free Press.

Hedley, B. (1977). Strategy and the "business portfolio". *Long Range Planning* **10**(1), 9–16.

House of Commons (1987). The UK motor components industry. Third report from the Trade and Industry Committee session 1986–87. Report, proceedings of the Committee, minutes of evidence and appendices. London: HMSO.

Hout, T., Porter, M. and Rudden, E. (1982). How global companies win out. *Harvard Business Review* **60**(5), 98–109.

Inter Company Comparisons (annual). *Business Ratio Report: Motor Components*. London: ICC.

Johnson, G. (1987). *Strategic Change and the Management Process*. Oxford: Basil Blackwell.

Lamming, R. (1989). The causes and effects of structural change in the European automobile industry. IMVP Working Paper, May, MIT, Boston, MA.

Levitt, T. (1965). Exploit the product life cycle. *Harvard Business Review* November/December, 81–94.

Nishiguchi, T. (1989). Strategic dualism, PhD thesis, Oxford University.

Ohmae, K. (1985). *Triad Power: The Coming Shape of Global Competition*. New York: Free Press.

Pettigrew, A. (1985). *The Awakening Giant: Continuity and Change in ICI*. Oxford: Blackwell.

Pettigrew, A., Whipp, R. and Rosenfeld, R. (1986). Competitiveness and the management of strategic management change processes: a research agenda. Presented at the Conference on the Competitiveness of European Industry: Country Policies and Company Strategies, European Institute for Advanced Studies in Management, Brussels, February.

Porter, M.E. (1980). *Competitive Strategy: Techniques for Analysing Industries and Competitors*. New York: Free Press.

Porter, M.E. (1983) *Cases in Competitive Strategy*, New York: Free Press.

Porter, M.E. (1985). *Competitive Advantage: Creating and Sustaining Competitive Performance*. New York: Free Press.

Porter, M.E. (1986). Competition in global industries: A conceptual framework. In M.E. Porter (Ed.) *Competition in Global Industries* (pp. 15–60). New York: Free Press.

Porter, M.E. (1987). From competitive advantage to corporate strategy. *Harvard Business Review* May/June, **65**(3), 43–59.

Porter, M.E. (1990). *The Competitive Advantage of Nations*. London: Macmillan.

Prahalad, C.K. and Doz, Y.L. (1987). *The Multinational Mission. Balancing Local Demands and Global Vision*. New York: Free Press.

Price Commission (1979). *Prices, Costs and Margins in the Manufacture and Distribution of Car Parts*. London: HMSO.

Roberts, J. (1990). Strategy and accounting in a UK conglomerate. *Accounting, Organisation and Society* **15**(1/2), 107–126.

SAC Enterprises (1991). *The Outlook for the German Automotive Supply Industry in the 1990s*. London: SAC.

Shimokawa, K. (1982). The structure of the Japanese auto parts industry and its contribution to automotive process innovation. Paper presented at the International Policy Forum of the MIT: Future of the World Automobile Program, 16–20 May, Hakone, Japan.

Skinner, W. (1978). *Manufacturing in the Corporate Strategy*. Chichester: John Wiley.

Slade, J.B. and Fordham, P.A. (1990). European automotive component industry in the 1990s, Consultants to Industry, Engineering Employers' West Midlands Employers' Association, Birmingham.

Wheelwright, S.C. (1981). Japan—where operations really are strategic. *Harvard Business Review* **59**(4), 67–75.

Womack, J.P., Jones, D.T. and Roos, D. (1990). *The Machine that Changed the World*. New York: Rawson Associates.

7

Strategies for Winning in International Manufacturing and Sourcing

PETER B. DIXON, BARRY D. HEDLEY

INTRODUCTION

The world is set upon a trend of increasing change in ownership and control of national markets and national enterprises. Established competitors are being displaced by new entrants from "non-traditional" locations. For example, many older competitors in the car industry have disappeared, while new ones have emerged. Prices, which were once relatively predictable, now vary erratically with exchange rate movements, causing harmful fluctuations in profitability and stock market valuation. Now, within the foreseeable future, the European Community (EC) is proposing currency union, to build upon the European Monetary System (EMS).

How is this going to change the environment for competitors in the EC—both EC-based and those outside the EC—and what will these organizations need to do differently to win? We shall specifically address issues to do with plant and service location, price determination and risk management. To answer these questions,

Strategic Renaissance and Business Transformation. Edited by H. Thomas, D. O'Neal and J. Kelly.
Copyright © 1995 John Wiley & Sons Ltd.

Braxton Associates has developed a rigorous framework for determining what has been driving these processes, and for formulating appropriate strategic responses. The purpose of this chapter is to demonstrate this basic framework. We shall show how competition takes place in an environment where economies are linked by exchange rates, and then consider how competition will be different if currency union takes place. Some of the insights may seem counterintuitive at first, but this is the "new reality" of international competition.

FRAMEWORK

An important point before moving on to describe the analytical framework itself: business activities in general fall into the four broad categories shown in FIGURE 7.1. Of these, manufacturing and R&D activities are those for which competitiveness at the international level is of the greatest concern. Competition in marketing, service or distribution activities is often national in character, or may even take place at a regional level within a country. (Note that both R&D and manufacturing are terms that can also be applied to operations in the financial and other service industries. These insights are not merely applicable in manufacturing organizations.) The framework that follows is relevant to considering the competitiveness of a company's manufacturing and R&D activities. But all major functions will also need to be aware of these phenomena, in order to develop appropriate financial responses. These activities deliver products into various regions or countries, so competitiveness in marketing varies as a function of the company position locally. Overall competitiveness in delivering products to a customer in a particular country will therefore depend on the overall balance of the company's competitiveness in the manufacturing/R&D activities (international), and the marketing/distribution activities (national or regional).

It is worth noting here that recent work by Michael Porter has validated our assertion that *activity* competitiveness is the key to international competitiveness, and that national industrial strengths derive from a clustering and reinforcing of key activities.

The basic framework addresses two key issues:

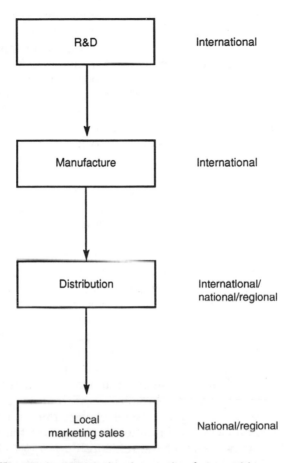

FIGURE 7.1   The activity perspective: international competition

1. What drives exchange rate movements, and hence what should exchange rates be in the future?
2. What do companies need to do to compete internationally in an exchange rate environment?

EXCHANGE RATES

Firstly, we need to see whether there is logic in exchange rate movements. Many economists reject the practicality of the purchasing power parity (PPP) theory, which says simply that the prices of baskets of tradable goods in two trading countries will be equalized over the longer term by the mechanisms of the exchange rate. These economists are wrong. Within limits, price parity of tradable goods is maintained in international trade.

In fact exchange rate movements *are* systematic, not random, and reflect fundamental shifts in average productivity. A convenient measure of real price levels and productivity in a country (and the best that we have been able to identify) is given by the wholesale price index (WPI). Its movement reflects two factors: firstly, productivity improvement drives "real" prices downwards; this is then (often more than) offset by structural national inflation. It is only the "real" component of the change that is strategically relevant over the long term in relation to international competition.

As an example, the data from Italy and Japan—two very differently performing economies—are shown in FIGURE 7.2. The second line in FIGURE 7.2a shows the ratio of the Japanese WPI to the Italian WPI over the past 30 or so years, arbitrarily indexed to a value of 1.0 in 1955. Obviously, on trend this ratio has decreased—the result of more rapid productivity improvements in Japan holding prices down there relative to those in Italy, together with rather higher inflation rates in Italy than in Japan during the 1970s. If the exchange arguments advanced hold true, one would expect the yen/lira exchange rate to be a perfect mirror image of the WPI ratio. The exchange rate is indeed a reasonable reflection of the WPI ratio, as shown by the top line in FIGURE 7.2a. The accuracy of the relationship is most clearly seen, however, by examining the multiple of the WPI ratio and the exchange rate over time. This is shown in FIGURE 7.2b, from which it is clear that an "equilibrium level" exists from which the multiple—most conveniently referred to as the real or "WPI-adjusted" exchange rate—has rarely strayed by more than plus or minus 15%. The "equilibrium" level is shown by the solid horizontal line.

Note that "short-term" fluctuations from the equilibrium—caused by interest rate differentials, balance of payments, politics, etc.—may last for three or four years, or more in the case of major continental blocks like the USA. It is crucial during these periods, if operating a business affected by the particular exchange rate, to have a good sense of where the current exchange rate lies in relation to the long-term trend, otherwise

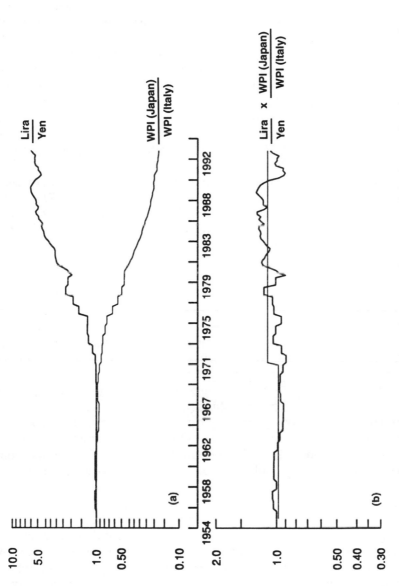

FIGURE 7.2 Wholesale prices and exchange rates, Italy and Japan, 1955–1992. Last data, 1992, fourth quarter; exchange rate = 10.5 lira/yen as of 5 October 1992; equilibrium exchange rate = 10.8 lira/yen. Reproduced by permission of IMP/Datastream

erroneous decisions can be taken in response to short-term pressures, or, indeed, to short-term profit "bonanzas". If these are related only to the current exchange rate and not the true long-term competitiveness at the equilibrium exchange rate, then the strategy that emerges from misreading the situation can be dangerously wrong. For example, we have worked with several clients in the UK to prevent closure of factories that were disadvantaged by what turned out to be the only temporary major deviation of the sterling exchange rate in 1980/81 and again in later periods of the decade.

The yen/dollar relationship (FIGURE 7.3) shows a different phenomenon: it appears that the WPI-adjusted exchange rate, which held very constant through the 1950s and 1960s, "floated" to a new equilibrium level when the Bretton Woods agreement was discontinued in 1971. The displacement of the post-1971 equilibrium relative to the earlier period suggests that the yen was undervalued by roughly 24% relative to the dollar during the Bretton Woods period. This obviously helped Japan's international cost competitiveness, and hence its rate of post-war industrialization.

It is tempting to search for a more detailed model of the reasons underlying shifts in these lines such as the 1971 change in the yen/dollar alignment. However, such endeavour is likely to prove somewhat sterile. The price of goods appears to be the best long-run determinant of exchange rates, and seeking a more complex model (including interest rates, etc.) is not likely to yield greater accuracy for *long-term* purposes. Hence, the best approach to the use of these relationships for business strategy depends primarily on developing an empirical view of the central tendency of the equilibrium exchange rate between two currencies, and on assessing the possible scale and duration of displacements from this tendency. There is likely to be no better guide to this than the actual historic behaviour as reflected in the pattern of the WPI-adjusted rate line.

Nevertheless, a few further comments about the factors underlying exchange rate relationships may be helpful as a guide to understanding. At any point in time, the value of one currency relative to another is, of course, affected by all of the factors influencing relative supply and demand for currencies. Trade is only one of these; capital flows seeking investment returns via interest rates are another, and these flows are influenced not merely by the apparent real interest rate but also by perceptions of the safety

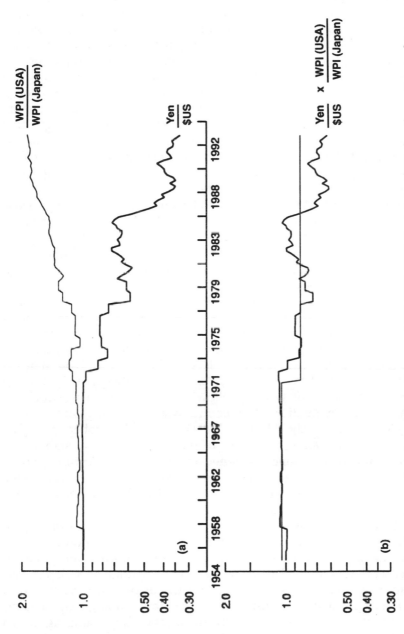

FIGURE 7.3   Wholesale prices and exchange rates, Japan and US, 1955–1992. Last data, 1992, fourth quarter; exchange rate = 119 yen/$US as of 5 October 1992; equilibrium exchange rate = 161 yen/$US. Reproduced by permission of IMP/Datastream

of those returns (e.g. as influenced by political stability), as well as by those speculative views of likely short-term exchange rate movements. In the short term—and this may mean for several years—capital flows can force the WPI-adjusted rate out of line. This usually causes adverse patterns in the country's balance on traded items, however, and in the long term the impact of this tends to reassert itself and the WPI-adjusted rate returns to equilibrium. Whereas the "real" economy used to drive the exchange rate, now both the "money" economy and the "real" economy interact through the exchange rate system: some would argue that the "money" economy now drives the "real" economy, to the latter's detriment. Indeed, the US government has recently called for a study of the effect of global funds flows on exchange rates and international financial stability.

The Deutsche Mark/sterling and Deutsche Mark/French franc exchange rates are also shown in FIGURES 7.4 and 7.5. Clearly, the pound varied significantly against the Deutsche Mark historically, but within the EMS, its fluctuations were much reduced. Note that the pound characteristically has deviated from its equilibrium for extended periods. Of all the currencies we have examined, the pound is one of the "worst" behaved, excluding some Third World currencies. However, it still remains true that the pound fluctuates around its equilibrium consistently, as do the other currencies (the equilibrium level is set by reference to "triangulation" with other currencies, hence the level in FIGURE 7.4). Note that the equilibrium level is DM 2.70/£, somewhat higher than its trading level at the time of writing following its recent release from the EMS, and devaluation. The pound was about 7% undervalued against the Deutsche Mark at 2.43 DM/£ on 5 October 1992. The French franc/Deutsche Mark relationship is more stable and shows the two currencies aligned for a considerable time period, following the 1971 realignment, and indeed reflects the comments of many observers regarding its undervaluation against the Deutsche Mark on "fundamentals" in September 1992.

Since this framework does give such a high level of insight into currency overvaluation and undervaluation at any point in time, we suggest that wide dissemination of this information would in fact serve to stabilize currency markets. Investors, speculators and traders would be able to see clearly the degree of deviation of a currency from equilibrium and hence draw rational conclusions about its future track on "fundamentals", thus damping down purely speculative flows. Economic policy itself would need to

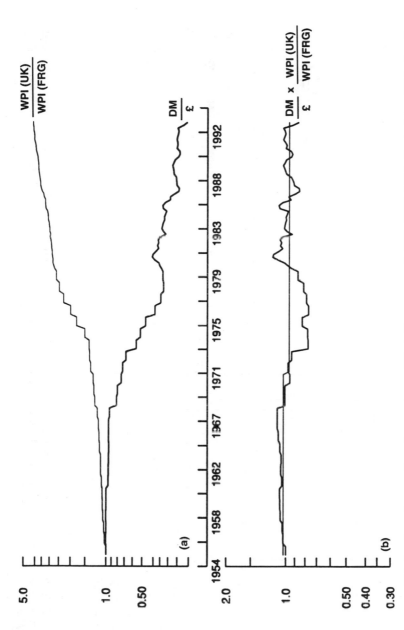

FIGURE 7.4 Wholesale prices and exchange rates, West Germany and UK, 1955–1992. Last data, 1992, fourth quarter; exchange rate = 2.43 DM/£ as of 5 October 1992; equilibrium exchange rate = 2.70 DM/£. Reproduced by permission of IMP/Datastream

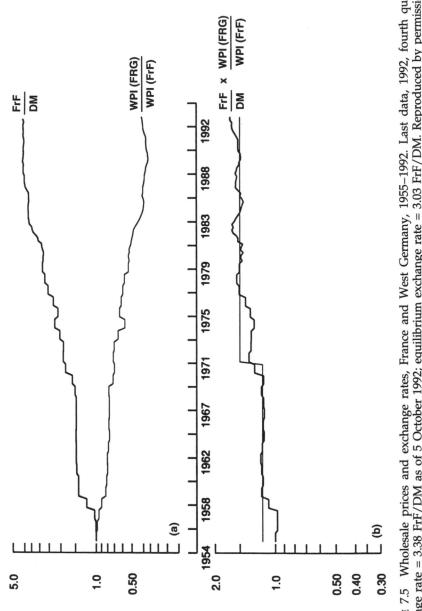
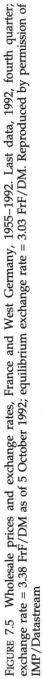

FIGURE 7.5 Wholesale prices and exchange rates, France and West Germany, 1955–1992. Last data, 1992, fourth quarter; exchange rate = 3.38 FrF̄/DM as of 5 October 1992; equilibrium exchange rate = 3.03 FrF/DM. Reproduced by permission of IMP/Datastream

focus then very clearly on the management of tradable goods' and services' price inflation and the rate of change of national productivity, an "innovation" that would surely appeal to many economists. (Note that productivity and inflation in the price of non-tradable goods and services impacts effectively the wealth balance, and not necessarily competitiveness directly.)

INTERNATIONAL COMPETITIVENESS

Half of the picture is now available. Exchange rates reflect national productivity differences and changes as well as structural inflation. But what must a business do to succeed?

For a business in a country, international competitiveness results not from outperforming an international competitor, but rather from performing better relative to its own economy than an international competitor does to its economy.

Schematically, this international cost relationship can be illustrated by reviewing a business setting within two countries (FIGURE 7.6). The analysis includes two competitors making "Product X". The competitor in the country with the low rate of real price decline (Country A) achieves a rate of real-cost reduction exactly equal to that for the average of the economy: from 100 down to 90 between 1970 and 1980. In absolute terms, the competitor in Country B does rather better, reducing real costs from 100 to 80 in the same period, perhaps as a result of superior growth or experience curve performance. If the two competitors were in the same country, then over time the competitor with the better absolute performance would be expected to achieve lower costs, and hence the better profitability. In international competition, this does not follow, because of exchange rate effects.

Because exchange rates tend to be driven by the average productivity for the economy, the exchange rate of 100 : 100 in 1980 will alter on trend to 90 : 70, since average price levels—reflecting average productivity—have dropped to 90 and 70, respectively. This will mean that the competitor in Country A, whose costs drop to 90 in Country A's currency, will have costs of 70 expressed (through the new exchange rate) in the currency of Country B. The competitor in Country A therefore has lower costs than the competitor in Country B even though the latter achieved better performance in absolute terms. The reason for this is that the

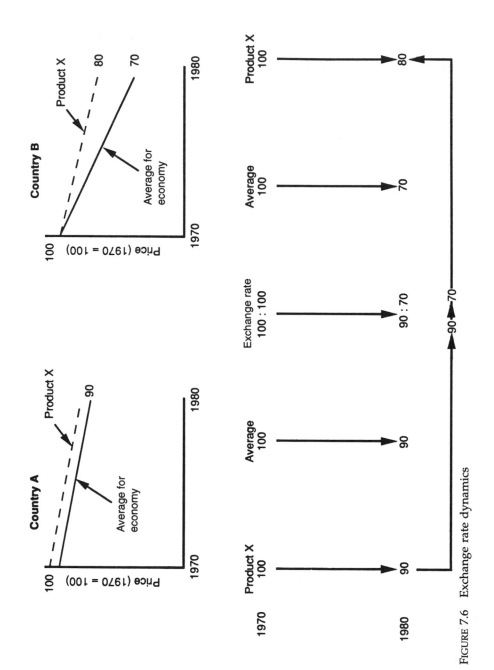

FIGURE 7.6 Exchange rate dynamics

competitor in Country A did better *relative to the economy* in Country A, than the Country B competitor did relative to its economy. For the Country B competitor to outperform its rival in international trade, it would have to outperform the economy in Country B—say by reducing real costs from 100 to 60 in absolute terms in Country B's currency.

So, how does this framework apply in practice? Taking the car industry as an example, we see that real average car prices in the US dropped by about 20% between 1946 and 1987, while in Japan they fell by about 80% (FIGURE 7.7). This is clearly a dramatic phenomenon, but misleading, since the prices are expressed in national currencies, dollar and yen. We must correct the analysis and use the above framework to do so, accounting for both exchange rate movements and national productivity effects.

It is possible to compare the performance of the Japanese car industry with Japan's national average by comparing the car price index with the national price index (the WPI). A time series plot

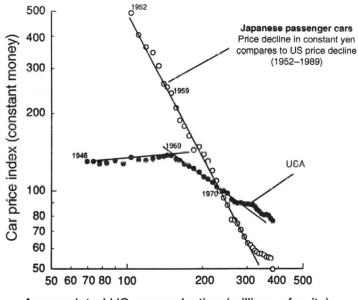

FIGURE 7.7   US and Japan passenger cars: price experience curve, 1946–1989. Japan price graphed to align with US year by year. *Sources:* US Department of Commerce, Ward's Automotive, SMMT, Bank of Japan

of the car prices relative to the national average is shown in FIGURE 7.8. This shows that Japanese car productivity has indeed been steadily—and dramatically—outperforming the national average over a long period of time. One of the reasons for the Japanese car industry's success relative to that of the US is apparent from this chart, which shows the US car industry's performance relative to the national average. This was roughly flat (i.e. car industry performance equal to the national average) during the 1950s and 1960s, but in recent years has been fairly steep. Indeed, since measurement relative to the national average effectively neutralizes exchange rate effects on trend, these curves can be overlaid because they are effectively in a common currency. Over the whole period the price pattern of the US car industry relative to the US national average has not kept pace with that of Japan relative to the Japanese national average. This "explains" much of the difficulty that the US manufacturers have had in achieving profitability.

As we have seen, productivity and growth are inextricably linked. What does this say about Japan's competitiveness in the car industry in the future? Domestic production of cars in Japan is predicted to decline in the future. FIGURE 7.9 shows the relationship between productivity growth and production growth in the car industry in Japan, and it can be concluded that with this decline in car production volume, the productivity of the car industry relative to the national average will inexorably decline, and thus lead to a continuing reduction in the competitiveness of domestically located car manufacture. Inevitably, therefore, Japanese car manufacturers will move manufacturing activities out of Japan and into the EC, the US and other (developing) parts of the world, and this strategy will contribute to the continuing decline of car manufacturing in Japan. This decline will accelerate quickly, and we should expect to see increasingly rapid withdrawal from car manufacture (or at least mainline assembly) in Japan.

SUMMARY SO FAR

The key points in this framework to remember are these:

- Exchange rate movements are systematic, not random, reflecting fundamental shifts in the average productivity of countries.

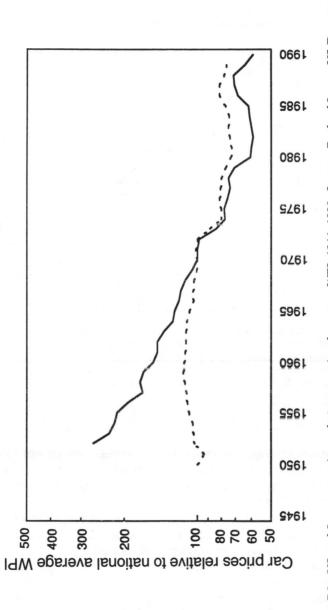

FIGURE 7.8 US and Japan car prices relative to national average WPI, 1946–1990. *Sources:* Bank of Japan, US Department of Commerce, IMF

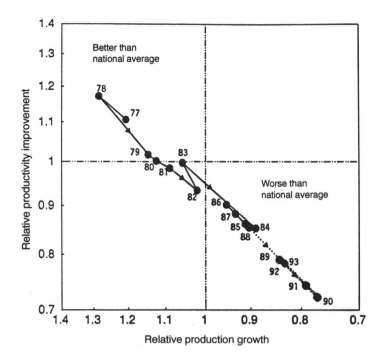

FIGURE 7.9   Japanese automotive industry: production and productivity in Japan relative to national averages; production growth/productivity improvement measured over previous four years

- For business, international competitiveness results not from out-performing an international competitor, but rather from doing better relative to one's own economy than an international competitor does relative to its economy.
- These effects must be considered as part of a system of interacting competitors and interacting economies in order to explain and forecast international competitiveness.
- Analysis of these international dynamics bears directly on issues of:
  - global pricing and marketing strategies
  - international sourcing and manufacturing
  - financial performance and resource allocation.

CURRENCY UNION

What impact would currency union within the EC have? First and foremost, there would be a reduction in the uncertainty caused by exchange fluctuations between economies. This is obvious. Many of the underlying phenomena that have driven international competition in the past would, however, continue into the future. Instead of competition taking place relative to the national average, what would now happen is that competitors would need to outperform the EC average against non-EC competitors, and would need to outperform regional averages within the EC.

This is best illustrated by an example—one that a client came to call the "Swindon effect". Swindon, in the UK, is a very popular place to invest. But faced with the choice between Swindon, and some other part of the UK with less exciting prospects, which should the client choose? Swindon is full of dynamic, rapidly growing companies. Wage rates are growing rapidly as the productivity of the companies within the Swindon area grows. In the alternative location, less investment was taking place, wage rates were altogether lower, and their rate of increase was lower. By locating in Swindon, the client would have needed to grow quickly just to keep up with the Swindon average. Locating in the alternative location meant that he could take advantage of the lower wage rates, and at any given level of growth always be more competitive in the future than in Swindon. These are questions that Honda may be reflecting upon, having established itself in Swindon, and with Toyota having located in Derby.

Generalizing this phenomenon, FIGURE 7.10 shows wage rates and wage growth rates in the UK for the period 1985–1988. Wage levels and wage level growth rates are radically different between regions of the UK. To generalize this further to the EC, it becomes clear that regional economics become paramount. Organizations will need to assess their competitiveness in terms of their performance relative to the driving forces of their particular region; in other words, how is the organization performing relative to all of the other organizations in its area? When locating a new facility within the EC, attention thus needs to be paid to the regional growth rates, for these will determine future competitiveness for that facility.

It will be particularly important for politicians to establish the right level at which to create union. The ideal would be for union

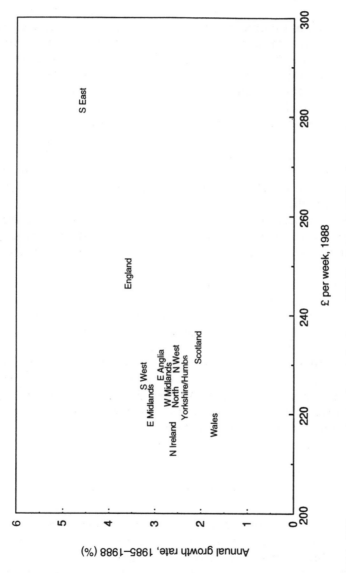

FIGURE 7.10 UK average wage rates and growth. *Source:* UK Department of Employment

to be established at exactly the equilibrium level. In practice, this is unlikely to be practical. Significant deviations on either side of an equilibrium level for a considerable period of time will, however, penalize or give advantage to companies within particular countries. Currency union between West and East Germany has produced the extraordinarily rapid demise of the East German economy. Choosing the right exchange rate on day one is very important, as many in the UK are painfully aware. Likewise, regional structural inflation tendencies (the UK, Italy, for example) will soon cause disadvantage unless these structural rates are reined into the overall EC average. Competitors in these regions will need to be particularly alert to the consequences of this inflation, which will rapidly give competitive disadvantage. Likewise, competitors in low structural inflation areas will quickly gain competitive advantage.

So, far from resolving all of the current problems and issues to do with exchange rates, currency union will introduce new and perhaps more difficult problems, at least in the short to medium term.

CONCLUSION

How, then, can businesses achieve long-term competitive advantage in a currency union region? The answer lies in developing specific marketing, production and financing strategies that reflect the new competitive dynamics but still retain many of the features of the old, which are still valid.

MARKETING

Many changes are being brought about by economic integration in Europe which will not be affected by currency union. Pricing, however, is likely to be profoundly affected. For all but those products that are priced on a "value in use" basis, price levels are likely to be competitively set, and to depend upon the cost levels of competitors and *their* location. Although these costs will be expressed in a common currency, the dynamics described in the previous section will apply; i.e. competitors' costs will be driven by their productivity performance relative to their region (as in the "Swindon effect" example). When setting pricing strategy, or making a long-term pricing forecast, therefore, managers will need to determine likely cost levels of competitors delivering to specific markets, not only on a "snapshot" basis, but also projecting out over time to capture the possible cost and price dynamics. We have found that this work is essential in many industries, ranging from the car industry to the chemical industry, and in some instances parts of the financial services industry. The difference between pre- and post-union is that one element of the calculation can now be missed out—the estimates of long-run exchange rates and current level relative to the equilibrium.

PRODUCTION

Two areas of production strategy will be significantly affected: balancing of production across manufacturing sites for competitive advantage, and determining the location of new facilities. In the first instance, because swings in exchange rates will no longer exist, production balancing will become easier, because decisions can be made on the basis of true relative costs and availabilities of capacity, rather than on the basis of temporary cost advantage given by an exchange rate movement. When making location decisions, managers will still need to ensure that their investments achieve adequate scale and focus to give competitive cost levels. But now, they will need to ensure that their factories maintain performance relative to *their* region. They need to take care, as always, not to underestimate investment costs, or overestimate achievable cost reductions. So, the search for a location for a new investment will involve identifying areas with favourable cost levels and trends versus regional averages, and then, once the investment is made, managing the business to ensure that cost competitiveness is maintained and, hopefully, improved.

FINANCE

Some of the uncertainty and cost of doing business within the EC will have been reduced or indeed eliminated altogether by currency union. The treasury department will be able to focus on transactions *outside* the EC—and can be considerably reduced in size to reflect the reduced volume of activity! A sharp eye will still need to be maintained to exploit interest rate advantages around the EC. It should be remembered, though, that significant currency exposure can still exist. Prices are set in international competition. Thus, if a competitor who is located outside the EC is a significant force in setting prices, then that price will vary as the competitor's currency varies against the EC's currency. This is often referred to as strategic or economic exposure—its impact often dwarfs other forms of currency exposure, but is rarely measured, let alone hedged. So, the treasury team's attention can be directed towards assessing the impact of strategic exposure to currencies outside the EC, and to developing strategies to mitigate the impact.

OVERALL

As mentioned earlier, uncertainty will have been reduced by currency union. The exchange rate levels at commencement are critical, because structural advantage or disadvantage will be built in at that point for some considerable time period. Many of the critical competitive factors in international competition will still be critical, though modified in impact, and so managers' reactions to these need to be modified to reflect the new competitive dynamics. Managers cannot afford *not* to understand these phenomena. By taking advantage of them, they will be able to win; not understanding them, or ignoring them, will lead to long-term defeat.

NOTE

This chapter has been developed from an article entitled "Currency union: What companies need to do differently to win", published in the *European Business Journal* of Quarter 1 1992, by the same authors.

ACKNOWLEDGEMENT

Notice
Datastream is a registered trade name, trademark and service mark of Datastream International Limited.

All data and graphs contained in this chapter and which have been obtained from the information system of Datastream International Limited ("Datastream") are proprietary and confidential and may not be reproduced, republished, redistributed or resold without the written permission of Datastream.

Data in Datastream's information system have been compiled by Datastream in good faith from sources believed to be reliable, but no representation or warranty express or implied is made as to the accuracy, completeness or correctness of the data. Neither Datastream nor such other party who may be the owner of any information contained in the data accepts any liability whatsoever for any direct, indirect or consequential loss arising from any use of the data or its contents. All data obtained from Datastream's system and contained in this publication are for the assistance of users but are not to be relied upon as authoritative or taken in substitution for the exercise of judgement or financial skills by users.

8

Information Systems in Global Business: Evidence from European Multinationals

MICHAEL J. EARL, DAVID FEENY

INTRODUCTION

In the literature of international business, a recurring theme is the need for coordination of operations and their management in global organizations. Such coordination is indeed central to the whole concept of globalization. Coordination of activity in order to achieve supranational efficiencies is argued by many writers to distinguish the global business from the "multinational" (Bartlett and Ghoshal, 1989) or "multidomestic" (Porter, 1986). And coordination in the strategic planning domain is at the heart of the "strategic intent" that defines global businesses for Hamel and Prahalad (1989).

These authors have expanded on the nature and complexity of global coordination required in the successful organizations

Strategic Renaissance and Business Transformation. Edited by H. Thomas, D. O'Neal and J. Kelly.
Copyright © 1995 John Wiley & Sons Ltd.

of the future. Such organizations, it is claimed, exhibit the simultaneous achievement of global scale, responsiveness to markets and governments, worldwide transfer of learning and innovation (Bartlett and Ghoshal, 1989; Prahalad and Doz, 1987). In place of organizational uniformity, each geographical unit will have a distinctive role within the overall business (Bartlett and Ghoshal, 1989; Hamel and Prahalad, 1985). In the "transnational" corporation of Bartlett and Ghoshal, the organization is neither centralized nor decentralized; it represents an integrated network in which there are intensive and complex interactions between physically remote but interdependent units.

As Porter (1986) recognizes, this necessary ability to coordinate globally is seen to be dramatically increased through advances in information technology (IT). The widescale use of IT is also implicit in Bartlett and Ghoshal's (1987) vision of the transnational as an organization in which there is "collaborative information sharing and problem solving, cooperative support and resource sharing, collective action and implementation". So information systems would seem to be an important component of global competitive strategy. Egelhoff (1988) has touched on this in his analysis of the complexity of global organizations. He has applied information processing models of organization, such as the work of Galbraith (1973), Huber (1990) and Thompson (1967), to multinational companies, and concludes that high information processing requirements are likely, but could easily be ignored in formulating international business strategies (Egelhoff, 1991). Hagström (1991) shows through case study research in SKF that information and communication flow requirements tend to grow as a multinational organization evolves.

However, there has been little empirical research done, through the information systems perspective (i.e. looking at IT applications and studying the information systems function). Ives and Jarvenpaa (1991) executed a survey to test emergent alignment of IS management with global business strategies, but otherwise there has been little examination of the practice of exploiting IT to enable coordination in a globally-managed business. In this chapter we examine some of the forms in which IT may contribute, the enabling conditions, and the obstacles to success, based on case study research in four European-based corporations.

THE POTENTIAL ROLE OF IT IN GLOBAL BUSINESS MANAGEMENT

Before exploring these case studies, we sought to establish more specifically what might be the theoretical contribution of IT. The starting point was consideration of the three imperatives of global operation identified above—global efficiency, local responsiveness and transfer of learning. In other words, we take a model of business strategy and speculate on the need for different sorts of information systems in the spirit of a model of strategic fit.

The search for *global efficiency* implies that the organization must be able, within each relevant function, to coordinate and consolidate its activity to achieve available economies of scale. A key requirement would seem to be the collection of comparative performance information from locations around the world to support decisions on how to effectively allocate resources and source requirements. This need may be facilitated by building a global data network, collecting and providing access to information that conforms to some globally applied data standards. Organizations often wish to go further, to implement standard application systems worldwide, in order to ensure the integrity of information, facilitate the transfer of activities and people, and perhaps achieve scale economies in systems development and processing. Conceptually, however, the base requirement is for the definition and communication of standard data.

Achieving *local responsiveness*, on the other hand, implies limits to standardization. The expectation is that organizations will want to identify some level of standard/core product, but also provide a variety of optional features, which may be present or absent in the delivered product depending on local legal or market conditions. Thus, the "world car" or "global TV" becomes tailored to suit the requirement of each market segment—"glocalization", in the vernacular. Global IT investment to support this environment may include production scheduling and control systems to support the management of high variety, and IT and communications networks to facilitate the efforts of dispersed marketing/ engineering/manufacturing groups who are tasked with developing the next generation of global core products or creating the required local derivatives. These capabilities would need to be planned and developed at global level, to interface with and supplement local systems that meet local needs.

The coordination required for *transfer of learning* would seem to be along functional dimensions, across multiple locations involved in research and development, marketing, service etc. Communication networks providing electronic mail, and computer and video conferencing facilities to support informal dialogue among professionals are the obvious IT contribution. Construction of globally accessible knowledge bases or knowledge systems may follow, as examples of best practice or scarce expertise are recognized and codified for distribution to others who can use or build upon them.

In addition, the potential IT contribution may be extended beyond the organization. For example, Ghoshal (1987) has described how an organization may extend its economies of scope through *external alliances* between companies with different skills and cultures. Inter-organizational information systems can provide new opportunities to operationalize this concept. In the vertical dimension, Benetton uses IT to support what Johnston and Lawrence (1988) call Value Adding Partnerships with manufacturers and retailers. In the horizontal dimension, Konsynski and McFarlan (1990) have described the global "information partnerships" between airlines, hotel chains, and car rental companies.

TABLE 8.1 summarizes these propositions on the potential contribution of IT to the pursuit of global business strategies. It served as a framework for analysing the history, current use and development of global information systems in our case study companies. The ideas it contains seem straightforward enough, but we were already aware from prior acquaintance with global businesses of a significant gap between the propositions and

TABLE 8.1 Global information systems

Business imperative	IT contribution
Global efficiency	Data networks, data standards, common systems
Local responsiveness	Production systems to manage variety, networks to support collaborative development, loal support systems
Transfer of learning	Functional communication networks, knowledge bases/systems
Global alliance	Inter-organizational systems

common practice. While this gap might be merely a function of deficiencies in the framework, an alternative explanation was that global information systems present difficult organizational and implementation problems. Consequently, information systems organization and management issues were also a focus of our fieldwork.

THE RESEARCH DESIGN

Given the complexity and emerging nature of the global business field in 1990–91, it was our view that a large-scale empirical study was inappropriate at this stage. Instead, we sought to build insights into the reality, potential and problems of IT contribution through in-depth investigation of a small number of businesses that were known to have pursued global management capabilities over a number of years.

Four such businesses were selected, to represent a variety of global business contexts and potential coordination needs. For the first, in re-insurance, transfer of learning was the primary global driver, with global efficiency of information processing a secondary goal. For the second, in electronics, supranational economies of scale in R&D and manufacturing were paramount. However, there were concerns about responsiveness to local market requirements and accordingly a possible need for sharing of learning both within and across functions—for example, from marketing to design. In the white goods industry our case study business was among those promoting global competition, seeking out economies of scale and scope while maintaining responsiveness to residual heterogeneity between national markets. By contrast, in the chemicals industry, the product was already a global commodity, but our case study business had set out to improve responsiveness in an industry traditionally organized to achieve efficiency.

Each of these businesses, therefore, was pursuing more than one global imperative; in this sense each business aspired towards the transnational positioning of Bartlett and Ghoshal (1989). The electronics and chemicals businesses were also in transition, which allowed us to explore more of the dynamics of becoming a transnational.

Our basic questions for these four businesses were:

1. What information systems (applications of IT) are in place or under development to support the global strategy of the business?
2. What IT infrastructures (networks, databases) are in place or under development to enable the desired levels of cross-border functioning?
3. How is the information systems function being managed in the global context, and with what results?

To address these questions, we conducted in each business a series of interviews at senior management levels, examined archival evidence of information systems evolution and plans, and documented experience of operational activity. General management executives were interviewed to establish an understanding of industry context, business strategy, and perceived and potential contribution of IT. Informations systems management was questioned about information systems history, strategy, organization and key issues. Operational management described usage of information systems in place, and experience of coordination needs, policies and problems.

CASE STUDY SUMMARIES

SKANDIA RE-INSURANCE BUSINESS

In 1991, Skandia International, a major insurance company within the Skandia Group, operated in 18 countries with 3800 employees. Only 350 of these employees were located in Sweden, the parent country, and the group's headquarters. Roughly 70% of Skandia International's revenues came from the re-insurance business which was the focus of the case study. Gross premium income from re-insurance was 9341 million Kr ($US1.5 billion) in 1990, placing Skandia fourth in the world behind the giant Munich Re, Swiss Re and General Re.

The re-insurance market was seen as naturally global, large (more than $40 billion) but mature and cyclical. The market was in slow decline as direct insurers reduced their purchases of re-insurance through backward integration. Entry barriers were low ("a tough mind and a pen") so that during cyclical upturns new entrants increased rivalry and created overcapacity. In 1991 there were an estimated 1250 competitors worldwide. In this difficult market, Skandia's strategy was summarized as follows by (former) CEO Hans Dalborg:

> We strive for profitability before volume and are realigning ourselves towards areas in which we can offer clients superior services. We are focusing our efforts on advanced actuarial techniques and products as well as on administrative and consulting services. At the same time we are introducing powerful computer and communication systems while making improvements on the personnel side. Together these measures will help us keep costs in check and will give us a base for new product development. The objective is to keep volume where it is, or expand in a controlled way in areas where profit potential is very good—concentrating on technically advanced niches.

Skandia operated a relatively flat organizational structure with most employees operating from a network of local offices as underwriters or support staff. Each local office was a profit centre, operating within the strategy and policies laid down by Stockholm headquarters. Monthly accounting figures were reported to Stockholm via a common general ledger package.

As can be detected from Dalborg's statement, these global policies extended beyond business goals and strategy to the field of information systems. In the words of the Corporate Controller Sten Lundqvist, "the essence of our offensive competitive strategy is to build information in a structured way over many years, and then take risk and return decisions". A corporately developed and owned system called SARA (System for Advanced Re-insurance Assistance) tracked re-insurance treaties and conditions; accounted for and managed money flows; stored treaties, risks and claims; and handled credit. SARA was available on-line at all local offices, supported by a standard set of analysis and enquiry tools. Underwriters accessed SARA for decision support, entered deals and updated the central database on-line to Stockholm. In 1991 Skandia was encouraging and coordinating experimental investments in expert systems, triggered by an initiative in the US, to help distribute underwriting expertise to new and dispersed staff. The database therefore was the repository of experience-based knowledge on risks, claims and prices. It was updated and disseminated to offices over the global data network. The decision support tools, some with resident expertise in them, enabled underwriters to be both responsive and shrewd in taking on risks. SARA and its related systems were thus fundamental to the global business strategy and operations of Skandia.

While IT resources and investment had reached a peak during the development of SARA, the company continued to regard IT as a strategic resource. Skandia was one of the three initiators of RINET, the value-added network being developed for information exchange in international insurance and re-insurance. Skandia set out to be a leader in improving information flows in the industry because it had an incentive to do so.

These examples demonstrate how information systems was itself a globally coordinated function within Skandia's re-insurance business. Corporate policy vested ownership of all local equipment and support staff with corporate information systems; there were globally defined technical architectures for the IT networks and applications; two preferred IT vendors were recognized worldwide, with central coordination of purchasing; a central register was maintained for all data and programs. This strong coordination of IT in the re-insurance business was very much a conscious choice, not a chance legacy of history. Indeed information systems and IT policy issues were formally taken at alternate board meetings of Skandia International. A recent proposal from the US business unit to devolve information systems responsibility had been firmly rejected by the board because it was felt that central control of information systems strategy, development and operations was essential if risk management was to be optimized, information processing costs minimized and, crucially, data managed as a corporate resource to transfer underwriting learning. By contrast, information systems organization for Skandia's Life and General insurance business had long been decentralized, in line with the nature of those businesses that were responding to a variety of local, national markets.

PHILIPS DISPLAY COMPONENTS

In 1991, Display Components (DC) was a major business unit within the components division of the Philips Corporation, with annual revenues of around fl.4 billion ($US2.3 billion). With global responsibility for development and manufacture of picture tubes for TV sets and computer monitors, Philips DC employed around 19 000 personnel in factories and offices around the world.

Like Skandia, Philips DC competed in a market that was large (100 million tubes p.a., worth $US15 billion), global in nature and relatively mature. Western Europe was the largest market area, followed by North America and Japan. Because of economies of scale in development and production, competition was concentrated, with four global companies accounting for more than 50% of industry output. Philips DC was the leading producer, closely followed by Toshiba and Matsushita. These same corporations were, of course, prominent in TV set making, but in practice set making and tube producing subsidiaries operated on a trading basis, with set making plants sourcing their TV tubes from producer plants in the same region.

The market for computer monitors was smaller, around $US9.5 billion in 1991, but growing strongly at around 25% per annum. The market was heavily concentrated in the Far East, reflecting that region's strength in microcomputer systems. Competition was less concentrated in this segment, with Philips DC perceived to be "one of the pack".

The strategic question for Philips DC in 1991 was summarized by executive management as "choosing where we want to be and what we want to have". The concern was that Philips DC was too influenced by Europe, where its dominant market share could only decline over time. Future business success was dependent on capturing market share elsewhere—particularly in the Far East, which included the largest Japanese TV market and the critical market for computer monitor tubes.

To this end, Philips DC had a number of strengths to deploy. Its current product offering was rated (at least in Europe) as better than the industry average on every customer criterion except price, and Philips was perceived to be technology leader over time. Philips already had a manufacturing presence in all of the four key continental markets of the world. But three aspects of market responsiveness were identified for special attention:

- Since success increasingly came from being the chosen partner of successful set makers, the Philips culture needed to develop further from a technology orientation to a customer one.
- "Closeness to the customer" must extend in a physical sense to the R&D function; poor performance in the Far East was linked to the lack of a development group based there to be able to develop local derivatives.

- Product time-to-market must be significantly reduced, with rapid handover from development to manufacturing despite the geographic separation involved.

Industry scale economies and globally orientated Japanese competition had resulted in Philips DC becoming the first business to move away from the corporation's historic emphasis on autonomous national subsidiaries. During the 1980s decision making was increasingly centralized into the Philips DC head office. However, by the end of 1991 a new organizational pattern had emerged to balance global coherence with customer responsiveness. Under this new regime (which also reflected wider corporate changes towards profit centre autonomy, cost and quality emphases), three levels of responsibility were emphasized:

- Business unit HQ was responsible for R&D and strategic marketing, therefore controlling the global core product stream.
- Four geographic regions were each responsible for the manufacture, sale and distribution of the core products within their territories.
- Each plant had a mission to manufacture and distribute one or more core products to customers in its region, tailoring core products where necessary to meet customer needs.

At the beginning of 1992, it was not clear that information systems was yet anchored securely in the new organization. A number of IT studies and developments were in progress but they were not explicitly focused on global issues or the emerging global business strategy. IT resources were thinly scattered across HQ, regional and plant levels; information systems managers were rarely embedded into the key management teams at each level; Philips DC was largely dependent for IT development and service on resources elsewhere, a legacy of the historic information systems structure, which was aligned to corporate, national and, more recently, divisional levels within Philips.

A further legacy of this structure was a set of common transaction processing systems across the corporation, notably in order processing, production planning and control, and logistics management. While the imposition of these systems in the 1970s and 1980s had caused resentment in some businesses, it did create an unusually coherent infrastructure, which—in principle—global business units could exploit to considerable benefit. For example,

Philips DC had no difficulty in taking an order from a customer anywhere in Europe and allocating it to whichever plant was appropriate. However, by 1991 a number of operational systems were due for replacement and questions were being raised over future levels of standardization. Could a regional requirement for the coordination of logistics, for example, be met through regional data standards and local systems, or did it necessitate a common worldwide logistics system?

A higher-order information management agenda was put forward by one member of the Philips DC executive management team, who believed that IT had a further and critical contribution to make in four areas:

- Enabling the coordination of increasingly geographically dispersed product development, based on distributed access to a consolidated design database.
- Providing information to support the optimization of supply versus demand, across the various production sites.
- Supporting goods flow management within the vertical manufacturing and supply chain.
- Providing better information to management on the global activity of competitors.

THE ELECTROLUX WHITE GOODS BUSINESS

With 43 factories in 15 countries and a turnover of more than $US5 billion, white goods was the dominant business of the Electrolux Corporation in 1991. It was also a pioneer of globalization in an industry where received wisdom had held that national differences prevented products such as refrigerators and washing machines from selling across borders. Electrolux had built its global business through more than 200 acquisitions, including large units like Zanussi (1984), White (1986) and Thorn EMI Appliances (1987). These acquisitions had been energetically and rapidly integrated into a complex new organizational structure. Despite setbacks (Bader-Fuller and Stopford, 1991), Electrolux had been sufficiently successful to convince others of the global potential of white goods, notably Whirlpool, with its acquisition of the domestic appliance business of Philips. The industry now comprised a combination of global giants such as Electrolux, Whirlpool and Matsushita, and aggressive national product specialists such as GEC's Hotpoint and Merloni's Ariston—which, in turn, were beginning to seek global alliances.

Electrolux has been a case study target for others interested in international business, including Ghoshal and Haspeslagh (1989) and Lorenz (1989), who wrote a series of articles that positioned Electrolux as the epitome of Bartlett and Ghoshal's transnational organization. Features of the organizational structure for white goods in 1991 included:

- Product divisions, responsible for development and manufacturing; each had a specific international mission, delivered through a number of dispersed sites.
- International marketing units, which each controlled a number of national and international brand names, working through nationally based sales companies that operated an arm's length trading relationship with product divisions.
- Country organizations, "headed by strong country managers" with "primary responsibility" for all of the development, manufacturing and sales units in their territory.
- Centralized service functions, including IT, which provided specialized expertises across the corporation.

In most respects the culture stressed decentralization, with production sites, sales units and service functions all operating as profit centres. It is clear that a number of tensions are built into such a structure, which can be pictured as a multidimensional matrix. But, according to Bartlett and Ghoshal (1990), Electrolux operated not as a formal matrix but through overlay of a series of microstructured mechanisms on top of a distributed asset structure! Certainly there was little evident coordinating bureaucracy: rather an emphasis on a culture that expected agreement seeking, galvanized by a series of corporate strategic initiatives, and monitored by a small number of high level executives such as the three responsible for international marketing.

The strategy that this "impossible organisation" was designed to deliver had the classic transnational components (Ghoshal and Haspeslagh, 1989):

- Achieving global scale volume to ensure long-term survival.
- Building/maintaining "adequate" share in all markets through local presence and responsiveness.

- Developing "insurmountable" competitive advantage through faster development of better products by multidisciplinary design teams, and through transferring and leveraging product concepts, components and manufacturing techniques across markets and borders.

This most transnational of our case studies also showed the most extensive exploitation of IT, at least in terms of the global information systems framework of TABLE 8.1. The Electrolux Forecasting and Supply (EFS) system supported business-wide coordination of demand, production and distribution—across functions, profit centres and national borders. A common Financial Reporting System (FCS) provided comparative information for performance assessment. Standardization of the ODETTE protocol for Electronic Data Interchange (EDI) allowed coordination of internal and external suppliers across different plants. The IT contribution to faster development was based on a common shared CAD system, and IT was integral to the extensive investments in flexible manufacturing systems made at the Susequana and Porcia plants in Italy to achieve flexibility of production. Only in respect of the transfer of learning was an IT contribution less in evidence, with little apparent enthusiasm, for example, for using the electronic mail system. But the presence of a group subsidiary to supply and install all factory level automation ensured transfer of functional learning within that field.

This alignment of IT investment with business need had been achieved even though the information systems function was not formally integrated into the organization and management structure of the white goods business. As already noted, the dominant unit in Electrolux's information systems function took the form of a corporate subsidiary and profit centre, with minimal IT resources being located in production and sales units.

A number of other factors, however, seemed to have enabled the alignment of information systems strategy with the white goods global business thrust:

- White goods were (by far) the dominant customer of the corporate information systems unit, and therefore critical to its success.
- Information systems initiatives consistently paralleled and evolved with major business initiatives (for example, EFS was first created in support of a corporate-wide inventory reduction

programme); this ensured the line management support required to implement tough changes such as the imposition of standard product coding.

- The centralized nature of the information systems group simultaneously ensured that a standard and coherent technical architecture was put in place as applications developed.
- The central information systems group remained lean (150 employees in a corporation of 153 000) and committed to pragmatic evolution rather than revolution; standards and new developments went no further than necessary. For example, EFS interfaced with existing local order processing systems.

Overall, the IT effort at Electrolux demonstrated the focus and drive that may be considered the hallmarks of effective information systems strategy making.

EUROCHEM

In 1991, Eurochem comprised four business units producing commodity chemicals with a combined turnover of around £2.3 billion. Each business unit had global responsibility for its product range, but a combination of scale and scope economies, history, health and safety, and environmental factors meant that the business units shared production sites. Indeed, in a common industry pattern, production sites and technologies and facilities were often shared with rival chemical companies. The company requested anonymity in our analysis on the basis that our findings were a fair representation but captured a business in transition.

The 1991 organization resulted from a series of evolutionary steps that had rationalized the acquisitions made in the 1970s and 1980s. The progressive emphasis in these steps had been devolution from a centralized, functional structure to business units with the aim of increasing accountability and cost control in a commodity-based industry. Most service functions had now been migrated to business unit control to establish value for money; one of the most recent changes was the devolution of the information systems function.

Alongside this process of decentralization, group business strategy continued to stress leadership in process technology as the route to cost advantage and market leadership. Since price was determined by market conditions, low-cost production was essential to long-term survival. However, a common ordering pattern was for customers to select a chemicals supplier to meet their forward needs during a contract period, with actual deliveries being made against call-offs, and at prevailing market prices. Therefore, in the shorter term and at business unit level, customer service was an important parameter of competitive strategy.

It was a particular attempt to create a service edge that had attracted our interest in Eurochem. In 1984 the company decided to develop a new computer-based order processing system, which would provide "comprehensive facilities to manage order processing, distribution, stock control, and invoicing" across the business, replacing a plethora of systems inherited through acquisition. In the classic pattern of IT innovation (Runge and Earl, 1988), the system was championed by a senior line manager in the commercial function, who saw it as the solution to a business problem ("we like your products, but we can't get hold of them"). He won the support of an executive sponsor, who steered the proposal through the Board. Another parallel with IT innovations elsewhere was set when the project development was put under the original champion, who contracted with external hardware and software suppliers to the exclusion of the in-house information systems department. For a number of reasons, the order processing system went through an often traumatic development history, with major overruns in timescale and budget, but by 1991 the system was installed and in use across the commodity businesses.

Opinions of the benefits and value of the system varied widely. In the opinion of the original champion, it had not only succeeded in putting Eurochem on a par with, or ahead of, the best chemical company and distributor competition, it had also been a stimulus to the internationalizing of the company. Others were much less convinced, complaining that it was a high-cost system that would be of limited value until it became a more authoritative source of inventory and market data. More mundanely, a sales office manager opined that the system was too slow to provide the planned immediate response to customer telephone calls. Some of the speciality chemicals businesses doubted that they required this sort of system.

With the latest changes to the information systems organization, the ownership of the system had been devolved from group level to the business unit processing bulk chemicals. With its thousands of customers and hundreds of products, this was the business where the system's capabilities were most relevant. The business unit agreed to provide the system service to its sister businesses, some of which were expressing dissatisfaction with it, expressing the belief that they could find a cheaper, better alternative to meet their own particular needs. Of course, if any one business discontinued its use of the order processing system, there would be adverse cost consequences for the others. The question would be asked more loudly of whether a common system had in fact been necessary for interfacing four distinct groups of businesses to the plants that served them. In short, the original rationale, the anticipated benefits and the current need for a common order processing system were not agreed across the chemical businesses.

While order processing attracted most of the attention, it was not the only common system in Eurochem. It had, in fact, been preceded by the creation of a management accounting database (MAS). More recently, a standard maintenance and materials system had come up for consideration, but a proposed common approach to payroll had been rejected as poor value for money. With seemingly ever stronger profit centre focus, and the accompanying devolution of most IT resources and responsibilities to business units, it seemed unlikely that new initiatives that involved cross-business coordination and cooperation would either emerge or be supported. A small IT policy unit was retained at the centre for a time, but was subsequently closed down as part of a downsizing exercise.

DISCUSSION

GLOBAL ALIGNMENT

Our four cases demonstrate more differences than similarities, as the research design intended. Collectively, however, we believe that they do suggest that information systems are necessary to support or enable certain global business strategies. In TABLE 8.2, we compare the descriptive evidence against our normative matrix presented in TABLE 8.1. Different levels of investment in information systems for coordination are evident, but each company has recognized at least some need. (The question marks represent systems not yet agreed and developed or systems that

TABLE 8.2 Investments in global information systems

Business imperative	Investment in information systems at:			
	Skandia	Philips	Electro-lux	Eurochem
Global efficiency	General ledger SARA re-insurance assistance system	Order processing logistics system Production, planning and control ?Supply/demand balance	EFS FCS CAD EDI	MAS ?Order processing
Local responsiveness		Order processing Logistics system ?Competitor information	EFS FMS EDI	?Order processing
Transfer of learning	SARA re-insurance assistance system Re-insurance decision support and expert systems	?Design database	?CAD	
Global alliances				

in principle could have supported a global business imperative.) Each type of global thrust, or business imperative, is represented except the development of global alliances. As we anticipated, companies differed in terms of their particular global strategies.

At Skandia, operating in a global market-place, the intent was to differentiate by building and exploiting a worldwide platform of knowledge within parameters of low-cost operation. SARA and the ledger systems therefore support global efficiency, but more particularly SARA and its surrounding decision support systems provide transfer of learning. Our model in TABLE 8.1 predicts these information systems investments, plus the emphasis on worldwide standards that the central information systems group enforced.

Electrolux also demonstrates the model fairly well. By design and some good fortune, they have developed or acquired information systems and technologies to support the three dimensions of the "transnational". EFS, the financial control system and EDI standards all facilitate the pursuit of global efficiency. EFS and EDI also provide the coordination to serve local responsiveness from one or two production sites. The flexible manufacturing technologies also aid responsiveness. The CAD system provides functional coordination across sites to transfer design and development knowledge.

In Philips DC, we find information systems present that are capable of supporting the same three transnational thrusts. However their management team, with new and increased responsibility through the parent's decentralization programme, were only just beginning to agree the critical success factors required to operate globally and perhaps therefore agree on information systems requirements. The systems' inheritance in production and logistics looked promising.

Eurochem neither fits nor deviates from our model because their (global) business strategy was not clear. Organizational devolution in response to corporate business was prompting hard questions not only about its strategy, but about the appropriate structure and the requisite information systems. This is not a context in which alignment is likely to be found, or be capable of evaluation.

Our study could have ended with the above descriptions and evaluation. We could have concluded that global business strategies are likely to benefit from or need investment in IT and information systems, and claimed support for our normative model of global information systems requirements. However, not all the companies were investing equally in IT, and two clearly demonstrated better adjustment between information systems and their global business strategy than the others. Indeed, collectively the four cases do not provide overwhelming evidence that a global IT platform is necessary to do business globally, as the industry hype often claims. We offer two explanations for this situation, one relatively commonplace, the other more novel.

Firstly, there needs to be a *global business vision* shared among the top management team. Skandia and Electrolux largely fulfilled this requirement. Philips DC and Eurochem did not. Now it is the gospel of consultants and many academics that before a firm can formulate its information systems strategy it needs a business strategy. So the need for a global vision may be only a special case of the wider problem. Indeed, it may not be just that information systems should not be forgotten in global strategy making, as Egelhoff (1991) suggests, but more fundamentally that you cannot consider appropriate information systems requirements until the vision of competitive strategy at a global level is developed and agreed.

However, it is well documented that information strategists often find business strategies absent, disputed or unclear (Earl, 1993). The information systems function often has either to work with the organization to explicate both levels of strategy or to await for them to emerge (Earl, 1993). Consequently, it is clear that whether an information systems strategy is derived from the business strategy, is formulated integrally with it or emerges by an incremental and evolutionary process, it only happens through organization.

The second condition, therefore, is that *information systems organization structure* promotes integration of business and information systems strategy. This integration was particularly clear at Skandia, where the information systems function's centralized structure and wide ranging powers both enabled and reflected its role in business strategy. At Electrolux the positioning of information systems as a service business and profit centre was consistent with corporate culture. More important, the dominance of the white goods business ensured that information systems gave the highest priority to understanding and meeting its needs. We are not clear that a smaller business unit would have been equally well served by these arrangements. In contrast, the other two case study businesses were clearly handicapped by a lack of organizational integration. At Philips, years of change had left the information systems function fragmented and struggling to catch up with the business unit structures. Lack of information systems representation on key management teams was a particular problem during a period of formative strategic thinking. Even the agreed IT initiatives were making slow progress, lacking resources and active support from business management. Finally, at Eurochem the information systems function faced a major repositioning challenge. From being a group-level function with executive support for development of the order processing system, it had to migrate to business unit level, where doubts about its contribution and performance had always existed. But unless it repositioned quickly and successfully, it would be unlikely to make much contribution to the group's new thinking and development.

The importance of a shared business vision and especially of alignment and integration of the information systems function may then seem simple or obvious propositions. However, it is not unusual for quite different issues to be emphasized by writers on global information systems management. For example, McFarlan (1992) stresses the disparity of standards in equipment, provision and service around the world. We suggest that this is no more than a technical, operational issue, the IT equivalent of the controller's need to handle multi-currency accounting. As in other functional areas, perhaps, the challenging issues are managerial and organizational. In the cases of IT and information systems, however, there is undue complexity, for information and information systems not only cross national borders, but also those between functions, business units, profit centres and sites. This is the inevitable corollary of the role of information systems in global businesses being that of coordination. Information management, as we discuss below, has to cross many levels and borders of the organization.

INFORMATION MANAGEMENT IN THE GLOBAL BUSINESS

The need for alignment between business and information systems organizations has already been noted in the global context by Ives and Jarvenpaa (1991), but this was a top-level mapping, associating different configurations of information systems and IT with the different globalization categories of Bartlett and Ghoshal, namely, international, multinational, global and transnational. Beneath these labels, and in contrast to the neat and tidy configuration implied by the familiar strategic business unit (SBU) of the 1980s, the organizational arrangements for global business management appear to us to be both varied and complex. Whereas the global business unit (GBU, perhaps) in principle has the characteristics of the SBU—product homogeneity, market delineation, identity of competitive forces, strategic control of resources—the four case studies demonstrate how organizational forms may vary as these ideas are played out across national borders. In Skandia Re-insurance, there is a relatively simple and single line of business, centre-driven strategy, profit centre discipline, hub and spoke configured organization. By contrast, Electrolux dub themselves "an impossible organization but the only one that works". The organization is multi-dimensional, with different market, product, functional and geographic axes, overlaid by a strong profit centre control architecture. It can be sensibly described at the level of the white goods business, but in reality it comprises many interacting entities, and its operation relies on myriad boundary-crossing activities and mechanisms. Meanwhile, in Philips and Eurochem, organizational history has left complicating legacies that hinder the working out of a neat and tidy configuration. The GBU, then, is apparently a complex phenomenon with which to achieve alignment.

The four case study businesses were all moving towards the transnational model of Bartlett and Ghoshal (1989), which involves simultaneous pursuit of several global capabilities. One consequence suggested by these authors and others writing on the history of international management is that the organizational design of functions becomes critical. Each function may have to be designed differently, dependent upon which global driver is most relevant to its domain. Since IT is a means to different ends—supporting these different functional activities or enabling them to be done differently—the information systems function has first to align with a mix of functional strategies. But, crucially, IT can then be instrumental in welding these organizational axes together. We emphasize once more that the coordination role is essentially this, the enabling of cross-boundary as well as cross-border integration and interaction. For example, at Philips and Electrolux, information systems were necessary in interfacing geographically based sales units into product based manufacturing plants; at Eurochem the interface was between product-based businesses and geographically orientated plants! So how to organize the information system's function to both align with and integrate across different functional strategies is both a critical and non-trivial question—and may be the single most important issue in understanding the implications of globalization for IT.

Curiously, achieving the required organizational fit may become easier if the question is first made more complex, if the different aspects of IT management are identified for potentially separate organization design decisions. We suggest that each of our case studies, even the more successful, might have benefited from adoption of Earl's (1989) distinction between three strands of information strategy:

- Information systems strategy: the choice of applications, of *what* is to be delivered to the business.

- Information technology (IT) strategy: the choice of technical platform, of *how* applications are delivered.
- Information management (IM) strategy: the adoption of policies that determine *who* holds what mission, authority and responsibility.

In particular, our case studies suggest that information management strategy must be determined at or above the top organizational level of the global business. Skandia had identified that because the re-insurance (as distinct from the insurance) business had global character with clear global information systems opportunities and needs, a very strong mandate had to be given to the IT director, together with appropriate administration arrangements. In Electrolux, the information systems function was corporate and so had little difficulty in taking an aggregate view of the white goods business. In consequence, at Skandia and Elect. olux, global information systems strategy was being delivered (for example the SARA and EFS systems, respectively), and global IT strategy was in place and robustly protected—not just by the information systems function but by top management. By contrast, at Philips DC and Eurochem, the information management issues were not yet resolved, and this helps to explain why the business information systems strategy connections were not consistently made, and why questions of whether certain applications should be common across the business were so difficult to address.

The rationale for this proposition about information management strategy ownership should be clear. From the case study evidence, we propose that global information systems are needed to cross both borders and boundaries within the transnational organization. To develop the appropriate information systems strategy, a business' vision must be set and shared at the level of the global business. To deliver the information systems strategy, an IT strategy/architecture is required—data standards, application interfaces, computer compatibilities, communications topologies—which is independent of any one function, country, profit centre or operating unit. Top-level ownership of information management strategy provides the platform, the decision framework, from which all of this can be achieved.

Having a global information management strategy does not, of course, mean that all applications must be global and common, or that every piece of equipment must be prescribed by a monolithic

TABLE 8.3 Information system ownership: system scope

System objective	Global	Regional	Local
Efficiency			
Responsiveness			
Learning transfer			

global architecture. On the contrary, a successful global information management strategy enables application and technology decisions to be made at various organizational levels without prejudicing global business strategy. The third framework developed during our research (depicted in TABLE 8.3) concentrates on these questions of information systems and IT strategy ownership level. Conceptually it might be employed after the global IT application set has been developed, perhaps assisted by using the model in TABLE 8.1 to explicate the information requirements. In practice, the framework seems to stimulate further application thinking in its own right.

Two examples can briefly illustrate the framework's use. At Electrolux, EFS is essential to delivering the global aspirations of the white goods business; both information systems and IT specifications must be set at global level. On the other hand, order entry is seen as a local application: its functionality (information systems aspects) can be determined by local management, but interface into EFS requires that each local system must be designed within a global technical (IT) specification. Secondly, at Philips DC, reorganization of the logistics function raises the question of what combination of information systems and IT responsibilities for the relevant applications will best align with daily operational control, which is local, and policy coordination, which is a regional responsibility.

We therefore suggest that our four case studies demonstrate something of the need for, and nature of, alignment between global business and information strategy. The resolution is not as straightforward as speculative practitioner and academic articles suggest (for example, Alavi and Young, 1992; Karimi and Konsynski, 1991; Reck, 1989). The frameworks we have introduced address the need to surface, analyse and action a set of information management issues as a function of the business strategy and organization. When Egelhoff (1991) calls for greater attention to information requirements in global businesses, we have to agree. However, firms may need the sorts of frameworks of analysis we have proposed to identify and justify requisite information systems. They certainly need to address information management strategy—the information systems organization and ownership questions—at the organizational design stage. The contrasting and changing contexts we have encountered emphasize the importance of this type of analysis. However, they also leave unanswered the question of whether the "transnational" is yet a robust prescription for the challenging economic environment of the 1990s. Nevertheless, information systems appear to be one important means for achieving the potential advantages implied by the transnational model.

IMPLICATIONS AND CONCLUSION

The aim of the study reported here was to explore how IT was being deployed in pursuit of global business strategies in four firms. Each case study business had some characteristics of the "transnational" and each was at a different stage of evolution. We now venture some implications of our findings for research and practice.

IMPLICATIONS FOR RESEARCH

The global information systems challenge appears to be more complex than commonly suggested, and the solutions far from neat and tidy. The critical questions seem to be ones of information management strategy, in particular about organizing the information systems function appropriately. These are not new questions, nor are they inherently technological; in some ways they are general management questions. It is perhaps interesting to note that Bartlett and Ghoshal (1991) recently argued that management and organization studies have contributed significantly to understanding international business. They may be of similar value in studying international aspects of information systems.

One way of doing such managerial research is through case

studies. They allow multidisciplinary, integrative enquiry. We suggest that they can also provide a necessary dynamic lens on global information systems. It seems likely from our four case studies that the archetypal IT applications—as, say, predicted by our framework in TABLE 8.1—are not yet widely in place. Firms are still discovering their global information systems requirements; thus IT applications are evolving. Longitudinal case studies—not least, further monitoring of events in the four firms reported here—therefore could be valuable if theory development is in part making sense of firms' actions.

Another direction for research is to extend investigations into the transnational organization. The multidimensional thrusts of the transnational form seem to involve high coordination and thus require intensive information processing. IT would seem to offer considerable potential in meeting these challenges. Our studies show some, but not widespread, investments in IT as transnational strategies unfold. Thus three related questions arise: what is the contribution of IT in practice *and* what other means of information processing—social and organizational in particular—are commonly deployed? Then it becomes important to know which mechanisms are more effective and yield more sustainable advantages.

Two other research opportunities may be mentioned. The use of inter-organizational systems to enable or support global alliances was not evident in this study. It still could be a rich area of enquiry. Finally, in examining how IT can enable new ways of doing and managing global business, individual IT applications may be a more fruitful level of analysis than the business unit.

IMPLICATIONS FOR PRACTICE

We have argued from case study evidence that there are no easy and straightforward prescriptions for practitioners involved with global information systems. However, we have concluded that a useful starting point is to formulate a global business strategy first, before any sensible IT decisions can be made. (We also have opined that few, rather than many, IT applications will be required.) "Strategy before systems" is a beloved adage of consultants and is hardly noteworthy advice. However, perhaps only one of our case firms, Skandia, had managed to adopt this rational approach, where a CEO had formed and pursued a business vision that was significantly dependent on IT.

Such top-down, business-led strategy making in IT is rare and difficult to achieve. Commonly a much more organizational approach is required (Earl, 1993), where management teams work continuously—or are specially brought together—to analyse business problems, agree business imperatives and identify a strategic theme, including the information systems requirements, which is implemented over several years. There were elements of this in Electrolux; it was perhaps beginning in Philips, and maybe it was needed in Eurochem.

This perspective on information systems strategy making leads to a third implication for practice. If a global business strategy is in place and the information systems strategy has been aligned with it, the information management strategy must then also match to ensure implementation and prevent global IT policies being eroded by local behaviours. Skandia is an exemplar. However, if the global business strategy is not yet clear and therefore no information systems strategy has been formulated— or if determination of the information systems strategy is hindered by legacies from the past—our cases suggest that attention is then best directed to information management strategy. By defining the roles, relationships and processes for managing information systems, alignment of global information systems and business strategies may then evolve. In particular, it seems crucial to ensure that these IT decisions are made at or above the level where global business strategy is to be formulated and debated.

The final recommendation for practice is that in resolving these questions, our frameworks for analysis may help. They were prompted and refined by the case study evidence and could help management identify and address the key questions of global information strategy.

CONCLUSION

Coordination of operations and management is commonly seen to be the hallmark of global businesses. IT in principle extends the horizons of coordination and reduces its cost; thus information systems are likely to be important investments for any global business. Some were present in each of our case study firms.

The coordination need is found to be across the three classical axes of international business: business units, functional boundaries and national (and regional) borders. Thus, information often becomes a shared and common asset and information systems have to cross many organizational domains. This creates considerable management challenges and organizational complexity for the IT function. It is this complexity—often in a context of slowly evolving global business strategy—that stands out. There may be some special difficulties in applying IT globally—regulatory constraints, national infrastructure development, multiple vendors, conflicting standards—but they seem likely to be trivial compared with the management and organizational issues that arise.

This complexity provides an opportunity for those firms whose competitive strategy is partly based on global IT applications. Sustainable advantage may be gained by those who effectively resolve these questions. The complexities of information management may also provide an arena for those researchers who wish to study the realities of how transnational organizations function.

REFERENCES

Alavi, M. and Young, G. (1992). Information technology in an international enterprise: An organising framework. In S. Palvia, P. Palvia and R.M. Zigh (Eds) *The Global Issues of Information Technology Management*. Harrisburg, PA: Idea Group Publishing.

Baden-Fuller, C W F and Stopford, J.M. (1991). Globalisation frustrated: The case of white goods. *Strategic Management Journal* 12, 493–507.

Bartlett, C.A. and Ghoshal, S. (1987). Managing across borders: New organizational responses. *Sloan Management Review* 29(1), 43–53.

Bartlett, C.A. and Ghoshal, S. (1989). *Managing across Borders: The Transnational Solution*. Cambridge, MA: Harvard Business School Press.

Bartlett, C.A. and Ghoshal, S. (1990). A new kind of organisation. *PA Issues* No. 10, London: PA Consulting.

Bartlett, C.A. and Ghoshal, S. (1991). Global strategic management: Impact on the new frontiers of strategy research. *Strategic Management Journal* summer, 5–16.

Earl, M.J. (1989). *Management Strategies for Information Technology*. Hemel Hempstead: Prentice Hall.

Earl, M.J. (1993). Experiences in strategic information systems planning. *MIS Quarterly* 17(1), 1–24.

Egelhoff, W.G. (1988). *Organising the Multinational Enterprise: An Information Processing Perspective*. Cambridge, MA: Ballinger Publishing.

Egelhoff, W.G. (1991). Information processing theory and the multinational enterprise. *Journal of International Business Studies*, third quarter, 341–368.

Galbraith, J. (1973). *Designing Complex Organisations*. Reading, MA: Addison-Wesley.

Ghoshal, S. (1987). Global strategy: An organising framework. *Strategic Management Journal* **8**, 425–440.

Ghoshal, S. and Haspeslagh, P. (1989). Note on the major appliance industry in 1988, INSEAD–CEDEP case library.

Hagström, P. (1991). *The "wired" MNC: The role of information systems for structural change in complex organisations*, Institute of International Business, Stockholm School of Economics, Stockholm.

Hamel, G. and Prahalad, C.K. (1985). Do you really have a global strategy? *Harvard Business Review* July/August, 139–148.

Hamel, G. and Prahalad, C.K. (1989). Strategic intent. *Harvard Business Review* May/June, 63–76.

Huber, G.P. (1990). A theory of the effects of advanced information technologies on organizational design intelligence and decision-making. *Academy of Management Review* **15**, 47–71.

Ives, B. and Jarvenpaa, S.L. (1991). Applications of global information technology: Key issues for management. *MIS Quarterly* March, 33–49.

Johnston, R. and Lawrence, P.R. (1988). Beyond vertical integration – The rise of the value-adding partnership. *Harvard Business Review* July/August, 94–101.

Karimi, J. and Konsynski, B.R. (1991). Globalisation and information management strategies. *Journal of Management Information Systems* **7**(4), 7–26.

Konsynski, B.R. and McFarlan, F. W. (1990). Information partnerships – Shared data, shared scale. *Harvard Business Review* September/October, 114–120.

Lorenz, C. (1989). Electrolux management. *Financial Times* 19, 21, 23, 26, 28, 30 June.

McFarlan, F.W. (1992). Multinational CIO challenges for the 1990s. In S. Palvia, P. Palvia and R.M. Zigli (Eds) *The Global Issues of Information Technology Management*. Harrisburg, PA: Idea Group Publishing.

Porter, M.E. (1986). Competition in global industries: A conceptual framework. In M.E. Porter (Ed.) *Competition in Global Industries*. Cambridge, MA: Harvard Business School Press.

Prahalad, C.K. and Doz, Y.L. (1987). *The Multinational Mission: Balancing Local Demands and Global Vision*. New York: Free Press.

Reck, R.H. (1989). The shock of going global. *Datamation* 1 August.

Runge, D.A. and Earl, M.J. (1988). Using telecommunications-based information systems for competitive advantage. In M.J. Earl (Ed.) *Information Management: The Strategic Dimension*. Oxford: Oxford University Press.

Thompson, J.D. (1967). *Organizations in Action*. New York: McGraw-Hill.

9

Strategic Alliance Evolution Through Learning: The Rover/ Honda Alliance

DAVID O. FAULKNER

INTRODUCTION

International strategic alliances have in recent years become a very fast growing cross-border organizational form due to a number of underlying forces in the current global business environment, in particular the globalization of markets and technologies. This chapter explores the transfer of learning as a key feature in alliance success with reference to one of the best known British/Japanese alliances, that between the car groups Rover and Honda.

It is likely that the next decade will see an economic world of larger trading blocs, lower tariff levels and dramatically shortened transmission times, both of products and of information. In addition, an increasing globalization of market arenas is developing in an ever widening band of industries (Ohmae, 1989), and coupled with this the development of global technologies, shortening product life cycles and a consequent ever increasing demand for investment resources to cope with this changing

Strategic Renaissance and Business Transformation. Edited by H. Thomas, D. O'Neal and J. Kelly.
Copyright © 1995 John Wiley & Sons Ltd.

environment. In these circumstances cooperative strategy becomes at least as important as competitive strategy in achieving competitive advantage, and a major form of cooperative strategy is the international strategic alliance.

Strategic alliances may be defined (Mattsson, 1988) as:

> A particular mode of inter-organisational relationship in which the partners make substantial investments in developing a long-term collaborative effort, and common orientation.

COOPERATIVE STRATEGY

Throughout the 1980s and into the 1990s, cooperative forms of doing business have grown rapidly, and continue to increase as firms of all sizes and nationalities in an increasing number of industries and countries perceive value in them. Collective or cooperative strategies and competitive strategies may now be thought of as being in a position of rough equivalence:

> Whether competitive or collective strategies prevail at any one point in time appears largely irrelevant for obtaining viability and long-term stability. What is relevant is the ability to react to instabilities by switching from more collective forms of strategising to more competitive ones and vice-versa.
>
> (Bresser and Harl, 1986)

Strategic alliances, joint ventures, dynamic networks, constellations, cooperative agreements, collective strategies—all make an appearance and develop significance. In tune with the growth of cooperative managerial forms, the reputation of cooperation, in the views of the commentators, is enjoying a notable revival, to set against the hitherto unassailable theoretical strength of the competitive model as a paradigm of resource allocation efficiency.

Globalization of markets is currently probably the strongest force leading to this development. Stopford and Turner (1985) reinforce the argument for globalization by adding the technology dimension, pointing out that all of what they describe as the meta-technologies, namely micro-electronics, genetic engineering, and advanced material sciences, are subject to truly global competition. They suggest that the major forces leading to globalization are:

1. Technology, principally through the micro-electronics revolution.
2. Cultural evolution, i.e. the homogenization of tastes through media and other forces.
3. The breaking down of barriers, e.g. deregulation and economic integration.

A major factor behind growing globalization of markets, then, has been the development of global technologies, which both dramatically reduce communication times, thus "shrinking" the world in Vernon's phrase (1949), and facilitate the design and manufacture of products with truly global appeal:

> Technology is replacing economic and financial considerations as the most common basis for international cooperation.
>
> (Osborn and Baughn, 1987)

Failure to appreciate this in the US may well have been a major factor leading to the growing predominance of Japan in international markets. US companies cooperate with Japanese ones, and export their technological know-how. The Japanese carry out the production function, while the US firms accept functional substitution, instead of engaging in organizational learning. The Japanese then improve the technology, quality and costs, and successfully attack the US market:

> The Japanese have become internationally competitive by a sustained emphasis on refining the products and processes invented in the West.
>
> (Zimmerman, 1985)

Technology has also been a key factor behind the dramatic growth of cooperative agreements in the 1980s. Osborn and Baughn's research showed that there were 189 cooperative agreements registered between Japanese and US companies between October 1984 and October 1986. Of these, 20% involved cooperative R&D and 50% crossed industry boundaries but still had a strong technological content. Friar and Horwitch (1985) also emphasize the growth of technology strategy as a key element in determining a firm's level of competitive advantage, and illustrate how this is frequently leading to inter-firm technology cooperation. An international alliance may be an effective way of spreading technology.

THE FEDERATED ENTERPRISE

The globalization of markets and technologies has also influenced organizational form, through a decline in the automatic choice of the integrated multinational corporation (MNC) as the only instrument appropriate for international business development. The movement away from the traditional concept of the firm is accentuated by the growth of "federated organizations" (Handy, 1992), of which perhaps the largest recent convert is IBM, one of the most powerful MNCs in the world. It decided in 1991, after experiencing a significant decline in performance, and suspecting a loss of competitive advantage, to restructure its operations radically, from that of an integrated worldwide firm with a strong single culture, to that of a federation of 14 potentially competitive companies. The culture shock was so great, and the immediate results so mixed that the chief executive has recently resigned, and his successor has come from outside the computer industry. The IBM of the future is likely to be a federated enterprise, although the company has clearly not yet successfully adapted to such a radically changed paradigm.

The concurrent growth of alliances approaches the flexible transnational structure from the other end, i.e. the amalgamation of previously independent resources and competencies in contrast to the federation of previously hierarchically controlled resources and competencies (FIGURE 9.1).

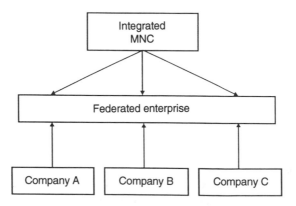

FIGURE 9.1   Federated enterprises are developing from both directions

Christelow's research (1987) indicates the growing importance of international joint-ventures to USA companies wishing to internationalize their operations. INSEAD research (Morris and Hergert, 1987) confirms the accelerating growth of all form of strategic alliance, as does recent UK research (Glaister and Buckley, 1992) which suggests that Europe has been the area of fastest growth in recent years (FIGURE 9.2). It is noticeable that the prime motor for growth since 1986 appears to have been with firms in the EU.

Contractor and Lorange (1988) also highlight the importance of joint ventures by pointing out that there were approximately 10 000 foreign wholly owned affiliates of US firms, but approximately 12 000 joint ventures in which US companies had between 10% and 50% ownership.

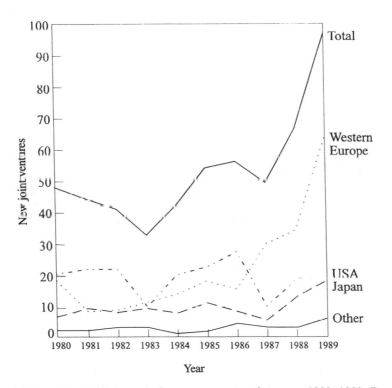

FIGURE 9.2 UK joint venture formation, region by year, 1980–1989. Reproduced by permission of *The British Management Journal* (Source: Glaister and Buckley, 1992)

THE LEARNING ORGANIZATION

This chapter suggests that strategic alliances are most frequently formed from resource dependency (Pfeffer and Salancik, 1978) motives, and that the ability of the partners to achieve and sustain competitive advantage in their chosen market is strongly influenced by the degree to which they place corporate learning as a high priority on their alliance agenda, and seek to cause the alliance to evolve in a direction based on that learning:

> A joint venture is used for the transfer of organisationally embedded knowledge that cannot be easily blueprinted or packaged through licensing or market transactions.
>
> (Kogut, 1988)

In a sense, corporate learning can be seen as the dynamic counterpart to the resource dependency theory of the firm. Thus, a firm will diagnose its resource and skill deficiencies in relation to a particular external challenge, and through the process of deliberate and planned corporate learning set about remedying its weaknesses.

Truly strategic alliances should be competence driven (Hamel, 1991); that is, explicitly adding to either the task or the knowledge system or to the organizational memory of each partner. The idea of the organization as a residuary for learning is a popular one. Decision theory emphasizes the importance of the search for information to enable organizations to make informed choices. Hamel stresses the role of learning as a source of competitive advantage, through the development of unique competencies. Senge (1992) describes learning organizations as the survivors of the future.

Corporate learning may be regarded as having two fundamental dimensions in the literature:

1. Individual learning
2. Organizational learning

Individual learning may be rational (how to work a computer) or intuitional (learnt unconsciously, like riding a bicycle). However achieved, individual learning adds to the competencies of the organization, but is in theory easily appropriated, as the individual with the developed competence is attracted into leaving the firm. Organizational learning develops at a level beyond that of the individual and becomes embedded in the rituals, routines and systems of a firm, in its culture. As such, it is more deeply rooted in its core competencies, and may therefore survive the tenure of individuals. Corporate organizational learning may be construed as consisting of both types described above.

THE FORMATION OF INTERNATIONAL ALLIANCES

Strategic alliances are formed for a wide variety of reasons. Firstly, there is generally an external stimulus. In the 1980s and 1990s this has been most commonly the globalization or regionalization of markets. Companies that had been equipped quite adequately to prosper in national markets suddenly found themselves having to cope in their home market with major global competitors. A number of factors brought this about, including the 1992 EC single market directives, and the dramatic improvement in communications, leading to the situation where in many industries the same products were to be found in department stores simultaneously in New York, Tokyo and London (Ohmae, 1989). Other external driving factors were the development of global technologies and ever shortening product life cycles. This led to the need for larger investment commitments as firms had to face the need to develop new products almost as soon as they had launched the last product. Few firms were adequately equipped to do this.

A further factor was the growing need to have a sufficiently large volume of sales to be able to take advantage of economies of scale and of scope that were available through modern automated manufacturing processes, in order to secure the low unit costs necessary to achieve competitive advantage. Additionally, the world economy had, since the oil shocks of the 1980s, become an increasingly turbulent and uncertain place, and only corporations of large financial strength had the flexibility to cope with such uncertainty. If they additionally felt the urgent need to get new products on the market to take advantage of major opportunities that might not remain long enough for their R&D to develop the products internally, and if they felt the need to economize with their finances and seek a partner to spread the risk, then they were strongly motivated towards seeking an alliance with an appropriate partner. Most companies, even the very large, faced these external forces with concern. Strategic alliances became an important item on their agenda, if they felt themselves to be deficient in global terms of resources, skills or what Prahalad and Hamel (1990) call "core competencies".

The partner selected for such an alliance would of course need to be one with complementary assets and capabilities, with identifiable synergies, with a compatible culture and with whom the firm believed it could achieve sustainable competitive advantage, which it could not achieve alone. In short, the partners would perceive their relationship as having a good strategic fit.

THE NATURE OF ALLIANCES

Strategic alliances come in many different forms and have been classified in the literature in a variety of ways. However, a classification by:

1. Nature
2. Structure
3. Membership

provides clear and simple categories of alliances. Thus, under "nature" the alliance can be classified as either focused or complex; a focused alliance is specific in its objectives, and may well involve only one activity from each partner's value chain (Porter, 1985). A complex alliance has more diffuse objectives, and may involve complete value chains, and lead to their reconfiguration. Under "structure" the alliance is either a joint venture with a separate legal existence or a collaboration without one. Under "membership" the classification is as a two-partner alliance or a consortium. Thus, a given alliance may be a focused two-partner joint venture, or a complex two-partner collaboration, or a focused consortium joint venture, and so on. Clearly, the three axes of the taxonomy give a possible eight alliance forms, as shown in FIGURE 9.3.

An analysis of 228 alliances (Faulkner and Johnson, 1992) showed two-partner joint ventures to account for 45% of the sample, consortium ventures 22.5% and two-partner collaborations 22.5%. Rover/Honda is a collaboration alliance.

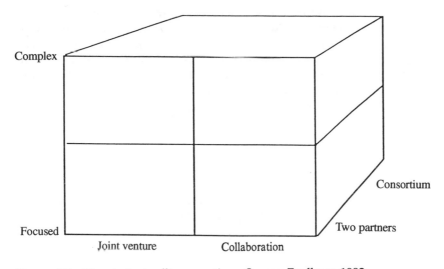

FIGURE 9.3   The strategic alliance options. Source: Faulkner, 1992

The life history of an alliance can be divided into three parts:

1. Formation
2. Management
3. Evolution

Stages 2 and 3 will overlap, as stage 3 emerges from stage 2. For an alliance to demonstrate the primary characteristics of success, it needs to evolve from the initial pact, and the process of evolution needs to be strongly influenced by positive attitudes to corporate learning held by the partners.

The selection of alliance form is also important, because different situations favour different forms. The collaboration form—the form chosen for the Rover/Honda alliance—may be most appropriate for situations where there is high uncertainty at the outset as to what tasks will be involved in the cooperative enterprise, and a consequent high need for flexibility between the partners. It may also be most appropriate where the partners do not immediately seek visible and specific initial commitments from each other, and where the alliance boundaries do not encompass specific assets or describe a clearly distinct business within the partners' portfolios.

In the most successful alliances the partners' intentions at or even before formation will be to learn from their partner, and hence remove some of their individual competence deficiencies. This does not, however, necessarily mean that their intention is to absorb all of their partner's know-how, and then subsequently establish themselves alone. This does happen in some alliances, but not in the most enduring and successful ones.

SOME BASIC PRINCIPLES IN THE MANAGEMENT OF INTERNATIONAL ALLIANCES

A genuine strategic alliance is formed for the long term:

> Strategic alliances are not tools of convenience. They are ... critical instruments in fulfilling corporate strategic objectives.
> (Roland Bertodo, strategic planning director of Rover and the key architect of the Rover/Honda alliance)

As such, the management system for running them needs to be established with as much care as that devoted to the choice of alliance form.

Important principles in this area involve agreeing good dispute resolution mechanisms, and if possible a "divorce" procedure to cater for the possibility that the alliance may cease to meet the needs of the parties. It is also important that the long-term goals of the partners should not be in conflict, although this does not mean that they need be identical.

Most importantly, attitudes need to be positive and flexible. For example, it is highly unlikely that the partners' companies or national cultures will be similar. If they are, of course, this may smooth the way for a harmonious working relationship. However, most strategic alliances are formed precisely because the partners are different, and valued the more for their difference. The cultural atmosphere in the partner company is therefore unlikely to be similar. A sensitive attitude to cultural differences is therefore necessary if the alliance is to prosper, since the cultural differences in ways of operating will inevitably lead to confusion in the partner company; if attitudes are positive, sensitive and flexible this need not have a negative impact on the alliance, and may lead to the partners absorbing what is best in each other's culture to their mutual benefit. Once more, learning from the partner is the key to success.

Two further attitudes are vital to success, namely commitment and trust. Commitment is showing the degree to which partners dedicate time and other resources to alliance matters, and are not discouraged by problems that arise. Trust is a more difficult area. Trust normally has to be earned in relationships, and this takes time. In alliances, however, it is suggested that an attitude which says, "I trust my partner, unless and until I have reason not to" is more likely to lead to positive results than the attitude which says, "I don't know my partner well. He will have to earn my trust over time".

A further important area is the establishment of systems to disseminate information throughout the company. In the absence of such systems the risk is high that the vital information, especially "know-how", will remain with the partner, and be merely used but not absorbed, or that it will go no further than the executives directly interfacing with their alliance partners, and not become embedded in the partner companies' tacit knowledge fabric:

> International joint ventures point to the transferability of each partner's capability as a critical determinant of the allocation of benefits of the venture.
>
> (Hamel, 1991)

Both Hamel and Grant (1991) stress the need for companies to appropriate the value they create, if they are to benefit from alliances in the future, and particularly if they are to maintain or increase their bargaining power in relation to their partner.

Thus we have the paradox that to gain from an alliance a partner needs to establish the ability to appropriate a substantial proportion of the value created by the alliance in the form of the successful internalization of new core competencies learnt from the partner. However, the more successful the firm is in doing this, the less it appears to need its partner, and hence the weaker the bonds of the alliance become. Fortunately for the inherent value of alliances, like all good paradoxes this is only an apparent contradiction and it arises from too static a view of an alliance. It assumes a finite set of competencies and skills, and that appropriation of value by one partner diminishes the pool available for the future.

ALLIANCE EVOLUTION

An important factor in the life of an alliance seems to be that, if it ceases to evolve, it starts to decay (Thorelli, 1986). Entropy is present in all networking, and needs to be actively fought on a continuous basis. Despite the continuance of the original agreement, management may start to lose interest in the liaison, if nothing new comes from it. The trading view, however, underlies a static "fixed set of goods" philosophy. Yet the reality of a successful alliance is that it not only trades competencies but also realizes synergies. Whereas the resource dependency perspective identifies a key part of a company's motivation for forming an alliance, the successful evolution of that alliance depends upon the realization of synergies between the companies, and the establishment of a durable competitive advantage for the partners, that each could not realize alone.

Evolution is about continuous value creation, which will, in a successful collaborative alliance, be appropriated by the partners in a balanced fashion. FIGURE 9.4 illustrates the stages by which this process may develop. Some value will emerge in terms of increased profits for shareholders, or for future investment, and some will emerge in the form of increased core competencies. But a third part will remain intrinsically dependent upon the continuance of the alliance and will form a strong bonding factor. For example, economies of scale and, to some extent, of scope would be difficult to realize by the partners separately, however adept their competence internalization. There may be joint patents and designs, and frequently joint development of assets of a tangible or intangible nature, which live naturally within the alliance, and are not subject to individual appropriation. In addition, over time, and with evolution, the alliance as an entity will begin to develop a life of its own, even more so in the joint-venture form of an alliance.

Alliance theory proposes that conditions for evolution include (Teramoto, Kanda and Iwasaki, 1991):

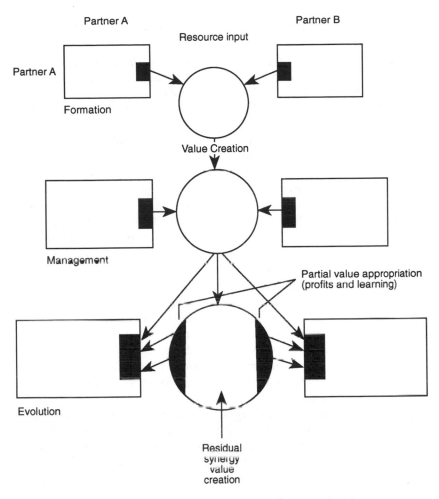

FIGURE 9.4 Evolution through value creation and appropriation

- Perception of balanced benefits from the alliance by both partners.
- The development of strong bonding factors.
- The regular development of new projects and responsibilities between the partners.
- The adoption of a philosophy of constant learning by the partners.

THE ROVER/HONDA ALLIANCE

In the Rover/Honda alliance a high level of strategic fit with mutual resource dependency existed at the outset in 1979, and continued to do so until the alliance was shaken in early 1994, when Rover's owners, British Aerospace, sold Rover to BMW. When the alliance was formed in 1979, Rover produced cars with a reputation for variable quality, had a management system based on confrontation and a poor labour relations record. It badly needed a new model for its mid-range, and to learn quality management processes from the Japanese company. Honda, for its part, looked to obtain low-cost, speedy and low-risk entry into Europe, access to Rover's surplus manufacturing capacity, an understanding of European taste and styling, and introduction to a well-developed network of suppliers. All of this was not on offer at the outset, or even appreciated by the partners, but it grew through the deepening relationship.

The collaboration alliance form met the needs of the partners very closely, as only this form provided total flexibility for development. At the outset it was uncertain what the alliance would involve in terms of areas of collaboration, and it was unlikely to describe a clear separable business area. Flexibility was the key, and this was demonstrated in the absence of legal agreements in the early years of the alliance.

In the area of alliance management, however, the Rover/Honda alliance had a mixed record. The alliance had been in operation since 1978, but it was only in the mid- to late 1980s that some of the key lessons in how to run an alliance were clearly adopted by Rover:

> It took us a long time to get our lines sorted out to pull together the learning and disseminate it throughout Rover. I would argue that of the first 10 years certainly the first 6 were wasted, in that they were spent really trying to understand Honda. We couldn't grasp what they were about. The cultural gap was very very wide.
>
> (Roland Bertodo, interview, 1991)

There was also very little attempt to set up a smooth dispute resolution mechanism, and a possible procedure for divorce was not ever discussed. However, the cultural issue was solved with the passage of time and increased working together. This was, in the Rover/Honda case, largely one-way progress:

I don't think we've had any impact on their culture at all. They did not set about to change their culture and they haven't. They set about learning, and if you look at their cars in terms of customer taste and values, with each evolution they became more Rover-like in terms of ambience.

(Roland Bertodo, interview, 1991)

However, trust and commitment were there from the outset and were demonstrated in the attitudes and behaviour of the partners. As Mr Hayashi, managing director of Honda (UK), puts it:

Both companies have a policy of strong commitment. If we broke apart we would be in competition with the same technology and the same products and suppliers—a duplicate of each other. This would not be sensible.

(Hayashi, interview, 1991)

Regrettably, the trust and commitment did not extend to the relationship between Honda and Rover's parent company, British Aerospace, and the alliance was destined ultimately to be damaged in 1994 when British Aerospace sold Rover to BMW.

During its lifetime, however, the alliance has produced major benefits for both Rover and Honda. Collaboration was limited to production processes, design, supplier sourcing and technology. In the sphere of marketing and sales, the companies competed and were very careful to avoid informal information transfer.

A key question had become whether the two companies had now learnt all they needed to know from each other. Thus in the Rover/Honda case, the argument would run as follows: as a result of the alliance, Rover have now learnt how to produce very high quality cars, to manage production processes more effectively, to adopt a more open attitude to learning, to increase productivity and to reduce the model life cycle to 4 years from 10. Honda has effected a successful entry into Europe, has developed a high quality network of European suppliers and has internalized its understanding of European taste and styling requirements. So why not say, "Thank you" and henceforth pursue separate developments? However, this brings us to a key aspect of successful alliances—continuous evolution.

Bertodo was always keenly aware of this and was conscious of the need to maintain a balance between the two companies' relative need for each other. He saw it as trading "packages" of competencies on a regular basis. There are five basic "trades" that can be identified over the life of the alliance, all leading to continuous evolution:

> As guardian of the company strategy ... I have got to have something ready to trade if the company decides it needs to trade, which will depend on how fast it is learning. I think we don't learn fast enough, but I would say that wouldn't I?
>
> (Roland Bertodo, interview, 1991)

Balanced benefits were achieved in the view of the partners. As Bertodo puts it:

> Buttressed by the ability to achieve better scale through joint manufacture and a spread of fixed overhead recovery over greater production volumes, manufacturing productivity has risen sharply over the period of the collaboration. Defect rates have shown a threefold reduction; the whole organization has moved away from a conventional hierarchical structure and self-contained functions towards an environment of personal interaction and fluid integration. Multi-functional, multi-skilled teams led by entrepreneur specialists became the rule, the payback has been a 10% reduction in administration burden and a halving of the human resource needed to achieve a given workload.
>
> (Roland Bertodo, interview, 1991)

For Honda, its establishment as a force to be reckoned with in the UK and Europe, and a growth of understanding of European tastes and styles, leading to the decline of the traditional Honda "box" style car, have resulted from the alliance. In addition, a £500 million inter-trading account between the two companies has developed. Bonding factors have been evident externally in the exchange of 20% of shares between the two companies, and internally by the establishment of close relationships at working team level in production, design and development functions between senior executives. An exchange of personnel between Honda and Rover has helped to cement this. Honda personnel have been seconded to Rover, and, for language reasons, Rover executives have been seconded to Honda USA.

A steady stream of new projects was evident over the life of the alliance and with it a growth of the closeness and cooperation between the two companies. What began as an arm's length knock-down kits licence for the Triumph Acclaim in 1979 progressed to real cooperative design development, and production of the Rover 200/400 series and the Honda Concerto, which includes cross-sourcing of components.

Finally, and most important, the philosophy of constant learning, which was already deeply embedded in the Honda culture, has been embraced wholeheartedly at least in the last five years by Rover. In the early days of the alliance Rover adopted an attitude towards the alliance which essentially saw Honda as being able to supply the deficient resources and capabilities that Rover needed. On this basis Honda would still have been valuable to Rover. It would have been able to provide Rover with a product that could be rebadged as Rover or Triumph (e.g. the Acclaim). This would have economized greatly on Rover's stretched R&D finances and enabled "new" models to be brought to the market at least two years earlier than could have been done using Rover's internal resources. In addition, Honda would have been able to take up some of Rover's excess manufacturing capacity and thus spread over-heads:

> I think Michael Edwardes saw it as a temporary alliance to plug a gap and to share costs so as to give us breathing space.
>
> (Roland Bertodo, interview, 1991)

However, an alliance on this basis would have been doomed to long-run failure since Rover would have become dependent upon Honda, and would have failed to learn and internalize any of the competitively advantageous skills that Honda had to teach. The transformation of Rover would not have taken place and the alliance would have done no more for Rover than temporarily and marginally improve its profit and loss account.

As the alliance continued, however, attitudes within Rover began to change, and an appreciation that alliances provide unique opportunities to learn and to improve skills and cap-abilities began to take over. By the time of the signing of the Statement of Understanding in 1985 the nature of the relationship had deepened:

> We had perceived the possibility of learning from Honda as they had perceived the possibility of learning from Rover, and joint development of a car was seen as bringing these common desires together and con-summating the relationship.
>
> (Roland Bertodo, interview, 1991)

From this point Rover did not look back. In fact, learning has become the touchstone of their new company culture, symbolized perhaps in the internal subsidiary Rover Learning Business, which is responsible for a wide range of training and for stimulating the living of the Rover Success through Learning policy. The Rover Learning Business is now extending its remit to the Rover dealer network, reminiscent of the Japanese Keiretsu attitude to suppliers and distributors as all part of the team.

Rover's learning and application has been dramatic in recent years, especially in view of the painful and difficult need to "unlearn" previous practices. Rover now includes just-in-time inventory management, through an intermediary third party buffer company, BRS, which maintains a constant flow of parts to the assembly line. Six end-of-the-line cold test stations with electronic function tests (in line with practice at Honda, Nissan and Toyota), multifunctional teams, single-source suppliers, and the flattening of the management hierarchy from 10 layers to 4 are further evidence of Rover's transformation. Managers up to director level are even donning Rover-logoed uniforms in characteristic Japanese fashion. So the traditional western attitudinal role of teacher has been replaced enthusiastically by that of student.

However, this is not to imply that there was total transparency of knowledge between the partners. Marketing and sales were areas of competition, and while Rover and Honda learnt to be good colleagues in R&D, design and production, they remained strong competitors once the marque badges had been fixed. This requires a strong self-discipline, more natural to the oriental than the western behavioural pattern. It is, however, vital to alliance success to retain separate identities and separate aspirational dreams while sharing a common bed, in Bertodo's picturesque phrase.

Beyond that, the two companies recognize that alliances only continue to evolve if this is valuable to the partners:

> There is no specific strategy between the companies in relation to the development of the alliance. We both look to an ongoing relationship to our mutual advantage.
>
> (John Bacchus, Rover's Director of Honda Collaboration)

> If we can grow together to our mutual advantage while maintaining our independence it will be a wonderful thing.
>
> (Mr Kume, President of Honda, 1991)

LEARNING AND EVOLUTION IN INTERNATIONAL ALLIANCES

Even faced with this evident success story of Rover/Honda, of the evolution of an alliance through mutual learning leading to competitive advantage, a perceptive analyst might still harbour nagging doubts about the role of value appropriation in the form of learning by the partners, and of the consequent stability of the alliance. Many commentators will in fact declare the alliance as a form to be an unstable and transitory arrangement, and undoubtedly, given opportunistic attitudes by the partners, it can be.

Further explanation of what is meant by learning and stability is probably merited. Perhaps due to the influence of the concept of "equilibrium" from the economists, stability is felt to be a state after which all wise organizations hanker. It is a "good" thing, but what do we mean by stability in a world that is constantly changing? Professor Teramoto of Japan puts it this way:

> It is often said that alliances are unstable. This is based on a failure to understand business life. Stability is in instability, and instability in stability. All are based on change, and this is the norm. Alliances are therefore no more unstable or stable than any other organizational form. All react by changing as they adapt to a constantly changing environment.
>
> (Teramoto, interview, 1992)

The often cited comparison of an alliance with a marriage is pertinent here. Marriages could be regarded as unstable, because they currently have a high failure rate. In fact, they have many of the qualities of strategic alliances. The partners retain separate identities but collaborate over a whole range of activities. Stability is threatened if one partner becomes excessively dependent on the other, or if the benefits are perceived to be all one way, but none the less, successful marriages are stable, and for the same reason as successful alliances. They depend upon trust, commitment, mutual learning, flexibility and a feeling by both partners that they are stronger together than apart.

Many businesses point to the need to negotiate decisions in alliances as a weakness, in contrast to integrated companies, where executives in hierarchies make decisions. This is to confuse stability with clarity of decision making, and would lead to the suggestion that dictatorships are more stable than democracies.

In this analogy, it is commitment to the belief that the alliance represents the best available arrangement that is the foundation of its stability. The need for resolution of the inevitable tensions in such an arrangement can as easily be presented as a strength, rather than as an inherent problem. It leads to the need to debate, see and evaluate contrasting view points. Ultimately, it would seem that British Aerospace valued the cash they could gain from the sale of the revitalized Rover more strongly than they valued the Rover/Honda relationship, and this therefore led to its decay.

How, then, is the learning issue resolved and does it influence alliance evolution? In terms of the possibilities presented by an alliance, there are a number of different types of learning, each with different implications:

1. Technological learning: a mixture of the technology describable in blueprints plus the know-how involved in using them.
2. Process learning: more deeply embedded in the culture of the partner, and therefore more difficult to transplant.
3. Opportunity learning: this involves practical matters such as: who are the best suppliers? What is the best way of getting skilled labour? Who are the best agents?
4. A learning philosophy: an attitude very difficult to translate but the most crucial to ultimate alliance success and the most guaranteed to transform the company.

The ease with which learning takes place within an alliance depends upon, firstly, the type of learning and, secondly, the relationship between the nature of the learning and the condition of the would-be receptor.

FIGURE 9.5 attempts to show the differences and strengths between Rover's condition, the learning opportunity presented to it, and the four types of learning. The ticks are made from Rover's point of view. The figure attempts to represent the situation by 1990, and would clearly be different, and with fewer ticks, in the early days of the alliance. In the figure:

> *Intent* represents the strength of the firm's determination to learn. Without that, there would be little advantage in terms of growth of core competencies, and the alliance would be largely limited to resource substitution from Rover's viewpoint.

		Technology transfer	Process learning	Opportunity taking	Learning philosophy
Condition of learning recipient	Intent	✓✓✓	✓✓	✓	✓✓
	Receptivity	✓✓✓	✓	✓	✓✓✓
Nature of knowledge	Transferability of knowledge	✓✓	✓	✓✓✓	✓
	Transparency of knowledge	✓✓	✓	✓✓✓	✓

FIGURE 9.5   Rover's knowledge absorbtion

Receptivity represents the condition in the company with regard to its level of sophistication and hence its capacity to learn. A low-tech company can only learn from a high-tech one, for example, after substantial education.

Transferability shows the ease with which the type of learning can be transferred: tacit knowledge is difficult, overt product knowledge easier.

Transparency is the willingness of a partner to release information and to explain difficulties.

FIGURE 9.5 therefore suggests that technical learning was relatively easy for Rover, particularly in the later stage of the alliance as Rover was receptive and keen to learn. The nature of technology transfer was clear, and Honda was willing to provide the information in joint learning working teams.

Process learning was more difficult, since by its nature it involves a lot of tacit knowledge, and cultural aspects related to Japanese paradigms. This was less easily transferred and less transparent, but as Rover's intent and receptivity grew, it became one of the success stories of the alliance from the Rover viewpoint, and processes were transplanted and "Roverized" (cf. just-in-time).

Opportunity learning was not a key area for Rover, but was a major concern to Honda; that is, identifying European opportunities and quality suppliers. Inherently, its transferability and transparency are high, but perhaps less durable than the other learning forms.

A learning philosophy is arguably the most important learning type of all, since it underlies the whole way in which a company is run. It meshes closely with the Honda philosophy of "continuous improvement". It is difficult to transfer, being part of Honda's essential cultural paradigm. However, there seems to have been little difficulty in transparency and, after Rover's intent and receptivity increased dramatically after 1985, the whole nature of Rover's attitude to itself, its personnel and its way of working became transformed, so that a learning philosophy came to underlie it.

LESSONS FOR MANAGERS

Many collaborative activities between companies are set up for short-term gains in order to deal with temporary situations. These obscure the nature of the true strategic alliance, in which the intent is a learning one, in the cause of joint sustainable competitive advantage and the extension of individual and joint core competencies.

From the evidence of the development of the Rover/Honda alliance a number of key points emerge of perhaps general value to managers wishing to set up and run international strategic alliances:

- The key to continued success is not skill (or product) substitution, but the ability and determination to learn from one's partners the competencies in which one is deficient.
- Sensitivity to cultural differences is vital to this process, but this is a different thing from the requirement for cultural similarity when selecting a partner. This latter characteristic may not be an advantage, since dissimilarities provide learning opportunities.
- To achieve genuine learning transparency is necessary, and this can only be brought about through positive inter-partner attitudes. In this regard commitment, trust and flexibility are the attitudes most necessary for success in an alliance. If some personal bonding can be achieved between the partners this also aids successful alliance development.
- It is obviously important to choose a partner with complementary assets and abilities, but after that point the alliance will only succeed through the mutually supportive behaviour of the partners, and a willingness by them to both learn and teach each other in the areas where they severally feel that they need to learn.
- Finally, and as it transpired most crucially, the commitment and trust must exist not only between the allies' top management, but also where appropriate between the top management of any relevant holding companies. The absence of this commitment between British Aerospace and Honda led to the ultimate decline of a very successful alliance.

However, given appropriate attitudes, and good strategic fit of the partners, it is suggested that strategic alliances can, through mutual learning, evolve into powerful global enterprises able to challenge the multinationals on their own terms and sometimes win.

REFERENCES

Bresser, R.K. and Harl, J.E. (1986). Collective strategy: Vice or virtue. *Academy of Management Review* **11**(2), 408–427.

Christelow, D.B. (1987). International joint ventures. *Columbia Journal of World Business* summer.

Contractor, F.J. and Lorange, P. (1988). Why should firms cooperate? The strategy and economic basis for cooperative ventures. In F.J. Contractor and P. Lorange (Eds) *Cooperative Strategies in International Business*. Boston, MA: Lexington Books.

Faulkner, D.O. (1992). Cooperating for competition: A taxonomy of strategic alliances. Presented at the Conference of the British Academy of Management.

Faulkner, D.O. and Johnson, G. (Eds) (1992). *The Challenge of Strategic Management* (1st Edn). London: Kogan Page.

Friar, J. and Horwitch, M. (1985). The emergence of technology strategy. *Technology in Society* **7**, 143–178.

Glaister, K.W. and Buckley, P.J. (1992). UK International joint venture: An analysis of patterns of activity and distribution. Unpublished work.

Grant, R.M. (1991). The resource-based theory of competitive advantage: Implications for strategy formulation. *California Management Review* spring, 114–35.

Hamel, G. (1991). Competition for competence and inter-partner learning within international strategic alliances. *Strategic Management Journal* **12**, 83–103.

Handy, C. (1992). Balancing corporate power: A new federalist paper. *Harvard Business Review* November/December, 59–72.

Kogut, B. (1988). Joint ventures: Theoretical and empirical perspectives. *Strategic Management Journal* **9**, 319–332.

Mattsson, L.G. (1988). Interaction strategies: A network approach, working paper.

Morris, D. and Hergert, M. (1987). Trends in international collaborative agreements. *Columbia Journal of World Business* summer.

Ohmae, K. (1989). The global logic of strategic alliances. *Harvard Business Review* March/April, 143–154.

Osborn, R.N. and Baughn, C.C. (1987). New patterns in the formation of US/ Japanese cooperative ventures: The role of technology. *Columbia Journal of World Business* summer, 57–64.

Pfeffer, J. and Salancik, G. (1978). *The External Control of Organisations*. New York: Harper & Row.

Porter, M.E. (1985). *Competitive Advantage*. New York: Free Press.

Prahalad, C.K. and Hamel, G. (1990). The core competence of the corporation. *Harvard Business Review* **90**, 79–91.

Senge, P.M. (1992). *The Fifth Discipline: The Art and Practice of the Learning Organization*. London: Century Business.

Stopford, J.M. and Turner, L. (1985). *Britain and the Multinationals*. Chichester: John Wiley.

Teramoto, Y., Kanda, M. and Iwasaki, N. (1991). The strategic alliances between Japanese and European companies – Cooperative competition, a growth strategy for the 90s, research report no. 91-05.

Thorelli, H.B. (1986). Networks between markets and hierarchies. *Strategic Management Journal*, **7**, 37–51.

Vernon, R. (1979). The product life-cycle hypothesis in a new international environment, *Oxford Bulletin of Economics and Statistics*, Nov., 255–267.

Zimmerman, M. (1985). *How To Do Business with the Japanese*. New York: Random House.

Section III

Managing Organizational Learning

Organizational learning, like any critical organizational process, must be carefully managed to assure its effectiveness. It is *not* just about learning from experience, since the past is not always the best predictor of the future. It *is* about a systematic approach to ensuring that all prerequisites for successful learning exist and are operational.

In his book *The Fifth Discipline*, Peter Senge suggests five elements (disciplines) that are essential to organizational learning. One is *personal mastery*—individuals' commitment to their own lifelong learning. Another is understanding our own *mental models*—how we, individually, understand the world around us, and how that understanding affects our actions. Next is *building shared vision*—a set of principles and values that will guide the organization's future. *Team learning* involves individuals thinking together, which not only produces superior results but also individual growth of team members. The fifth discipline, *systems thinking*—recognizing how one event/action affects and is affected by others—integrates the other four into a coherent whole.

Although Senge's five disciplines are largely personal, having to do with our desires, how we think and how we interact with others, he argues that the fundamental learning unit in organizations is the team. If teams cannot learn, the organization cannot learn.

The chapters in this section reinforce some of the established perspectives on organizational learning, as well as adding new points of view.

Lorange and Løwendahl present some key dimensions in organizational learning, and suggest an approach to the study of how organizations learn based on observations of organizational learning and change at the Norwegian School of Management. Key dimensions include an organizational culture where commitment to the organization is broader than the formal authority; incentive systems tailored to allow for learning; ability to "see" the environment in a more common way; and top management's role, particularly when financial and/or portfolio concerns are pressing for the short-term results.

Jalland and Gunz maintain that the new emphasis on organizational learning requires a closer look at the way in which organizations select, develop and promote key strategic decision makers. They argue that the upper echelon perspective proposed by Hambrick and Mason (1984) provides too limited a view of managers engaged in strategic management. This chapter offers a 2 × 2 matrix showing how organizational structure (diverse versus similar operating units) and internal mobility barriers (high versus low) lead to four types of "organizational career logics" (OCLs): command-centred, evolutionary, constructional and parochial.

Gratton describes the issues encountered by senior executives in one multinational firm as they restructured from a bureaucratic, centralized organization to a decentralized, team-based one. Her chapter addresses the challenge of an incumbent executive team reconfiguring its own skills, behaviours and competencies to facilitate and reinforce the transformation process.

Based on an in-depth field study of one company, Overmeer challenges the assumption that interactive learning will happen automatically during strategy implementation. He suggests that, under conditions of major change, strategic learning is likely to be very difficult. He proposes joint inquiry prior to a major shift in the environment, and discusses the role of consulting-based research in the process.

Eden and van der Heijden seek to reinforce the significance of understanding strategy from an emergent strategizing view, and explore alternative ways in which the emergent strategizing of an organization can be made explicit.

Learning, like academic discovery, is about answering questions; solving problems. Although theories, by initiating further questions and illuminating additional problems, exert a powerful influence on learning, much of the most effective learning is from practice, involving real problems and real people.

In either case, those seeking an answer to a particular question consider various alternatives before arriving at a possible solution (a "theory"). Logical next-steps include: (i) testing the theory; (ii) collecting the results; (iii) analysing the results—attempting to determine what they are showing; and (iv) considering how well the results address or answer the original question ("reflection"). The next step may involve rephrasing the question, or asking another, followed by another theory, and so on. Whether done by academics or business practitioners, this process is universal, and represents an ongoing learning process—we learn from what we do; from what works and what doesn't work.

Accepting the premise that virtually all individuals engage in ongoing learning means acknowledging that continual learning takes place within most organizations, whether by design or not. The extent to which organizations benefit from individual learning is dependent upon the degree to which it is recognized and managed by the organizational actors. Not capitalizing on this potential may waste some of an organization's most valuable, and scarce, resources—knowledge, experience, information, ideas and individual commitment. On the other hand, reframing how the organization promotes individual and organizational learning can help to operationalize and capitalize on some of its most potent corporate assets.

10

Organizational Learning in Academic Institutions

PETER LORANGE, BENTE R. LØWENDAHL

INTRODUCTION

We have recently seen an increased interest in organizational learning among both researchers and practitioners, and clearly an improved understanding of how organizations learn will be of great interest in strategic management. This chapter looks into learning as an increase in the competence assets of an organization. First, it discusses the types of competence assets in an organization as well as how these may be enhanced, then it presents examples of organizational learning within an academic institution, based on the experiences and observations of the authors within the Norwegian School of Management.

This chapter represents the early stages of our work in progress, and is primarily based on our own observations of organizational change and learning processes in what was our own organization. Hence, it is relatively unorthodox in terms of data collection, because we were both participants involved in the processes, as opposed to "objective" observers studying the processes with a particular research project in mind. We certainly do not claim to provide systematic and unbiased observations of

Strategic Renaissance and Business Transformation. Edited by H. Thomas, D. O'Neal and J. Kelly.
Copyright © 1995 John Wiley & Sons Ltd.

organizational learning and change. Rather, we suggest some potentially fruitful insights, which may serve as a basis for future (and more traditional) empirical studies of strategy, organizational change and organizational learning in academic institutions.

ORGANIZATIONAL LEARNING AT MULTIPLE LEVELS

Partly as a result of the increased emphasis on competence as a strategic resource (Barney, 1991; Conner, 1991; Itami, 1987; Prahalad and Hamel, 1990; Rumelt, 1984; Teece, Pisano and Shuen, 1990; Wernerfeld, 1984), managers as well as academics within the strategy field have recently put substantial emphasis on understanding organizations' competencies as well as how these competencies may be enhanced. Based on Nordhaug (1993), Løwendahl (1992) discusses six types of competence assets in organizations, three of which exist at the individual level and three of which exist at a collective level. FIGURE 10.1 illustrates these six types of competencies.

Collective competencies may exist on group, division and/or strategic business unit (SBU) levels within the organization. In addition, both individuals and organizations are strongly influenced by the existing competence level of the task environment surrounding the organization, as illustrated in terms of clusters of organizations in Porter (1990) and in terms of the influence of

Competence assets

Individual	Collective
Knowledge	Client-specific databases Technology
Skills	Routines Methods Procedures
Aptitudes	Organizational "culture"

FIGURE 10.1   Types of competences in organizations

professions on individuals as well as organizations in Løwendahl (1992).

An increase in the organization's competence assets may result from the addition of new members with competencies supplementing those that the firm already has, from the learning of individual members of the organization such that their competencies are enhanced or from improved competencies at the organizational level. At the individual level, learning may involve new knowledge or new skills, and the latter may only be learned through improved ways of doing things. Aptitudes cannot be taught or learned, but can certainly be activated and mobilized in ways that improve the performance of the individual as well as the organization. Knowledge may be transferred through a number of different means, including written documents such as books, reports and internal memos, or through oral presentations such as seminars, courses and meetings.

At the collective level, knowledge may exist in terms of technologies, and may also be developed by individuals as the result of new insights and innovation. Skills, however, are transferred through "learning-by-doing", and the process may be accelerated if a mentor–apprenticeship relationship is established whereby those who have already acquired the skills assist other organizational members in the process of learning. In most cases, active participation of the individual who is learning is required in order for competence enhancement actually to happen. More often than not, the process also involves at least one more individual who transfers some of his or her competence to the other(s)—patented solutions, and so on, or in terms of information such as customer or client databases, aggregated market data, etc. Organizational skills, as discussed at length by Nelson and Winter (1987), involve organizational ways of carrying out operational activities, including routines, standard operating procedures, management practices (to the extent that these are organizationally determined, rather than individually based) and so on. In terms of organizational knowledge, competence enhancement may occur as the result of information gathering and/or technology development, either as the result of activities specifically focused on the increase of knowledge, or as a by-product of the firm's operations (Itami, 1987). Similarly, organizational skills may be improved as routines or procedures are altered in response to changing operational requirements, or as the result of pre-planned explicit activities aimed at improving organizational skills. In the former case, practices may be changed locally, without management or people other than those involved in the operations knowing about the changes. In the latter case, changes are designed first and implemented later, such as when an organization develops a new set of quality control standards and procedures and later implements these throughout the entire organization.

A third type of organizational competence contains elements that are difficult to enhance directly through pre-planned and explicitly designed learning processes, similar to individual aptitudes. Part of the organizational "culture" may fall into this category as some organizations are clearly better than others at finding new solutions etc. beyond capabilities explained by knowledge and skills. Yet, like aptitudes, it may be possible to mobilize a larger part of an organization's potential, thus enhancing this dimension of organizational competence.

The total competence of an organization, therefore, depends on both the competence of individual members, the ability of the organization to mobilize these individual competencies at the highest possible level of performance—including finding the person and/or combination of people for each task and hence mobilizing synergies—and also the collective competence. The competence of the organization, then, is more than just knowledge; it also includes skills and innate aptitudes. The total competence of the organization is also more than the sum of individual competences, because competence may be added at the collective level. However, organizational competence in use may be much less than the total stock of competence available in the organization, because people may have competences that they are not given the opportunities to use. In addition, groups may be put together or entire organizations designed in such a way that the competence of one person inhibits the competences of others. You may get negative synergies rather than a positive sum.

We suggest that, within the resource-based perspective, organizational learning may be viewed as an increase in the organization's stock of mobilizable competences, at the individual as well as at the collective level. Hence organizational learning can occur in at least four different ways:

1. When individuals learn, and the sum of individual competences is increased.
2. When new people with additional competence are recruited.

3. When people with obsolete competence are substituted by people with new competence.
4. When collective competences are added, developed or improved.

However, when we analyse organizational learning in a strategic context, in our view it is also critical to consider two additional factors, beside the sum total of the learning that has taken place in the organization. Firstly, organizational learning should be linked to the strategy and prioritized tasks of the organization, such that learning is analysed in terms of its relevance for organizational value creation. Learning may take place in a number of areas which may be irrelevant to the performance of the organization, or may even be dysfunctional. Secondly, organizational learning may be more or less appropriable by the organization. To the extent that individuals learn valuable and transferable skills, the organization has only increased its competence level as long as the individuals prefer to continue to provide their inputs to the same organization. If the employee leaves, so does the competence. Organizations may experience a "brain drain" leading to a reduction in competence—a deskilling—and hence, what may be seen as negative learning from the collective point of view.

To date, the strategic management literature on the resource-based perspective of the firm (Barney, 1991; Teece, Pisano and Shuen, 1990; Wernerfeld, 1984) has primarily focused on the competence assets that are fully owned and controlled by the firm. Given such an emphasis, organizational learning will primarily involve the information seeking and routine improvement processes of the organizations, as described in detail in the literature based on the behavioral theory of the firm (Cyert and March, 1963). In our opinion, organizational learning involves both individuals and the entire organization, as well as sub-units of the organization, and may be both positive and negative relative to the value creation process of the organization in focus.

ORGANIZATIONAL LEARNING AND STRATEGIC DIRECTION

Strategic management involves setting the direction of the evolution of the organization. Hence, the strategy of the firm should fundamentally affect the learning processes that take place in the organization. It is not enough for the organization to be learning and improving its competencies. It also needs to be *learning the right things*, as seen in a long-term strategic perspective. Improved competencies as the result of organizational learning processes do not automatically lead to improved organizational performance on whatever key dimensions of performance are relevant to each particular organization. In fact, if the learning is substantial and in the wrong direction, as seen from a strategic perspective and in terms of the overall goals of the main stakeholders of the organization, the learning process may significantly shift the power structure away from the dominant coalition (Thompson, 1967). The results of an unmanaged organizational learning process may be that one group of stakeholders of the organization is able to shift the core competencies of the organization to a considerable extent, through suboptimal learning processes, so that the competitive advantage is eroded. The consequence may be a very different type of organization, and even inability to survive.

It is the responsibility of top management of all organizations to manage the organization such that the overall goals of the organization are attended to in the best possible way. As a result, even the learning processes and the competence enhancement of the organization have to be managed, and the management of these processes requires substantial top management attention, time and energy. The visions, ambitions and intentions of top management significantly affect the flavour of the learning activities, both in terms of how much is learned and what is emphasized in the learning process. In addition to the direct effect of leadership on learning within the organization, top management controls a number of organizational elements by which they set the framework of the organizational activities, including the learning processes. Fundamental elements include the design of the organizational structure, the strategic control dimensions (Lorange, Scott Morton and Ghoshal, 1986), the incentives systems and guidelines for recruiting. Top management can also impact organizational "culture" in several indirect ways, such as allowing for experimentation, allowing norms for accepting diversity, and providing incentives to get broader viewpoints beyond one's own "kingdom". In addition, top management has the opportunity to directly focus incentives on issues that are related to organizational learning, particularly when it comes to group incentives, or for achieving pioneer strategy type breakthrough, etc. The issues having to do with choosing the strategy itself and providing for different underlying critical assumptions, so as to allow for different types of learning, thus represent opportunities for top management. Organizational learning is also a managerial task!

Based on the above discussion, the effect of organizational learning involves at least three fundamental dimensions: the amount of learning, the strategic relevance of the learning, and the individuals involved in the learning process. All three dimensions need to be analysed from a strategic management perspective, regarding where in the organization the learning takes place, including whether it is individual or collective.

The framework developed by Chakravarthy and Lorange (1991) may serve as a starting point for discussing the strategic context within which organizational learning takes place. At the business unit level this framework distinguishes between the ability to see unique opportunities where others may not see them, and the ability to mobilize internal strategic resources, above all human resources and their competences, in order to pursue such opportunities. FIGURE 10.2 illustrates the framework.

Four different business level strategic intents emerge thereby. The first is "pioneer", where new opportunities are explored. Learning is likely to be highly experimental. If successful, the next stage may be "expand", where the new projects or ideas are implemented and institutionalized, in order for an increased activity level to make the innovations profitable. At this stage, learning is likely to be centred around transfer of knowledge and

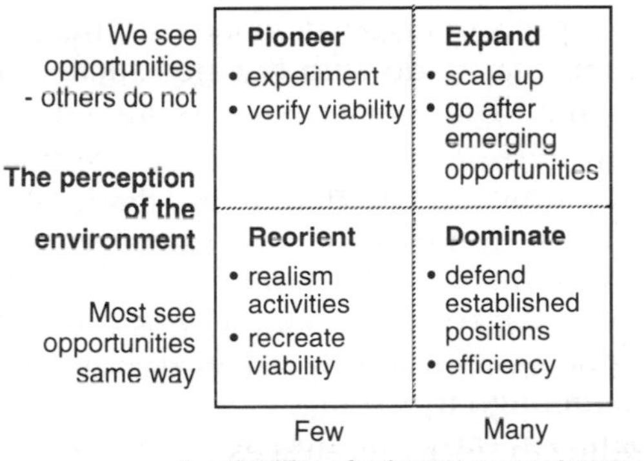

The perception of the environment	Pioneer	Expand
We see opportunities - others do not	• experiment • verify viability	• scale up • go after emerging opportunities
	Reorient	Dominate
Most see opportunities same way	• realism activities • recreate viability	• defend established positions • efficiency
	Few	Many

Availability of relevant competences

FIGURE 10.2 A framework for tailor-made strategies at the business level

skills from the individual champions who developed the ideas, and the development of efficiency-enhancing routines in order for the expansion to be profitable on a larger scale. Recruitment is also likely to take place, adding competences that enable the organization to exploit the opportunities. The third strategic intent is "dominate", which primarily emphasizes efficiency-enhancing improvements at all levels, through better routines, more efficient divisions of labour and a routinization of tasks. This stage is likely to be dominated by what Argyris and Schon (1978) describe as single-loop learning. The fourth and final strategic intent is "reorient", where learning may be an eclectic blend of single-loop and double-loop learning, depending on how management decides to reorient the business.

In the following section, we present three recent examples of organizational changes, and hence implicit organizational learning, in the Norwegian School of Management (NSM). Subsequently, we analyse the organizational learning from the perspective of the model presented in FIGURE 10.2. All three examples represent processes that have not come to an end. Hence, our case descriptions represent only temporary snapshots of ongoing changes. It is much too early to evaluate the total impact of these changes on organizational learning at NSM.

EXAMPLES OF ORGANIZATIONAL LEARNING

The following are concrete and specific examples from our own research/practice at the Norwegian School of Management (NSM) which illustrate aspects of organizational learning.

Our first example has to do with the introduction of a Master of Science programme. This started out as an effort inspired by several of our faculty members and the president, based on a number of initial observations regarding needs. In fact, learning had to do with seeing the need to create more graduate level courses, to have a number of courses on offer that were more closely linked with the research interest of our faculty, and so on. Thus, both external market forces and internal organization motivations were triggering factors.

It was recognized early on that for NSM to attract foreign students we needed to have high quality courses that would be taught in English. It was also recognized that a large number of faculty members would have to be involved in the course development process, to increase broad topical coverage as well as organizational buy-in.

The outcome of this predominantly bottom-up course design process was a choice of three Master of Science programmes, one in Energy Management, a second in International Marketing and Strategy and a third in Euromanagement. A number of other offerings were considered, but were turned down. This was done partly as a consequence of the president's desire to have one programme predominantly identified with each of the School's three academic departments to ensure commitment to "deliver". Partly, too, it was based on a "first come, first served" basis, whereby a few committed "champions" had come forward early and demonstrated a willingness to do the preparatory work. Finally, it was partly a consequence of the political strength (or lack thereof) of the faculty members proposing these programmes.

Initially it was hoped that the programme development would lead to a set of courses that could be used interchangeably. It turned out, however, that it was virtually impossible to develop the necessary synergies between the various programmes. Individual faculty members and groups instead created their own approaches based on *their* notions of what would be the most appropriate. The relatively strong resistance to the creation of a common meta-structure resulted in a high resource expense level. With the subsequent lack of performance of two of the three programmes in the market-place, it thus became natural to reorient the programmes into one graduate school "catalogue" that would provide the flexibility to offer a number of more tailor-made specializations, all within an overall meta-structure. This led to the creation of resource-saving synergies—although delayed—and a better pulling together of the faculty team. One price of learning was that of emphasizing how synergies develop more easily under times of stress and resource shortage. Creative faculty teams tend to do their developmental work more easily with emphasis on "focus in the small" rather than in the large—resource-expansive fragmentation rather than meta-structured synergies.

It also became clear that linking the educational programmes with broad research programmes was difficult because the focus on the market's needs then tended to become biased. Particularly with corporate programme sponsors (which was the case for the Energy master), the issue of relevance was a source of debate.

Still, these tensions turned out to be a major advantage for enhancing the richness of the programmes. The Energy programme turned out to be a particularly flexible vehicle for achieving this, which was not to the same degree the case in the other two programmes, where the stress factors were less strong.

From this we see that organizational learning, and how it relates to different degrees of complexity, had changed, for example, regarding simple, free-standing courses versus synergetic, new programme packages that involve new norms and ways of seeing things. Thus, the effort to develop a Master of Science programme proved to be a rich source for organizational learning within our School, with the gradual realization that the broader organizational issues were harder to learn about than learning in an independent manner by each faculty member. But the dynamics of learning—leading to a better understanding of the importance of an overall concept rather than merely individual pieces—was perhaps the most interesting.

Although the initial overall results were mixed, they led to important organizational learning that thus can be stated in different ways. The specialization that worked best was the Energy Management programme. Here Norway has a comparative advantage with a strong competence base. This made the marketing of the programme easier. Our faculty also has a broad-based competence here, as well as the ability to draw on other international networks. The need to establish such a realistic closeness to the market, in a broader sense, turned out to be an important learning insight.

The other two programmes were not as clearly positioned relative to specific markets. In the eyes of prospective students they were rather graduate level programme offerings, competing with several well-established offerings from a number of distinguished schools internationally. The unique *raison d'être* was not there. Consequently, few students applied. It was also difficult to establish close corporate sponsorship support and interest, given the generality of these programmes' themes. Finally, it was hard to establish a broad linkage between the programmes and common research programmes for large faculty groups within our school.

Let us now consider a second example. This one differs from the previous in that it was largely a top-down initiated project, where organizational learning was induced much more directly as a consequence of shifting overall pressures facing the school's organization. This example involves organizational learning as it relates to the School's executive lifelong education programmes.

Executive lifelong education has long been part of the product portfolio of NSM courses. This programme activity had in the past been provided with a relatively loose support organization and relatively little overall institutionally standardized efforts when it came to development and marketing. It had had a heavy reliance on individual faculty members' initiative, interest and drive, and offered an opportunity for faculty members to generate more income to themselves directly as well as to their research activities. Marketing of such lifelong learning was done primarily through advertisements that focused on each individual partici-pant as a customer.

The traditional overall portfolio mix of activities within NSM puts heavy emphasis on providing learning to new students seeking university level education. It was recognized, however, that this market was becoming less growth orientated, due partly to demographic shifts and partly to the build-up of additional capacity in the public education sector. It took a financial mini-crisis to make the organization realize that the portfolio mix of educational activities might have to be significantly changed, with a relatively large strengthening of lifelong learning to counteract the falling traditional markets. This mini-crisis was induced by an unexpected large increase in free student seats in the public education sector, which took away approximately 10% of the students in NSM's primary business segment overnight.

The resulting re-examination of lifelong education, and its relation to organizational learning, reveals several interesting issues:

Firstly, marketing of the product portfolio needed to be directed to major private and public institutions, so as to cater to the needs such institutions have to develop their own core competencies in a systematic manner through lifelong learning. To market to indi-viduals directly would only satisfy this issue indirectly, and would probably only address particularly motivated individuals and not necessarily the ones that organizations would prefer to participate in lifelong learning. In order to be able to meet the larger customers an elaborate network of corporate contacts would have to be set up through a network of "partnerships" with specific business organizations and the executives dealing with these issues in these organizations. Our traditional faculty resources were generally not—we found—well equipped to deal with this rather different marketing challenge. New talents would have to be brought in, and the organizational learning took place primarily within *this* new subgroup of people, and *not* within the broader NSM organization, as had been hoped.

Secondly, the product offerings would have to be significantly modified. Here, we thought that synergies with various offerings from established programmes might be built upon. It seemed important that professional skills at the state-of-the-art level within various faculty milieux in the school should systematically be exposed to lifelong learning offerings. It turned out, however, that course design pedagogical approaches, teaching styles, etc. were very different for this type of programme, thus a considerable learning effort was called for. We underestimated the added energy, time and stress this took. Thus, even though many of the same topical issues that had been introduced in the modified master level offerings were also given in lifelong learning, it took a virtually new learning effort to do this. We had underestimated the need to learn in depth the handling of each distinct type of teaching activity. We had thought that more learning could be transferred.

Thirdly, while the compensation for lifelong learning teaching had previously been primarily an extra incremental benefit to each faculty member, lifelong learning was now redefined as part of the general compensation package linked to the overall duties of each faculty member. Additional incentives were, however, still preserved but at a lesser scale, so as to maintain additional inducement to meet the "hardships" of teaching more mature executives. In essence, faculty members were no longer asked to "compete with their school". A lot of resistance resulted from this, which demonstrated that "unlearning" of practices that were no longer part of the strategy can be very difficult in practice.

In terms of more general learning experiences from this example, we would like to point out three additional issues. Firstly, assessment of the situation, the organizational changes that were made, the actions that were initiated and the resulting organizational learning were much more a direct consequence of top management's intervention and ameliorating efforts, stemming from the immediate overall portfolio and financial pressures that the institution was experiencing. This is in contrast to the earlier example, where few such pressures existed and where the consequences for the learning process were much more firmly based on bottom-up induced activities. Secondly, it was critically important to establish clear links with the market-place in this case too. Such links involved explicit relationship building with new field organizations, so they could become part of the organization's strategy for competence building. Earlier, individual links to particularly keen lifelong learners was not enough. Learning from the market-place was key here too, but organizational fragmentation make it difficult for sufficiently broad learning to take place.

Thirdly, the issue of creating synergies was, again, a critical one for providing meaningful utilization of scarce faculty capacity and competencies. While each course previously tended to have an element of individual faculty ownership and to be sheltered from other faculty members, a more systematic development of courses linked intellectually with developments in other parts of the school's curricula (particularly the masters studies) proved feasible, but only after a broad-based realization within the organization that there was a sense of crisis and urgency. Building on pedagogical synergies with traditional programmes turned out to be an impossibility.

Let us now discuss a third and final example, one that deals with organizational learning that took place relative to various internal management processes at NSM. This is in contrast to the organizational learning that took place in the earlier two examples, where it related directly to particular teaching programme strategies, induced in either a bottom-up way or in a top-down way. This third example has to do with the introduction of a planning and incentive system for individual faculty members.

A set of prices had evolved over time whereby faculty workload tasks were assigned on a more or less incremental basis, largely based on each individual's preferences and initiatives, and above all as a function of how tasks had been carried out in the past. Similarly, incentives were primarily given in an indirect way, in the form of extra pay generated as a result of one's own initiatives in lifelong learning, through bringing in special research projects, and so on. These incentives were essentially individualistically focused and short term. They did not address such questions as how to generate synergies, how to develop new business, how to develop new relevant academic competencies, how to establish and manage the balance between research, teaching, lifelong learning action involvement, and so on.

As a consequence of several of the shifts in programme emphasis within the school, including what we saw from the two examples just discussed, it became clear that the management processes relating to faculty members' planning and how they were provided incentives no longer worked as desired. Organizational learning had indeed taken place when a systematic examination of the consequences from all these major programmatic changes was undertaken. This provided the basis for a new initiative to work out modifications of the workload assignment and incentives processes. Thus, the organizational learning relating to a management process change was a function of previous shifts in the business strategies and portfolio of the organization. It was lagged organizational learning.

The planning activities of each faculty member were strengthened in such a way that they were asked to undertake plans that specifically indicated research efforts, teaching efforts, outside involvements, and so on. These plans were then more carefully coordinated at the academic department level and were reviewed carefully with the department chair and the school's top management. A process of annual follow-up of the plans relative to what had actually been achieved was also established, and bonus incentives were given to those faculty members who achieved their goals in a satisfactory manner.

What were the main elements of our organizational learning when it comes to this initiative? Firstly, it seems critical that faculty members accept that planning and incentives of these types provide a basis for the execution of more involved "higher level" strategies, enhancing such challenges as achieving synergies, providing innovative programmes to more demanding customers, and expanding internationally. It was a major organizational learning that workloads, incentives, pay, etc. were issues that must be dealt with in the context of the School's current strategy, and not as independent, seniority-driven issues. The organization learnt this slowly—many parts of the organization have probably not learnt it yet. Our strategic ambitions could hardly be realized if the School's efforts were nothing more than the mere sum of each individual faculty member's undertakings.

Secondly, as before, a feeling of crisis seemed necessary to instil a systematic examination of what had been going on, thus providing an organizational learning basis for change. Again, the shifts in the School's financial situation, as well as a perception of the need to change the strategic portfolio balance of activities, were very important inducements here. Finally, top management again played a very important direct role in accentuating changes and stimulating organizational learning.

THE STRATEGIC INTENT FRAMEWORK APPLIED TO THE THREE EXAMPLES

As indicated above, organizational learning in an academic institution such as our School requires not only that someone in the organization has learned something, but also that this learning be relevant relative to the shifting strategic context. The examples illustrate how different strategic changes that take place in the organization may be more or less followed by an organizational learning process, aimed at increasing the probability of success of each of the strategic changes. However, the task of explicitly and strategically directing and supporting organizational learning activities is more complex than just creating an organizational change context where learning is supposed to take place. Organizational learning needs to be directed according to, firstly, the strategic goals of the organization and, secondly, the type of strategic intent governing the organizational change process at any given point in time. Projects as well as entire organizations evolve, and may move from "pioneer" through "expand" and "dominate" to the "reorient" stage, e.g. as a result of the life cycle of the programme or service offered. There may be specific key insights that can be learnt about this dynamism. We did not see this, however. Rather, we were underestimating the stability-prone working mode of our academic organizations. Some programmes or services seem to be very stable, such as our undergraduate "Siviløkonom-program", which has been—and clearly will remain for a long time—in the "dominate" cell of FIGURE 10.2. These stable programmes dominate our learning. But for new programme innovations and strategic portfolio changes, the cycle seems to move from "pioneer" through "expand" to "dominate". Our planning and learning focus did not seem to be sufficiently prepared for these shifts in emphasis. Let us go back to the three examples for an illustration:

In the MSc programme, the pioneer stage was dominated by a number of champions protecting their own ideas ("babies") as well as their own way of developing the programmes. However, the three programmes were very different in nature. The programme in Energy Management addressed a niche not yet explored in Norway, and an area with strong demands, where the international community was ready to accept our new programme. The combination of faculty and staff champions, good programme design, advertising in appropriate journals, and close cooperation with key stakeholders such as the major oil companies, led to an early implementation and expansion of the programme. Speed and dynamism was thus a reality.

The programme in Euromanagement got off to a slow start. There was no apparent strong outside demand. As the result of strong faculty champions with their own networks, as well as a very good programme design, it still started out with some success. The programme in International Strategy and Marketing was even more difficult to get started, as it had no clear market advantage. It was anchored in two faculty groups, marketing and strategy, and nobody emerged with the necessary time and enthusiasm to become an energetic champion.

In the pioneer stage, the programme with the appropriate champions as well as the clear market demand naturally succeeded faster than programmes that were more non-distinct *vis-à-vis* the market-place and more like "orphans" without any obvious champion willing to put in a lot of energy in order to secure their success. However, push from the top by both the administration and the president also played a role. This process of pioneering within the organization was thus a rich process of learning, where both faculty and staff had to learn how to develop such new programmes, in English, across faculty groups, marketed across national borders. As a result, NSM experienced a major shift from being predominantly a Norwegian undergraduate business school, to becoming a more international school, with programmes that are of interest to students from all over the world. So, key elements in learning during the "pioneer" phase are:

- Learning resulting from an induced procedure from the market.
- Learning being catalysed via a programme champion.
- Learning resulting from top-down support and insistence.

Let us now take a closer look at the learning process when we shift from "pioneer" to "expand". We recall that in our first example, programmes developed primarily through faculty members with the relevant interests and networks, and the major challenge was to target organizational learning towards the development of common core courses and administrative structures, in order to reduce costs for the "expand" period—i.e. synergies creation, a hard task! Our second example, considering the shift from evening courses for individuals towards advanced programmes for middle managers paid for by their employers, was to a much larger extent top-down orientated. The strategic change was perceived as critical by top management, programmes were designed primarily by administrators with the support of relevant faculty members, and finally programmes were "sold" both to potential students and to faculty members who were asked to contribute. For these programmes, the institutionalization of the organizational learning across programmes was thus taken care of at the early stages, hence the move to an "expand" phase was in this sense rather easy. However, whereas in the first case, the challenge was the shift from pioneer to expand through a targeted organizational learning effort emphasizing the development of administrative routines and efficiency enhancing synergies across programmes, for the second programme the challenge was rather to mobilize or develop the necessary faculty competence for such programmes. The faculty members with experience and/or potential for such executive education were typically already more than fully booked for other graduate programmes, whereas the faculty members with some slack capacity were not trained in the specialities required. In terms of organizational learning, this was a rather difficult period, but the results achieved were still acceptable, through a combination of recruiting, overtime input of key faculty members, and training of faculty members with potential for such teaching. In addition, the administrative staff did an unusual job in terms of providing support for the overworked faculty. In brief, faculty support was developed through an unusually effective faculty–staff interaction, where both faculty and staff experienced positive learning, which also helped to enhance both the cost efficiency and the external effectiveness and programme quality perceived by the students (executives). To summarize, when it came to learning when going into a rapid "expand" mode there were three lessons:

- Organizational learning about how to create synergies and be resource effective and organized was going slowly in the bottom-up programmes, and was better understood in the top-down programmes.

- However, individual *resistance* to learning was higher in the top-down induced programmes than in the bottom-up programmes. Thus the resulting organizational learning was perhaps not too different in the two cases.
- Staff support was a key catalytic ingredient in speeding up learning at the expand stage.

Our third example is different in the sense that it focuses entirely on efforts directed at the improvement of internal procedures. The previous two examples were both driven by and legitimized by the direct demands of the market. On the contrary, the third example was motivated by resulting internal needs for improved control and direction of faculty member activities, including both research and teaching. It was obvious that the linkage between teaching efforts required by the strategy of the School and the teaching interests of some faculty members was not always coordinated. As a result, as a School we were facing the challenges of how to guide top-down the priorities of faculty members, while at the same time allowing for sufficient bottom-up faculty generation of activities prioritized by them as a scarce resource. Thus, by changing the process context facing the faculty there was an *indirect* way of enhancing focused learning in the "pioneer" and "expand" segments.

This example illustrates one of the challenges involved in the management of academic institutions, namely that the internal context within the School can be managed in such a way so as to enhance learning.

It seems to be the case that strategic directing of organizational learning is not only possible but also desirable. A key vehicle for this might be the planning and incentive process. However, for faculty members to accept and prefer such an enhancement of direction setting by top management, it needs to be supported by a learning process that develops a deeper understanding of the strategic realities and challenges. Maturity in the learning outlook seems to be key!

From our examination of the experiences we had at NSM regarding the introduction of various strategic initiatives—in the form of both teaching programmes and administrative support—we can make several tentative conclusions, or perhaps more appropriately, observations. We should keep in mind the unsystematic, experimental, action-research nature of our data, and the clear limits this gives for us to draw conclusions. Still, we feel that it seems to be the case, when we observe how key strategically induced programmatic and administrative initiatives were taking place in practice, that a lot was hinging on organizational competences, and how to rapidly ameliorate critical gaps through learning.

It seemed to be useful to think about this competence gap-filling and learning as *both* organizational and individual, and many types of competences were involved, from specific knowledge and technology for offering a modern executive education programme to changed attitudes and culture shifts when it came to working for oneself as an individual or as a member of an organization. The various dimensions of FIGURE 10.1 were useful as a means of better mapping out what was going on.

The model of FIGURE 10.2 also seemed to be useful in emphasizing the importance of different learning contexts, depending on the newness of the task ("pioneer", "expand").

Several dimensions seemed to enhance learning, but in different ways depending on the context:

- market push
- the champion-catalyst
- top-down and administrative support

Finally, we saw that major internal administrative procedures, such as workload planning and incentives, can themselves impact the context for learning regarding the direct academic task of creating value through programmes.

REFERENCES

Argyris, C. and Schon, D.A. (1978). *Organizational Learning: A Theory of Action Perspective*. Reading, MA: Addison-Wesley.

Barney, J.B. (1991). Firm resources and sustained competitive advantage. *Journal of Management* **17**(1), 99–120.

Chakravarthy, B.S. and Lorange, P. (1991). *The Essence of Strategy: Managing the Process*. Englewood Cliffs, NJ: Prentice Hall.

Conner, K.R. (1991). A historical comparison of resource based theory and five schools of thought within industrial economics: Do we have a new theory of the firm? *Journal of Management* **17**(1), 121–154.

Cyert, R.M. and March, J.G. (1963). *A Behavioral Theory of the Firm*. Englewood Cliffs, NJ: Prentice Hall.

Itami, H. (1987). *Mobilizing Invisible Assets*. Cambridge, MA: Harvard University Press.

Lorange, P., Scott Morton, M.F. and Ghoshal, S. (1986). *Strategic Control*. St Paul, MN: West.

Løwendahl, B.R. (1992). Global strategies for professional business service firms, PhD thesis, The Wharton School, University of Pennsylvania, Philadelphia, PA.

Nelson, R.R. and Winter, S.G. (1982). *An Evolutionary Theory of Economic Change*. Cambridge, MA: Belknap.

Nordhaug, O. (1993). *Human Capital in Organizations*. Oslo: Scandinavian University Press.

Porter, M.E. (1990). *The Competitive Advantage of Nations*. New York: Free Press.

Prahalad, C.K. and Hamel, G. (1990). The core competence of the corporation. *Harvard Business Review* **63**(3), 79–91.

Rumelt, R.P. (1984). Towards a strategic theory of the firm. In B. Lamb (Ed.) *Competitive Strategic Management* (pp. 556–570). Englewood Cliffs, NJ: Prentice Hall.

Teece, D.J., Pisano, G. and Shuen, A. (1990). Firm capabilities, resources, and the concept of strategy, working paper, University of California at Berkeley, Berkeley, CA.

Thompson, J.D. (1967). *Organizations in Action*. New York: McGraw-Hill.

Wernerfeld, B. (1984). A resource based view of the firm. *Strategic Management Journal* **5**, 171–180.

11

Strategies, Organizational Learning and Careers: The Fall-Out from Restructuring

R. MICHAEL JALLAND, HUGH P. GUNZ

INTRODUCTION

This chapter examines one aspect of a topic that has traditionally been at the heart of strategic management: the link between general managers and strategies. We argue that the new emphasis on organizational learning requires a closer look at the way in which organizations select, develop and promote key strategic decision makers, and in particular how these managers accumulate experience and capabilities on their career paths through organizations. We argue that the upper echelon perspective (Hambrick and Mason, 1984) provides too limited a view of managers engaged in strategic management. Although a major advance on earlier theoretical approaches in which the focus was solely on the chief executive officer (CEO), it does not deal with the constraints acting on strategic change.

Strategic Renaissance and Business Transformation. Edited by H. Thomas, D. O'Neal and J. Kelly.
Copyright © 1995 John Wiley & Sons Ltd.

Delayering and restructuring have become typical features of the renaissance of companies around the world, making this topic particularly relevant now. It is generally believed that different assumptions about the shape of organizations, about career paths and about the capabilities necessary to carry out newly defined jobs have changed the context within which general managers are developed. Strategy issues are being framed differently, often by new managers subject to many pressures novel to them and their predecessors.

Thus, there is something paradoxical about the frequent calls for "learning organizations": they come at a time when devastation is more prevalent than development. As a result, organizations are faced with some difficult questions:

- What kinds of career history and experience produce appropriate general managers?
- What link is there between career systems and organizational learning?
- What impact will changing career contexts have on strategy formation?

We present a framework for examining these problems and point to opportunities for research. The implications for general managers and for organizations are also explored.

The Relationship between Careers and Strategies

Traditionally, the general manager's role has been conceptualized as that of an "integrator", pulling together the efforts of specialists who cope with the changing environment of the business. In relationships with superiors the communication of proposals and the building of understandings about goals strategies and resources are key competencies (Jalland, 1991). Perhaps for this reason, the study of general managers, their responsibilities and their decisions has long been at the heart of the field of strategic management. Although journals and conferences now include a wide range of topics covering both content and process issues, the central assumption remains: at various levels of the firm there are a limited number of key decision makers who are the carriers of the strategy frameworks that guide the enterprise (Andrews, 1971).

More recently, increased emphasis has been placed on the dynamics of the role: the responsibilities for change management and the execution and adaptation of strategies as they evolve. The general manager has been identified as an important actor in the processes of organizational adaptation and learning.

Cognitive aspects of strategy making have also become a focus of interest: calls for increased managerial adaptation and experimentation force renewed attention to the neglected domain of judgement. Once again, this directs regard to the role of the general manager because of the questions it raises about values and choice in the development and adoption of strategies. If experiments demand the interpretation of situations and the impact of organizational actions, then the frameworks that general managers bring to the task are an important area for enquiry.

Until recently, however, little attention has been directed to the antecedents of these frameworks and the way in which the experiences of general managers shape judgements about strategy. Although "values" have been seen as an important input to strategy choices since the early days of business policy as an area of academic study, discussion has been about types of values rather than their sources. The emphasis is on "personal desires, aspirations and needs" and their consequences, and the need to reconcile divergences among senior managers. Little has been written about where these personal desires, aspirations and needs come from.

Some attention has been paid in the literature to the effect of the CEO's background on the direction a firm takes. For example, a number of researchers have tried to see whether their functional backgrounds are reflected in their firms' strategies: are firms with CEOs who have made their careers in, say, marketing more likely to have market-driven strategies than firms led by CEOs with production or finance backgrounds? But much of this work is comparatively atheoretic, and (as in many other undeveloped areas of management theory) prescriptive. For example, it has been argued that the different life cycle stages require different approaches to leadership, so that at a certain point in a growing firm's life, a transition from "entrepreneurial" to "professional" is likely to be needed. The prescription that flows from this is that the situation calls for a change of general manager, because one person is unlikely to be good at both approaches (Gerstein and Reisman, 1983; Gupta, 1984; Porter, 1980; Szilagyi and Schweiger, 1984). These prescriptions are also consistent with the "Formulation → Implementation" paradigm, which until recently dominated thinking about strategic management. Decisions about staffing, structure and systems follow the choice of strategy. The problem with this branch of the literature is, of course, that it tells us little about the origins of the managers who are to be selected. It simply presupposes that they are available in suitable numbers when they are needed.

Much of the systematic work on the relationship between careers and managerial behaviour has been at the individual level of analysis. Managers' career backgrounds are held to have a strong influence on the kind of managers they turn out to be, and the characteristics that they acquire over the course of their careers shape their approach to managing (Bouchet, 1976; Dearborn and Simon, 1958; Walsh, 1988). These individual characteristics are also reflected in their preferences for certain types of strategy over others (Chandler, 1962; Gabarro, 1985) and in the strategic behaviour of their organizations (Ibrahim and Kelly, 1986; Reed and Reed, 1989; Song, 1982).

Upper echelon theory is an important departure from this approach to the field. By focusing on the firm's dominant coalition, it draws attention to the variety of managerial inputs to strategy and strategic change represented in the top management team (Hambrick and Mason, 1984; Virani, Tushman and Romanelli, 1992; Wiersma and Bantel, 1992). The characteristics of the top management team are linked to strategic choices in order to provide causal explanations of organizational progress. Demographics, tenure and the distribution of backgrounds among the key managerial group' are examined for their linkages to the firm's performance.

But upper echelon theory is, in many ways, an extension of the individual level of analysis. It pays little attention to the organizational factors that influence the development of the characteristics of the top management team: the organization is regarded as an externality and part of the "objective situation", but is not explicated further. The organizational variable typically used is the functional track, which dominates the background of a team member and provides one source of variance between managers; yet we know that "functional track" is a comparatively ill-defined concept, given the variety of work experience managers typically have over the course of their careers (Gunz, 1989). Furthermore, restricting the focus to "upper" echelons risks ignoring the contribution of the wider group of "middle" managers to strategy development in the enterprise. There are two reasons why this contribution matters to developing an understanding of the influence careers have on strategic behaviour. Firstly, many writers have pointed out that a realized strategy is the product not only of the efforts of the top management team, but also of the wider group of managers who are responsible for the initiation and execution of strategy initiatives. Secondly, this cadre of managers is also likely to be a major recruitment source for the top management team.

The model we outline in the next section attempts to address these concerns. Its central proposition is that career systems produce the management cadres whose frameworks shape strategies. These career systems are in turn influenced by the realization of these strategies, defining a hitherto neglected mechanism for organizational learning.

A Model of the Linkages between Careers and Strategies

Central to the model in FIGURE 11.1 is the concept of what have been called managerial *rationalities*, or dominant logics (Prahalad and Bettis, 1986). These constitute the way in which managers make sense of their business world. A particular rationality renders certain actions and possibilities "sensible" and "rational", while others are ignored or considered "unrealistic" (Whitley, 1987); the concept is closely linked to that of organizational culture (Schein, 1985) and is, in a sense, a subset of that phenom-

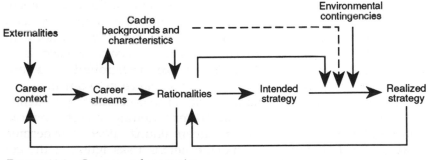

FIGURE 11.1 Careers and strategies

enon. We shall argue that rationalities should be affected by career systems in a number of ways. Firstly, we shall trace the role that rationalities play in the development of the firm's strategic behaviour.

We can expect rationalities to have an important main impact on the firm's intended strategies. For example, if a top management team's interests focus on growth by acquisition rather than organic growth, it would be surprising if their intentional strategies for the company were not of the same kind. But in addition to this main effect, we can also expect a moderator effect between intended and realized strategies. Suppose that a firm has officially decided to become more "customer-orientated". Many large bureaucracies have found to their cost that the success of this programme depends not only on the intentions of the top management team, but also on the beliefs lower down in the organization about what it is there for—that is, the rationalities of managerial cadres other than the upper echelon (Hambrick and Mason, 1984). Indeed, it is not unknown for official declarations to be at odds with the top management rationality. So we can expect rationalities not only to influence intended strategies directly (the main effect), but also their success in becoming realized strategies (the moderating effect).

So how might rationalities be influenced by career systems? In FIGURE 11.1 we show two influences, the first coming from the backgrounds and characteristics of managerial cadres and the second from what we label *career streams*.

Most people would regard the link we have shown between background and characteristics as self-evident: a particular kind of work history is bound to develop certain characteristics in the people who have gone through it. Someone who has spent a lifetime in marketing must, surely, know a lot more about marketing than someone who has not. Here, of course, we are describing an individual-level organizational learning process: people learn from the work they do. They become habituated to select certain approaches to complex situations (March and Simon, 1958) which, for the organization, is manifest in certain kinds of strategic intentions. Our marketing manager, for example, is likely to interpret the situations that he or she encounters as "marketing" problems needing a "marketing" approach (Dearborn and Simon, 1958), and if he or she becomes CEO this is likely to affect the strategic behaviour of the company. More controversially, in the sense that the evidence for the link is very thin (Gunz, 1989), backgrounds may also have an effect on managers' personalities. Jobs in which there is little room for discretion, for instance, may lead to the development of more rigid personalities than those with more room for manoeuvre (Kohn and Schooler, 1983). But if we do accept that managers' backgrounds have an effect on the kinds of managers they are, we can also expect backgrounds to influence the rationality of the group in which they work. For example, managers who have a background in R&D are likely to have a number of characteristics in common, such as a preference for developing innovative technical products. They are likely to reinforce each other in the belief—the rationality—that new product development is "good" management, while cost containment and concentration on marketing existing product lines is "bad".

We have also shown a moderating effect that individual characteristics have on the link between intended strategies and realized strategies (Mintzberg and Waters, 1985). The success of a company, for example, which is trying to diversify into something new is going to be very much influenced by whether or not it has managers who know anything about the new business. American firms trying to open up businesses in Japan need to have managers—or have access to them—who know something about Japan. In other words, managers' characteristics also affect the success with which intentions are realized.

The problem is that the evidence for these linkages is not as evident as one might expect. Not only is the link between background and personality not at all well understood, but the much-quoted finding of Dearborn and Simon, that managers interpret complex situations in terms of their work roles, has proved difficult to replicate (Walsh, 1988). We are not arguing for throwing out the baby with the bathwater, however, but simply for the point that although there is highly likely to be a managerial characteristics–strategy link, it is a little understood one about which too many assumptions should not be made lightly.

So how might careers affect rationalities? At the organizational level of analysis we show a link between career streams and rationalities. Career streams are the patterns of people flows through the hierarchy. The flows may be in many different directions. Traditionally, they are thought of as vertical ladders: systems of progression in which one advances by moving to the next rung up as it falls vacant. But there are many different kinds of move possible in organizations other than straight up. Companies typically have systems for developing their junior staff which involve the staff getting experience in a variety of different functional areas. In mid- to late-career it is common for executives to be moved laterally, for instance to take advantage of their experience or expertise or to cope with the problems of career plateauing. An organization's career streams are the patterns discernible in these flows. The patterns may be sharply defined, such as when the predominant move is upwards through clearly defined hierarchies, or more fuzzy, as in companies in which many different kinds of lateral moves can be found at all levels.

In any organization certain streams typically lead to top positions, while others do not. In some companies it is the "bean counters" who succeed at the expense of their more product-orientated colleagues, while in others it is the engineers. Each stream tends to have its own way of defining good management and sound business practice; that is, its own rationality. But career streams have their origins in the points at which people join organizations, and we can also expect the thinking of more junior managers aiming to move up a particular stream to be affected by the stream's rationality. Proposals reaching the upper echelon will be shaped by the beliefs of its would-be successors about what it is that the upper echelon is interested in.

In order to close the loops shown in FIGURE 11.1, we need to consider briefly how career streams are shaped by contextual factors, one of which might be the firm's realized strategy.

Career contexts are the organizational contexts in which careers take place: the structures over which executives move in order to build their careers, and the systems that shape the careers. For instance, managers in a decentralized, multi-divisional company are likely to encounter the general management role sooner than they might in a centralized, functional organization, if only because in a decentralized structure there are many more general management posts available at more junior levels. A growing organization obviously has more career opportunities than a static one, but equally a diversifying firm will provide opportunities of a different kind from those in a non-diversifying one.

The "career context" is our label for the sum of the factors that make careers in any given organization distinctive of that organization or type of organization. It is, in a sense, the analogue of an organization's environment, sharing with environments the same problems of reification. Just as organizations enact their environments in an attempt to make sense of a puzzling, equivocal world (Weick, 1979), so managers may enact their career contexts in order to make sense of the way control, power and prestige are distributed in their firms. Furthermore, organizations are not closed systems: people join them and leave them at many points in the structure. External labour markets are one way in which externalities affect organizations' career contexts. Others include macroeconomic factors affecting the performance of the firm, legislative changes (especially when they concern employment law) and changes to the age structure of populations.

Realized strategies are one of the influences on the firm's career context. We show this process mediated by rationalities. Firstly, to the extent that the career context depends on observable "facts" about the firm such as its structure, changes to the context depend on managers recognizing that change is needed and deciding on the form the change should take. Managerial rationalities are clearly central to this process in just the same way as they are central to the process of developing intended strategies. Secondly, rationalities must also play a part in the process of enactment to which we argued career contexts are subject.

Because the loop closes we have defined a mechanism of organizational learning, in the sense that the organization's past actions constrain and enable its future ones. Individuals are involved, of course, as their backgrounds shape their characteristics and as they learn the culture (here, the rationality). But our focus is on learning at the organizational level: the way in which organizational phenomena like career contexts, career streams, rationalities, and intended and realized strategies develop over time.

It is important to recognize that the model does not imply that the learning is necessarily what a rational observer would interpret as "good" learning. We explained above that career contexts are enacted by their participants as they try to make sense of why it is that some people make it to the top and others do not. Rationalities come into play here, as we show in FIGURE 11.2, because the way in which people interpret what has "really" happened depends on what their view of "reality" is. Thus, a top management that is bent on a particular course of action will typically interpret everything that happens in such a way as to reinforce their view that they are right, and as a result the career context will continue to nurture the development of people who support them in this view.

SOME IMPLICATIONS OF THE MODEL

CAREERS AS THE ANTECEDENTS OF STRATEGIES

The model describes what we see as some important (and neglected) antecedents of strategy, namely the career-related factors that influence the rationalities of the middle and upper management cadres of organizations. In particular, we are drawing attention to the need to examine more closely the nature of the experiences that constitute a "career" and move beyond simplistic assumptions that functional perspectives dominate managerial thinking. Career paths provide exposure to a variety of situations and project initiatives, which involve a manager in different tasks and roles and develop different characteristics.

These paths across organizations are not easily captured: the histories of successful managers give no indication of routes that lead to less prominent positions. Managers are good at describing their own track records but less able to give other examples and generalize. Spectacular examples of promotion or demotion tend to dominate popular legend in the corridors. Similarly the human resources manager will tend to cite instances where the career paths provide evidence of good company practice, consistent with human resources policies. Thus, methodologies are required that gather data from a wide variety of sources.

The methodologies also need to capture not only the past histories of career streams but also the career prospects for managers, since these are an important set of driving forces influencing the nature of the cadres available to an organization. Most models of motivation agree that people's behaviour is influenced strongly by what they believe will be rewarded. So career prospects are relevant from the broader perspective of the linkage between careers and strategies. What managers expect to be able to achieve in their careers will affect the collective rationalities that are the source of the judgements about intended strategies and about their execution.

STRATEGY VERSUS STRUCTURE

The dynamics of the model are consistent with the basic propositions of the traditional strategy–structure–performance paradigm. The processes of strategy generation, execution and adjustment take place in the right-hand loop of the model (rationalities → intended strategy → realized strategy → rationalities). The feedback from realized strategies via the left-hand loop (rationalities → career context → career streams → rationalities), involving changes in career structures, depends on the adjustment of rationalities. These changes may be lagged and stressful if managements do not recognize the need to act to modify the career context. The stresses arise not just because the tasks of the organization are performed inappropriately, but also—and more perniciously—because of the persistence of the obsolete dominant rationalities that the managers have accumulated. Their experiences have been reinforced by the career expectations established in the old organization. Thus in situations where there is some continuity in management, "structure" may indeed drive strategy, as Peters claims (Peters, 1984).

The model also lends strength to the arguments of those who call for the building of strategies on the basis of "competencies", here identified as part of personal characteristics. In particular, it supports those who argue for a long-term investment in development in managerial cadres (Kerr and Jackofsky, 1989). It draws attention also to the need for careful consideration of the career streams within which those competencies will be developed and enriched; in service industries especially, the retention of those with special talents is a key issue.

CAREERS AND STRATEGIES

The benefit of the model is that it provides a general organizing framework for highlighting what we see as a neglected aspect of strategic management: the importance of career streams as a contributing factor to the generation of strategies. In order to operationalize the model some further clarification of the concepts of career streams and strategies and of the linkage between them is required.

CAREER STREAMS: STRUCTURE AND PROCESS

Earlier, we described career streams as the patterns of people flows through the hierarchy. However, not all posts in the hierarchy are equally open to a manager at each stage of his or her career. The accessible structure in any given organization is defined by the organizational context, which constrains the paths that managers can follow. Operations managers typically find it difficult to move to marketing posts. Divisional boundaries are often marked by unbridgeable chasms, so that transfers even within the same job category are unheard of.

The metaphor that we have found useful to capture the dynamics of this system of structures and flows is the "climbing frame" (UK usage) or "jungle gym" (US usage). Each organization has a set of these laid out within an organizational "playground". Managers move across the climbing frames and a few progress to the routes that lead to the top management team. The shape of the formal structure, the human resources systems, and the changes in these through time dictate the connections or bridges between the climbing frames, and where transitions are likely to be difficult. They also define the openings points for access for entrants from external labour markets.

In previous empirical work Gunz found regularities in the structures and career flows that tend to lead to the top in organizations, and labelled them "organizational career logics" (OCLs) (Gunz, 1989). Four dominant types of OCL have been identified, which differ in terms of the diversity of the operating units in the organizational structure, and the barriers to internal mobility for managers (FIGURE 11.2). The OCLs are:

- Command-centred: firms such as chain retailers or retail banks, in which there are many similar posts, should have OCLs in which managers move from one similar post to another, and if they are successful each post will have larger responsibilities than its predecessor (e.g. a bigger store or bank district). Internal mobility barriers tend to be low, as the firm seeks to move managers around.
- Evolutionary: firms that have typically grown by starting new ventures (growth into the unfamiliar) should have a series of separate career streams which develop as each venture's

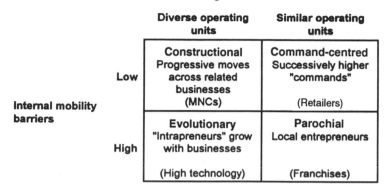

FIGURE 11.2   Organizational career logics

founders build their own business. Operating units are diverse and barriers to mobility are high. Top management emerges from successful venture managers, as at 3M.

- Constructional: firms that have grown into familiar territories but have developed complex structures in which there is a great variety of kinds of managerial job are predicted to have career logics in which managers tend to amass many different experiences over the course of their careers. Mobility is high and there are often well-mapped pathways used by fast track cadres, who move quickly to senior management posts. Large related diversified companies like Shell and Unilever have such structures.
- Parochial: firms where growth comes from local success and few internal career moves are made. Operating units are similar and mobility is low. Top management is recruited from outside for specialist expertise. Franchises and fast food chains tend to have these OCLs.

It is important to note that these OCLs constitute the *dominant*, or modal, patterns: other career logics may well exist in parts of the firm, for example where a retailer is setting up a new venture in manufacturing, or in some technical support function known in the firm as a career "backwater". The dominant logic is the pattern that most closely maps the career stream leading to top management posts.

STRATEGIES AND CAREER STREAMS

Many frameworks have been used to conceptualize strategies in discussions of strategies and careers. Two approaches, narrow and broad, can be distinguished based on the "degree of comprehensiveness or integrative pattern" of the dimensions (Hambrick, 1980).

The "narrow" approach includes the life cycle stage of the firm (Gerstein and Reisman, 1983; Ibrahim and Kelly, 1986; Porter, 1980; Stybel, 1982; Wissema, Brand and Van Der Pol, 1981), "build" *versus* "harvest" strategies (Gupta, 1984; Gupta and Govindarajan, 1984) and Porter's Generic Strategy framework (Gupta, 1984; Porter, 1980). At the corporate level of analysis, product market scope or degree of diversification has been the favoured dimension (Bouchet, 1976; Leontiades, 1982; Smith and White, 1987; Song, 1982; Reed and Reed, 1989; Tichy, Fombrun and Devanna, 1982).

The "broad" or multivariate approach that has dominated enquiry in the area of the relationship between careers and strategy has been the business level multivariate model of Miles and Snow (1978; see also Gunz, 1989; Gupta, 1984; Sonnenfeld and Peiperl, 1988). Although based on the organization's positioning responses it also includes variables relating to its operational competencies and administrative structure and process. It is useful for our purpose because Miles and Snow set out explicit assumptions about the administrative solutions that each of the types tends to adopt.

When we map the OCL types described above onto Miles and Snow's typology we find some interesting relationships.

Firstly, the Prospector characteristics appear to provide an appropriate context for the Evolutionary OCL. The firm operates in dynamic product-markets and promotes venture managers. Managers prove themselves by their successes in finding and exploiting new opportunities. Low formality and decentralization mean that direct interaction is required to resolve conflicts and maintain coordination. Since there are a high proportion of professionals, external mobility can be high, offset by the limitations imposed by the narrowness of the competencies and knowledge acquired while competing in specialist domains.

Secondly, the Defender context is one where the Command-centred OCL is likely to be found: the stable environment and pursuit of efficiency lead to predictable internal promotion paths.

Centralization, an emphasis on planning and relatively high formalization mean that communications are vertical and roles are well defined.

The Analyser context, with its trade-offs between stability and growth, make the Constructional OCL an appropriate way to develop a wide experience base in its managerial cadres. Matrix structures and the variety of control mechanisms often found in such organizations mean that many different sets of managerial competencies are required. However, transferring managers so that they learn inhibits the pursuit of efficiency. At the same time the benefits of the tighter coordination of the Prospector are lost.

CAREERS, STRATEGIES AND LEARNING

The concept of learning has been introduced already at various points in this chapter. As others have noted, this is an elusive concept, subject to a wide variety of interpretations and applied at several levels of analysis (Weick, 1992). Here we are concerned with a model at the organizational level of analysis, and one that has three "loops" of learning (FIGURE 11.1).

The right loop is the sequence of adaptation as rationalities are modified—or not modified—during the application of strategies. The firm's managers observe the outcomes of realized strategies and learn from them; as we have argued, the learning can be either "good" or "bad", depending on the extent to which the process is one of learning from mistakes or confirming prejudices. The left loop describes a process of building experience into the organization through its career processes. Rationalities influence career contexts, in turn affecting the shape of career streams. These build certain kinds of experience into the firm's managers (cadre backgrounds and characteristics) and have direct impacts on the rationalities themselves. The overall learning loop, combining both right and left loops, is the process by which organizations adjust the context for managerial careers as rationalities respond to developments in strategy.

This perspective implies that the process of "fitting managers to strategies" is more complex than the personnel selection task implied in much of the literature. This is not to say that recruitment and appointment processes are unimportant, or that matching job requirements to a manager's characteristics is unnecessary. Rather, it highlights what appear to be some unanticipated consequences of disruption and change.

The starting point for a discussion of these consequences is the observation that the model described above is largely an equilibrium one; that is, firms are in some steady state condition as Prospectors, Defenders or Analysers. They have enough capability to adapt to the domains that they have chosen. The career systems tend to generate appropriate cadres of managers from which appropriate appointments can be made.

The pathologies or potential sources of imbalance in each of the types are indicated by Miles and Snow: market shifts threaten the Defender, wasted effort and resources undermine the Prospector and bad trade-offs topple the Analyser. Still, the inference is that new and purposeful leadership is capable of re-establishing the mix of elements that will lead to renewed growth. This view is consistent with the strategy model, which proposes that organizations go through periods of convergence, when they adapt incrementally, and frame-breaking change, when they go through revolutionary disruptions and reorientate themselves (Tushman, Newman and Romanelli, 1986). The convergence phase is one in which competencies are developed and efficiency and effectiveness improve.

The drawback is, of course, that continuing success leads to self-reinforcing patterns of behaviour and widely shared norms and values. In the context of our model this translates to strong and shared rationalities, which then inhibit change or which allow for only partial responses to the new situation; people make substantial personal investments in their careers, which can strongly inhibit their receptiveness to something new, and the learning they have acquired over the course of their careers may have a similar effect. Career processes, in other words, take place over a long time span, and their effects can be enduring. Even if new strategies are adopted, then it is not clear that new approaches to career systems will be created: right-loop learning takes place but is not linked to left-loop change.

FRAME-BREAKING CHANGE

Frame-breaking change has become accepted as a normal, if infrequent, stage of the strategic management process. Mintzberg's studies support the notion of patterns of progressive modification of strategies interspersed with dramatic moves (Mintzberg, Raisinghani and Theoret, 1976). The events of the 1990s have also reinforced the idea that dramatic shifts in strategy may be required as organizations have faced not one but two phases in the double dip recession. These developments have followed a period in which "speed, simplicity and self-confidence" have become commonplace aspirations, and the search for task redefinition and administrative efficiency become widespread. Continuous process improvement, like other waves of reform to sweep through organizations, has few detractors. Delayering has become common.

From our perspective the interesting questions are then about the return to equilibrium or convergence. Since the successful execution of the new strategy depends on the establishment of new rationalities, much depends on the abilities of the new management to bring about internal reform. Clearly the advent of managers from other organizations, the import of familiars through networks, and appointments of incumbent managers who appear to share the same values are key processes. Anecdotal evidence from, or inspired by, the efforts of Jack Welch at GE supports this and also indicates the importance of management development activities as frame-changing mechanisms (Tichy and Charan, 1989).

However, many managers remain who have been shaped by their previous career experiences and the process of integrating them into the new way of thinking may be a long one. They are likely to be most persuaded by the behaviour of the organization, rather than by "flavour of the quarter" rhetoric, that they should align their long-term aspirations with those of the new leadership. This has conventionally been seen as a problem of reward systems and incentives. Career expectations and prospects are catered for through strategic staffing and the selection of managers according to a human resources plan. The assumption is that managers will respond to the new realities and adapt accordingly.

Our observation is that succession planning is remarkably difficult: even in steady states, departures are only partially predictable, the needs of managers change, for example due to family circumstances, and anticipated high fliers turn out not to be. Thus creating and maintaining an organizational career logic is a continuing task, since an OCL is largely an emergent consequence of the career context.

MANAGERIAL IMPLICATIONS

Restructuring, then, potentially leads to the demolition of the existing career logics. The re-establishment of credible career systems is crucial in the path to restored equilibrium. The key to this process is clarity about the kinds of OCL that the organization wishes to encourage. This then becomes the "vision" which guides the career decisions. In an emergent situation where predictability and planning are inappropriate the approach has to be one of "crafting", an approach now widely discussed in the area of strategic management generally (Mintzberg, 1987). The aim is produce a cadre of managers who together comprise a "pool" of learning.

The prescription that follows from this analysis is that at the business level the dominant OCL should be the one that corresponds to its strategy configuration, so that Prospector businesses, for example, set up the career context to facilitate evolutionary career streams. It is important to note that several OCLs will exist in an organization: within some functional areas a command approach is likely to be the best response to career pathing. In others, such as R&D, career streams may be evolutionary. Some managers will follow a constructional fast track. The OCL that emerges as dominant will generate a pool of managers whose rationalities make them more likely to encourage particular strategies.

The emergence of an inappropriate OCL brings dangers for the organization. Firstly, the response to pressures for strategy change may be limited or slow. In situations where new approaches are required, a manager who has learned in a command career stream may find experimentation difficult. Secondly, the lack of prospects for managers in the non-dominant tracks may bring problems of trust and motivation. The loss of some managers may be expected, but a continuing drain will reduce the variety in the pool of managers.

Similarly, the adoption of a constructional career logic has its dangers. While job rotation and exposure to different parts of the organization can be beneficial, it can also result in superficial acquaintance with the job and its pressures. In situations where in-depth understanding of technologies or processes is crucial for the survival of a business, a pool of peripatetic managers is not likely to provide sustainable competitive advantage.

At the corporate level the problem is more complex, since a variety of business strategy configurations may exist. It is likely that some form of constructional career logic will be in place in order to provide the pool of managers from which the senior executives will be chosen. It will be in the corporate interest to ensure that a wide variety of managerial experience is available to meet the changing needs within the portfolio. This implies special efforts to ensure that entry to this career stream is not restricted to managers from one type of OCL. It follows from this logic that excessive devotion to producing entrepreneurial business-building managers, as seems to be the fashion in current prescriptions for corporate revival, is likely to produce an imbalance in the available pool that a corporation requires for long-run survival.

During the period of readjustment after restructuring, the crafting approach to career stream management requires the regular mapping and monitoring of OCLs. Only if the organization is aware of the quality of the learning pool that is emerging will it be able to make appropriate decisions about management development. Perhaps more important, ongoing OCL diagnosis may provide important signals about the mismatch between the intended and actual career logics in the organization. In an era when careers have become so uncertain and trust between management levels is under threat, a gap between promises and expectations can undermine the best laid recovery plans.

NOTE

A fuller version of this chapter appears in P. Shrivastava, A. Huff and J. Dutton (Eds) (1993). *Advances in Strategic Management*, Vol. 9 (pp. 193–216). Greenwich, CT: JAI Press.

ACKNOWLEDGEMENTS

Our thanks to our colleagues, Martin Evans and Joe D'Cruz, who have made helpful comments during the preparation of this chapter.

REFERENCES

Andrews, K.R. (1971). *The Concept of Corporate Strategy*. Homewood, IL: Richard D. Irwin.

Bouchet, J.-L. (1976). Diversification: Composition of the top management and performance of the firm. Presented at the EGOS Conference on the Sociology of the Business Enterprise, Oxford.

Chandler, A.D., Jr. (1962). *Strategy and Structure*. Cambridge, MA: MIT Press.

Dearborn, D.C. and Simon, H.A. (1958). Selective perceptions: A note on the departmental identification of executives. *Sociometry* **21**, 140–144.

Gabarro, J.J. (1985). When a new manager takes charge. *Harvard Business Review* **63**, 110–123.

Gerstein, M. and Reisman, H. (1983). Strategic selection: matching executives to business conditions. *Sloan Management Review* **24**(2), 33–49.

Gunz, H.P. (1989). *Careers and Corporate Cultures: Managerial Mobility in Large Corporations*. Oxford: Basil Blackwell.

Gupta, A.K. (1984). Contingency linkages between strategy and general manager characteristics: A conceptual examination. *Academy of Management Review* **9**(3), 399–412.

Gupta, A.K. and Govindarajan, V. (1984). Business unit strategy, managerial characteristics, and business unit effectiveness at strategy implementation. *Academy of Management Journal* **27**, 25–41.

Hambrick, D.C. (1980). Operationalizing the concept of business-level strategy in research. *Academy of Management Review* **5**(4), 567–575.

Hambrick, D.C. and Mason, P.A. (1984). Upper echelons: The organization as a reflection of its top managers. *Academy of Management Review* **9**(2), 193–206.

Ibrahim, A.B. and Kelly, J. (1986). Leadership style at the policy level. *Journal of General Management* **11**, 37–46.

Jalland, R.M. (1991). Evergreen planning: Formal planning systems revisited. Presented at the Strategic Management Society Conference, Toronto.

Kerr, J.L. and Jackofsky, E.F. (1989). Aligning managers with strategies: Management development versus selection. *Strategic Management Journal* **10**, 157–170.

Kohn, M.L. and Schooler, C. (1983). *Work and Personality*. Norwood, NJ: Ablex.

Leontiades, M. (1982). Choosing the right manager to fit the strategy. *Journal of Business Strategy* **3**(2), 58–69.

March, J.G. and Simon, H.A. (1958). *Organizations*. New York: John Wiley.

Miles, R.E. and Snow, C.C. (1978). *Organization Strategy, Structure and Process*. New York: McGraw-Hill.

Mintzberg, H. (1987). Crafting strategy. *Harvard Business Review*, **65**, 66–75.

Mintzberg, H. and Waters, J.A. (1985). Of strategies, deliberate and emergent. *Strategic Management Journal* **6**, 257–272.

Mintzberg, H., Raisinghani, D. and Theoret, A. (1976). The structure of "unstructured" decision processes. *Administrative Science Quarterly* **21**(2), 246–275.

Peters, T.J. (1984). Strategy follows structure: Developing distinctive skills. *California Management Review* **26**, 111–125.

Porter, M.E. (1980). *Competitive Strategy: Techniques for Analyzing Industries and Firms*. New York: Free Press/Macmillan.

Prahalad, C.K. and Bettis, R.A. (1986). The dominant logic: A new linkage between diversity and performance. *Strategic Management Journal* **7**(6), 485–502.

Quinn, J.B. (1980). *Strategies for Change and Logical Incrementalism*. Hemel Hempstead, Irwin.

Reed, R. and Reed, M. (1989). CEO experience and diversification strategy fit. *Journal of Management Studies* **26**(3), 251–270.

Schein, E.H. (1985). *Organizational Culture and Leadership*. San Francisco, CA: Jossey-Bass.

Smith, M. and White, M.C. (1987). Strategy, CEO specialization, and succession. *Administrative Science Quarterly* **32**, 263–280.

Song, J.H. (1982). Diversification strategies and the experience of top executives of large firms. *Strategic Management Journal* **3**(4), 377–380.

Sonnenfeld, J.A. and Peiperl, M.A. (1988). Staffing policy as a strategic response: A typology of career systems. *Academy of Management Review* **13**(4), 588–600.

Stybel, L.J. (1982). Linking strategic planning and management manpower planning. *California Management Review* **25**, 48–56.

Szilagyi, A.D., Jr. and Schweiger, D.M. (1984). Matching managers to strategies: A review and suggested framework. *Academy of Management Review* **9**(4), 626–637.

Tichy, N. and Charan, R. (1989). Speed, simplicity and self-confidence. *Harvard Business Review* **5**, 112–119.

Tichy, N.M., Fombrun, C.J. and Devanna, M.A. (1982). Strategic human resource management. *Sloan Management Review* **23**(2), 47–61.

Tushman, M.L., Newman, W.H. and Romanelli, E. (1986). Convergence and upheaval: Managing the unsteady pace of organizational evolution. *California Management Review*, **29**, 29–44.

Virani, B., Tushman, M.L. and Romanelli, E. (1992). Executive succession and organizational outcomes in turbulent environments: An organization learning approach. *Organization Science* **3**(1), 72–91.

Walsh, J.P. (1988). Selectivity and selective perception: An investigation of managers' belief structures and information processing. *Academy of Management Journal* **31**, 873–896.

Weick, K.E. (1979). *The Social Psychology of Organizing*. Reading, MA: Addison-Wesley.

Weick, K.E. (1992). Conceptual options in the study of organizational learning. Presented at the Learning in Organizations Workshop, University of Western Ontario.

Whitley, R.D. (1987). Taking firms seriously as economic actors: Towards a sociology of firm behaviour. *Organization Studies* **8**, 125–147.

Wiersma, M.F. and Bantel, K.A. (1992). Top management team demography and corporate strategic change. *Academy of Management Journal* **35**, 91–121.

Wissema, J.G., Brand, A.F. and Van Der Pol, H.W. (1981). The incorporation of management development in strategic management. *Strategic Management Journal* **2**(4), 361–377.

12

The Development of Empowering Leaders: The Anatomy of a Fast Track

LYNDA GRATTON

INTRODUCTION

The corporate transformations that result in new organizational structures, cultures and working practices are central to the means by which senior executives in many multinational companies strive to achieve competitive advantage. While the popular press may focus on leaders who come in and turn a company around, we know that for these less drastic ongoing corporate transformations, the development and learning is usually the responsibility of senior incumbents (Wiersema, 1992). This places real emphasis on the capability of the current and future executive cadre to refigure their own skills, behaviours and competencies to facilitate and reinforce the process of transformation.

This chapter reports on how the current senior executive group in one multinational company faced up to the challenge of re-aligning executive competencies to meet the needs of transformation, and describes the issues and problems they encountered in doing so. The core of the transformational process in the company

Strategic Renaissance and Business Transformation. Edited by H. Thomas, D. O'Neal and J. Kelly.
Copyright © 1995 John Wiley & Sons Ltd.

was a gradual re-alignment from a bureaucratic, command-and-control structure to one in which responsibility would be devolved into team-based, networked businesses. The transformation involved many changes, which included the movement from hierarchical layers to team-based activities; from narrow single-task jobs to whole process multiple-tasks; from a management role of direction and controlling to one of coaching and facilitation; from top-down leadership to sharing with the team; from job processes based on management planning and control to team planning and learning.

It was argued within the senior executive group that this team-based, networked structure would require executive competencies and behaviours very different from those that had previously flourished. The current executive cadre had evolved in what Jaques (1989) has termed the "accountability hierarchy", in which they had been motivated and rewarded to behave as highly autonomous individuals who find a common ground of accountability to pursue their ambitions, need for achievement and personal enhancement. To understand in more detail the likely requirements for future executives, the company had commissioned a future-orientated executive competency profile (Boyatzi, 1982). This revealed that while the well-understood executive competencies of strategic vision, impact, action-orientation and negotiation had a role to play, they were balanced by an emphasis on a whole new set of competencies. These included team building, networking, empowering and influencing. The results of the future-orientated competency profile mirrored the views of those researchers who, in the past decade, have described these "new" competencies. For example, Bennis (1985) believes the task of those executives involved in transformation is to enable significant employees to feel that they make a difference and are joined in a common purpose; Burke (1986) describes them as rewarding followers informally with personal recognition; Conger and Kanungo (1988) as expressing confidence in their subordinates, fostering opportunities for them to engage in decision making and providing autonomy from bureaucratic constraints.

One of the key issues this senior executive group faced was the current and future capability of their executives to behave in these "new" ways. To understand this issue further they engaged in a whole in-depth diagnostic survey of the strengths and development needs of the current and future executive cadres.

KEY ASPECTS OF THE COMPANY'S EXECUTIVE DEVELOPMENT SYSTEMS: THE FAST TRACK

Before describing the results of the diagnosis it may be useful to describe briefly the human resource processes that currently support the selection and development of senior executives. This company, like most large companies (Granick, 1972; Poole et al., 1981), selects the majority of senior executives from the internal labour market with limited recourse to the external labour market. This has the advantage of creating executive cadres with both a breadth and depth of company knowledge, who are well networked and who have high company loyalty. The implication for executive change is that the majority of people who will be taking leading roles in creating the organization 15 years hence are already in place.

The appraisal, reward and development of this critical high-potential group is managed in this company through a process often referred to as a "fast track". This process, which has been widely adopted in both American and European companies (Brooklyn Derr, Jones and Toomey, 1988) has a number of characteristics, the benefits of which are described in TABLE 12.1.

Five major characteristics are presented. In the first characteristic, the identification of management talent from the total population takes place when individuals are in their mid- to late 20s. This early intervention allows rapid career progression, which ensures that maximum time is available for varied job experience. (Thompson, Kirham and Dixon (1985) quote an average time in each job of 12–36 months.) The early identification of talent also has the benefit of creating a strong psychological contract with the individual, who is treated in a special way and can begin the long process of deferred gratification, where short-term inconvenience through mobility and job pressure is offset against the possibility of long-term promotion, power and resource gains (Roche, 1975; Stinchcombe, 1983; Veiga, 1981). The second characteristic, the tournament process, encourages high-potential individuals to compete with each other to remain on the fast track. Regular "cullings" of less successful fast-track incumbents takes place at about three-year intervals. This ensures that only those people with the necessary drive and determination (often perceived in hierarchical companies to be key attributes of success) progress to senior positions in the organization (Rosenbaum, 1979). The tour-

TABLE 12.1   Executive development: characteristics and benefits of the fast track

Characteristics	Benefits
1. Early identification of high-potential talent by the line manager	Maximizes possibility of career intervention
	Creates psychological contract
2. Tournament process	Maximizes drive and determination
	Keeps talent pool manageable
3. Cross-functional and international job placement	Creates breadth of knowledge
	Creates networks across executive group
4. Accelerated vertical progression	Ensures rapid grade ascent
	Strengthens psychological contract
5. Extended senior executive interest and support	Establishes mentor and coaching relationships
	Ensures cross-business job experiences gained
	Reassures through the provision of a "visible" talent pool

nament also has the advantage of keeping the fast-track pool to a manageable size.

A third characteristic and key outcome of the fast-track process is the delivery of varied and cross-functional job experience, often linked with the acquisition of international experience. Individuals are moved across functions and across businesses, spending a limited time in each place. Cross-functional and international experience has the real benefit of ensuring that people have a breath of understanding and are capable of taking a multi-functional approach to the complex problems with which they are faced. The breath of experience also creates the networked relationships that are so critical for implementing change (Moss Kanter, 1984). This breath of job experience is closely integrated with the fourth characteristic, accelerated vertical promotion. To get to the top, and progress through multiple job levels fast-track individuals realize that they must keep to a rapid career progression; any flattening of the trajectory will result in them missing their target job. This rapid promotion also has the advantage of strengthening the bonds of the psychological contract, the rate of promotion playing the role of a key intrinsic reward.

Interwoven through all of these activities is the amount of senior-management attention enjoyed by fast-track participants. This, the fifth characteristic, is expressed through both close mentoring and coaching relationships, and the provision of formalized senior management committees in which the potential and career paths of high-potential individuals are discussed. This senior-management involvement is often critical to the success of the process. The relationship between the current and future senior executives creates important mentoring and coaching roles, while the proximity of the senior executives provides a series of role models. The presence of a cross-business committee tasked with the corporate development of high-potential people increases the likelihood of participants moving across businesses. Without this process, the "barons" of the individual functions and businesses concentrate on developing the potential in their own "patch". The visibility of future executives to current executives can also go some way to reducing current executives' fears and anxiety about the future of the company. Individuals in the fast track are a high profile and constant reminder that the company (and the human resource function) cares about the future and is making adequate provision.

This fast-track process, with its accelerated promotion for high-potential individuals, was designed 20 years ago to meet the needs of an organization very different from that envisaged in the transformational process. A critical issue for the senior executive group was the capacity of the process to develop and reinforce the "new competencies". How capable are those on the fast track at behaving in the team-based, involving, empowering manner that would be so critical to future success?

A number of studies have highlighted the possibility that these behaviours may well be underdeveloped and not part of an executive's "formulae for success". This evidence comes from observation of executive behaviour (Luthens, Rosenkrantz and Hennessy, 1985), insights from questionnaire and psychometric analysis (Drath, 1990; Norburn and Schurz, 1984) and in-depth executive studies (Kaplan, 1990; Kofodimos, 1990).

In the study by Luthens, Rosenkrantz and Hennessy, the researchers report that while those executives who have experienced most rapid promotion were observed to spend significantly more time networking, they spend significantly less time performing activities classified as motivating and reinforcing. These included giving credit, listening, delegating, backing a subordinate and letting subordinates determine how to do their own work. Similarly, Drath (1990) reports that the executives he has studied scored low in the area of "confronting others skilfully" or "dealing with problem subordinates". He argues that when interpersonal feeling becomes personal and less task-based executives tend to run away from conflict or deal with it aggressively. They are not able to operate constructively through intense, immediate emotion. A study in 1984 by Norburn and Schurz of 450 UK managing directors reported that the executives were "more likely to be authoritarian. They do not consider social adaptability, concern for people, loyalty and lateral thinking are likely to enhance executive success". Kaplan (1990) has described executives as seeking achievement and with a distinct and separate sense of self, frequently at the expense of intimate relationships. This striving for mastery, power, achievement and self-assertion can have negative consequences. Kofodimos (1990) has described some of the executives she observed as hyperactive, impatient, callous, insensitive, overly confident and ambitious and self-serving.

It has been argued that many executives are at what Kegan (1982) has described as the institutional stage of development with a highly established sense of self-autonomy and "self authorship". Interpersonal relationships are externalized and objectified, and in doing so the feelings connected to interpersonal relationships lose their power to shape and reflect the self, and instead are reflected on by the self. In objectifying feelings, executives are able to make effective interpersonal relationships (Gabarro, 1987). They are good at communicating with each other, can generate respect in a hierarchy, can be object and tough in decision making and are well equipped for working relationships based on mutual respect and performance of duty. But, as Drath (1990) has argued, the difficulty they have with empowering and team building is around sharing responsibility and control with their subordinates and their organizations.

To summarize, experiences of executives in other situations suggests that the behaviours required of team-based, networked structures are not well developed in the general executive population. The senior executive group were keen to understand the particular configuration of competencies within their own future senior executive cadre.

THE COMPETENCIES OF THE HIGH-POTENTIAL CADRE

To answer this question the strengths and development needs of the company's high-potential cadre was examined in some detail. The findings come from a group of 109 people who represent 60% of those on the fast track; their age ranged from the youngest (28) to those at the end of the programme (45), after which people come off the track and enter senior executives roles. The group are multinational, with the majority (52%) employed at middle management grades.

The diagnosis consisted of a 360° feedback process in which the views of bosses, peers and subordinates of the high-potential group were collected (1038 people in total). Each individual filled in the "Collegiate Review" for themselves and selected up to 10 people to send it to. They were encouraged to send it to their boss (or bosses), peers and subordinates. The completed questionnaires were returned to the researcher, who provided in-depth data to the individual and synthesized group data to the senior executives. The Collegiate Review contained a questionnaire and an open-format section.

Questionnaire

The 41-item questionnaire contained seven sections referring to strategic vision and direction; action orientation; problem analysis and decision making; networking and building channels of communication; team building and empowering; personal impact; and adaptability and independence. Performance was rated on a six-point, behavioural anchored scale. Examples of items from the first and last section are shown below:

Demonstrates, with actions and behaviour, a clear strategy for where his/her group is going.	Appears to have no strategy of where his/her group or function is going.
Prepared to take an independent view, to question the status quo.	Inclined to agree with others; does not question the status quo.

Open-Format Section

Observers were also asked to describe "in their own words" the individuals' strengths and development needs. The resulting textual information was content analysed into 92 bi-polar categories. The majority of these bi-polar categories represented a strength at one end and a development need at the other. Examples of the bi-polar categories are:

Joint problem solving:
Engages in joint problem solving.

Fails to take into consideration others' views when problem solving.

Problem analysis:
Takes time to analyse problems.

Fails to take time on analysis, jumps to conclusions.

To provide an overview of the qualitative data, the 92 categories were further clustered into 22 themes. The top 10 ranked themes are shown in FIGURE 12.1 (strengths) and FIGURE 12.2 (development needs). These figures also illustrate the rater group differences, with the percentage of each rater group who used the categories in the theme to describe an individual. The bars show the mean across all of the rater groups and the asterisk those themes with significant statistical rater differences (analysed by cross-tabulations with chi-square).

The quantitative data from the questionnaire allowed sophisticated statistical manipulation of the information and provided insights into the relationships between the observer groups. The qualitative information, from the written comments, provided an opportunity for individuals to highlight areas they deemed important using their own words and concepts. The richness and depth of this information gave real insights into the ways in which the groups were perceived. (See Gratton and Pearson (1993) for a more detailed description of the methodology and results.)

KEY FINDINGS FROM THE DIAGNOSTIC PROCESS

From quantitative and qualitative data three key findings emerged that were particularly interesting for the senior

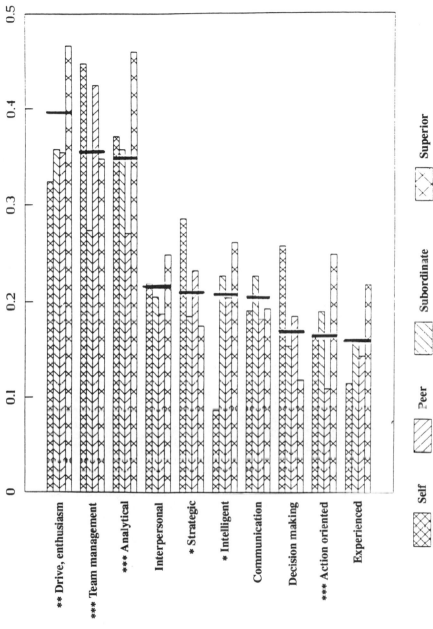

FIGURE 12.1 Strengths: the 10 most frequent themes, percentage of raters to cite each theme

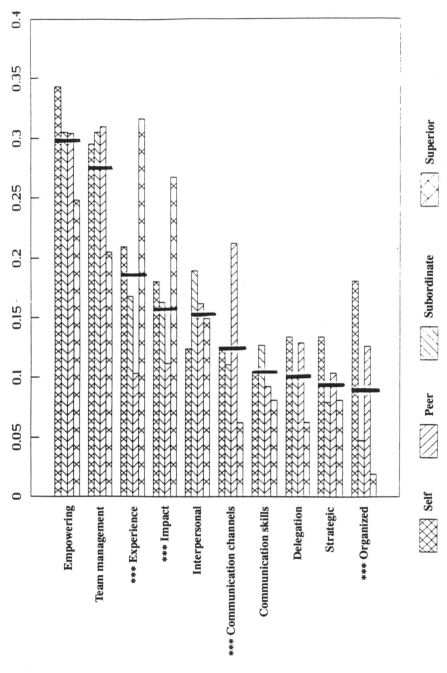

Percentage of raters to cite each theme

Themes (order of total group frequency)

Empowering
Team management
*** Experience
*** Impact
Interpersonal
*** Communication channels
Communication skills
Delegation
Strategic
*** Organized

 Self Peer Subordinate Superior

FIGURE 12.2 Development needs: the 10 most frequent themes, percentage of raters to cite each theme

executive group. These findings are summarized briefly as follows:

- Finding 1: the strengths of the high-potential cadre reflected individualistic, goal orientated behaviour. Their "winning formulae" derives from intelligence, drive, action orientation and commitment. Their development needs reflect the difficulty they may have in team building, delegation and involving others.
- Finding 2: however, contrary to past research, which has suggested that individuals have limited awareness of their development needs, many of this high-potential cadre realize that their team and empowering skills require substantial development.
- Finding 3: the bosses systematically gave higher performance ratings than any other observer group and were the least likely to believe that the cadre's team building and empowering skills needed development.

A more detailed description of the findings and their implications are presented in the following section.

FINDING 1: "WINNING FORMULAE" BASED ON TALENT AND MOTIVATION

The "winning formulae", or the five top ranked strengths as described by all four groups (the individuals themselves, their bosses, peers and subordinates), are:

1. Energetic and hard-working (72)
2. Analytical ability (63)
3. Intelligence (46)
4. Ability to communicate (43)
5. Determination and commitment (40)

The figures in brackets refer to the number of the group for whom two or more people (including themselves) described the category as a strength. Clearly much of the success of this high-potential group comes from the individual talents and motivations they bring to their jobs. The team-based, empowering skills, which the senior executives group believed to be so critical to the future success of the transformed company, are not currently a central means by which the group or their colleagues believe they achieve success. On the contrary, two of these team-based empowering behaviours are seen as major development needs. Looking at the top ranked development needs, 42 of the high-potential people are described by two or more people as expecting too much, and being impatient and insensitive, and 26 as being abrasive. A proportion of the group were described by two or more people as failing to take others' views into consideration (29), unable to build teams (28) and unable to keep communicating channels open and share information (22).

With regard to their broader development needs, they needed more experience managing people (42), more commercial experience (31) and more functional or technical experience (26).

Implications of Finding 1

This diagnostic data was explored and discussed by the senior executive group who believed it had a number of fundamental implications for the transformation process:

• The transformational process must be accompanied by a far-reaching review of the way in which executives are selected, promoted, rewarded and developed. In particular, the fast-track model must be scrutinized to ascertain its appropriateness to the transformed company and its ability to develop and reinforce team-based and empowering behaviours.
• In the short term, the team building and empowering capabilities of the high-potential cadre must be addressed through a series of internal and external programmes, some of which are discussed later.

FINDING 2: HIGH LEVEL OF SELF-AWARENESS

It has been widely assumed that individuals' tend to overestimate their own performance and underestimate their development needs (Mabe and West, 1982; Thornton, 1980). For this high-potential group this was not the case. As FIGURES 12.1 and 12.2 demonstrate, the individuals are as aware as their peers and subordinates of their empowering and team management development needs.

Implications for Finding 2

This high level of self-insight reinforced for the senior executive group the key role that the individual could play in his or her own development. In the past this company, like many others, had operated development processes that were essentially paternalistic. Development was something that was "done" to an executive, and to a large extent the management of an executive's career was outside his or her sphere of responsibility. These findings reinforced the importance in the transformed company of moving from this paternalistic attitude to one of involvement and "partnership". The involvement of individuals in their own development was judged to be one of the centre-pieces of the re-aligned fast track.

FINDING 3: THE VIEWS OF THE BOSS

The third critical finding to emerge from the diagnosis was the very particular view taken by the boss (in most cases current senior executives). It was clear that compared to peers or sub-ordinates, the boss had a rather different view of the high-potential individuals' performance. This is perhaps best illustrated with a statistical analysis of the results of the 41 questions from the first part of the questionnaire. A factor analysis of the questionnaire revealed five underlying factors, which were termed team leadership; independence and decisiveness; energy and effort; adaptability and pragmatism; and strategy and vision. For the first three of these clusters the bosses' average rating was significantly higher than the rating of any other group. Further, a multi-trait multi-rater correlation matrix (which examines the correlation between all three observer groups), showed that the highest correlations existed between the ratings of peers and subordinates (factor correlations ranged from 0.30 to 0.42) and the lowest between peers/subordinates and the boss. This shows clearly that the response of the bosses (the current senior executive group) to the high-potential cadre (the future senior executive group) is rather different to the responses of peers or sub-ordinates. This difference is further explored in FIGURES 12.1 and 12.2, which relate to the open-format information. Bosses are less likely to comment on development needs in the areas of empow-ering, team management, communication skills, delegation and organizing. In comparison, the peer and subordinate groups have rather similar views of performance and are more likely to cite development needs in the empowering, team building and com-munication areas.

Why do the differences between the views of the boss, peer and subordinate groups arise, and what, if anything, does this tell us about these people? It may be that when rating perfor-mance or describing strengths and development needs, the observer groups compare against their own idiosyncratic "models" of executive effectiveness (Tsui and Ohlott, 1988). The model of effectiveness used by peers and subordinates, for example, may have empowering and team building as central aspects. In contrast, the bosses' model of what makes for effec-tiveness places emphasis on drive, enthusiasm, analytical skills and action orientation. An alternative explanation would be that observers differ in their opportunity to observe and, in parti-cular, peers and subordinates have greater opportunity to observe at more revealing times when team-based skills could (or count not) be shown (Latham and Wexley, 1982; Lawler, 1967). Or perhaps, the high-potential group places greater emphasis on managing upwards to their bosses (who are conse-quently more impressed), than downwards to subordinates or across to peers.

Implications for Finding 3

When rating or describing the performance of these future senior executives, current senior executives do not appear to emphasize empowering or team management as highly as other groups. As such, their view is not as complete as that gained by 360° feedback.

Secondly, as a consequence, the boss is not necessarily in the most appropriate position to rate or comment on empowering, teamwork or lateral communications. This has implications for the way in which an individual's potential performance and develop-ment needs are described and appraised. More specifically, it emphasizes the role played by the team and peers in performance management and upwards feedback.

In their discussion of these diagnostic findings, the senior executive group believed that a re-alignment of the executive development architecture was required. It was realized that while the process had worked well at promoting and shaping executives who were capable of effectiveness in the pre-transformation company, it would be much less able to service the post-transformation needs.

Furthermore, the very characteristics that brought the benefits described in TABLE 12.1 had, to some extent, created an administrative heritage ill suited to support the development of a team-based, networked company. In particular, the five characteristics had implications that would need to be addressed.

Characteristic 1

The early identification of high-potential talent by line management favours those people who mature early and consequently reduces the diversity of the "gene pool". Further, it could be argued that the central role played by the line manager in identifying potential underplays team-based, empowering skills, and overplays upward management skills.

Characteristic 2

The tournament process focuses "contestants" on "looking good (which is assessed) rather than performing (which is not)" (Hirsch, 1985). It also curtails the frank and open exchange that these high-potential individuals could have about their real needs, aspirations and motivations.

Characteristic 3

Cross-functional and international job placement and the rapid job movement associated with it can have perhaps the most damaging impact on the development of team building, empowering skills. With such rapid movement, high-potential individuals focus on short-term projects that lead to dramatic results rather than team involvement and development (Thompson, Kirkham and Dixon, 1985). Too rapid movement and promotion can emphasize short-termism and upward focus and management, and can also reduce the learning opportunities around tough people issues. Drath (1990) is one of a number of people who argue that the development of open-empowering behaviours must take place over time and in a team where the manager learns to empathize, trust and delegate. For many high-potential people in this and other companies, the rapidity of their job movements has the result that they move jobs before this empathy develops and before they have to deal with tough people problems, like motivating underperforming team members. As a consequence they rely on their innate aptitude as their "winning formulae".

Characteristic 4

Accelerated vertical progression has the impact of putting pressure on young executives to remain mobile throughout the early part of their career. This can have a very negative impact on those with young families or in dual careers. By making these personal compromises they develop an emotional "shield", which can reduce their ability to emphathize.

Characteristic 5

The extended senior executive interest and support enjoyed by the high-potential group increases the emphasis on upward management and reinforces the paternalistic, hierarchical nature of the organizational structure.

After reviewing the diagnostic information the senior executive group came to a number of conclusions about the human resources processes supporting executive development. They agreed that while the current executive development processes and fast-track process had worked well in supporting the pre-transformational hierarchical company, they were not well placed to serve past-transformational requirements. In the review of the executive development architecture, the senior executive group agreed to place emphasis on three processes to support the needs of the transformation.

PROCESSES TO SUPPORT THE TRANSFORMATION

The decision was taken to make three major interventions: the creation of personal development plans, the increasing use of 360° feedback and the re-alignment of the fast-track process.

PROCESS 1: CREATION OF PERSONAL DEVELOPMENT PLANS

Executives capable of succeeding in the transformed company must have a greater level of awareness of their own strengths and development needs, their career aspirations and how these can be fulfilled. From this self-awareness comes a learning agenda that creates flexibility and an emphasis on teamwork and the development of trust. To support this each high-potential individual participated in a process designed to increase their self-awareness through structured 360° feedback and a series of psychometric and personality tests. Following this heightened self-awareness individuals became more able to understand their own skills and develop team awareness.

PROCESS 2: PERFORMANCE MANAGEMENT AND THE USE OF 360° FEEDBACK

It is apparent from the data discussed earlier that the boss is not necessarily in the best position to make an accurate judgement of an individual's empowering or team-based skills. In the past, the central role played by the boss in the appraisal process served to reinforce upward management behaviours and the hierarchical power structures of the organization.

The decision was taken to make increasing use of 360° feedback (i.e. from peers and subordinates) to provide information for development appraisal and performance management. This would form a central mechanism to appraise and reward the maintenance of team-based, empowering behaviours.

PROCESS 3: RE-ALIGNING THE FAST TRACK

The review of the fast-track process suggested that a number of re-alignments should take place.

Job assignments, particularly at the beginning of the career, should be lengthened, with greater use made of projects, task-forces and lateral job moves. This was designed to encourage people to come to terms with people issues, to gain confidence from teamwork and to develop empathy and trust.

The personal development plans should play a central role in career discussions between individuals and senior executives to ensure that partnership rather than paternalism was reinforced.

The one entry tournament fast track should be abandoned and replaced by a cohort approach (Demb and Brooklyn Derr, 1989) that allows talent to emerge at any career stage and reduces the level of competition between people.

The reward and grade system should be re-aligned to reinforce team rather than individual performance and emphasize lateral skill-based development rather than vertical promotion.

DISCUSSION

The means by which the senior executive group re-aligned the human resource systems to meet the needs of the transformed organization highlights a number of issues and observations.

THE ROLE OF DIAGNOSTIC DATA

This chapter reports on a series of fundamental changes to the career development, training and performance management processes of a company. A major catalyst for this change was the in-depth diagnosis of the future senior executive cadre. This diagnosis demonstrated to the current senior executive group the gap between the future requirements of senior executives (described in the future-orientated competency profile) and the ways in which the current high-potential cadre gained success (described in the 360° feedback). More importantly, it became clear to the senior executive group that the current executive competencies, human resource and career systems placed a real threat to successful completion of the organizational transformation. This sense of risk and urgency unleashed management energy and commitment, which allowed the rapid instigation of the range of interventions described earlier.

THE GENERALIZABILITY OF THE FINDINGS

How generalizable are these findings, in particular the limited prevalence of empowering and team-based competencies in this high potential group? The process of collecting 360° feedback has since been repeated in four other large companies. Similar results were found, and in the case of two companies (with a highly developed technical talent pool), the empowering and team building capabilities were at a significantly lower level of development. I would argue that, except in those companies that have actively created processes to reward and develop team and empowering competencies, the results reported here are generalizable. This would suggest that executives in most large, hierarchical companies have limited team-building and empowering skills. Unless this issue is raised and addressed they and the human resource processes that support them have the potential to create a major resistance to change in the longer term.

THE ROLE OF HUMAN RESOURCE PROCESSES IN CORPORATE TRANSFORMATION

It has been my experience of corporate transformation that too little attention is paid to the human resource systems and processes, both in terms of their ability to be a major force for change, or, as in this case, a major force against change. In the case described earlier, it became clear to the senior executive group that fundamental changes in the fabric of the human resources processes had to occur. However, in my view, too often transformation is attempted against a backdrop of antiquated and hierarchical appraisal systems, reward systems that reinforce individual competitiveness, promotion systems based on competitive tournaments, and training focused simply on technical skills (Gratton, 1994).

ACKNOWLEDGEMENT

I would like to thank Jill Pearson for her support in collecting and analysing the data.

REFERENCES

Bennis, W. and Nanus, B. (1985). *Leaders*. New York: Harper & Row.

Boyatzi, R. (1982). *The Competent Manager: A Model for Effective Performance*. New York: John Wiley.

Brooklyn Derr, C., Jones, C. and Toomey, E.L. (1988). Managing high-potential employees: Current practices in thirty-three US corporations. *Human Resource Management* 27(3), 273–290.

Burke, W. (1986). Leadership as empowering others. In S. Srivastra (Ed.) *Executive Power* (pp. 51–77). San Francisco, CA: Jossey-Bass.

Conger, J.A. and Kanungo, R.N. (1988). The empowering process: Integrating theory and practice. *Academy of Management Review* 13(3), 471–482.

Demb, A. and Brooklyn Derr, C. (1989). Managing strategic human resources: Leadership for the 21st century. *European Management Journal* 7(2).

Drath, W.H. (1990). Managerial strengths and weaknesses as functions of the development of personal meaning. *Journal of Applied Behavioral Science* 26(4), 483–499.

Gabarro, J.J. (1987). The development of working relationships. In J.W. Lorsch (Ed.) *Handbook of Organizational Behaviour*. Englewood Cliffs, NJ: Prentice Hall.

Granick, D. (1972). *Managerial Comparisons of Four Developed Countries: France, Britain, United States and Russia*. Cambridge, MA: MIT Press.

Gratton, L. (1994). Implementing strategic intent: Human resource processes as a force for change. *Business Strategy Review* 5(1), 47–67.

Gratton, L. and Pearson, J. (1993). Empowering leaders: The evidence for their existence, working paper, Centre for Organisational Behaviour, London Business School.

Hirsch, W. (1985). Flying too high for comfort. *Manpower Policy and Practice* 1.

Jaques, E. (1989). *Requisite Organization*. Kingston, NY: Cason Hall.

Kaplan, R.E. (1990). *Character Shifts: The Challenge of Improving Executive Performance Through Personal Growth*, report no. 143. Greensboro, NC: Center for Creative Leadership.

Kegan, R. (1982). *The Evolving Self: Problems and Processes in Human Development*. Cambridge, MA: Harvard University Press.

Kofodimos, J.R. (1990). Using biographical methods to understand managerial style and character. *Journal of Applied Behavioral Science* **26**(4), 433–456.

Latham, G.P. and Wexley, K.N. (1992) *Increasing Productivity Through Performance Appraisal*. Reading MA: Addison Wesley.

Lawler, E.E. (1967). The multi-trait, multi-rater approach to measuring managerial job performance. *Journal of Applied Psychology* **51**, 369–381.

Luthens, F., Rosenkrantz, S. and Hennessy, H. (1985). What successful managers really do. *Journal of Applied Behavioral Science* **21**, 255–270.

Mabe, P.A. and West, S.G. (1982). Validity of self-evaluation of ability: A review and meta-analysis. *Journal of Applied Psychology* **67**, 280–296.

Moss Kanter, R. (1984). *The Change Masters: Corporate Entrepreneurs at Work*. London: George Allen and Unwin.

Norburn, D. and Schurz, F.D. (1984). The British boardroom: Time for a revolution. *Long Range Planning* **17**, 42.

Poole, M., Mansfield, R., Blyton, P. and Frost, P. (1981). *Managers in Focus: The British Manager in the Early 1980s*. Aldershot: Gower.

Roche, G.R. (1975). Compensation and the mobile executive. *Harvard Business Review* **53**(6), 53–62.

Rosenbaum, J.E. (1979). Tournament mobility: Career patterns in a corporation. *Administrative Science Quarterly*, June.

Stinchcombe, A.L. (1983). *Economic Sociology*. New York: Academic Press.

Thompson, P.H., Kirkham, K. and Dixon, J. (1985). Warning: the fast track may be hazardous to organisational health. *Organizational Dynamics* spring, 21–33.

Thornton, G.C. (1980). Psychometric properties of self-appraisals of job performance. *Personnel Psychology* **33**, 263–272.

Tsui, A.S. and Ohlott, P. (1988). Multiple assessment of managerial effectiveness: inter-rater agreement and consensus in effectiveness models. *Personnel Psychology* **41**, 779–803.

Veiga, J.F. (1981). Do managers on the move get anywhere? *Harvard Business Review* **59**(2), 20–42.

Wiersema, M.F. (1992). Strategic consequences of executive succession within diversified firms. *Journal of Management Studies* **29**, 20–40.

13

Strategy Design, Learning and Realization: Exploring Designing under Conditions of Major Change

WIM OVERMEER

CONVERGENCE ON THE IMPORTANCE OF STRATEGIC LEARNING

Over the past decade an increasing number of mature companies have experienced difficulties in responding to environmental shifts that require a major change in their corporate strategy. By the early 1990s, there were two broad frameworks, developed to help executives. The "rational" approach prescribes a design process driven by the corporate office, aimed at "positioning" the company in relation to its competitors (Porter, 1980, 1985). To fully exploit a niche in an evolutionary fashion (Andrews, 1971), the approach focusses on "coherence" among business unit plans and on implementation through administrative systems. The

Strategic Renaissance and Business Transformation. Edited by H. Thomas, D. O'Neal and J. Kelly.
Copyright © 1995 John Wiley & Sons Ltd.

"natural" approach describes a design process grounded in "creative" actions of managers anywhere in the organization (Mintzberg, 1987; Mintzberg and McHugh, 1985; Mintzberg and Waters, 1982). In "revolutionary" times, such actions can become emerging strategies that form the basis for a new configuration.

To address the difficulties firms have in making a major change in corporate strategy, these frameworks have converged on the importance of "strategic learning" through an interactive process between formulation and implementation, or between deliberate and emerging strategy. However, the idea for this interaction is often presented in passing, at the end of theorizing. How it *actually* occurs in everyday practice, what difficulties company executives encounter during this process, and how these may be effectively addressed is not yet well articulated. Based on an in-depth field study, this chapter probes beyond this prescription and inquires into the assumption that interactive learning will occur during *realization* of strategy. It points to powerful underlying organizational dynamics undermining the interaction and preventing strategic learning.

THE RESEARCH PROJECT

This chapter reports on how one very successful company, a medium-sized, east coast, real estate development firm with the pseudonym Citadel actually organized itself when making a major strategic change. It was selected because (i) the firm had repeatedly made successful major strategic changes in response to environmental shifts, typically about every 10 years over the past 4 decades, and (ii) the CEO granted access to senior management in exchange for advice on how to address an escalating conflict between two divisions—a new hotel division that plans and operates hotels, and a project management division that actually builds them. The conflict between the divisions had emerged after a major strategic change.

Three years after the change, the researcher and the corporate planner conducted 42 interviews with all senior managers, several key business partners (such as architectural firms) and two academic consultants to top management. This chapter reports on how senior executives designed a new strategy through a rich and complex process of strategic experimentation when they faced a major shift in the environment. This process is considerably different from the rational approach, and is more in line with the natural approach. This chapter also reports on how at the same time executives were relatively unaware of the experimental aspect of the design process, how they had contradictory assessments of the design, and how they neither discussed nor inquired into their differences. As a result they left a key resource in learning a new strategy untapped and failed to grasp a stable set of rules for design of strategy which the firm had used for a long period of time and which accounted for its success. Executives were initially unaware of a mismatch between these design rules and the new corporate environment, and did not appreciate a set of complex organizational issues during the realization of a new strategy. Their lack of access to the firm's actual design rules led to an emerging conflict among themselves about the firm's direction, which, in turn, led to escalating interdivisional conflict. Mutual adjustment among managers, central to the natural approach, was very limited.

In the end the conflict involved all senior managers and led to strategic and organizational decision making geared at relieving the firm of conflict without addressing a mistaken fundamental design assumption. Top management retreated into its own private considerations, excluding major actors from the strategy making process. This was the opposite of interactive learning, and this chapter explores the causes of this process.

FRAMES OF PRACTICE AND STRATEGY, AND THEIR INCONSISTENCIES

A first probe into the conflict between the project management division and the hotel division quickly revealed a conflict between two very different frames of real estate development practice— between crafting "unique projects" through an open-ended process, and cranking out "cookie cutting" projects through a design constrained from the beginning.

These views of practice were closely linked to frames of strategy design. Proponents of "unique projects" not only saw their position as a relatively accurate account of what the company had done successfully in the past, they also thought that the firm's ability to do those projects constituted its core competence. Therefore, they argued, the firm should do those kinds of projects in the future, if not in its home town, then elsewhere. The proponents of "cookie cutting" projects, mostly hired recently from major hotel chains, acknowledged the construction competence but considered it an overkill for creating a profitable chain of first-class "suites hotels."

A first probe also revealed several important inconsistencies in both positions:

1. The company not only had done "unique" projects but, until recently, also "cookie cutting" housing projects.
2. "Unique" projects, while seemingly built from scratch every time, were in fact architectural designs draped around a pre-arranged but flexible structural design.
3. While the hotel program was framed as a cookie cutting activity, the first hotel project had been a unique project.
4. Cookie cutting projects required, at times, considerable adaptation to a local site, making them more like unique projects.

To the extent that members of the firm were aware of such inconsistencies, they tended to ignore them.

Finally, the first probe indicated that as a result of increasing conflict, senior managers in both divisions were no longer on speaking terms with each other. While expressing respect for the competence of the other division, each side believed it could no longer influence the other by discussing differences.

Strategic learning had become seriously undermined. How had this happened? This question not only had great importance for the practitioners involved, it also questioned the prescription for strategic learning of the "rational" and the "natural" frameworks of strategy design.

A View from the "Outside In"

Faced with contradictory claims and a vexing frame conflict, the researcher undertook a second probe. He focussed on actual company behavior reported in a long list of all completed projects and constructed a view from the "outside in." When all projects (more than 100) were grouped based on similarity, 12 groups emerged. When these groups were plotted over time, 12 series of similar projects emerged (FIGURE 13.1). Assuming that a series of similar projects represents sustained strategic attention to a specific market opportunity (FIGURE 13.2), then each series constitutes an emerging strategy (Mintzberg & McHugh, 1985). A seemingly disjointed flow of projects displayed a surprising consistency over time.

No one in the firm had ever drawn such a map. It revealed a much richer and more complex corporate development, which included series of unique as well as cookie cutting projects. It partly confirmed and disconfirmed both views of the firm's strategic development. Moreover, it confirmed what many insiders to the industry knew; Citadel was good at learning new strategies in a volatile environment. How could the firm accomplish this?

A LIMITED SET OF STABLE RULES FOR STRATEGY DESIGN

With the help of the map we inferred a limited set of 14 rules for strategy design that was stable for more than three decades. These rules govern the strategic conversation between the firm and its changing environment, and help the firm to generate stable patterns in a volatile environment. These rules fall into five subsets.

Subset 1: Probe and Shape Specific Initiatives

In response to specific federal or local government initiatives, Citadel develops a series of similar projects, which eventually leads to a "signature in the urban fabric," identifiable by insiders in the industry as a "typical" Citadel project. Such a series is a medium-term development program in the form of an "emerging" strategy, resulting over time in a *company-specific type of project*. We infer the following design rules, geared to learning a new strategy:

- Follow changing local and federal legislative agendas *closely*.
- Engage *early on* in resulting initiatives by bidding for a project.
- Do a series of *similar* projects as a way of probing into and shaping an initiative.
- Make each project in a series of similar projects a *limited improvization* on a previous project in that series.

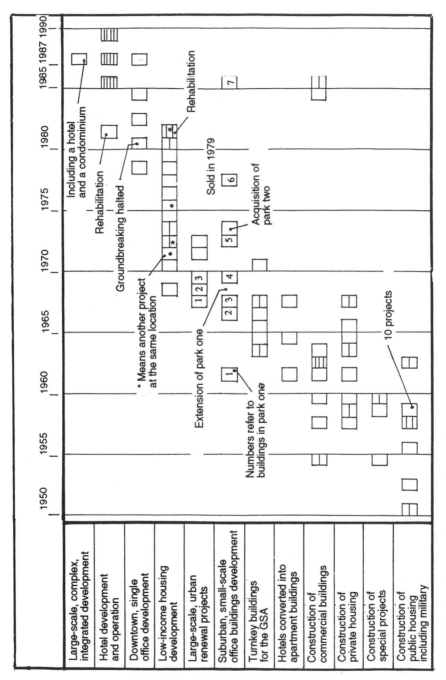

FIGURE 13.1   Similar projects grouped over time

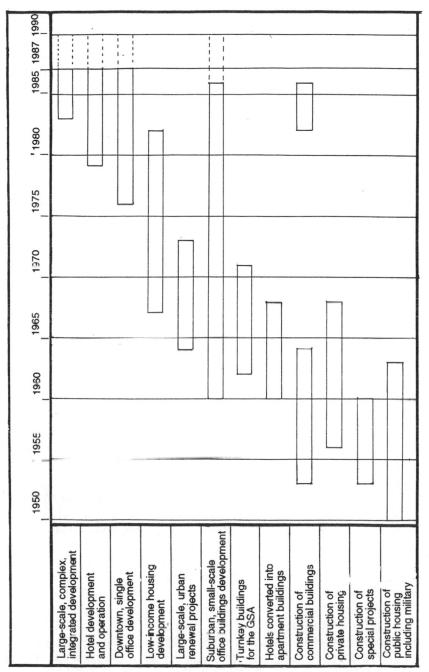

FIGURE 13.2 Types of projects as emergent strategies

Subset 2: Stage Projects

When Citadel embarks on a new series of projects, it stages them; after planning and overall design of the first project, top management directs its attention to the next project. This allows top management to (i) focus on the overall negotiations and design for a project, (ii) bring new lessons immediately to bear on new projects, (iii) delegate daily supervision to project managers, (iv) closely monitor the work, and (v) intervene at times in the field. Moreover, management breaks up large projects into smaller pieces and takes them on in the same fashion. Finally, the firm will never "walk away" from a project. Three projects stand out; even under extreme adversity, the firm stuck to them, turned them around and completed them in crisis conditions. They subsequently became *prototypical* projects for the firm, forming a deeper improvizational basis for types of projects to come. We infer the following design rules for organizing the learning of a new strategy:

- Undertake *partly* overlapping projects within a series.
- *Break up* large projects into sequentially built parts.
- *Stick* to a project, even under extreme adversity.

Subset 3: Keep a Dual Focus

At any time Citadel develops *a steady but changing core* of three to six series of projects. Yet, despite this diversity, it has a sharp dual focus: all series of projects fall into two broader groups, housing and offices. The development of several similar types of projects leads over time to a *general type of project*. In the case of office buildings, for instance, industry insiders point to the recurrent high quality of architectural design, often making them landmarks. This suggest a combination of deeper component design practices that allows the firm to draw on previous experience and build a *distinguishable* practice of real estate development. Against this background, new specific types of projects are improvizations on previous types. They stretch, challenge and develop a set of component design practices. We infer the following design rules for building on and expanding on new strategies:

- Develop *multiple* types of projects simultaneously in different stages of their life cycle.
- Develop *related* types of projects, whereby each new type is a limited improvization of a previous type.

Subset 4: Keep Moving by Switching Attention

Citadel focusses only on *two domains*: (i) privately financed, luxury office buildings, and (ii) publicly financed, low-income housing projects. By switching between these counter-cyclical domains, the firm *keeps moving* in a volatile corporate environment, resulting in a continuous flow of projects. It avoids dependency on one domain that occasionally may experience a severe cyclical downturn. We infer the following design rules for continuous learning:

- Do only projects within two *counter-cyclical* domains of real estate development practice.
- *Switch* strategic attention between domains depending on initiatives at the federal and local level.

Subset 5: Strengthen Competence Continuously

Citadel's two general types, housing and office buildings, are highly complementary, feed on each other, and strengthen the firm's competence. For instance, unique office projects with an open-ended design process are a kind of R&D in real time, challenging managerial competence. Newly acquired competence is then used to make cookie cutting housing projects more competitive. Up-front government subsidies for housing projects were a welcome additional source of financing office projects in difficult times. In addition, Citadel has steadily increased its control over the life cycle of projects by expanding its role from construction subcontracting to turnkey development, to development for own account, to operating the business inside its real estate. Finally, the *increasing portfolio* of buildings is used as (i) a source of specific feedback on performance, (ii) a feeler in specific real estate markets, (iii) a way to stabilize income, and (iv) a source of new activities such as renovation that can serve as a work buffer during cyclical downturns. We infer the following design rules for strengthening the learning of core competencies:

- Pursue *complementary* general types of projects feeding on each other.
- Increase *control* over the development process by internalizing new forms of ownership.
- *Hold on* to completed projects and use them as source of intelligence and a way to stabilize in a volatile environment.

These 14 design rules were remarkably constant over three and a half decades, and were at the core of learning new strategies. However, in our discussions with senior managers, no one was aware of the entire set and they had never put their sense of these rules together. Hence, a significant part of the firm's design knowledge was tacit.

THE LIMITS OF STRATEGY DESIGN RULES

While corporate behavior shows a remarkable consistency over time, it also displays significant discontinuities:

1. The company has a pulsing pattern of geographical expansion and retreat.
2. Its sales go up and down in parallel to the geographical pattern, with a quantum leap in the early 1980s.
3. By developing for its own account after 1960, Citadel's portfolio of completed projects is rapidly increasing.
4. Several big unique projects had not met expected profits or had failed, jeopardizing the firm's continuity.

These discontinuities suggest two related organizational dilemmas:

1. Out of state, federal projects reduce dependency on the home town but top management wants to remain closely involved in the design part of projects (in particular of "unique" projects) and bring its own competence to bear on each project (in which it is personally at risk).
2. A growing portfolio of completed projects gradually shifts the strategic attention from development to property management.

Both dilemmas challenge the espoused theory of management that the firm is "an investment builder which owns what it builds and manages what it owns". The firm could respond by:

- either selling of property in violation of the key norm, "managing for its own account" (central in attracting investors), or
- developing increasingly more projects at a faster pace, requiring more delegation by top management in violation of the norm of "close involvement," or
- reducing the need for close involvement by resorting more and more to cookie cutting projects, in violation of the norm of dual focus.

All three responses were becoming visible in the early 1980s. However, while senior managers mentioned these discontinuities, there was no evidence that they sensed the inherent dilemmas.

STEADY STATE AND EXPERIMENTAL DESIGNING

Continuities and discontinuities in company behavior put together into one map reveal that Citadel's strategic development is made up of periods with a steady pattern of behavior, punctuated by episodes of experimental designing during the early 1950s, 1960s, 1970s and 1980s (FIGURE 13.3). The length of steady periods was shorter than reported by Tushman, Newman and Nadler (1988) and Mintzberg and Waters (1982) and longer than reported by Mintzberg and McHugh (1985).

Episodes of experimental design occurred in response to a discontinuity in the environment and company behavior (starting and halting series of projects) is in large part a continuation of periods of steady behavior. Therefore these experimental episodes can be viewed as natural experiments in practice, superimposed on a process of ongoing design.

In summary, the inquiry into the conflict between Citadel's project management division and hotel division revealed that during almost 4 decades, the firm had pursued both cookie cutting and unique projects in a symbiotic way through an intricate set of design rules that, as a set, was largely tacit.

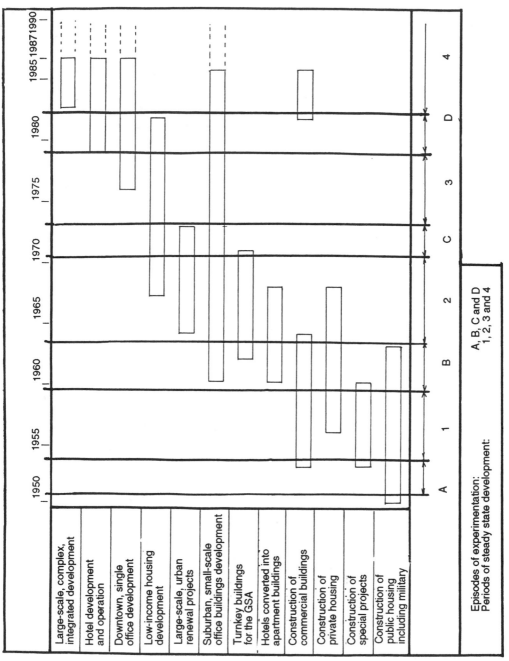

FIGURE 13.3 Citadel's strategic development: episodes of experimentation and periods of steady behavior

A VIEW FROM THE "INSIDE OUT"

How had executives lost sight of this symbiotic relationship during the episode of experimental design in the early 1980s? This third probe goes beyond behavior in terms of completed projects and constructs a view from the "inside out" based on accounts of executives. This led to the following script-like version of the latest episode in the early 1980s during which Citadel entered the hotel business. For a detailed description see Overmeer (1989).

AN EPISODE OF EXPERIMENTAL DESIGNING

By the end of the 1970s, Citadel's main line of business was "cookie cutting," federally subsidized, low-income housing projects, producing a steady stream of one project per year. However, the federal program was rocked by scandals and got a bad reputation. The government not only imposed more regulation, it also reduced the size of projects so as to allow smaller non-union companies to compete. When they began to lose projects that they had never lost before, management concluded that Citadel, with its "non-union mind," had become too large for this type of housing project. At the same time, by developing a unique medium-sized downtown office building, top managers became aware that the local market for luxury offices was poised for a revival. However larger out-of-town competitors were moving in with the resources to deal with increasing city regulations. Citadel's executives experienced a *strategic predicament*; the firm was either too big for housing or too small for offices and *could not switch* from one domain to another.

After a strategic planning process along the lines of Andrews (1971), top management decided to grow and professionalize the firm so that they could focus on unique downtown office skyscrapers. However, while designing the first skyscraper, executives could, to their surprise, "not make the numbers work" for an existing office building on the site (designated as a landmark that could not be demolished). After studying alternative uses, management concluded that a luxury hotel could work. They had never developed or intended a hotel, but under pressure of competitors eager to step in, they took on a unique hotel development. It was a creative improvization in the margin of a larger project and a minor anomaly in its strategic development. Then, when Citadel began development of a second skyscraper on an adjacent site, executives, again to their surprise, could not get the necessary city approvals. Management concluded that their unwillingness to make an (illegal) contribution to the re-election fund of the mayor would make it impossible to pursue further projects in their home town. Thus, with a housing program withering away and an office program stalled, Citadel could *not switch domains*, and again experienced a *strategic predicament*.

The company responded in several ways. Firstly, again to the surprise of Citadel's executives, the hotel made a profit in the first year (industry practice was five years) and the company became aware of a local niche for luxury hotels. As they tried to pursue more projects, an initial anomalous project became the basis for a strategic invention. Secondly, they persisted in bidding for large skyscraper projects while integrating hotels in their design proposals. Even though they lost every bid, each time they were forced to think through the design of a very unique, large-scale, multi-use, integrated project. According to the managers closely involved, it led to "maturing" of the newly appointed president of the firm. Thirdly, top management switched its attention to a neighboring region in which they had worked before. As they began development of a skyscraper, they also explored the possibilities for renovating hotels with major hotel chains as well as for renovating suburban office buildings in the same town. None of these efforts was, however, successful and the company faced an *acute strategic predicament*; it was now running out of work.

In response, top management began, with great reluctance, to lay off people for the first time in the firm's history. With its back against the wall, top management retreated to its home town and reacted in a variety of ways. Firstly, it began construction work for other development companies so as to keep people at work. Secondly, it began developing an additional building in one of its local, suburban office parks to keep some key people at work. And finally, top management discovered that the local niche for luxury hotels was in fact a regional, if not national, niche. When the product champion of a "revolutionary" hotel concept, based on double rooms called "suites," was ready to leave a major hotel chain and "ride the wave of the future" with Citadel, the firm set up a hotel division to enter the market "quick and big" and to pre-empt other regional developers. A strategic invention, derived from a unique project had turned into a strategic commitment for cookie cutting suites hotels.

KEY FEATURES OF THE DESIGN PROCESS

While the first steps in the process of strategic change follow the "rational approach," in particular Andrews's prescription (1971) of matching opportunities with distinctive competence, most of the process is not captured by that approach. The shift from anomaly, to strategic invention, to strategic commitment is more like an emerging strategy described by Mintzberg (1987). However, while Mintzberg invokes the metaphor of the potter, quietly potting at her wheel, Citadel's management went through a very different kind of process. Firstly, at the core of the strategy design process was the repeated failure of the switching rule, resulting in repeated strategic predicaments. In the face of these predicaments, executives had to act, often under the pressure of compelling deadlines in specific projects, and faced high uncertainty and a steep downside. Secondly, while fraught with failure and predicaments, the design process involved multiple moves as part of a rich and complex process of experimentation, involving different forms of real estate development. Thirdly, this process was triggered by surprise ("can't make the numbers work") and led to a creative improvization in the margin (i.e. developing a hotel). Fourthly, initially the design process was not very different from the limited improvizations that the company routinely displayed when developing projects during a steady state period. Fifthly, experimentation led to a window on an unfamiliar environment, the hotel market, and to the discovery of a major shift in that environment. Finally, only through repeated and deeply felt crises, in which the central norms of the firm were challenged ("no illegal election contributions") and violated ("a closely held family company firing dedicated employees"), top management decided to enter a new market.

While executives demonstrated an extraordinary ability for drawing on existing resources in the face of repeated failure, the process was not without hazards. At the end of the episode, top management saw the new hotel program as "counter-cyclical" to Citadel's office program, and "repetitive" like its housing program, although they did not know the hotel market. They also saw the hotel development process *as* building luxury offices and the management of the hotels *as* leasing housing projects. Moreover, they saw the hotel program *as* a sure fire strategy, based on a "unique" and "revolutionary" concept, presenting "the wave of the future." When granted an "exclusive" franchise, they decided to enter "big and quick" so as to gain "critical mass" and "pre-empt" competitors.

Hence, as they entered an unfamiliar context, top management framed that context as familiar by *seeing* the hotel program *as if* it was a combination of the housing and hotel program, a combination of what the company already knew how to do. Moreover, it assumed this to be largely correct. Hence, executives carried their old frame into a new context, and worked from it while trying to realize a new design for corporate strategy.

REALIZING THE HOTEL PROGRAM

What happens when an old frame is carried into a new context? A fourth probe centered on the problems Citadel encountered during the realization of its suites hotel program. Early on, when negotiating deals, Citadel was forced to develop several other types of hotels. Moreover, suites hotel development turned out to be more expensive, forcing Citadel to develop more than the five initially envisioned, and at a higher pace. Finally, due to negotiation delays, unexpected site problems (contaminated soil), and pressure to speed up due to competitors' moves, the hotel group began to commit itself to five hotels in the same developmental phase, breaking with the rule of "staged" projects.

Other design rules were challenged as well. Soon after it had started the hotel program, its home town changed mayor. After 10 futile bids, the company was suddenly awarded two very large projects, extensions of the office program. Their size, complexity, and timing, presented a major challenge to the firm, and the president of the firm (attending to the office program) wanted to switch the company's attention back to the office development domain. However, a second member of top management (attending to the hotel program) argued that there was only "a brief window of opportunity" for this type of hotel, that the firm needed to establish a critical mass quickly, and that experienced hotel executives had been hired with the promise of setting up a chain. This presented a new strategic predicament for the company. Parallel pursuit of two development programs and simultaneous development of several new types of hotels were profoundly mismatched to the way the firm had been learning new strategies over the past three decades.

THE EMERGING PREDICAMENT OF PARALLEL DEVELOPMENT

How did top management respond to the predicament of parallel development programs? A study of minutes of meetings and consultant reports led to a fifth probe, which revealed the following.

Firstly, shortly after entering the hotel market the president called in an organizational consultant with a psychoanalytic perspective, who conducted a traditional strategic planning exercise. Senior management focussed on defining the corporate mission and struggled with how to square "opportunistic hits" with long-term development. Unable to agree after three meetings, the co-founder/CEO stated the mission. Hence, the emerging rivalry was framed as a problem of corporate identity but did not lead to further action.

Then, after nine months, the president and the CEO felt a sense of urgency and reframed the problem as one of defining the "critical mass," "the rate of growth," "the financial risk and exposure," and a "balanced portfolio." A third member of top management, who attended to the hotel program, proposed an escape by acquiring a low-budget hotel chain and using a tax loophole so as to "cool off" the hotel division. But this only evoked new questions: would the loophole remain, was an acquisition not merely a "quick hit," and how to square the chain's low building quality with Citadel's pursuit of high quality? The corporate planner wrote to the consultant that:

> [an acquisition] would have serious implications for the company ... we are indeed at a crossroad.

Next, the president called in a strategy consulting firm to look at the hotel group strategy. It identified an "unhealthy internal growth imperative" that would "outstrip market opportunities" due to higher than expected overheads, as well as an incentive structure geared to operational profits from hotel operations rather than long-term real estate value appreciation. Again, top management avoided immediate action and focussed on making deals as the franchiser had given in to Citadel's demand for more projects.

After three years, the pursuit of both programs had led to an unexpected amount of work and the firm was stretched to its financial and managerial limits. Escalating conflict around the scarce resources left the hotel group and the project management group, whose leaders were not invited to the planning sessions, increasingly bewildered.

Finally, in separate interviews, the president stated the hotel program was *"planned,"* the manager attending hotel program stated that the program was *"personal challenge,"* and the CEO maintained that Citadel's strategic development was *"an evolution without a grand plan"* whereby entries into markets were "not very calculated decisions." It turned out that:

1. They had very different perceptions of the strategic development.
2. They had never sat down and discussed their differences.
3. As a result, they had never wondered how to account for them and explored how to test them.

In summary, through an extraordinary design process in the face of repeated strategic predicaments and failure, management had discovered an unfamiliar context, seen that context as familiar, and assumed it was largely correct. When realizing the new design, some of the firm's most important design rules such as "switching between counter-cyclical domains" and "staging projects" were mismatched to the new company environment. This resulted in an emerging predicament of parallel development programs. Strategic learning as an interactive process between formulation and implementation, between deliberate and emerging strategy had become problematic. Traditional strategic management methods, based on the "rational" approach, appeared to be largely ineffective for addressing this dilemma. On the other hand, "mutual adjustment," based on the "natural" approach, occurred only in a very limited way.

THE VIEW FROM THE "INSIDE IN"

When traditional techniques failed and mutual adjustment hardly occurred in the face of a strategic dilemma, how did executives respond? By the time the planner and the researcher had held three feedback sessions with top management, the disappointing results of some of the first hotels had come in, while at the same time the conflict among the divisions had begun to affect top management. Top management began to address both issues during the meetings, making it possible to construct a view from the "inside in"—the thinking of top managers *while* addressing a strategic predicament and the ensuing conflict. This became a sixth probe.

Firstly, in response to disappointing results, the president (attending to the office program) argued that the hotel business was "a repetitive activity, counter-cyclical to offices." He advocated a return to a protected home market with a focus on large-scale integrated projects. The top manager (attending to the hotel program) argued, "you can't be right all the time, you can't be precise, and you can't have a perfect view of the future." He advocated that the company should actually develop more hotels so to offset a few, less successful projects, and not limit the program even though it might lead to dominance of the program. A third top management member thought that the firm should not "become dependent" on one dominant program, and advocated that "the pendulum" should swing back so as to "keep forces in the middle."

Secondly, in response to the effect of the division conflict on them, the president had called in a psychoanalytically-oriented consultant (hired several times before) to assess the leadership of the hotel division. The consultant reported that although the hotel leadership came across as "strong and assertive," the conflict had revealed that they "were insecure," "lacked maturity," "worried about their authority," "didn't have a seasoned background," "wanted the golden brass," and "had bravado." He concluded:

> They are a fortress. In the future it will be harder to penetrate. They are a Siamese twin requiring surgery before it is too late.

In response top management sensed "chaos in the company" stemming from "a struggle for palace power" with the danger of "the daughter taking over the mother." Toward the end of the meetings, top management retreated to the private realm of the family and stated the need for "a united and uniform view regarding the basic policy issues."

Several weeks afterwards it decided to change the organizational structure of the hotel group by separating hotel development from operations and having these activities report to different members of top management. Soon afterwards, it severed its relation with a still wavering franchiser and acquired another regional, closely-held and family-owned hotel suites development company working in the south east and south. In doing so, Citadel established a national chain. It was the first time Citadel had acquired a company and it was the first time it had achieved national prominence. By 1988, however, top management publicly announced that it had put the hotel group up for sale, only to come back on the decision half a year later.

RESPONDING TO A STRATEGIC DILEMMA

At the time of this research a gradually emerging strategic predicament based on erroneous assumptions in the design stage had taken the form of a genuine strategic dilemma. The most striking features of top management's efforts to come to terms with the dilemma were the following.

Firstly, the problem was initially not framed as a predicament and a design problem, but as a problem of switching attention and resources from the hotel program back to the office program. However, no matter what top management did to address the strategic predicament, it could not invent adequate solutions. The way in which it framed the strategic problem seemed to make the problem resistant to actually addressing it. For a year and a half, it avoided dealing with the problem and, in the meantime, the problem became more and more pressing and took the form of a dilemma.

Secondly, whenever top management met to address problems, it reframed them. However, it did not reflect on the effectiveness of the way it framed the problem, nor on its problem solving. As the problem became more and more pressing, top management retreated more and more into the private realm of the family, and excluded key players from its deliberations.

Thirdly, top management never framed the parallel development problem as a corporate strategy design predicament but as a problem with the hotel program and of curbing its growth and expansion out of fear that "the daughter" would come to dominate "mother."

Fourthly, eventually, after several attempts to frame the problem without leading to action, the strategic dilemma turned into an issue of control over the strategic direction of the firm. While the acquisition of another hotel chain was a way "to cool off" the hotel group, to free up resources for the office program, and to address the hotel group's "critical mass" problem, decision making was framed as a corporate strategy control problem leading to a power struggle with clear winners and losers rather than a corporate strategy design problem.

Fifthly, while top managers realized that they had avoided taking action early on, they never addressed (i) their failure to act, (ii) their own contribution to creating a "control" problem, (iii) the effectiveness of a structural intervention that would split up the hotel group into a development and an operations group, and (iv) the likely rivalry that will emerge between those two groups.

Finally, when top management excluded key players in the firm and used a psychoanalytically-oriented consultant, it bewildered the hotel group's management. They felt that the "ground rules" for cooperation were unilaterally changed. Most likely, this will make a productive interaction and strategic learning even more difficult in the future.

An Amendment to Design Approaches

Prior to 1980, Citadel, a mature firm with an entrepreneurial senior management, showed an extraordinary competence for learning new strategies interactively. During this period of three and a half decades, the firm *confirmed* the advice of the "rational" and the "natural" approach for strategic learning through an interaction between strategy formulation and implementation, or between deliberate and emergent strategy. However, when a major shift in the environment required major strategic change in the early 1980s, that interaction became problematic, *partly disconfirming* the prescription of both frameworks.

The design process deviated from the "rational" approach during the implementation, when the core of the formulated strategy ("develop downtown skyscrapers") became challenged. By responding in real time, the firm engaged in an episode of experimentation during which it interactively generated an emergent strategy—the idea to create a hotel program. When realizing the hotel program, the firm again developed that program interactively. But, unlike the prescription of the "natural" approach, the interaction between deliberate and emergent strategy through mutual adjustment between managers hardly took place. Strategic planning techniques such as defining a corporate mission, finding sensible trade-offs within a portfolio, and cooling off a division through acquisition (all central to the "rational" approach) were neither adequate to address the emerging strategic dilemma nor were they "the paraphernalia of the strategy industry" that got in the way (according to the "natural" approach). Strategic change was neither a swift change of plan during a brief episode followed by seamless implementation (according to the "rational" approach), nor was the "reconfiguration" (according to the "natural" approach) fast. To the extent that reconfiguration began to take place toward the end of the research, it took some six years from the first hotel or more than three years from the moment the firm decided to enter the hotel business. An in-depth study of one case, then, suggests that authors need to specify more accurately (i) what they mean by interactive learning and strategy learning, and (ii) how to bring it about under conditions of a major shift in the environment.

The Citadel case suggests that successful firms are, indeed, good at interactive learning during steady state periods; that is, they are good at learning a strategy through an interaction with a specific opportunity in the environment. This is, what Argyris and Schon (1978) call, "single loop organizational learning" or learning a new strategy without changing deeper norms. Citadel was also good at "deutero single loop organizational learning"— that is, it had learned to learn new strategies. However, the case also suggests that a firm's strategic knowledge reflected in its design rules as well as in its ability to improvise on those rules (together, its theory-in-use for strategic action) is likely to be partly tacit. Senior managers may not know the complete set, may have conflicting versions explaining the firm's strategic development, may have never explored their differences, may have never tested their differences, and may not know how to test them.

The case suggests that limited access to design rules and tremendous pressure to act may lead senior managers to see new opportunities as a known combination of old programs, and not to appreciate the differences in time. In doing so, it makes an unfamiliar context familiar, but also assumes a continuation of causality in the new context (anti-cyclicality) and an implicit match of design rules. Limited access to these rules may prevent top management from grasping early on the predicament, created by its entry into a new business, and from framing it as a corporate design problem. Such a strategic predicament may express itself initially as a difference and later on as a rivalry between two members of top management. The resistance of a strategic predicament to the repertoire of traditional strategic management solutions (such as defining an overall mission, finding sensible trade-offs, cooling off a division) may cause delays. This, in turn, may increase pressure up to a point that the predicament becomes a strategic dilemma and turns into a "control" problem for top management. A firm's extraordinary improvisational competence, central for strategic learning, is of limited use in addressing such a strategic predicament. Tampering with one division will neither lead to addressing the underlying causes of the strategic dilemma (parallel development in Citadel's case) nor to finding creative solutions.

Citadel's problem is part of a class of organizational problems called "double loop organizational learning" problems (Argyris and Schon, 1978); that is, one or more central design rules are challenged to which the firm managers do not have ready access. Such problems may occur within firms that have been very successful at "deutero single loop organizational learning" for a long time. To the extent that design knowledge has been accessible, it may have become largely tacit. Typically, the theory of action perspective (Argyris and Schon, 1978) predicts that when such knowledge is mismatched to a new situation, it will give rise to conflict among top managers. To the extent that the behavioral world of the firm does not allow open confrontation of such conflicts, the design knowledge may remain undiscussable, and tacit, thus aggravating an already difficult re-design problem, eventually requiring "framebreaking" (Tushman, Newman and Nadler, 1988).

How, then, can the "rational" and "natural" approach help managers to bring about strategic learning when a firm faces a major shift in its environment? A consulting-based research approach suggests that if senior managers of a successful firm have only partial access to what makes the firm successful in learning new strategies (such as the 14 design rules) or if they hold one or more erroneous assumptions (such as anti-cyclicality when there is none), then any approach needs to inquire into the ways a firm has been learning strategies and map the rules that inform this, as well as publicly (in the sense of a large team of senior managers) surface and test central assumptions of individual managers about specific events, situations and strategies. The Citadel case shows three specific cases in which a researcher/consultant can help.

Firstly, the best moment is *prior to a major shift* in the environment. Successful firms typically have developed an ability for learning to learn new strategies ("deutero single loop organizational learning") and their members typically have limited access to the design rules for strategy. A combination of mapping the firm's strategic development together with testing management's assumptions, centered around successful and failing projects or products, will begin to surface critical assumptions, strategies and norms. By getting access to how the firm actually designs new strategies, executives will develop a much better understanding of the process of experimental design when facing a major shift. Rather than facing merely failure- and predicament-inducing events, driving the organization to do more of what it has done before in a limiting fashion, these events can become valuable sources of strategic information, which can be used to jointly test strategic assumptions.

Secondly, when confronted with *a strategic predicament in its acute form*, such as a major conflict between two divisions, the consultant/researcher should help management to try getting underneath the conflict by constructing a map of actual corporate behavior and using it to test the espoused theories that executives hold. At this stage, the central idea is that managers (as was the case with Citadel) are often locked into rather rigid ideas and ignore the inconsistencies in their own reasoning. Inquiry into their reasoning, surfacing inconsistencies and providing alternative ways of viewing their situation may lead them to step back and begin to reflect on central assumptions they hold, leading to unfreezing.

Thirdly, as the Citadel case has pointed out, with the help of a consultant/researcher, by the time the firm is facing a strategic dilemma, managers have most likely made a series of ineffective and perhaps aggravating moves. Management needs to reflect on how it contributes to the making of the organizational problems it frames, and on its ineffectiveness in addressing these problems. Moreover, for strategic learning to occur in the future, senior managers need to begin to test their inferences among a broader team of managers.

Finally, future research into these issues will likely take the form of consulting-based research, in practice, with practitioners, and for practitioners. Such research needs to focus on what prevents practitioners from jointly reflecting on failing projects and on design situations, while simultaneously exploring what interventions will help practitioners to engage in joint problem setting and solving.

REFERENCES

Andrews, K.R. (1971). *The Concept of Corporate Strategy*, Homewood, IL: Richard D. Irwin.

Argyris, C. and Schon, D.A. (1978). *Organizational Learning*. Reading, MA: Addison-Wesley.

Mintzberg, H. (1987). Crafting strategy. *Harvard Business Review* July/August.

Mintzberg, H. and McHugh, A. (1985). Strategy formation in an ad-hocracy. *Administrative Science Quarterly* **30**, 160–197.

Mintzberg, H. and Waters, J.A. (1982). Tracking strategy in an entrepreneurial firm. *Academy of Management Review* **25**, 465–499.

Overmeer, W.J.A.M. (1989). Corporate inquiry and strategic learning: the role of surprise and improvisation in organizing major change, doctoral dissertation, School of Architecture and Planning, MIT, Cambridge, MA.

Porter, M.E. (1980). *Competitive Strategy*. New York: Free Press.

Porter, M.E. (1985). *Competitive Advantage*. New York: Free Press.

Tushman, M.T., Newman, W.H. and Nadler, D.A. (1988). Executive leadership and organizational evolution: Managing incremental and discontinuous change. In R.H. Kilmann, T.J. Covin and Associates (Eds) *Corporate Transformation, Revitalizing Organizations for a Competitive World* (pp. 102–130). San Francisco, CA: Jossey-Bass.

14

Detecting Emergent Strategy

Colin Eden, Kees van der Heijden

INTRODUCTION

In his address to the Strategic Management Society conference on strategic renaissance, Richard Pascale (1990) suggested that "strategic intent" is more often than not a retrospective device. This is one way of understanding the notion of emergent strategy. The retrospective designation of intentions is an efficient way of describing both organizational and personal action. In saying this one is adopting a view close to that of Weick when he developed his thesis for the relationship between thinking and acting, "how do I know what I think until ... I see how I act" (Weick, 1979, p. 133). Similarly Mintzberg (1990) argued that "emergent strategy means unintended order" (p. 152)

The expression "emergent strategy" (Mintzberg and Waters, 1985) is linguistically consistent only if strategy is understood as "the art of using plans" (*Collins Dictionary*). Thus the expression signifies an active process (which might be better named "emergent strategizing"), which can be detected by understanding emerging behaviour, *patterns* of decision making and problem solving, "theories-in-use" (Argyris and Schon, 1978) and themes. This interpretation means that emergent strategizing is located primarily in the institutional language, as it categorizes and provides a wider *meaning* to the pattern of events as they unfold.

Strategic Renaissance and Business Transformation. Edited by H. Thomas, D. O'Neal and J. Kelly.
Copyright © 1995 John Wiley & Sons Ltd.

Note that, with a little rearrangement of the ideas, Lindblom (1959) got there first with his treatise on "the science of muddling through".

This chapter first explores the nature of emergent strategy in this processual context, then explores its significance, then discusses how it might be captured, and finally suggests implications for a strategy development process. It takes a stance that relates organizational recipes and emergent strategy to the nature of managerial cognition (Huff, 1990) as set within the context of a socially *constructed* reality informed by the culture of the organization.

THE NATURE OF STRATEGY IN ORGANIZATIONS

In seeking to understand strategy as it is pursued by organizations, the notion of emergent strategizing is powerful because it highlights the supposition that organizations in their "muddling through" are guided by a subconscious framework. This derives partly from the active process in organizations of socially constructing reality (Berger and Luckmann, 1966) and "making sense" of the world (Kelly, 1955), and partly from relatively consistent purposeful behaviour of managers driving problem solving. This consistency derives from stable tacit assumptions and a "world-taken-for-granted", which underlie espoused values, which in turn drive cultural artefacts (Schein, 1992). The basic underlying assumptions are reinforced through cognitive and emotional feedback loops in an organizational setting (Bougon, 1992) through which they become shared. Relative consistency of problem solving behaviour suggests to the outside world a sense of direction. This is influenced by the values and culture of the organization, based on these taken-for-granted assumptions. This influence is largely unconscious, to the extent that the assumptions are treated as taken-for-granted reality. Thus it is implied that any organization, large or small, uses a stable long-term (strategic) framework to solve today's problems.

"Visions tend to be tacit, taken-for-granted, they are seldom made explicit, they operate in the background" (van der Heijden, 1993). For alignment of basic underlying assumptions to emerge in organizations there needs to be a common meta-level world-view on purpose and meaning, through which shared reasoning (Kelly's "sociality corollary") as to why one assumption might be better than another can emerge. Strategizing implies the development of a shared meaning about how the world is to be interpreted (Scheper, 1991). Meaning is shared through language. This is based on strategic concepts, generated in the past as categorization of historical patterns of events, in order to cope with past breakdown situations. It will almost by definition stop short of completely describing new reality. Strategic thinking needs to be continuously renewed if it is to remain effective.

This shared meaning "can develop in all kinds of unusual ways, as people interact, mutually adjust, learn from each other, conflict and develop consensus" (Mintzberg, 1987). Through this process individuals increase the degree of overlap between their "mental models" (albeit often by the use of "cryptic constructs", which are left vague to allow this overlap to take place (Bougon, 1992)). As a result of this shared understanding the organization will structure itself accordingly (in terms of organizational structure and other cultural artefacts, as well as norms and role recognition), increasing further the stability of the underlying meaning structure (Schein, 1993). Due to these structures, frameworks for action are in place which create the alternative meaning of the term "emergent strategy", not in terms of retrospective interpretation, but as firmly embedded recipes for current and future behaviour.

STRATEGIC FLEXIBILITY

Because the emergent strategy is an organizational phenomenon it is tantamount to an organizational "recipe", set within the context of an "industry recipe" (Spender, 1989). Due to internal reinforcement processes institutional mental models tend to filter out weak danger signals, and it often takes considerable overall performance deterioration before existing "recipes" are perceived to be wanting (Grinyer and McKiernan, 1990). However, if the recipe is socially efficient it can be instrumental to an organization's success. It will be unique to the organization and so may represent an unrecognized "distinctive competence". Competencies in this domain are distinctive precisely because they are tacit and therefore not open to designed emulation by competitors.

However, society is dynamic and what is socially efficient today may be obsolete tomorrow.

If so, and the organization is to survive, then the emergent strategy needs to change. This requires that the current emergent strategy and competences need to be articulated and considered consciously. This leads to a managerial paradox, namely that identifying and reflecting upon organizational recipes may make you stronger (more adaptable) and, at the same time, weaker (imitable). The appropriate balance to be struck depends on the degree and rate of change in the organization's business environment. However, at some time or other, most organizations need to renew their models of the business environment and themselves (de Geus, 1988) through a process of reflective learning (Argyris and Schon, 1978).

The embedded framework drives real behaviour (problem solving—tactically linked to strategic, decision making—cultural routines and artefacts) of members of the organization. If patterns of behaviour become obsolete and the need for change arises the embedded framework must be acknowledged and articulated so that it can be worked on. Therefore we need to be clearer about what an emergent strategy is, both conceptually and practically. The idea can be more valuable if it is more adequately defined. Such tighter definition is best attempted by operationalizing it, for example by attempting to detect formally the emergent strategy of an organization.

With the embedded framework driving behaviour, enacting thinking is dominant, rather than thinking then acting. It is for this reason that detecting emergent strategizing as a "world-taken-for-granted" is so difficult. Deep knowledge needs to be accessed as theories-in-use, rather than accounts of behaviour or hypotheses about future behaviour ("espoused theories").

POLITICAL FEASIBILITY

Assumptions about emergent strategy that develop without acknowledgement of the emergent strategizing *process* may not be backed up by the mental models of some key actors in the organization. In this way "implementation problems" are experienced, caused by institutional disparities. These often arise through the existence of cryptic constructs in managers' mental models. These cryptic constructs play an important role in maintaining the "strategic conversation" (the explanation of meaning to each other in the organization), but when real action is considered discrepancies in interpretation of concepts surface and are put to the test. These can underlie significant issues in developing political feasibility for any strategy.

Negotiating order is the most crucial element of political feasibility. There are two elements to negotiated order: social negotiation among members of a group to create order determined by the needs of the organization as differently perceived by each member of the group ("socially negotiated order"), and acknowledgement that organizations and groups exist within an established order of social relationships ("negotiated social order"). The first acknowledges that a social procedure of one sort or another is always used to make decisions; and the second acknowledges that any organizational change has an impact on negotiated social relationships (Eden, 1989).

The second of these contributes to people having difficulty saying what they think ought to be done because to do so might have undesirable consequences for social relationships. It leads to "groupthink" (Janis, 1972) and a dominance of "Abilene paradox" type outcomes (Harvey, 1988), where a group decide to go to a place that no one in the group wanted to go to. In organizations, "the goals we seek are changes in our relations or in our opportunities in our relating; but the bulk of our activity consists in "relating itself" (Vickers, 1983, p. 33). To negotiate order implies developing shared meaning and organizational alignment (Bartunek, 1988). Indeed, transformation of organizations focuses on changes in shared meanings, belief and values (Bartunek and Moch, 1987; Pettigrew, 1977; Sims and Gioia, 1986).

EMERGENT STRATEGY IN PRACTICE

We argued earlier that the best form of definition of "emergent strategy" should develop from considering the practice of detecting it. Emergent strategy seen as emergent behaviour, emergent theories of action and decisions introduces conceptual notions that are difficult to identify as units for analysis. However, emergent strategy is also about detecting a stream that has a recurring pattern rather than detecting and analysing individual units, a task for which human intuition is better equipped. We suggest that in the same manner as a person can "act thinkingly" (Weick, 1979) so can an organization strategize thinkingly. Following Weick's model for "thinking action" it is appropriate to explore strategizing through an exploration of assumptions, mental models and "world-taken-for-granted".

The task of detecting emergent strategy, in this way, needs to get at deep knowledge and embedded wisdom, the theories-in-use. Not espoused theories or the rhetoric of strategy, but the embedded norms and values, role definitions and the "organizational recipe" all need to surface. All of this has been shaped by historical events. The task of surfacing requires a clear recognition of the role that history and language play in forming deep knowledge (Ackermann et al., 1992) and developing theories-in-action (Argyris and Schon, 1978).

In this way detecting emergent strategy is similar to the processes of discovering "grounded theory" (Glaser and Strauss, 1967; Strauss and Corbin, 1990) about purpose, vision and strategic problem solving. Or, alternatively, strategy development becomes "action research" (Eden and Huxham, 1995; Susman, 1982; Susman and Evered, 1978), which is intended to guide action, with the research process guiding reflection.

ELICITATION

We consider four different, but related, approaches to this process of discovery:

- Approach 1: analyse the concrete record of strategic intentions, through, for example a study of the documentation designed to direct behaviour.
- Approach 2: analyse decision making in action, get involved in the organization (an anthropological or participant observer approach); watch decision making, listen to stories.
- Approach 3: work with managers, as action researchers, on strategic breakdown situations; become immersed in the thinking and the social process of "strategic firefighting".
- Approach 4: use well designed trigger questions in interview situations to replicate closely the immediacy and relevance so

that theories-in-use can be detected. Follow interviews with feedback to individuals and to the team.

APPROACH 1: ANALYSIS OF DOCUMENTATION

The first approach can be very revealing of the way in which the organization manages its bureaucracy, but the process of analysing recorded statements can be a poor representation of emergent strategy. The analysis of formal procedures through written documentation reveals one important slice through the strategic life of the organization but misses the social processes of negotiation and bargaining about the future, and misses the aspects of thinking and acting that documentation often attempts to rationalize away. The observer can describe what is seen and felt, but meaning cannot be reconstructed, because it is unknown whether important assumptions are reflected. It is especially dangerous to try to infer the deeper assumptions from artefacts alone as in this approach it is only the observer's models that can be used for interpretation (Schein, 1992).

The appropriate ways of analysing documents so that they reveal an action orientation (seeking out theories that were in use) can follow those used by Bonham and Shapiro (1976) and Axelrod (1976). There is no shortage of attempts by academic researchers in using this approach; however, it is very rare for the output to have any implications for the organization to which it relates.

It is not always necessary to get to this deep interpretation in order to make productive progress in an emergent strategy *facilitation* project. In such a case Approach 1 can be useful providing it is used dialectically and so can be informed by the debate it generates. For example, Eden and Cropper (1992) spent four years working with the director-general of the England and Wales Prison Service, seeking to understand the patterns and coherence of strategy statements used across the organization. The project was designed to observe statements made by senior staff to Ministers and to different but interrelated parts of the service, in order to understand the strategic significance of the framework underlying the emergent system of reporting by the staff responsible for managing prisons. In many respects the project was successful in enabling the director-general to understand and reflect upon the strategy of the service as it was delivered through the reporting about strategic direction and problem solving. As the work progressed, the analysis of emergent strategy sat in tension with deliberate strategy making. It was this dialectic between two understandings that provided the drive towards more effective strategy development. In such circumstances the extent to which the particular slice of detected emergent strategy was complete or "true" was less important than its role as a dialectical device.

APPROACH 2: PARTICIPANT/OBSERVER

The second approach gets away from trusting documentation and seeks to understand the social processes of decision making, relating and strategy in action. However, it is more time consuming than the first approach and has the added disadvantage of displaying little added value to the management team until all of the data has been collected and understood. In our experience of work with dozens of organizations, in both the public and the private sectors, other approaches are more practical in most cases.

APPROACH 3: WORKING WITH "PAIN"

The third approach is more promising because it wraps up the process of detecting emergent strategy within another activity that demands immediate attention from the top management team. Locking into real strategic problem solving is likely to provide the best assurance of detecting theories-in-use. However, it does depend upon such opportunities presenting themselves at the time when strategy making is regarded as important and relevant.

The approach depends upon work with managers who "feel pain" about a situation that they believe has strategic consequences. Attention to strategic transformation often only arises from crisis. Crises normally are not about strategy, but about strategic issues. One very powerful way of detecting emergent strategy is by deliberately seeking to uncover the embedded theories-in-action that are used through the analysis of these strategic breakdown situations.

For example, we used an interactive modelling technique for strategic problem solving, triggered by study of particular issues, but subsequently taken more widely into strategy development. By introducing a self-monitoring conversational interactive modelling tool as the problem solving support mechanism, beliefs and values gradually become explicit and recorded as an aggregated system of theories-in-use. One approach uses a methodology known as Strategic Options Development and Analysis (SODA) (Eden, 1993a), which uses *cognitive* mapping as the formalism for recording beliefs and values. The model is used as the device for negotiating a way forward in the crisis, building consensus-seeking behaviour (Lindblom, 1959), and developing commitments. The approach deliberately uses equivocality in the social construction of reality as the basis for social and psychological negotiation towards new strategies, following the framework for negotiation suggested by Fisher and Ury (1982) and Fisher and Brown (1988). Because a map is amenable to analysis through its structure and content (Eden, Ackermann and Cropper, 1992) it provides an opportunity to extract assumptions and values that are a part of the organizational recipe for strategic transformation.

FIGURE 14.1 shows the example in practice. Here individual members of the top management team had each commissioned

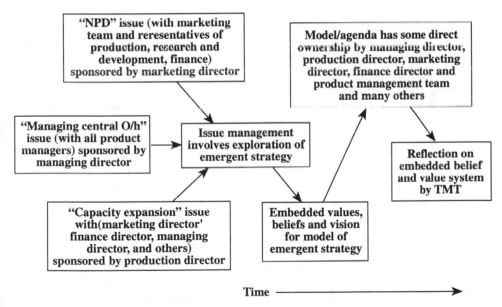

FIGURE 14.1   Detecting emergent strategy from issue management

the use of group decision support as a way to deal with (assumed separable) strategic problems. The same approach to group problem solving using a group decision support system (Eden and Ackermann, 1992) had been used in each case, and so slices of emergent strategy in practice could be merged together to form a single model.

This model of emergent strategy was then introduced to all of the top management team as something about which they might be curious. The feedback of their aggregate theories-in-action formally presented and analysed as a strategy map (in effect, a cognitive map for the organization), as these applied to specific problem solving episodes, had a profound effect on their understanding of their implicit management of their strategic future. As the figure indicates, this model became the basis for their wanting to proceed with strategy development that recognized the past (as expressed by the initial model) and their wishes for the future (as expressed in contrast to the initial model).

Approach 4: Interview and Feedback

The fourth approach involves using well-designed trigger questions in interview situations, followed by structured feedback to individuals and to the team, to replicate immediacy and relevance so that theories-in-use can be detected.

When the opportunity to work on a strategic crisis does not exist, interviews with key actors become a substitute. The extent to which the interview procedures are specifically designed as a substitute for working on a strategic breakdown situation will determine the success of the interviews in uncovering a world-taken-for-granted. The principle involved is to present the interviewee with unexpected and non-confirming perspectives, triggering articulation of their own mental map in an attempt to rectify the (mini-)breakdown created by the interviewer.

The model for this approach to detecting emergent strategy is set out in FIGURE 14.2. The procedure is iterative and depends upon the careful use of a number of techniques at the various stages of the process. Thus, as FIGURE 14.2 shows, the elicitation cycle is built on responses from well-designed triggers. The process uses dialectic and non-confirming statements, and involves the cycle of:

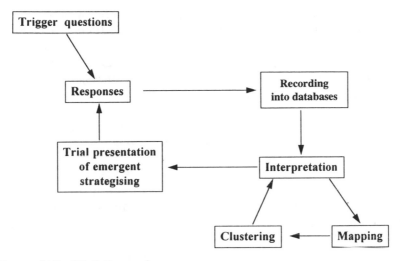

FIGURE 14.2   Elicitation cycle

- triggering responses
- recording responses
- interpreting and relating responses (creating theory of action)
- feeding back the resulting strategic framework
- back to triggering responses

The iterative process converges after a few cycles. It can be speeded up by the use of skilfully designed initial trigger questions. Following the interviews, the record is analysed and interpreted by the facilitators, after which the next iteration can take place. In further iterations, through team feedback, the underlying divergence of views in the team is a powerful trigger for further articulation of views on the world-taken-for-granted. For this reason it is important that the initial interview is a personal one, to ensure the maximum degree of initial range of views. Teams almost invariably underestimate the range of views existing within the team (the process thus creates a "natural dialectic" (Eden, 1992)), and are strongly triggered into action if this is perceived in a feedback session. Debate ensues on the relative validity of the views expressed, leading to a considerable degree of exposure of tacit strategic assumptions.

A good example of a management team discovering emergent

strategy through exploiting this type of dialectic was an intervention in an upstream oil exploration and production company (van der Heijden, 1992). Following the initial interviews, the first feedback meeting showed clearly the lack of consistency between the following three views of the business, espoused in the initial personal interviews:

- the traditional business definition as oil producers and traders
- the stock-in-trade strategic management models
- the intuitions about success in the business.

This proved a strong incentive to try to re-frame the situation. The tension created made the team concentrate on what became known as the competitive "moment of truth". It seemed that success or failure were much more conditional upon having access to the most favourable reserves, where significant mining rents could be earned, than on competitive positioning in the commodity crude oil market. It was finally agreed that the real moment of truth takes place when the deal is struck with government, particularly relating to the share of the rent left with the company developing the resource. Looked at in this light, companies are providers of a service to government, which can be defined as realization of a mining rent stream.

This new definition put a different perspective on the business. What had been known intuitively fell into place. Reasons for organizing in particular ways became more widely understood. Cultural and managerial dilemmas became discussable and more manageable. In general, the ability to articulate the strategic driving forces had a strong enabling effect on rational strategic dialogue within the company. This realization had come from detecting the emergent strategy and reflecting upon it through exploring the dialectic generated across team members.

IMPLICATIONS FOR THE STRATEGY DEVELOPMENT PROCESS

As discussed, many organizations will reach a point in time when capturing emergent strategy is useful. Those who set out to affect the emergent strategy need to address the question of how to improve the mental agility of the organization. They can be most productive in focusing on the process elements in strategy formulation through facilitation of the conversational process.

The strategy development process is a negotiative and social business. It is emotional and cognitive (Eden, 1993b; Raimond and Eden, 1990). The development process needs to acknowledge each of these four characteristics:

- social negotiation
- negotiating new social relationships
- building cognitive, or reasoned, commitment to the strategy
- attending to the need for emotional commitment to the strategy

This process of strategizing is continuous, therefore the strategy facilitator is never finished.

Our argument, as illustrated in the examples quoted and based on many experiences of working with top management teams, is that the task of facilitation of emergent strategizing will have the following elements:

- It starts with creating overall awareness of hidden processes of organizational decision making, their strengths and weaknesses, and the attention and time they require.
- The next step involves surfacing the decision makers' definition of the strategic breakdown situation at hand and their assumptions and mental models of the world around it. The strategic breakdown may be simulated by the setting up of dialectic tension between different viewpoints.
- By using the language of strategic management, decision makers can be helped in conceptualizing and categorizing aspects of the situation, recognize patterns and discover the deeper structure of their assumptions (their emergent strategy).
- Dislodging obsolete mental models and recipes requires making the organization discuss and think in terms of multiple futures (Ingvar, 1985). This will happen with greater enthusiasm when it is grounded in the emergent strategy rather than in the intellectual case to do so.
- The conversational process can be helped by opening lines of communication in the organization and ensuring appropriate participation by those with relevant knowledge or power to act (Harvey-Jones, 1988).

Whatever steps are selected, an important early part of the process is the surfacing of the current mental models. As Lindblom (1959) has suggested, these are often kept tacit in order to avoid confrontation and to maintain flexibility in the negotiation that strategy development entails. On the other hand, tacit models slow down the negotiation process and sometimes disable it. If the breakdown situation requires a fast response and a degree of deliberate strategy it is important to acknowledge the existence of embedded patterns that guide strategic problem solving. A more efficient process may be required, based on early surfacing of knowledge, views and positions, and the resulting emergent strategy.

CONCLUSION

Like any language, strategic management concepts have been generated in the past as categorizations of particular patterns of events, in order to cope with specific historical breakdown. It is the basis of any categorization of aspects of new situations, but will almost by definition stop short of completely describing new reality. Strategy needs to be continuously remapped if it is to remain socially efficient. This requires a flexible and dynamic conceptual framework of underlying assumptions in use in the organization. This focuses attention on the continuing process of strategy development.

We have argued that the processual approach to strategic management can be a more powerful lever than other levers that are aimed directly at strategic outcome and that ignore the organization as a socially negotiated enterprise. We have considered the idea of emergent strategy from a processual perspective. Given that the latter assumes intervention to improve the strategy process, we have argued that the concept of emergent strategy can be helpful if it is interpreted to represent the organizational reality of an underlying assumption framework. Any intervention approach starts from discovering this organizational reality through exploring actual breakdown situations, real or simulated, using dialectic methods in order to surface emergent strategy.

The methods and concepts of a grounded theory approach to management research are helpful in devising approaches to detecting emergent strategy, which is tantamount to detecting grounded theory. But, as illustrated, the processual approach to strategic management goes beyond that into exploring proactively the grounded theories in collaboration with the research subjects (the top management team), aiming at creating a dynamic assumption set that leads to an emergent strategy which continues to be socially efficient.

REFERENCES

Argyris, C. and Schon, D. (1978). *Organizational Learning: A Theory of Action Perspective*. Reading, MA: Addison-Wesley.

Axelrod, R. (Ed.) (1976). *Structure of Decision: The Cognitive Maps of Political Elites*. Princeton, NJ: University of Princeton Press.

Bartunek, J.M. (1988). The dynamics of personal and organizational reframing. In R.E. Quinn and K.S. Cameron (Eds) *Paradox and Transformation: Toward a New Theory of Change in Organization and Management*. Cambridge, MA: Ballinger.

Bartunek, J.M. and Moch, M.K. (1987). First-order, second-order, and third-order change and organization development interventions: A cognitive approach. *Journal of Applied Behavioural Science* 23, 483–500.

Berger, P.L. and Luckmann, T. (1966). *The Social Construction of Reality*. New York: Doubleday.

Bonham, G.M. and Shapiro, M. (1976). Explanation of the unexpected: The Syrian intervention in Jordan in 1970. In R. Axelrod (Ed.) *Structure of Decision: The Cognitive Maps of Political Elites*. Princeton, NJ: University of Princeton Press.

Bougon, M. (1992). Congregate cognitive maps: A unified dynamic theory of organization and strategy. *Journal of Management Studies* 29, 369–389.

Bryson, J., Ackerman, F. and Finn, C. (1992). Critical incidents and emergent issues in the management of large scale change efforts. In D. Kehl and H. Brinton (Eds) *The Strategy of Public Management*, Baltimore, MA: Johns Hopkins University Press.

de Geus, A. (1988). Planning as learning. *Harvard Business Review* March/April, 70–74.

Eden, C. (1989). Operational research as negotiation. In M. Jackson, P. Keys and S. Cropper (Eds) *Operational Research and the Social Sciences*. New York: Plenum Press.

Eden, C. (1992). Strategic management as a social process. *Journal of Management Studies* 29, 799–811.

Eden, C. (1993a). Strategy development and implementation – Cognitive mapping for group support. In J. Hendry and G. Johnson with J. Newton (Eds) *Strategic Thinking: Leadership and the Management of Change*. London: John Wiley.

Eden, C. (1993b). From the playpen to the bombsite: the changing nature of management science. *Omega* 21, 139–154.

Eden, C. and Ackermann, F. (1992). Strategy development and implementation: The role of a group decision support system. In B. Bostrom, S. Kinney and R. Watson (Eds) *Computer Augmented Teamwork*. New York: Van Nostrand Reinhold.

Eden, C. and Cropper, S. (1992). Coherence and balance in strategies for the management of public services: Two confidence tests for strategy development, review and renewal. *Public Money and Management* **12**, 43–52.

Eden, C. and Huxham, C. (1995). Action research for management research. *British Journal of Management*, forthcoming.

Eden, C., Ackermann, F. and Cropper, S. (1992). The analysis of cause maps. *Journal of Management Studies* **29**, 309–324.

Fisher, R. and Brown, S. (1988). *Getting Together: Building a Relationship that Gets to Yes*. Boston, MA: Houghton Mifflin.

Fisher, R. and Ury, W. (1982). *Getting to Yes*. London: Hutchinson.

Glaser, B.G. and Strauss, A.L. (1967). *The Discovery of Grounded Theory*. Chicago, IL: Aldine.

Grinyer, P.H. and McKiernan, P. (1990). Generating major change in stagnating companies. *Strategic Management Journal* **11**, 131–146.

Harvey, J. (1988). The Abilene paradox: The management of agreement. *Organizational Dynamics* Summer, 17–34.

Harvey-Jones, J. (1988). *Making It Happen*. London: Collins.

Huff, A. (Ed.) (1990). *Mapping Strategic Thought*. Chichester: John Wiley.

Ingvar, D. (1985). Memories of the future, an essay on the temporal organisation of conscious awareness. *Human Neurobiology* **4**, 127–136.

Janis, I.L. (1972). *Victims of Groupthink*. Boston, MA: Houghton Mifflin.

Kelly, G.A. (1955). *The Psychology of Personal Constructs*. New York: Norton.

Lindblom, C.E. (1959). The science of muddling through. *Public Administration Review* **19**, 79–88.

Mintzberg, H. (1990). Strategy formation – schools of thought. In J.W. Fredrickson (Ed.) *Perspectives on Strategic Management*. Grand Rapids, PA: Harper Business Books.

Mintzberg, H. (1987). Crafting strategy. *Harvard Business Review* July/August, 66–75.

Mintzberg, H. and Waters, J. (1985). Of strategies, deliberate and emergent. *Strategic Management Journal* **6**, 257–272.

Pascale, R.T. (1990). *Managing on the Edge*. New York: Simon and Schuster.

Pettigrew, A. (1977). Strategy formulation as a political process. *International Studies in Management and Organization* **7**, 78–87.

Raimond, P. and Eden, C. (1990). Making strategy work. *International Journal of Strategic Management* **23**, 97–105.

Schein, E.H. (1992). *Organizational Culture and Leadership* (2nd Edn). San Francisco, CA: Jossey-Bass.

Scheper, W. (1991). Group decision support systems: An inquiry into theoretical and philosophical issues, thesis, Katholieke Universiteit Brabant, Tilburg.

Sims, H. and Gioia, D. (Eds) (1986). *The Thinking Organization*. San Francisco, CA: Jossey-Bass.

Spender, J.C. (1989). *Industry Recipes, An Enquiry into the Nature and Sources of Managerial Judgement*. Oxford: Basil Blackwell.

Strauss, A. and Corbin, J. (1990). *Basics of Qualitative Research*. London: Sage.

Susman, G.I. (1982). Action research – a socio-technical systems perspective. In G. Morgan (Ed.) *Beyond Method*. Sage: London.

Susman, G.I. and Evered, R.D. (1978). An assessment of the scientific merits of action research. *Administrative Science Quarterly* **23**, 582–603.

van der Heijden, K. (1992). Corporate culture for competitive edge, strategy of international oil exploration and production companies. Presentation given at the Planning Forum Annual Meeting, 3–6 May 1992.

van der Heijden, K. (1993). Strategic vision at work. In J. Hendry and G. Johnson with J. Newton (Eds) *Strategic Thinking: Leadership and the Management of Change*. Chichester: John Wiley.

Vickers, G. (1983). *The Art of Judgement*. London: Harper & Row.

Weick, K. (1979). *The Social Psychology of Organizing* (2nd Edn). Reading, MA: Addison-Wesley.

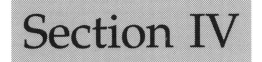

Section IV

Managing the Processes of Strategic Change

The changes around us are such that the experiences of the past no longer provide appropriate solutions. New pressures and new opportunities are leading to major transformations of the strategies of corporations and of the industries in which they operate. Many industries and sectors today are going through irreversible changes in their dynamics. To succeed with business transformation in this environment, organizations must recognize and deal with discontinuous change. The characteristics of discontinuous change include the certain knowledge that continuing to do what you are currently doing, or incrementally improving it, will not close the performance gap—a situation where not taking action is "using up your future" (Richard Pascale).

Blumenthal and Tichy describe how success can be hazardous to a firm's long-term health (success sclerosis), and assert that top management must be able to recognize and cope with change whenever market shifts require it. This involves redefining the role of management and changing management behaviour (genetic re-engineering), and includes leadership at the board level.

Bogner, Thomas and McGee explore significant changes in an industry's competitive patterns as reflections of multidimensional environmental changes, and the extent to which the new competitive patterns that emerge are the competitive responses to these changes. They use a "reverse lens" perspective to look back at the environmental and competitive factors that changed significantly in the time period preceding major changes in the patterns of industry competition.

Lockett examines the factors behind successful strategic change when the change includes a significant element of information technology (IT). He proposes a framework for managing strategic change with a significant IT component, based on a combination of research into business success in IT-related projects, and consultants' experience implementing change in large organizations.

Markides examines an apparent trend of the 1980s toward diversified firms refocusing on their core businesses and reducing the extent of their diversification. His study attempts to provide systematic evidence on the extent of refocusing and the nature of refocusing firms. His findings suggest that the relationship between diversification and profitability is not linear, but curvilinear: at low levels of diversity it is positive but, once a firm diversifies beyond some optimal level (perhaps a function of its resources and its external environment), the relationship becomes negative.

Chapter 15	Learning to Cope with Success *Barbara Blumenthal, Noel Tichy*
Chapter 16	Technological Forces as the Source of Industry Change: An Industry Study *William C. Bogner, Howard Thomas, John McGee*
Chapter 17	IT and Strategic Renaissance *Martin Lockett*
Chapter 18	Causes and Consequences of Corporate Restructuring *Constantinos C. Markides*

Discontinuous change is also about facing change that is vast in both scope and depth. It involves setting out on a path that leads to not knowing the answers and, in some cases, not even knowing the questions. As a result, the apparently safe and attractive option of returning to what we know has worked in the past (i.e. getting back to basics) may not work. Getting back to basics may mean arriving at the station after the train has left. Time has moved on, the market has caught up, customer expectations have evolved. Those once successful leaders who espouse getting back to basics forget that they were originally successful because they broke the mould of the existing market-place.

A strong case for action must also exist. The gap between current performance and aspiration or survival has to be powerful and quantified—and it does not apply in every situation. Turn-arounds, for example, are not necessarily transformational. Keys to successful business transformation include:

- A major event or crisis occurs that generates widespread recognition that things cannot continue as before (which begs the question, "can a successful business transform itself without first enduring crisis?").
- A vision that captures the imagination of employees may be necessary to harness their emotions about and commitment to the type of change that will likely be personally demanding and may mean the loss of many jobs.
- New leadership often finds it easier to challenge the existing order than do those who are burdened with the baggage of the past.
- Leadership of transformation means managing the present as though you are living in the future—living the vision.

If these are some of the keys to successful business transformation, what are some of the actions necessary for success? Based on what we have learned so far, some stand out clearly:

- Give the organization a shared vision about its strategic intent and about the process for getting there, before releasing the behavioral agenda. This higher order vision must then be clearly defined and quantified at each level of activity, so work-place actions can be guided and measured.
- Encourage people who are excited by the vision, at all levels, to challenge the status quo. This can create the tension required to stimulate restructuring the organization and re-engineering the processes.
- Set up teams of senior managers to design the future, and make them stakeholders in the design.
- Involve all employees in implementation of the design. Harness

their desire to contribute and their intimate knowledge of how things are done and how they can be improved.
- Recognize that transformation is not always a linear process, and generate a leadership style that encourages independent thinking, trial-and-error, and learning from mistakes.

15

Learning to Cope with Success

BARBARA BLUMENTHAL, NOEL TICHY

Under the intensive pressures of rapid change in the global market-place, scores of large firms in the past 15 years have been forced to transform their organizations. While some companies moved quickly and effectively, others did not. Among those that have had the greatest difficulty accepting the need for fundamental change and implementing ambitious change programs are some of the household names of world industry, firms with long histories of success and dominant market positions.

After more than a decade of concerted effort, both General Motors (GM) and Sears continue to lose market share and have as yet been unable to convince investors that a turnaround is on the horizon. In the mainframe computer industry IBM is struggling to restructure and restore profitable growth under vastly changed conditions. DEC was woefully late to react and under new leadership has begun an urgent restructuring process. Tenneco suffered huge losses before bringing in new leadership to embark on a fundamental restructuring of its operations. In Europe, similar problems beset Philips, which waited until large losses threatened its future before beginning a transformation effort.

The dramatic rise and fall of so many dominant firms raises intriguing questions. Why do large, successful firms have difficulty recognizing the need for change? Are there special

Strategic Renaissance and Business Transformation. Edited by H. Thomas, D. O'Neal and J. Kelly.
Copyright © 1995 John Wiley & Sons Ltd.

characteristics associated with success that make it difficult to mobilize an effective response? This chapter argues that success can be hazardous to a firm's long-term health. The greater the past success and market dominance of the firm and the longer the period of superior performance, the greater the risk that management will be slow to recognize and react to fundamental change (Tushman, Newman and Romanelli, 1986). It is a condition that we call *success sclerosis*.

Diagnosing a case of success sclerosis is the easy part. The far more difficult challenge is to cure it—to transform an organization so that it adapts to change whenever major market shifts require it. Yet, most transformation efforts do not address what we call corporate self-renewal. Instead they downsize, rightsize, flatten hierarchies, focus on customers, lower costs, and improve quality. In many instances, performance improves and the firm announces its transformation a success. But how well equipped is the firm to respond to the next major challenge in its markets? Has its experience actually cured it of success sclerosis?

To better understand the unique role of corporate self-renewal, it is necessary to compare it to the goals and levers used in more common types of transformations. The General Electric (GE) transformation is used to illustrate the process of corporate self-renewal, and the critical role played by the CEO. Finally, we offer advice for the board of directors, who must deal with the effects of success sclerosis—sooner or later.

THE ROOT CAUSES OF SUCCESS SCLEROSIS

There are undoubtedly unique aspects of each firm's history that can create barriers to change. Yet an examination of successful firms that have difficulty responding to change reveals common values, beliefs, structures and processes that pose clear impediments to change.

Some of the most important beliefs in successful firms are those that explain the firm's long period of success. Unfortunately, managers and employees tend to give undue credit to management practices, and not enough emphasis to factors beyond their control. Rarely do you hear a manager credit patents, proprietary systems, rising barriers to entry, or simply historical accident or luck as the reasons for the firm's success. Two beliefs can become widespread:

We are not threatened by our competitors.

In part because the reasons for success are not well understood, the firm assumes that its success can last forever. Inadequate efforts are made to collect external data that might paint a different picture, or to create internal debates that challenge the firm's strategy. Successful firms also tend to believe:

There is one right way to do things—the XYZ way.

The firm's success may leave it unable to appreciate that there are a variety of approaches that can be successful, or that a particular approach may not be appropriate for other conditions (Prahalad and Bettis, 1986). Intolerance of diversity is reinforced by the tendency in successful firms to recruit employees at a young age and promote from within, so that most managers lack other experiences and perspectives. It can become a central issue in managing acquisitions and joint ventures, since the acquired firm or joint venture often faces very different competitive conditions, yet the parent firm may insist that its management systems be used (Blumenthal, 1989).

Taken together these beliefs paint a picture of what others see as "arrogance"—managers who are excessively inward, inflexible and insufficiently alert to outside events. To compound the problem, many successful firms develop large bureaucratic hierarchies to cope with their phenomenal and rapid growth, resulting in decision processes that are slow and risk averse. Over time, bureaucratic structures and decision processes produce dysfunctional norms of behavior. At firms like GM in the 1980s, "no mistakes" was the surest way to advance up the ranks, so few risks were taken. At Tenneco there is now a drive to replace "best efforts" with accountability and keeping commitments. Jack Welch found that GE managers showed a tendency to put the best face on negative signals or data, and now cajoles managers to "face reality."

TABLE 15.1 summarizes the beliefs, behaviors and structures that are the root causes of success sclerosis, and proposes changes that have been identified as effective antidotes (Tichy and Sherman, 1993; Weitzel and Johnson, 1991).

TABLE 15.1 Diagnosis and cure for success sclerosis

	Success sclerosis	Desired state
Beliefs	Not threatened One right way	Changes can threaten us Keep looking for a better way
Goals	Internal targets Not a stretch	External benchmarks World class
Behavior	Don't question or criticize Don't look for threats Don't accept responsibility Risk averse Withhold information	Challenge strategy, practices Encourage debate Face reality, accept criticism Hold managers accountable Take risks Share information, teamwork
Structure	Many levels Large central staff	Few levels Reduce staffs, decentralize
Roles	Managers direct and control	Managers coach and facilitate
Rewards	Small differential	Large differential Based on performance

COMMON TRANSFORMATION PROCESSES

Three types of transformation processes are used to address specific mismatches between the capabilities of the firm and the requirements of the market-place: restructuring the corporate portfolio, operations improvement and strategic transformation.

RESTRUCTURING THE CORPORATE PORTFOLIO

This process is triggered by a change in business unit performance, a change in corporate strategy to increase or decrease the relatedness of the business units, or a change to the financial objectives of the firm. Management must decide which businesses to be in and how to develop core competences that will sustain each business.

This is often the first phase of a larger transformation effort, and can have a significant impact on the financial performance of the firm. In the early 1980s, Jack Welch sold $US9 billion of assets and acquired $US18 billion, steps that helped to dramatically improve GE's financial performance and stock market value (Tichy and Sherman, 1993). Typically, the process is triggered by the appointment of a new CEO or a financial crisis. Portfolio decisions are clearly the domain of top management and typically involve a relatively small group of senior managers of the firm.

In most instances, the standards for corporate performance are raised, expressed as higher return on investment (ROI) targets, market position, or contribution to building core competences of the firm. Divesting businesses on this basis sends a clear message to employees and managers of the remaining business units that they are not immune from scrutiny.

OPERATIONS IMPROVEMENT

Operations improvement is called for if the diagnosis reveals that the business unit's strategy is sound, but cost, quality, or service must be improved to compete. The solution is typically to redesign the business unit's processes across the organization, supported by changes to structure, skills and behavior. Such programs are often referred to as "bottom-up" change because they rely heavily on employee involvement in both the design and implementation of changes. While the change process is by no means simple, there are many examples of successful programs and many interventions that have proven to be effective.

Top management's role in this process is to set targets for improvements, allocate resources to the line managers who will lead the change effort, and finally to congratulate the division when the results are achieved. The CEO plays a more active role if the program is corporate-wide and designed to attack a problem common to all business units. In 1981, Jack Welsh initiated a program throughout GE to improve total cost productivity in response to competitive pressures from Japan. Mike Walsh at Tenneco initiated a corporate-wide quality program within a few months of taking over in 1991.

Strategic Transformation

Many organizational changes are triggered by a shift in business strategy. Often, management must adjust the components of the organization—its structure, processes, people and culture—to fit the new strategy and competitive conditions, as success depends on the internal consistency of the various components.

When the general direction of market and competitive changes is clear it is often not difficult to conceive of an appropriate strategy. The primary challenge is in implementing the changed strategy, because it involves wholesale changes to the systems and procedures of the organization, and frequently calls for new behavior by managers and employees. Many firms have successfully faced such challenges, and the key steps of the change process have been well documented (Greiner and Bhambri, 1989; Nadler and Tushman, 1989; Tichy, 1983; Tushman, Newman and Romanelli, 1986).

There are numerous examples of successful strategic transformation, either for an entire firm such as Motorola and Hewlett-Packard, or a division such as GE Locomotive. K-Mart and Sears are in the midst of strategic repositioning in the rapidly changing retailing industry, while mainframe computer firms are struggling to redefine their competitive formulae.

How Does Corporate Self-Renewal Fit In?

A firm suffering from success sclerosis is likely to need the three transformation processes discussed above *and* corporate self-renewal. An organization that does not demand excellence and tolerates inefficiencies is a good candidate for operations improvement, perhaps in every business unit of the firm. A lack of attention to industry trends and competitors suggests that some of the business units will be in need of strategic transformation. And if the competitive situation in some of the business units look particularly bleak, there may be a need for divestiture and re-evaluating the corporate portfolio.

All four transformation processes are similar in that they create non-incremental change in the organization. They differ by the type of vision, the organizational levers used to institutionalize

TABLE 15.2 Comparison of transformation processes

	Corporate portfolio	Operations improvement	Strategic transformation	Corporate self-renewal
Define the vision	Who we are	Cost, quality productivity	How we compete	How we manage
Levers to institutionalize change	Set goals Buy, sell	Redesign processes, roles	Redefine products and markets; structure, processes, systems	Redefine decision process, roles, rewards, structure; Develop leaders
Leadership role	Top management	Bottom up	Top management or division management	Top management
Time frame	1–5 years	6–24 months	1–5 years	3–10 years

change, the leadership role, and the time required for the transformation to succeed (TABLE 15.2). The summary shows that many of the same organizational levers are used in each of the transformation processes. A cost reduction program may target layers of middle management and staff as extra expense not incurred by the firm's competitors. Such layers may also be a primary target of strategic transformation, because they can interfere with innovation and responding to customer needs. And the same changes are essential to corporate self-renewal to make the organization more flexible and speed the decision process.

Perhaps the most important reason for removing layers is to speed the transformation process itself. Changing management behavior can be painfully slow, as each level of management must convince and coach the next. Where there are many levels, passive-resistors can flourish and outlive the tenure of most change-minded CEOs. With fewer levels in the hierarchy, the spotlight is put on managers who are either unable or unwilling to change. A major breakthrough in the transformation at GE occurred when Jack Welch removed a layer of senior managers.

Strategic transformations are typically concerned with positioning products and services, developing skills and competences, and building the capability to deliver. Thus a strategic transformation leaves the firm better able to compete in today's market, but not necessarily better able to adjust to tomorrow's market.

While there may be overlap with other processes, corporate self-renewal is unique in several respects. Firstly, it is the only process that attacks management behavior at the corporate level. Secondly, it addresses the quality of the firm's goals and the behaviors required to meet higher goals. While facing reality, exploring alternatives, and accepting criticism are necessary to find solutions in each of the transformation processes, only corporate self-renewal seeks to institutionalize this behavior.

EXAMPLES OF CORPORATE SELF-RENEWAL

The evidence shows that few firms attempt to create a more fundamental type of transformation, and even fewer firms succeed (Kotter and Heskett, 1992). Two cases illustrate the difference. By most accounts, GM has not succeeded in creating the type of fundamental change required to compete in the 1990s. During the same period, GE has gone through a sustained effort to recreate itself in order to remain competitive and responsive to changes in its markets. While it may be premature to judge the results of these efforts, the difference in approach and leadership are striking.

GM, faced with eroding market share and profitability throughout the 1980s, tackled its decline on several fronts. It changed its structure, improved quality, lowered costs, diversified, and experimented with new management practices. And yet many observers think that the fundamental problems have not been addressed:

> GM is undeniably a different company as it approaches the end of the decade. It is impossible for a company to be slammed against the wall of change with such velocity and not become different in fundamental ways. But a car crash can break your nose, and still leave your head intact, and the dramatic gestures of the 1980s may not have necessarily shifted the cultural reality for the better.
>
> (Keller, 1989)

Take the NUMMI project, a joint venture with Toyota begun in 1983 to build small cars in a GM assembly plant using Toyota's management approach. While GM professed to be interested in learning about Japanese management and manufacturing practices, there has been little effort to transfer the lessons to the rest of the firm. Can GM transform itself through change programs at the plant or division level without attacking the underlying management processes, behaviors, and beliefs that continue to dominate the firm? Can GM performance improve over the long run without a systematic, painful, and sustained attack to change its genetic code?

When Jack Welch became CEO of GE in 1981, he declared that the firm needed a revolution, and set out to create it. He initiated actions to restructure the corporate portfolio, improve productivity, and in a few cases redefine business strategies.

But from the beginning, his primary target was the GE management system itself. He began with the corporate structure and decision process—cutting the central staff in half and pushing authority for most decisions to the businesses. However, much of the rigidity and complacency remained in the businesses themselves. While on the one hand Welch tried to give the business leaders much more autonomy, he also pushed them to simplify the review and control processes, eliminate work and reduce management and staff. Between these efforts and a major push for productivity improvement and improved earnings, the result was a total of 170 000 positions eliminated from 1980 to 1991, net of acquisitions and divestitures, while revenues grew from $US25 billion to $US60.2 billion.

From the beginning, Welch articulated his ideas about a new style of management required for GE to regain its competitive strength. He discussed management behavior at every opportunity and began a process to formalize the firm's values to drive this behavior in 1985. He publicized examples of management behavior that he saw as role models, and coached his direct reports and other managers with whom he had contact.

Promotion decisions were a potent weapon to create change. Welch made promotions with an eye not only to a manager's business performance, but also to how he or she achieved results. In 1989 formal performance evaluations began to use adherence to the firm's values as an important criteria.

Despite the changes in style occurring at senior levels, Welch was frustrated that changes were slow to develop in the middle management ranks, and searched for ways to reach this critical group. In an organization the size of GE, the normal mechanisms were inadequate. Managers who had their own doubts about the new values were not reliable coaches for their subordinates, and corporate training was effective but limited to a small percentage of the population. The solution was the Workout program, begun in 1989 to reach directly to the lower levels of the organization and force middle managers to "walk the talk." Workout sessions presented a forum for employees to challenge management, make suggestions for improvements, and solve problems as a group, while giving managers a quick lesson in the importance of listening.

While substantial progress has been made at GE in ridding the firm of success sclerosis, the transformation is far from complete. Welch estimates that creating a value-based organization to guide behavior may take until the year 2000, just as he will be reaching retirement age. It is fortuitous that Welch was a young man when the Board appointed him CEO in 1981.

The GE story offers important clues about why corporate self-renewal is so often overlooked as executives re-examine their corporate portfolio, begin strategic transformation and launch several operations improvement processes. That is because corporate self-renewal begins at the corporate level, and is the only process that seeks to change the way in which senior managers work. Such change is not only threatening, but close to home. As Jack Welch discovered, many of his colleagues, including people whom he put into senior positions, were not suited for his new system of management. Painful as it may seem, the CEO must be willing to create a revolution in his own backyard.

LESSONS FOR THE BOARD OF DIRECTORS

The board of directors can play an important role in both the prevention of success sclerosis, and the cure, when necessary. While there have been calls for more effective boards of directors for years, there are recent signs that directors are becoming more active, at least when a firm's situation is clearly deteriorating. The GM board took over the direct management of the firm after years of declining performance. The directors of DEC and Tenneco recruited new CEOs. But can the board play a more constructive role than simply waiting for the CEO to fail and replacing him?

In a recent paper, Lipton and Lorsch (1992) make a strong case that boards can and should do better: "By acting early and effectively, directors can prevent small problems from growing into a major crisis over many years." They go on to propose several changes to the practices of boards, which can help them to be an effective monitor of management's performance. One proposal is for the board to evaluate the firm's performance each year relative to the firm's goals, philosophy, and competitors' performance. They also suggest that boards be given a broader range of performance measurements such as market position, productivity, product leadership, and employee attitudes.

While new types of information suggested by Lipton and Lorsch will help, they provide board members only a glimpse of the internal workings of the firm. Meetings, particularly informal discussions with managers from all levels, provide another important window, and may reveal signs of arrogance, failure to face reality, and failure to challenge and explore alternative approaches. Yet, while an alert Board may be able to spot signs of trouble, they cannot force management to take corrective action of the type described here. The only direct impact the Board can have is to prod the CEO—through aggressive questioning—to be more realistic and less complacent.

The choice of CEO is the Board's critical contribution to fighting success sclerosis. If they select someone who understands the need for change and is capable of leading it, they have performed a valuable service. Frequently, this means not choosing the logical internal candidate, who may be terrific at managing operations, but not at leading a fundamental and long-term transformation. Thus, boards of directors, as much as top executives, must be alert to the signs of success sclerosis, and understand the nature of the transformation required to overcome it.

REFERENCES

Blumenthal, B. (1989). *The acquisition of small high technology firms: A study of merger implementation*, PhD dissertation, University of Michigan.
Greiner, L. and Bhambri, A. (1989). New CEO intervention and dynamics of deliberate strategic change. *Strategic Management Journal* **10**, 67–86.
Keller, M. (1989). *Rude Awakening*. New York: William Morrow.
Kotter, J. and Heskett, J. (1992). *Corporate Culture and Performance*. New York: Free Press.

Lipton, M. and Lorsch, J. (1992). A modest proposal for improved corporate governance, *Directors Monthly* **17**, 1–5.

Nadler, D. and Tushman, M. (1989). Organizational frame bending: Principles for managing reorientation. *Academy of Management Executive* **3**, 194–204.

Prahalad, C.K. and Bettis, R.A. (1986). The dominant logic: A new linkage between diversity and performance. *Strategic Management Journal* **7**, 485–501.

Tichy, N. (1983). *Managing Strategic Change*. New York: John Wiley.

Tichy, N. and Sherman, S. (1993). *Control Your Destiny or Someone Else Will*. New York: Doubleday.

Tushman, M., Newman, W. and Romanelli, E. (1986). Convergence and upheaval: Managing the unsteady pace of organizational evolution. *California Management Review* **29**, 29–44.

Weitzel, W. and Johnson, E. (1991). Reversing the downward spiral: Lessons from W.T. Grant and Sears Robuck. *Academy of Management Executive* **5**, 7–22.

16

Technological Forces as the Source of Industry Change: An Industry Study

WILLIAM C. BOGNER, HOWARD THOMAS, JOHN McGEE

INTRODUCTION

Technology represents just one of several interdependent contextual factors that determine an individual firm's strategy and the overall structure of an industry. Over time, the relative positions of firms within an industry may change as the firms alter their competitive strategy in response to significant changes in the competitive environment, including major technological changes. However, these technological changes seldom occur in isolation; other aspects of the task environment are usually changing as well. The thesis of this chapter is that the competitive impact of major technological changes on both firms and industry structure is often significantly distorted by other dynamic factors in the environment. The impact of technological change will only be understood when the interaction with all other changes is understood as well.

Prior longitudinal research has shown a relationship between technological change and the relative competitive positions of

Strategic Renaissance and Business Transformation. Edited by H. Thomas, D. O'Neal and J. Kelly.
Copyright © 1995 John Wiley & Sons Ltd.

firms (Ghazanfar, McGee and Thomas, 1987; Tushman and Anderson, 1986). Specifically, these studies have shown that significant shifts in industry technology are followed by changes in industry leadership as some firms opportunistically reposition themselves. It is anticipated that other types of environmental changes can disrupt the stable competitive structure of an industry as well. Legal, political, and regulatory changes, as well as fundamental changes in the competitive practice of a member firm, could all similarly disrupt industry stability. We suggest, however, that changes in industry environment seldom occur in isolation. Consequently, the resulting changes in firm strategy and intra-industry structure are seldom driven by a single factor. In this chapter we explore significant changes in an industry's competitive pattern as a reflection of multidimensional environmental changes.

We focus first on major changes in the pattern of competition observed in the US pharmaceutical market. At each of three instances we look back at all of the environmental and competitive factors, including technology, that changed significantly in the preceding time. Through this "reverse lens," we not only capture the major technological change that occurs, but other areas of change as well. This enables us to explore how the totality of these changes caused the major disruption in industry competition that we observed.

DIFFERENT TYPES OF EXTERNAL CHANGE

Competitive patterns within an industry tend to be fairly stable in the short term. Industry leaders tend to retain their positions and rivalry among members is relatively predictable. Modest change does occur during these periods of relative stability. Tushman and Anderson (1986) call this "competence enhancing" change; Gersick (1991) calls it "Darwinian gradualism." The "deep structure" (Gersick, 1991) of competition, including key elements of the value chain and their interactions, customer and producer perceptions about what needs exist, the ways in which a product or service can satisfy customer needs, and how providers should actually provide the satisfying goods and services, remain stable. Leading firms can cope with such changes due to their organizational slack and their experience in managing the factors underlying the turbulence.

Ongoing competitive strategies are grounded in the beliefs about the deep structure of competition. Traits such as technological trajectories (Pisano, 1989), standard operating procedures (Cyert and March, 1963), and organizational structure (Chandler, 1962) become learned, established, and institutionalized consistent with the deep structure of an industry. Tacit knowledge and core competencies evolve along these trajectories, allowing industry leaders to sustain their competitive advantage in a dynamic environment (Bogner and Thomas, 1994). Further environmental changes simply represent further opportunities for leaders to replicate the dynamic management that has put them in the lead in the first place.

In recent years interest has shifted to those less common events in which the deep structure of the competitive environment is shattered. These "frame-busting" (Tushman, Newman and Romanelli, 1986) or "competence destroying" (Tushman and Anderson, 1986) events actually destroy some or all of the deep structure on which a firm's competitive strategy is built. Importantly, the traits of the firm are not destroyed; the asset base of the firm remains and the firm often continues pursuing its past strategy. But the competitive context with which the strategy was aligned has been significantly altered. Those organizations whose strategies are most strongly tied to the old structure (logically the best performing firms) suffer most. Conversely, those firms that had not built a tight alignment with the prior deep structure are more likely to respond quickly and effectively to the opportunities that change brings.

Technological changes can alter the deep structure of competition by significantly altering consumer demand, the ways in which demands can be satisfied, or the competitive methods that firms can employ. However, the existence of other competitive forces with the potential to disrupt industry structure creates two scenarios for major changes in competitive patterns that involve technology. Firstly, technological change alone may be significant to cause frame-breaking change, with the interaction of other environmental changes altering the impact of the technology shift on competition. Secondly, technological change may not, in and of itself, be sufficient to destroy the deep structure of competition. However, when combined with other changes, these surrounding changes interact and "lever-up" the technological change, creating an overall impact that is sufficient to change the industry structure.

In both cases the scope of the change interacts with the speed of the change. A larger shift occurring slowly over time may give leaders sufficient opportunity to react. Conversely, smaller aggregate change that happens quickly may overwhelm the leaders' ability to compete.

In this study we want to observe the ways in which technological change interacts with other changes in the industry environment when frame-breaking changes occur. In order to do so we will look at three major changes in the competitive structure of the modern pharmaceutical industry. In each case technological change was a major force in creating new market opportunities. However, in each of these situations other significant changes also occurred in the environment. In examining each change period we will focus on these three research questions:

1. To what extent are the major changes in the pattern of industry competition preceded by both significant technological changes and significant changes in other environmental factors?
2. To what extent do the patterns of competition that have emerged following these periods of change reflect the interaction of technological and other changes, rather than only the technological change?
3. To what extent could the technological change have produced "competence destroying change" in the industry in the absence of simultaneous, non-technological changes in the competitive environment?

INDUSTRY FOR ANALYSIS

For this study we will look at the modern pharmaceutical industry in the US. Our analysis focuses on US and eastern European firms during the post-war period. Because of the public and often controversial nature of the industry, there exists a significant amount of research on industry competition in the literature from industrial organization economics (Steele, 1964; Temin, 1980) and strategy (Cool and Schendel, 1987). In addition, there are well-developed accounts of the development of medicines (Sneader, 1985) as well as specific firm histories (Carlisle, 1987; Cray, 1984). Three major shifts in competition patterns were identified as a result of this review.

The first shift identified was the emergence of the powerful "antibiotic houses" after the war. In the pre-war era the ethical drug business was dominated by "fine chemical" firms (e.g. Merck) or large organic chemistry firms for whom drugs were largely a side line (e.g. Hoechst and ICI). After the war, antibiotic technology was the driving force in the industry and the firms that emerged as industry leaders after the war (e.g. Pfizer, Upjohn) gained their positions as a result of the war-time breakthroughs in antibiotic research.

The second period of major industry change occurred during the second half of the 1970s. This era saw a weakening of the performance of the whole industry (Cool and Dierickx, 1993) and increasing emphasis on non-antibiotic drugs. Many of these drugs were entering the market as products of "rational drug design." Swiss firms (Hoffman-LaRoche, Ciba-Geigy, Sandoz) were strong performers and US firms that had not participated as fully in the antibiotic era (e.g. Merck) had regained leadership positions. Conversely, the relative performance of the antibiotic firms had diminished significantly from their 1950s and 1960s levels.

The third period of change is the late 1980s and early 1990s. It is clear that the primary technological change seen shaping the pharmaceutical industry at this time is the emerging biotechnology. This research began in earnest on a very basic level following breakthroughs in recombinant DNA technology in the 1970s. By the late 1980s over 1000 biotechnology firms existed in the US alone. The most visible response to this technology has been the "strategic alliance." These long-term relationships between established pharmaceutical firms and biotechnology start-ups have been attributed to several factors associated with biotechnology, including its high risk, the inability of traditional organic oriented labs to shift research trajectories to biochemistry, and the control of tacit knowledge by a few scientists. However, factors unrelated to technology, such as the globalization of markets, also present a rationale for such alliances.

ANALYSIS OF EACH CHANGE PERIOD

EVENT 1: THE LATE 1940s

This period saw the emergence of firms such as Pfizer and Squibb as leaders in terms of growth and profitability. All of the firms that emerged as major participants in the post-war industry had existed prior to that time, trading in areas related to health care, including fine chemicals, vaccines, and proprietary remedies. In spite of their various pre-war backgrounds, the key distinction among firms after the war had to do with their relationship to the development of deep-tank fermentation processes for penicillin production.

Technological Change

At the dawn of World War II the UK government and its pharmaceutical industry had begun to coordinate efforts for supplying war needs. Although penicillin research was proceeding on many fronts it did not receive significant government support. Sneader (1985) notes that the British government took penicillin's potential lightly enough to allow early research results to be published in the *Lancet* in 1940 and 1941. (Apparently the Axis powers did not think much of the research either, given their complementary lack of interest in taking advantage of this public information.)

In 1941 the US government agreed to allow several firms, universities, and independent researchers to cooperate in an effort to develop a new technology that would replace the low-volume, shallow-tank fermentation methods by which penicillin had been grown since its discovery. This process of innovation involved the testing of a very large number of soil samples and the chemical modification of promising mould strains. The search was successful, and large production plants were built in the US during the war for the manufacture of penicillin.

After the war, six firms that had participated directly in developing deep-tank technology—Squibb, Pfizer, Lederle Labs of American Cyanamid, Abbott, Eli Lilly, and Parke-Davis—acquired many of the plants. Through their research efforts these firms had acquired a large store of knowledge about antibiotic activity in nature, as well as processes for isolating and mass producing various desirable antibiotic strains. Other firms, notable Merck, had also been studying antibiotic activity in nature. Merck's support of Selman Waksman at Rutgers helped lead to the isolation of streptomycin. The firms that built up antibiotic research skills during the war were in the best position to exploit the soil-screening research. Not surprisingly, in the years following the end of the war these firms went on to develop synthetic penicillins and related antibiotics far more effectively, taking leadership of the industry.

Here the story seems straightforward: a group of American firms acquire the new, key skills for developing antibiotics, which leads them into a period of sustained growth and profitability. Other firms were relegated to second-tier performance for a significant time. The leadership change was driven by the development of new competencies. However, a broader analysis of the industry and its economics suggests that the incentive to exploit this technology did not exist after 1945. Two significant legal changes in the US, and their associated economic consequences, were the catalyst needed for the successful economic exploitation of the new skills.

Non-Technological Change

Two legal changes altered the economics of developing and marketing pharmaceutical drugs in the United States. The first was the granting of drug patents and the second was the requirement for prescriptions from physicians. Temin (1980) and Hirsch (1975) describe in detail how these environmental factors facilitated high industry profitability in the 1950s and 1960s. Their impact is described briefly here. The first decision was made by the US Patent Office on the drug streptomycin. In 1948 the US patent office decided that *synthetic* penicillins and other antibiotics derived from living organisms (e g the cephalosporins) were eligible for product patents in spite of their related existence in nature.

The ability to lock in large profits held out the promise of large returns from investments in R&D and capital facilities during the life of the patent. However, the patents would produce only small profits if the therapeutic variation among competing patented products was insignificant. Indeed, many of the synthetic, patent-protected antibiotics were only slight variations of one another. Therefore, a further bar to competition by close substitutes was needed in order to avoid price competition. This barrier was provided in the form of the "prescription only" requirement.

Prior to the 1938 Food Drug and Cosmetic Act (1938 Act) products sold in pharmacies in the US did not require a prescription, except in the case of some narcotics. A year later a regulation was promulgated under the Act to the effect that if a drug's safe use was too difficult for a layman to understand, then it could not be safely labeled and, hence, could only be sold through a physician's prescription. The US Supreme Court upheld this regulation's validity in a 1948 case (*United States* v. *Sullivan*, 332 US 689 (1948))–the same year as the patent ruling on streptomycin. The economic impact was to transfer to the physician the power to choose from among patent-protected substitutes. When the physician chooses without respect to the price that the patient will be charged, the profit potential for patent-protected drugs could reach monopoly levels. The resulting relationship between pharmaceutical firm, patient, pharmacy, and physician is illustrated in FIGURE 16.1. This system suggests that the *physician* should now be able to exercise "gatekeeper" power and extract the economic rents of the firm's patent in return for the writing of the prescription. However, due to ethical restrictions (and no easy way to extract the payments) the physician largely allows the monopoly profit from the sale to pass through to the patent holder. The pharmacy also has no bargaining

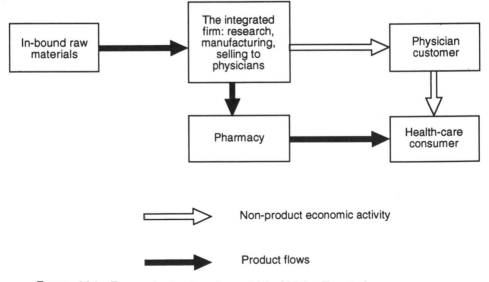

FIGURE 16.1   Economic structure in post-World War II period

power when filling a prescription under this system, due in part to further dispensing limitations imposed by state governments in the 1950s (Hirsch, 1975; Steel, 1964). Thus, in the US retail setting the manufacturer was able to capture the economic profits in the activity chain through its wholesale price (Measday, 1971).

Interactions

The interactions of these changes can be seen by looking at the value system represented in FIGURE 16.2. Technological competencies developed during the war provided knowledge for creating new drugs (the second box), which can be patented (the third box) and, hence, become unique. Through the rigidity of the "prescription only" requirement and the conduct of physicians (the fourth box), competition from close substitutes was blocked in the retail purchase setting (the fifth box). The critical activities in the value chain for this strategy were the research and development of new products, and the detailing (marketing) of the drugs to the physician prescribers. The lower part of FIGURE 16.2 shows how the legal and technological changes just described simultaneously changed multiple elements of the value system.

The interactions of technological and legal changes not only favored the emergence of a group of firms (the antibiotic firms), but also shaped these firms' internal structure. The firms that engaged in the antibiotic research during the war were primarily upstream firms, which needed expertise in downstream activities, particularly in the selling of branded products. For example, two firms, Pfizer and Merck, mainly upstream operations, acquired Rorer and Sharpe & Dhome, respectively, both with downstream selling skills. Note that if technology was the key activity and if the economic profits of the new value system could be captured through the technological competence alone, then there would have been no need for control of downstream functions. But in order to exploit their new patents from the new technology, firms also needed competence in the marketing to physicians. The research and technological skills of the antibiotic era were only made economically viable when simultaneous legal and regulatory changes raised potential returns on the new antibiotic drugs to a higher level.

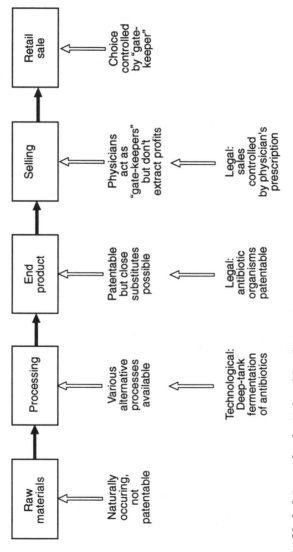

FIGURE 16.2 Underlying technological and legal impacts

EVENT 2: THE MID1970s

Unlike the antibiotic era after World War II, much less attention has been given to the decade that brought the most significant overall changes in the industry to date—the 1970s. The decade has not entirely been ignored, but most of the attention had focussed on consumer issues dealing with generic substitution and retail price advertising issues in the US market. While these were important, they do not give a full or sufficient explanation of the changes that swept through the competitive strategies of the firms. A change in technology (the emergence of rational drug design) and its impacts on the industry have been largely under-emphasized.

Technological Change

Entering the 1970s firms earned a good portion of their returns from older products, including those that were never patented or on which patents had expired, due to the economic relationships between the firms, the physicians and consumers as depicted in FIGURE 16.1. (The competitive situation in this time period is more fully detailed by Measday (1971).) These cash flows were critical to the industry because fewer new patent-protected products were being produced. The introduction of new chemical entities had been falling in the US since 1959. This was due, in part, to a fundamental R&D problem: newer generations of products required more complex and expensive research, but the underlying biochemical knowledge needed to develop more sophisticated treatments was lacking.

Historically, research did *not* begin with an understanding of the biochemistry of the human body followed by the development of a chemical compound to fit that need. Instead, mass-assay screening of potential compounds was done. Promising insights and observations from clinical practice led to systematic chemical modification in a search for improved efficacy, the removal of side effects, and, eventually, new products, such as diuretics and oral anti-diabetes treatments (Sneader, 1985). Rational drug design emerged in the 1970s as the technology that would change this discovery process. In effect, rational drug design allowed desirable therapies to be pursued based on new understandings of the human biological and chemical processes involved.

An example of how rational drug design changed R&D can be seen in cardiovascular drugs. Drug treatment for high blood pressure in the period before the 1970s included extensive use of diuretics. Typical of earlier drug development processes, these drugs were developed in the 1950s after physicians observed heavy diuresis from patients treated with sulfa drugs. Firms such as Merck and Lederle manipulated the chemistry of existing sulfa drugs to produce new drugs that maximized the diuresis while eliminating other effects. By the 1970s, however, the process by which blood pressure rose was well understood. One such activity, which leads to angina and hypertension, is driven by the excessive flow of calcium ions, leading to undesired levels of heart muscle contractions. From this knowledge drugs were developed to block the entry of the triggering calcium ion, breaking the sequence. This "rational" drug development represents a total departure from prior methods of drug discovery.

Rational drug design changed drug research in two ways. Firstly, the process was expensive. Secondly, opportunities expanded for new drug development in a variety of therapeutic classes. As long as the high cost of the R&D could be borne, firms could more systematically diversify their product lines. Further, they could develop new and more effective patent-protected drugs to replace the old therapies, which were subject to generic competition. Such an R&D agenda favored firms whose existing cash flows were sufficient to fund multiple new projects across several therapeutic classes. Hence, the ability to squeeze higher margins out of older products became more critical.

Non-Technological Change

During the 1970s the changes with which the US market was most often associated were those affecting retail prices. The system that was presented in FIGURE 16.1 had generally been maintained until the 1970s. Through the rules against generic substitution by pharmacists, it allowed for maintenance of monopoly price levels even after patent expiration and the entry of generic substitutes onto the market. Given the drop off in new drug development and the aging of the highly profitable anti-biotics, this ability to protect non-patent-protected (older) drugs from price competition grew in importance. Legal and regulatory changes, however, cut into this cash flow just at the time it was needed to fund rational drug design projects.

The first change was a state-by-state trend that permitted pharmacists to substitute a generic equivalent when filling prescriptions for non-patent-protected drugs, unless expressly forbidden from doing so by the physician. But while the generics were often much cheaper, consumers were often unaware of the difference due to restrictions on price advertising. Because many pharmacists charged a fixed mark-up (often set by professional rules) economic incentive to use higher cost products continued to exist even where substitution was permitted. Then in 1976 the second change occurred. The US Supreme Court ruled that restrictions on price advertising were unconstitutional restraints on the freedom of speech (*Virginia State Board of Pharmacy* v. *Virginia Citizens Cons. Council*, 425 U.S. 748 (1976)). Newly informed consumers could now assert pressure for low-priced generic equivalents. Retail stores wishing to advertise low drug prices as part of their competitive posture increased the price pressure on manufacturers. The most effective retail drug price competition would involve a switch to the use of the lowest cost generics. Together these legal changes caused prices to fall sharply, and cash flows were squeezed.

Interactions

These changes in the legal environment for retail sales interacted with the shift toward rational drug design in the laboratory. While the primary impact of rational drug design was on the *cost* of *new* drugs, the primary impact of retail price competition was on the *revenue* from *old* drugs. The combined effect was to shift the overall product mix sought by drug firms *and* the speed with which they sought to embrace the new technology. A stylized representation of the interactions of the legal and regulatory changes with rational drug design is presented in FIGURE 16.3. Not only was rational drug design creating new opportunities for patent-protected products, but changes in the retail drug market meant that these new patent-protected drugs would increasingly have to be the source of the cash flows that would feed future R&D programs. The number and regularity of drugs coming out of a research program had to increase because the number of

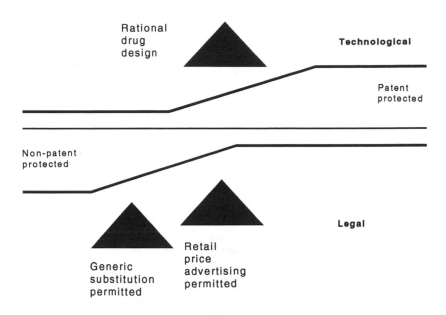

Shifting impacts on product and research postures

FIGURE 16.3   Shift in retail focus in the 1970s

years for which a big discovery would produce cash was reduced. Rational drug design put new products within R&D departments' reach just when legal changes required more patent-protected cash flows for financial viability. FIGURE 16.3 represents the shift in what constitutes a viable, ongoing product profile for a firm. This shift favored the larger firms, while also giving rise to a much larger generic drug industry in the US. A study by Bogner and Thomas (1991) illustrates the patterns of competition within the industry that resulted from these events. That study used FDA and US Patent Office data, and grouped US and western European firms based on their patterns of drug introductions and new pharmaceutical patents. These "strategic groups" cluster firms with similar strategic profiles within the same group. The groupings that they developed for the 1981–1983 period are presented in TABLE 16.1.

TABLE 16.1 shows that the dominant group in the early 1980s was the third group, made up of large chemical firms and some former antibiotic firms all with a large number of new patents

TABLE 16.1   Strategic groups in the US pharmaceutical market, 1981–1984

Group 1	Group 2	Group 3	Group 4
Boots	American Home Products	American Cyanamid	Barr
ICN	Bristol-Myers	Beecham	Bolar
Marion Labs	Burroughs-Wellcome	Ciba-Geigy	Par
Merrell	Glaxo	Eli Lilly	Mylan*
Norwich-Eaton	Johnson & Johnson	Hoechst	Zenith
Rorer	Robins (A.H.)	Hoffmann-LaRoche	
	Schering-Plough	Imperial Chemical	
	Searle (G.D.)	Merck	
	Smith Kline and French	Pfizer	
	Syntex	Sandoz	
	Warner-Lambert	Squibb	
		Sterling	
		Upjohn	

Source: Adapted from Bogner and Thomas (1991).
Note: Ward's (1963) clustering algorithm was used on seven variables for each firm: actual number of patents (logged), patents adjusted for firm's size, concentration of product line by research relatedness, concentration of product line by therapeutic relatedness, concentration of product line in clinical settings, concentration of product line in chronic care and new products relative to industry-wide introductions. Abbott Labs was also included but was clustered as an outlier.
*Mylan realigned to generic group.

and a broad mix of products under patent. Group 2 represents firms that were weaker on these traits, yet had still maintained good competitive positions. Group 1 represents firms much more severely disadvantaged by the environment shifts of the 1970s. These firms had smaller product lines made up of older products. At the same time rational drug design was demanding more R&D dollars, their sources of cash (older off-patent drugs) were being damaged by increased retail competition. The elevated research levels needed for continued competition were especially difficult for these firms. Group 4 includes some fast growing generic firms.

An overview of the patterns of competition in the US that followed the groupings in TABLE 16.1 highlights further the impact of the changes. Four of the six firms in Group 1 were acquired, Marion and Merrell by Dow Chemical, Norwich-Eaton by Proctor and Gamble, and Rorer by Rhône-Poulenc. Of the remaining firms ICN remains a small player and Boots is considering exiting new drug research. From among the stronger firms in Group 2, Smith Kline and Bristol-Myers have merged with Group 3 firms, while Robins has been acquired by American

Home, Searle by Monsanto, Syntex by Hoffman-LaRoche, and Burroughs-Wellcome by Glaxo. The other Group 2 firms remain independent, although Glaxo and Burroughs-Wellcome clearly are following distinctive competitive strategies from the others (Bogner and Thomas, 1991). The firms trying to remain independent and keep up with the Group 3 firms have clearly struggled. These include Schering-Plough, Syntex, and Warner-Lambert. Conversely, while not all Group 3 firms have had excellent results, these firms were among the leading performers in profitability and investment returns in the late 1980s and early 1990s as their patent-protected products of rational drug design dominated the market.

EVENT 3: THE MID1980s AND BEYOND

The third significant change in how firms compete in the US pharmaceutical industry is currently under way. The most significant feature of this new pattern of competition is the "strategic alliance." A strategic alliance goes beyond a traditional contract for inputs or sale of outputs. An alliance addresses what traditionally were often intra-firm activities (such as R&D) and blurs the lines that distinguish organizations from each other. Alliances such as the recent attempt by Sanofi and Sterling to cover all products in the US and Europe are seen as reshaping the boundaries and scope of pharmaceutical firms in the same way as they are reshaping firms in the airline and automobile industries.

Technological Change

Many of these alliances focus on the emerging biotechnology industry: drug products based on recombinant DNA, monoclonal antibodies, and related capabilities. This had been a basic research area in the 1970s when manipulation of the "sticky ends" of DNA (in 1972) effectively allowed practical laboratory creation of alternative living structures. The biotechnology revolution entered the applied stage with an explosion of new ventures that were formed in the early 1980s, although by 1988 only nine biotechnology engineered products had been approved in the US.

Biotechnology can be seen as an extension of the technological evolution of rational drug design. It involves more of an emphasis on employing biologic processes than organic chemical reactions to accomplish its end, but it is driven by the ever enlarging knowledge of human biochemical activity. In this way the opportunities pursued by biotechnology start-ups in the 1980s represent the next generation of research beyond the organic drug designs of the 1970s.

Non-Technological Change

The other major change the industry underwent in the late 1980s and early 1990s was a change in drug marketing. This change was heralded by the marketing of ranitidine (Zantac) by Glaxo in the early 1980s. Prior to that launch Smith Kline's cimetidine (Tagamet) had built close to $1 billion in sales and accounted for almost 25% of sales and 50% of the firm's profits. Although ranitidine was only slightly different and was entering the market years after cimetidine was established, Glaxo was able to usurp Smith Kline's number one position in the market, taking away literally billions of dollars of potential sales in the years since. Glaxo's technique was described as having involved "marketing shock troops deployed with [s]peed and overwhelming strength", selectively employed "with [p]roducts ... intelligently, and forcefully, sold through a worldwide strategy with as close to simultaneous launches as possible" (Teitelman, 1989, p. 68). Importantly, Glaxo did not need to spend either the time or the money to build the sales force needed in the US. Instead they "rented" the established, trained, but under-utilized US sales force of Hoffmann-LaRoche.

Glaxo's activities illustrate the ability of marketing alliances to cut the cost while increasing the speed in accessing the global market. Indeed, no firm had the ability to launch a product such as ranitidine globally without alliances and marketing agreements. But the pinched cash flows on non-patented drugs increased the need to exploit new drug discoveries as fully as possible during patent life. In addition to the cost of sales forces in every country, firms had to address national variations in drug licensing processes, in drug promotion methods, and in physician use. The use of marketing alliances speeds the entry of drugs into markets via local partners with skills in local drug detailing, while cutting marketing expenses and maximizing pre-patent expiration cash flows.

Interactions

The use of strategic alliances has been tied recently to attempts by firms to focus their competitive strategies on their core competencies—the activities that they do best (Quinn, 1992). In both the R&D and the marketing alliances partner firms are seen as attempting to take advantage of the skills that they have while using external alliances to acquire skills in areas where they are weak, and taking advantage of environmental opportunities that would otherwise be beyond the scope of the firm. This is true even for the large firms. For example, in 1987 Merck and Repligen, a biotechnology firm, formed an alliance to pursue an HIV vaccine (Whittaker, 1991). Merck had not only the cash that Repligen needed to continue funding its research, it also had established marketing and drug approval experience in genetically engineered vaccines (hepatitis B). Here, each firm had unique competencies in one or more activities involved in bringing the drug to market, of which biotechnology was only one. Together, through the alliance, the firms hope to be able to bring a key drug to market more effectively (and profitably) than either would have been able to do without the alliance.

The key skills in R&D alliances are those held by the scientists who are on the cutting edge of research. At this stage the knowledge cannot be decoupled from the researcher for exploitation. Therefore, in order to capture this knowledge an alliance needs to be formed with the scientist, or, more likely, the scientist's start-up company. In a four-country sample of 20 firms that share over 30% of the global pharmaceutical market, Whittaker and Bower (1991) found that 24.3% of the products in their current R&D pipeline were collaborations, while their existing major products were only 6.4% collaborative.

Alliances are reshaping both firms and the industry, and those firms who master them will emerge as leaders. The R&D alliance is just one of the types of alliance that have impacted the industry. Still, although alliances in one area (R&D) may facilitate alliances in another (marketing), the different types of alliance may not have equal impact on the long-term structure of the twenty-first-century drug firm. Given the closeness of the R&D agreements to the cutting edge of drug development, and given the constant pressure for new drugs in order to maintain viability while reducing risk and controlling costs, the overall alliance structures of firms could become centered around core R&D alliances.

DISCUSSION OF THE RESEARCH QUESTIONS

Each of the three situations presented here analyzes a competitive situation where the structure of the pharmaceutical industry has been significantly altered. In each situation the preceding events included technological change as well as changes in other parts of the competitive environment. Now we look back across the three periods *in toto* and discuss the research questions.

RESEARCH QUESTION 1

The first research question looked for the various sources of change in the environment preceding changes in the patterns of competition. Technological precursors occurred in all three cases. While this was anticipated with respect to the first event, the antibiotic era, it had not been the primary focus of previous research on the second era.

In all three situations we also found simultaneous non-technological changes occurring. Only in the awarding of the streptomycin patent in 1948 was an "other" event related to the technological change. The other legal and regulatory changes, and the changes in marketing tactics in the later periods, occurred independently of the contemporary technological change. Thus, a strong suggestion is raised that industry changes following technological change are not solely shaped by the technology change.

RESEARCH QUESTION 2

The second research question looked at the extent of the interaction between technological changes and other factors in producing the resulting patterns of competition. In the first two cases the interaction of technology and other changes explains the structure of industry competition that followed. In the first era the change in technology was seen as ineffective in changing the long-term structure of the industry: it was the regulatory change that enabled the antibiotic discoveries, as well as other drugs, to be exploited.

Similarly, the patterns of competition emerging from the second era show a clear interaction of environmental factors. The cash "squeeze" put on medium and small research firms by all of the changes was significant. Surprisingly, the impact of the technological change has been largely under-discussed here. The ability of rational drug design to allow firms to "remake" themselves with new pharmaceuticals was important, particularly given the legal and regulatory impacts on older drugs.

The total impact of the interactions in the third era remains to be seen. Clearly the form of the traditional pharmaceutical firm has been changed by alliances, and research alliances in particular have been a major force behind this. Still, there are other types of alliances that are significant in shaping the firm of the future, as was seen in the Sanofi–Sterling case. It is, therefore, quite likely that here too the interaction of the different forces for different types of alliances will help to shape the firm of the twenty-first century, in spite of the true dominance of biotechnology among these arrangements.

RESEARCH QUESTION 3

In the light of the prior conclusion that all of these periods of change were shaped by interactions of technological change with changes in other factors, we now project the way in which technological change would have reshaped the industry in the absence of the non-technological changes. In other words, was each technological change a "competence destroying change," even in the absence of the other changes in the environment? Only in the third case can we say it was. In the other two periods we are not only saying that the competitive outcome was dictated by the interaction (as just discussed for question 2), but also that it was the other non-technological changes interacting with technological change that raised the overall level of industry turbulence (speed and scope of change) to the point where long-term changes in competitive patterns resulted.

The facts from the first era support this conclusion. Contrary to the much touted "antibiotic revolution," mass-screening and trial-and-error techniques based on observed side effects or chemical reactions remained the basis for drug research. It was only when those closely related products were tied to patents and the "prescription only" class of drugs was in place that the antibiotic firms were able to take the lead in growth and profits.

Our conclusion is also supported by analyzing the second era. Clearly, the new knowledge from biology and chemistry would have presented new opportunities for larger firms to pursue new drugs. However, the incentive to pursue expensive new patent-protected drugs would not have been so great had it not been for the margin pressure on their older drugs. The small firms would have benefited from the absence of regulatory change at the time of technological change. Firstly, it would have reduced the direct threat from increased generic competition; secondly, less aggressive R&D responses by their large competitors would have given them the time to replace old drugs. Rationally designed drugs would still have entered the market at a slower pace. With both larger flows of cash coming in from older products and less pressure for research dollars for new product development, the smaller firms would have fared much better.

Only in the third period of change do we conclude that the technological change has been so great as to bring about the larger, competitive changes in and of itself. Even though the impact of biotechnology has yet to be completely played out, the major shift in the technological trajectory away from organic chemistry and toward biotechnology would require significant changes such as alliances to keep pace, even if changes in patterns such as marketing were not also forcing more alliances on firms. Interestingly, unlike the other two eras of change, this era has seen a large number of new entrants, which are having a significant impact on the industry. This suggests a single dimension of change, one that could be focussed upon and exploited by a thinly resourced start-up.

CONCLUSIONS

As in other studies, this analysis shows that technological change preceded changes in industry structure. However, by looking backward from the resulting structure we observed other precedent events occurring in addition to the technological change. Managers attempting to anticipate future industry structure or set future competitive strategy based on technological change alone may well be fooled. We do not want to understate technology's role. Indeed, we have suggested here that the role of technological change in the 1970s has been understated in most analyses of the pharmaceutical market in the US. However, managers must take into account the interactions with and dynamics of other forces shaping their environment prior to acting. Indeed, the significance of the subsequent shifts in industry competition underscore the scope of the error of not doing so.

REFERENCES

Bogner, W. and Thomas, H. (1991). A strategic group study of the competitive positions of European firms in the US pharmaceutical market 1969–1988. Paper presented at the Academy of International Business, Miami, Florida.

Bogner, W. and Thomas, H. (1994). Core competence and competitive advantage: A model and illustrative evidence from the pharmaceutical industry. In G. Hamel and A. Heene (Eds) *Competence Based Competition*. Chichester: John Wiley.

Carlisle, R. (1987). *A Century of Caring: The Upjohn Story*. Elmsford, NJ: Benjamin Co.

Chandler, A. (1962). *Structure and Strategy*. Cambridge, MA: MIT Press.

Cool, K. and Dierickx, I. (1993). Rivalry, strategic groups and firm profitability. *Strategic Management Journal* **14**, 47–59.

Cool, K. and Schendel, D. (1987). Strategic group formation and performance. *Management Science* **33**, 1102–1124.

Cray, W. (1984). *Miles 1884–1984: A Centennial History*. Englewood Cliffs, NJ: Prentice Hall.

Cyert, R. and March, J. (1963). *A Behavioral Theory of the Firm*. Englewood Cliffs, NJ: Prentice Hall.

Ghazanfar, A., McGee, J. and Thomas, H. (1987). The impact of technological change of industry structure and corporate strategy: The case of the reprographics industry in the United Kingdom. In A. Pettigrew (Ed.) *The Management of Strategic Change*. Oxford: Basil Blackwell.

Gersick, C. (1991). Revolutionary change theories: A multilevel exploration of the punctured equilibrium paradigm. *Academy of Management Review* **16**, 10–36.

Hirsch, P. (1975). Organizational effectiveness and the institutional environment. *Administrative Science Quarterly* **20**, 327–344.

Measday, W. (1971). The pharmaceutical industry. In W. Adams (Ed.) *The Structure of American Industry* (4th Edn). New York: Macmillan.

Pisano, L. (1989). *The Emergence of Biotechnology: Institutions and Markets in Industrial Innovation*. New York: St Martin's Press.

Quinn, J. (1992). The intelligent enterprise: A new paradigm, *Academy of Management Executive*, VI: 48–63.

Sneader, W. (1985). *Drug Discovery: The Evolution of Modern Medicines*. Chichester: John Wiley.

Steele, H. (1964). Monopoly and competition in the ethical drugs market. *The Journal of Law and Economics* **12**, 131–163.

Teitelman, R. (1989). Pharmaceuticals. *Financial World* 30 May, 54–71.

Temin, P. (1980). *Taking your Medicine: Drug Regulation in the United States*. Cambridge, MA: Harvard University Press.

Tushman, M. and Anderson, P. (1986). Technological discontinuities and organizational environments. *Administrative Science Quarterly* **31**, 439–465.

Tushman, M., Newman, W. and Romanelli, E. (1986). Convergence and upheaval: Managing the unsteady pace of organizational evolution. *California Management Review* **29**, 29–44.

Ward, J. (1963). Hierarchical grouping to optimize an objective function. *Journal of the American Statistical Association*, **58**, 236–244.

Whittaker, E. (1991). R&D networking: Merck's strategy to combat AIDS, working paper no. 11, Heriot-Watt Business School, Edinburgh.

Whittaker, E. and Bower, D. (1991). The global winds of change in the pharmaceutical industry, working paper no. 3, Heriot-Watt Business School, Edinburgh.

17

IT and Strategic Renaissance

MARTIN LOCKETT

INTRODUCTION

Information technology (IT) is becoming recognized as an important business weapon. As well as traditional data processing applications designed to increase business efficiency through cost reduction, IT is being used to improve effectiveness, for example through improved information for decision making and faster speed of response to the customer. More radically, IT can be a key component in doing business in new ways and even transforming a business or sector. For example, State Street Bank abandoned much of its traditional banking business and became a leading world supplier of specialist trust and custody services, as opposed to remaining a medium-sized regional bank in the north-eastern USA. Reuters' transformed itself from a news agency into the world's leading financial information provider, and is now becoming a global alternative to traditional financial markets.

This chapter examines the role of IT in such "strategic renaissance". It argues that successful exploitation of IT is, and will continue to be, a necessary but by no means a sufficient condition for achieving the radical business change that we are seeing in leading organizations. Today, the availability and cost of IT are not the major constraints on its effective application in business. The potential applications of IT that can be cost-justified and are

Strategic Renaissance and Business Transformation. Edited by H. Thomas, D. O'Neal and J. Kelly.
Copyright © 1995 John Wiley & Sons Ltd.

technically feasible far exceed the capability of organizations to exploit these opportunities. But while this potential is large, there are many cases of projects that fail to meet their objectives and produce limited business benefits, as well as exceeding budgets by large margins. Cases in which millions or tens of millions of dollars have been spent on IT systems with little or no result exist in many organizations. Ineffective use of IT can therefore not only incur the costs of missed opportunities but also damage the health of today's organization.

So the capability of IT is less of a limiting factor than the recognition and implementation of business opportunities for change involving IT. Given this context, determining the factors behind success (and failure) in innovations making use of IT is an important precondition for effective use of IT for business advantage and for organizational learning about how to achieve business benefits. This chapter therefore focuses on how to exploit IT as part of an overall business change. It does this by looking at two levels: the first is the individual *project* level, and the second an overall *programme* of change in an organization.

SOURCES

This chapter is based on a combination of research and consultancy work, the conclusions of which have been consistent. The research was undertaken personally and with colleagues at the Oxford Institute of Information Management in the late 1980s, as well as at Nolan, Norton & Co. in the early 1990s followed by analysis of AMS (American Management Systems) experience of major change programmes to achieve breakthrough performance. The personal research projects on which the chapter is based are:

- Success factors behind 30 innovative projects involving IT in a major multinational, employing expert systems, sales and marketing systems and production management systems (Lockett, 1990).
- The changing role of the IT director in major corporations, based on interviews with senior business and IT executives in a dozen major organizations (Earl et al., 1988).
- Business information management in three major banks, based on interviews and case studies with senior business and IT

executives—used as a basis for developing executive education programmes on the management of IT and business redesign.

I will draw also on associated projects specifically:

- Measuring business performance in the organization of the future, a project undertaken jointly with 12 major North American corporations on the need for new measures of business performance, which put forward the "balanced score-card" approach to measurement (Nolan, Norton & Co., 1991).
- An analysis of strategic projects involving IT in 50 top US corporations, which looked at the reasons behind their success and failure.
- The *Impact Programme*'s research into the relationship between the chief executive and IT director in major UK organizations.

This formal research is supplemented by the personal experience of working with a variety of organizations, primarily in the financial sector, in Europe and East Asia. These consulting projects have been involved with developing business-driven IT strategies; redesigning business processes based on customer needs; developing new balanced measures of business performance; clarifying business strategy and priorities; and executive workshops to enable managers to take responsibility for the business exploitation of IT. The conclusions from this research and consultancy have been remarkably consistent across both different organizations and different regions, though of course influenced by both organizational and national cultures.

STRUCTURE OF THE CHAPTER

This chapter first outlines the demands faced by business and the IT function. This stresses the extent to which competitive success depends on simultaneously achieving low cost, high quality and fast speed of response. The effective use of IT is a necessary but by no means sufficient condition for this competitive success—and this in turn depends on major changes in the way in which IT is managed and delivered to the business. It is argued that this demands integrated business change, of which information and systems are one component, the other major components being (i) the redesign of business processes, and (ii) new roles, skills and organization.

The next section looks at the *project* level, and the factors behind success and failure in specific IT projects. Research shows that these are little different from other technological innovations in business. This means that organizational rather than technical factors are critical to success, for example the commitment of project champions and sponsors. As a result, business ownership of IT projects is critical to success, combined with appropriate project management, the style of which changes over the life of the project.

In the penultimate section, the *programme* level is examined, where an organization is seeking major change. If organizations are to be transformed, then this will be through a programme of change guided by a clear strategy, which together tackle the linked areas of people, process and technology.

THE DEMANDS ON BUSINESS AND IT

THE BUSINESS DEMAND

The rate of change in business is faster than ever, and the pace is increasing rather than decreasing. Successful business formulae are lasting for shorter periods before they are overtaken by new approaches to satisfying customer needs better and at lower cost. Indicators such as the duration of product life cycles and the movement of companies in and out of the *Fortune 500* demonstrate this rate of change. While this is widely accepted, many of the assumptions of the mass production era are being challenged. In particular, the idea of inevitable trade-offs between *cost, quality of product/service* and *speed of response* has been destroyed by the recent experiences of many sectors.

In place of this cost/speed/quality trade-off has come the reality that doing business in new ways can create a combination of:

- low cost
- high quality of product and service
- fast speed of service and response to the market

This is best illustrated by examples of sectors where this has happened over recent years. The first is the car industry; the second, personal computers; and the third, financial services for the personal customer.

THREE EXAMPLES

Car Industry

Japanese car producers have clearly shown how *cost*, *quality* and *speed* go together in the automobile industry. For example research based at MIT showed how Japanese companies such as Toyota had combined low cost assembly with high quality, in contrast to most European and US car producers, as shown in TABLE 17.1 (Womack, Jones and Roos, 1990, p. 92). Such differences exist in both the mass and the luxury car markets. In the latter, it is said that Mercedes-Benz has relatively more staff in quality inspection and fault repair than its competitor Lexus has to produce a car of similar or higher quality. In addition, there is *speed*; the lead time to deliver a customized car to a customer in Japan is under two weeks compared with the 6 to 12 weeks of most European producers.

Cost, *speed* and *quality* can also be seen in the design cycle for new cars. Japanese producers cut lead times, as shown in TABLE 17.2 (Womack, Jones and Roos, 1990, p. 118). Japanese companies have been able to do this with designs for both mass and niche markets. Examples of the latter include the Mazda *Miata* (also known as the *MX-5*), whose engine noise was designed to meet

TABLE 17.1 Productivity and quality in the car industry

	Japan	US	Europe
Productivity (hours per vehicle)	17	21	36
Quality (assembly defects per 100 vehicles)	60	82	97

TABLE 17.2   The design cycle for new cars: cost, speed and quality

	Japan	US	Europe
Productivity (million engineering hours per new car)	1.7	3.1	2.9
Quality (months to return to normal quality level)	1	11	12
Speed (lead time in months)	46	60	57

customers' expectations of a small sports car, and Toyota's *Lexus*, whose features were designed in detail to meet customer preferences—from the quality of the key to the sound of closing a door. Today, US and European producers have responded and are replicating many of the innovations in production and design that were made in Japan. There can, however, be no doubt that a successful car producer must combine low cost with high quality and fast speed of response.

Personal Computers

In personal computers, one of the fastest growing markets for IT hardware, this trend can be seen again. The premium that can be charged by leading brands such as IBM, Compaq and Apple has been reduced substantially over the past five years. In terms of *cost*, all three of the above market leaders have been faced with producing and selling at low cost in order to retain market share against both other brands and low cost "clones", which consumers realized were functionally equivalent and could be half the price. The result was a major restructuring at Compaq to reduce cost, dramatic reduction of margins by Apple and, in the case of IBM, the creation of competing brands both within and outside the IBM mainstream (the *ValuePoint* and *Ambra* lines, respectively).

In terms of *quality*, basic product quality is now accepted as a given in the market-place. Indeed, recent quality surveys have often shown direct sales companies beating the market-leading brands on service and reliability as well as price. The response from companies like Compaq has been to provide three-year warranties as standard to reassure the customer. And in terms of *speed*, the lead time between availability of a new technology (such as a processor chip) and its general availability from "clone" manufacturers in Taiwan has been steadily reducing over the past decade from a couple of years to a couple of months. As a result, the life of a personal computer model has declined rapidly: in the case of Apple from several years to under a year in some cases.

Financial Services

A third example is banking and other financial services for the personal customer. In the UK, the core product (current accounts for everyday transactions) is unprofitable for most banks in most of their customer base. The *costs* of the largest banks are high as they service customers through an extensive branch network, with tens of thousands of staff backed up by large investments in IT. *Quality* is perceived to be low, with a combination of errors, unfriendly attitudes and poor service. *Speed* and responsiveness are also seen as weak points by customers. Much the same is true of major players in other areas of the market, notably insurance companies.

A number of new entrants to the market have shown that it is possible to combine low cost with high service quality and fast response. Based on telephone service, they give extended opening hours, quick answers and lower pricing than major competitors. Examples include:

- *Direct Line*: a direct sales insurance company, initially specializing in car insurance. Only serving customers by phone, their pricing is typically significantly lower than traditional competitors, although their underwriting is more sophisticated and so certain risks are priced higher. As a result, they obtain the customers they want from a business perspective; have a lower cost base than companies working through brokers and area offices; and offer faster service with instant quotations and cover.
- *First Direct*: a 24-hours-a-day, 365-days-a-year bank with very keen pricing but doing all of its business by phone. Established

by Midland Bank (now part of the Hong Kong and Shanghai Bank Group) in competition with its existing branch network, it regularly comes top of customer service surveys. Again, its speed of response is faster than through a branch and the cost base much lower, although it is still repaying its investment costs.

Examples such as these, as well as highly focused organizations in market niches, have shown the level of change that financial services must undergo. If anything, the major difference between financial services and other sectors such as retailing is that the banks have only just begun the restructuring that others have faced up to for a decade.

THE ROLE OF IT

Could these transformations of organizations in cars, computers and financial services have been accomplished without the extensive use of IT? In the initial stages, perhaps, as was shown by the Japanese car industry in the 1970s. But the current levels of performance cannot be sustained without extensive use of IT. In the car industry, the design process has been changed dramatically by the advent of computer-aided design, linked to simulation of the characteristics of a new car while still on the computer "drawing board". No longer are clay models of a car required for early testing of designs. Computer designs can then be transmitted directly to automated manufacturing facilities either within the organization or in a supplier. In the computer and electronics industries, such design technology is as essential to microchip design as it is to a car. In both industries, IT is behind the speeding up of response and cutting of costs in the supply chain from supplier through manufacturer to customer.

In a financial sector example like First Direct, it can only afford to provide 24-hour, 365-day service through concentrating its operations while providing customers with distributed access. This results in a service which is *personalized*, in that the staff know all of your personal history from the information stored in its IT systems, without the costs, variability and lack of availability of a truly *personal* service through a branch network. While this may look technology-driven, such technology has been available for years and implemented in branch networks by far-sighted banks such as Wachovia Corporation in the US. Although not leading edge in most of its systems, First Direct does use sophisticated information systems to maximize cross-selling of products into its customer base. It also uses advanced phone systems to monitor its service levels and make staff aware of these in "real time", for example how many seconds it takes to answer incoming phone calls.

Although IT has made certain features of these transformations possible, it would be totally misleading to see it as the main driver of change. The connection between high spending on IT and business results is tenuous. Indeed, there are many cases where large amounts have been spent on sophisticated systems that attempted to reproduce the current way of doing business, which have been costly, slow and not done the job that was wanted. This is graphically illustrated by a 1994 Siemens advertisement in *Business World*, which boasted how, "Weeks before a car is due to be delivered to a customer, our computers set the precise day and time of assembly—down to the hour". In contrast, the Japanese competitor has simplified its processes to get the total response down to a few days, which in turn reduces the complexity of the systems required to schedule production. And in the case of personal computers, Toshiba reduced the level of production automation because it turned out to be quicker for people to adapt to new models than for machines to be reprogrammed.

This leads to a fundamental point: that in most organizations, IT is as much a "disabler" of rapid business change as an "enabler". This was put bluntly by the Director of Management Services of John Lewis, a major UK retailer and user of IT, who stated that, "It takes less time to build a warehouse than a warehouse system" (quoted in *Computing*, 28 April 1994). IT is all too often on the critical path in terms of response time, while IT costs have increased as a proportion of the cost base. In businesses like banks, which spend 10–30% of their expenses on IT and associated costs, line managers often see both technology and their systems people as "out of control" from a business perspective. This was graphically illustrated by an interview with a director of one of the largest UK banks, who stated, "If a customer managed their business with information like ours, we would not lend them money".

Research by the *Impact Programme* reinforces these conclusions—and that top management will no longer sanction continually increased IT spending or slow response to business needs. A summary of the chief executives' views could be characterized as:

- "Cut the cost of IT radically."
- "If you can't do things quickly, don't do them at all."
- "Give me an adaptable infrastructure."
- "Incremental improvements rather than major projects."
- "Provide timely, accurate, relevant management information."
- "Give me some benchmarks (or I'll make some up myself)."

So, it is essential that IT is delivered to the business with the same improvements in *cost*, *speed* and *quality* that are demanded of the rest of the organization. This implies that the successful delivery of business results from *IT projects* is critical to overall business success. But it is not just a question of sorting out the delivery of IT projects. Looking at the design of cars, computers or financial products, organizations that have reduced lead times and development costs have not necessarily invested as heavily in IT as their competitors. Rather, it is change in business *processes* and *people* that have been primary. Cross-disciplinary teams who actually take responsibility for results are behind much of the reduction in lead time. Such a team with shared objectives is far more effective at anticipating problems and resolving them than an inter-departmental steering committee. Other innovations in design include sending design engineers on an intensive programme to use or sell the current generation of products before starting the design of the next. As a result, the products meet customer requirements more closely and design decisions are far more likely to be based on customer preferences than on internal views of what the customer "should" want.

This implies that it is *integrated business change* rather than just IT that is behind transformation. My research has shown that there are five main components in this change. The first three— *people* (including skills and organization), redesign of business *processes* and information *technology*—have already been outlined. To these three, I would add two others: *infrastructure* (where work is done, including the channels to the customer) and *control and regulation* (internal or external rules that determine what is permitted). Thus IT projects only contribute to strategic renaissance when they form part of an overall programme of business change linked to strategic objectives.

To summarize, IT has made possible the scale of business transformation that we have seen, and will continue to do so. However, it is by no means the major driver, and must be combined with other components of an integrated business change if performance is to be improved at the rate demanded by customers and competition. Success will depend upon both (i) the effective delivery of IT at the level of a specific *project*, and (ii) the integration of IT into a *programme* of integrated business change in an organization. I will consider these two levels in turn.

PROJECTS: SUCCESSFUL INNOVATION

What lies behind successful IT projects that aim to make a significant impact on the business? This section is based primarily on research to identify the factors behind successful innovation in projects involving information systems in a large multinational company, combined with work in other major companies and financial institutions to develop and implement business-driven IT strategies (Lockett, 1990). This covered about 30 projects with a range of technologies and success in terms of impact on the business.

The success factors at the project level were found to be similar to the success factors in other areas of technical innovation. In particular, organizational issues were much more important than technological ones. Major factors behind successful projects were:

1. Limiting the technology risks involved.
2. A project champion in a business function, combined with appropriate sponsorship.
3. A development team bridging the gap between the IT function and the business.
4. Prototyping in the early stages of a project.
5. Transition between two management styles, from a "flexible" development phase to a "tight" implementation.

LIMITING THE TECHNOLOGY RISKS

The results confirmed that the availability and cost of technology were not the major constraints on using IT for business advantage. In 70% of the projects, cost was not a significant constraint. While there can be no doubt that cost-justification of IT investment is important, the cost of the technology is not a major constraint on successful innovation. Rather, it was identifying and realizing the benefits from projects whose pay-off is substantial relative to the technology costs. These benefits come from the business change that technology makes possible, which typically came from innovative use of technology already available in the market-place, not the exploitation of leading-edge technology.

New technology from the viewpoint of users and system developers was associated with technical problems in the project, longer lead times and greater cost overruns. However, the newness of the technology in itself had a small positive association with project success. Thus, there is little evidence that the newness of technology *itself* has a major impact on overall business success and failure of IT innovation. Rather, it was limiting the risks to those areas necessary to achieve the business objectives of the project that drove successful projects. This often meant changing the technology used in the project once or twice during its development—indeed, changing the technology midway was positively associated with project success in business terms. In some cases, this led to a choice of "older" technology because it was easier for projects to succeed when they built on existing systems and infrastructure rather than requiring major new investment, especially when the system was to be used by customers.

CHAMPIONS AND SPONSORS

If new technology does not explain the success and failure of innovative IT projects, what does? The clearest factor to emerge from the research was the existence of a project *champion* within the business. Almost all projects without a clear champion failed to deliver significant business benefit. The moving of a project champion to a new role in the business was also directly linked to the subsequent failure of the project in cases where the new incumbent did not take over the role of champion. But why are champions so important?

A champion in the business rather than the IT function is able to coordinate the project and guide it towards relevant business goals. This increases the chances of success for two reasons: (i) by influencing the design of the system to make it meet business and user needs more closely; and (ii) by sustaining momentum for the implementation of the project. Such a champion therefore manages the project in a way more likely to achieve business objectives than one that either is championed from within the IT function or has no clear leadership.

In the event of problems during the development of the project, a strong champion is able to gather support for the project if he or she believes it to be viable. However some champions are not at a sufficient level in the organization to be able to allocate adequate resources on their own initiative. A second role of sponsor is important here—a senior manager who takes an interest in the project, makes some commitment to it, and reviews its progress. Two patterns emerged that were associated with successful project development: either (I) a relatively senior champion; or (II) a more junior or less enthusiastic champion backed by a more senior sponsor. While sponsors are important, they are no substitute for a champion actively involved in a project.

Another role of a champion was to stop projects that were unlikely to meet business objectives. There are many examples of IT projects that have continued well beyond the stage where those directly involved recognize that failure is likely, if not inevitable. All too often, these continue for months before someone sufficiently senior is prepared to press the "stop button". The research identified that strong business champions tended either to stop or to refocus projects at a much earlier stage than was the case with weak champions or strong ones from the IT function. Indeed, the latter could well complete development of the system but find that it was little used, or even rejected.

In short, ownership of the project had to be in the business rather than the information systems function. Thus, the existence of a champion, combined with a sponsor where appropriate, was the single most important factor for success. This confirms the findings in technical innovation research, as well as the experience of many companies in implementing both IT strategies and other programmes such as quality. However good the technology or strategy methodology, it is actually business commitment to change that has the greatest influence on business success or failure.

BRIDGING THE BUSINESS–IT GAP

The ability to understand business problems and develop appropriate IT-based solutions depended on the nature of the development team. In particular, success depended on bridging the gap between (i) business managers who often knew little about information systems and had not been involved in previous projects, and (i) IT professionals often unaware of detailed business needs. In successful projects, this gap was bridged within the development team—there had to be no significant gap in understanding and communication between those involved. The most critical area was converting business needs into functional specifications of information systems requirements, for example a production manager specifying the information needed to analyse plant performance.

Here past experience of a project champion was useful in some of the projects—though they were regarded as tough customers to please by the IT function. Where this was not the case, someone else had to fulfil this role—typically by either someone from the business area being moved into the IT function in mid-career, or by an IT professional with a long working relationship in the business area. So, in the early stages of a project the quality of the staff in the development team is more important than the quantity. Also, it is essential that the development team is truly cross-functional rather than being essentially from the IT area.

PROTOTYPING AND ITS PROBLEMS

The use of prototyping methods was associated with project success. Prototyping in this context is the development of small systems of restricted scope and/or functionality that users can test for themselves. The system design develops through an iterative process of evaluation followed by a further prototype system. Particular gains come from enabling business managers and staff unfamiliar with information systems to see what can be done and thus to refine the specification of the functions of a desired system. Prototyping also enabled user interfaces to be tested before they were finalized, thus meeting user needs better.

Using prototypes enabled changes of approach to be made at an earlier stage in a project. This meant that the cost of change was lower as the technical design of the system was still undecided. It also enabled business users to see if IT could produce benefits without the cost of trying to specify and produce a full system, thus making it easier to stop a project that turned out not to be as promising as expected. However, analysis of the research results indicated that while a certain amount of prototyping gave positive results, a high level of prototyping gave no more benefit—and probably gave less. Why was this?

There were two main problems that arose from prototyping, both connected with the transition between the development and implementation stages of a project. The first was the nature of prototyping tools, which are intended to enable rapid development (within days) of prototype systems. While these tools were highly productive at the early stages of projects, they were often inappropriate for future commercial working systems. For example, prototyping tools tended to be inefficient in the use of computer hardware, leading to higher operational costs and response time problems. Also, they were usually not the best tools for future maintenance of the system.

The second problem of prototyping was that associated with the "freezing" of a specification at an appropriate stage. Having had the freedom to make changes quickly and easily in the early stages, there was a problem in moving towards a final system that would be more stable. This was necessary not only for the technical reasons outlined above, but also for business reasons such as needing a final design to train users. In very few cases was it appropriate to continue prototyping methods into the implementation of the project. Thus, while prototyping was a useful tool in the early stages of the project, there was a need to move away from this approach later on.

CHANGING MANAGEMENT STYLES

In recent years great stress has been placed on the need for formal controls over IT projects—starting with formal approval, and followed by structured development methods with formal project structures. This degree of formalization has been intended to avoid the problems of cost and time overrun. However, my research showed formalization to be positively associated with both cost and elapsed time overruns. This was particularly true of projects using formal project management structures. Further, there was little association between these formal structures and success or failure. Thus, at first sight, formal management processes appeared to have done little, if any, good!

A detailed examination revealed a more complex pattern, in which formalization in the later stages of a project was associated with success while early formalization had the opposite effect (cf. Kanter, 1985, on technical innovation). This was confirmed by numerous cases of success that took place outside the "proper" channels for approval and systems development. In these a champion often worked informally with the IT function to produce a prototype or initial working system. On the other hand, in two of the projects with the earliest formal approval and highest visibility, there were serious problems with systems implemented late and rejected by users.

The best explanation is in the costs of exit from projects that are not meeting business objectives. Early formalization tends to freeze a project in a particular form and to make it more difficult for those involved to stop because this involves "public" admission of failure. Real checkpoints tend to be months apart on large projects. In contrast, unapproved projects using discretionary resources have to gain continual approval from those involved. Also, deciding not to pursue the idea does not count as a "failure" because it is less visible. In such projects, it is also easier to change approach: for example, the focus of the project or the IT tools used. Such changing of approach was associated with project success. But during project implementation, formalization becomes important as lack of formal approval, poor project management and failure to integrate with business planning substantially reduce the impact of the project on business results.

Finally, while shifting from a flexible to a tighter management style is essential, new issues emerge. On the management side, the marketing of the project becomes critical in ensuring that it will actually be used both internally and sometimes externally, especially for projects in the sales and marketing area. Technically, the requirements of the system change to include reliability and its delivery to users in a suitable form.

IMPLICATIONS FOR MANAGEMENT

What are the practical steps that could be taken to increase both the level and chance of success of IT innovation with substantial business benefits? To conclude this section, I propose ten steps to promote successful IT innovation:

1. See IT projects as innovation whose benefits come from the business change which IT makes possible, not primarily as the technical implementation of systems.
2. Allocate part of your IT budget to R&D. Focus this resource on high quality IT staff working with managers on business needs.
3. Ensure different management processes and controls at different stages of projects—looser for development, tighter for implementation phases.
4. Insist on a cross-functional project team involving both IT and all relevant areas of the business. Ensure the right mix of skills to bridge the business–IT gap.
5. Only use new technology if it is absolutely necessary to achieve the business benefits—there is huge potential in what you already have and what is widely available in the market-place. Go for "clever use of technology", not "clever technology".
6. Be prepared to experiment with alternative technology approaches and to change after an initial review. Even try two alternatives competing against each other.
7. Explicitly include personal commitment and organizational factors in assessing projects, as well as ensuring clear accountability for achieving the benefits. Remember that a business champion is the number one factor in success and the easiest way to stop a wayward project.
8. Be prepared to stop projects early, and refocus others rather than ploughing ahead. The bigger the project, the more necessary and the more difficult this is!
9. Split IT development into "bite-sized chunks" with a deliverable after a maximum of a few months, and do not move forward unless the business recognizes that value has been delivered.
10. To build a long-term capability to innovate successfully, reduce the barriers between business and IT by educating

senior management on how to manage IT, developing
business awareness of IT staff, and increasing the interchange
between IT and other functions in the business, particularly
for high-fliers.

PROGRAMMES: IT AND STRATEGIC CHANGE

Delivering business benefits from investments in IT projects is a
necessary but by no means sufficient condition for strategic
renaissance. Dramatically increasing the level of business performance demands design and implementation of a wide range of
linked projects with varying levels of IT involvement. This section
outlines a framework for making strategic change (FIGURE 17.1)
based on research and consulting experience.

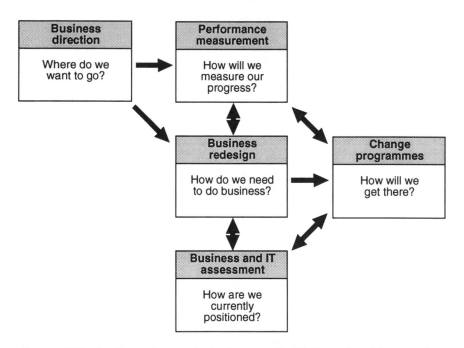

FIGURE 17.1   Implementing strategic change with IT. Reproduced by permission of Nolan, Norton & Co.

THE NATURE OF STRATEGIC CHANGE

This framework identifies five main stages in designing and implementing programmes of strategic change involving IT. These are:

- Business direction
- Performance measurement
- Business and IT assessment
- Business redesign
- Change programmes

Each of these will be outlined in turn to show where IT is an essential element in strategic change.

BUSINESS DIRECTION

The starting point is a clear vision of where the business should go, which is distinctive and easily understandable by everyone in the organization. Such a vision must be communicated widely in the organization to have a major impact, so it must also be memorable! This converts a business strategy into a set of ideas to which the work of everyone can be related. One of the best was President Kennedy's 1961 vision for NASA: "before this decade is out, of landing a man on the moon and returning him safely to the earth". The performance of NASA before and after the first moon landing clearly demonstrates the power of a clear, communicated vision. In addition, the high-level vision must be supported by high quality strategic and market analysis—but the best analysis will not motivate an organization's managers and staff to action by itself. This stage has little to do with IT, except that the formulation of strategy must take account of the opportunities that IT offers in various dimensions, including its use in the product, customer service and internal organization.

PERFORMANCE MEASUREMENT

Converting the vision and strategy into consistent action requires not just communication but also reinforcement through the measurement of business performance. This was clearly identified in a recent study by Nolan, Norton & Co. (1991; see also Lockett, 1993; Norton and Kaplan, 1992). This study found that performance measurement was of increasing importance arguing that, "The degree to which we succeed in installing new performance measurement systems will determine how well we are able to guide our organizations to the 21st century". The "balanced scorecard" framework proposed (FIGURE 17.2) has been applied in a wide range of organizations to motivate and monitor management in line with business direction. It stressed that financial measures were insufficient to do this in today's business world—and would become less valuable as the rate of change increased. Therefore, it was essential to measure not only financial performance but also non-financial performance in the key areas that drove success in creating future customer and shareholder value. Specifically, it recommends that measures are balanced, covering four aspects:

- *Financial*: high level financial measures focused on the creation of shareholder value.
- *Customer*: performance in the eyes of the customer and what they value most.
- *Process*: the performance of key internal business processes in terms of quality, speed and productivity.
- *Learning*: the ability of the organization to continuously improve and innovate in its products, services and processes.

These measures must be validated against the business strategy, and hence can be used as a basis for setting targets and judging the business case for strategic change. They will therefore express the aspects of cost, speed and quality that will really drive future success.

BUSINESS AND IT ASSESSMENT

To be realistic, any plans for strategic change must be realistic and based on an assessment of the strengths and weaknesses of today's organization. Many well-known concepts and approaches can be used to conduct such an assessment, which

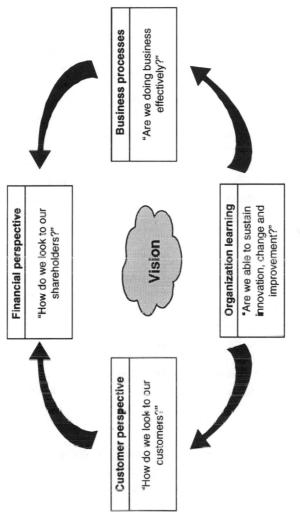

FIGURE 17.2 The "balanced scorecard" approach. Reproduced by permission of Nolan, Norton & Co.

is then used to identify strengths that can be leveraged and weaknesses to be remedied. Examples of such approaches are benchmarking and evaluation of core competences.

BUSINESS REDESIGN

All of the strategic direction, measurement and assessment in the world will be of no use if they do not drive the design and implementation of new ways of doing business. The next step is therefore the design of the future. Five aspects of this can be identified, and these must be integrated if the maximum performance improvement in cost, speed and quality is to be obtained. These are:

- *Process*: the way in which work is done, using the perspective of end-to-end processes that create value for customers.
- *People*: the roles, skills and organization of the people involved in the redesigned processes.
- *Information*: the information—and hence IT—that supports and makes possible the new business processes.
- *Infrastructure*: the physical structure of where work is done and the infrastructure necessary to support this.
- *Control*: the fundamental regulatory and business requirements that must be met in order to comply with regulation and ensure control over the business.

Experience from consulting suggests that focusing on IT will not generate the highest value solutions in terms of performance improvement. On the other hand, IT makes possible opportunities for change that would not have been sustainable in the past. For example, telephone banking like First Direct is dependent on relatively advanced and reliable telecommunications. Where these do not exist, as in most parts of Africa, different solutions are needed. And where IT solutions do exist, such as satellite, they frequently come up against regulatory barriers, which are then the major constraint. Such business redesign is best undertaken by cross-functional teams that cross both business barriers as well as the business–IT boundary.

CHANGE PROGRAMMES

Redesign is easy by comparison with the implementation of major change. Any substantial redesign will involve a range of projects with greater or smaller IT involvement. Some will be essentially IT projects, while in others a small IT input is needed as part of a business project. This linked set of projects can be seen as a *programme* of change, in which it is necessary to ensure: (i) the consistency of direction in projects; (ii) the completeness of the projects in achieving the desired business results; and (iii) the practical fit of projects with each in terms of resources, dependencies and so on. This demands *programme management*, which is driven by a business champion backed up with high level sponsorship. In practice, this depth of commitment is often absent at the early stages of an idea—unless it is the chief executive's! As a result, it is necessary to steadily mobilize commitment and hence resources to the programme of change.

The model shown in FIGURE 17.3 shows what can happen to gain the commitment of senior management when they do not give full commitment from the start. Having got the idea on the sponsor's agenda, the champion pushes through an experiment or pilot whose benefits can be used to persuade senior management to commit themselves to the implementation of the project as a whole.

The implication of this approach to strategic change is that IT is just one aspect of an integrated business change. Just as successful IT projects are dependent on bridging the business–IT boundary, this is true on a larger scale in programmes of strategic change, which must also bridge the boundaries between different business functions. But can the IT organization of today make the contribution to the strategic renaissance that is demanded by the business?

CONCLUSION: TRANSFORMING THE IT CONTRIBUTION

This chapter has argued that businesses are facing the challenge of dramatically improving their performance simultaneously in different ways, of which cost, speed and quality are the most important examples. IT has enabled new ways of doing business

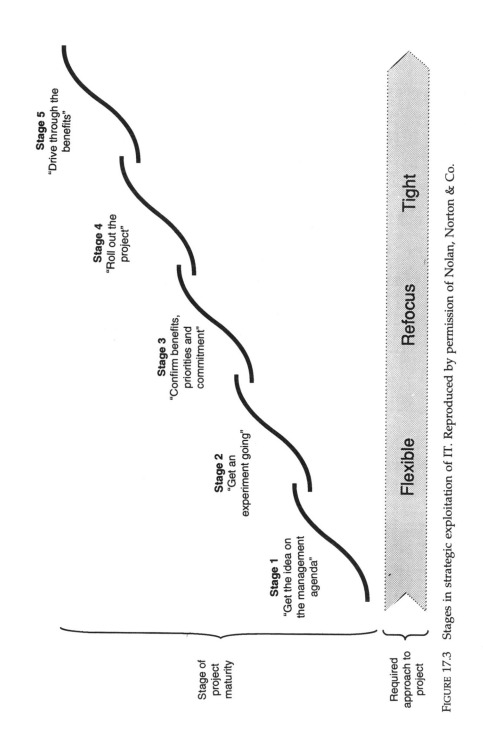

FIGURE 17.3 Stages in strategic exploitation of IT. Reproduced by permission of Nolan, Norton & Co.

but the current performance of the IT function in most businesses is poor. Often, IT staff are locked into past ways of developing systems; they lack business knowledge and are not integrated organizationally or culturally with the business; the range of their technical knowledge is limited and may be dated, and so on. While there are exceptions, this picture is true of many large organizations. Thus, to transform business performance, the IT function itself must change radically.

The dimensions of this change will be remarkably similar to those on the operational side of the business, and will involve the five components of business change that were outlined above:

- *Process*: redesigning how systems are developed to gain business results, rather than focusing on technical aspects of IT.
- *People*: restructuring roles, skills and organization to prioritize business and interpersonal skills, together with awareness of the range of technologies available in the market-place.
- *Information*: using and managing information and technology well within the IT function itself.
- *Infrastructure*: moving from a function located in one place to being dispersed in business units while maintaining coordination.
- *Control*: moving from a "control" mentality with respect to IT towards a facilitation and influencing role.

There will be no one model of IT organization that will succeed. Some will outsource much of their work, becoming buyers and integrators of external suppliers as well as consultants to the business—a pattern emerging in a company like BP Exploration in the oil industry. In others, more work will be done in-house working closely with business users. In either case, the business demand is for IT performance to improve at least as fast as that of the business. Success will be when IT is no longer a blocker of low cost, fast and high quality business change.

REFERENCES

Earl, M.J., Feeny, D., Hirschleim, R. and Lockett, M. (1988). Information technology, strategy and leadership. In M.J. Earl (Ed.) *Information Management: The Strategic Dimension* (pp. 242–253). Oxford: Oxford University Press.

Kanter, R.M. (1985). *The Change Masters: Corporate Entrepreneurs at Work*. London: Unwin.

Lockett, M. (1990). The factors behind successful technology innovation. In M. Warner, W. Wobbe and P. Brödner (Eds) *New Technology and Manufacturing Management: Strategic Choices for Flexible Production Systems* (pp. 239–252). New York: John Wiley.

Lockett, M. (1993). Do you measure up to the best? In *1993 Annual Review* (pp. 2–5). London: Nolan, Norton & Co.

Nolan, Norton & Co. (1991). *Measuring Performance in the Organization of the Future*. Boston, MA: Nolan, Norton & Co.

Norton, D.P. and Kaplan, R.S. (1992). The balanced scorecard – measures that drive performance. *Harvard Business Review* January/February, 71–79.

Science Policy Research Unit (1972). *Success and Failure in Industrial Innovation*. London: Centre for Study of Industrial Innovation.

Womack, J.P., Jones, D.T. and Roos, D. (1990). *The Machine that Changed the World*. New York: Macmillan.

18

Causes and Consequences of Corporate Restructuring

Constantinos C. Markides

INTRODUCTION

> While headlines proclaim megamergers, hostile takeovers and proxy fights, something far less visible but just as noteworthy is occurring at hundreds of American companies. Much like overweight people ... these corporations are working off excess weight. They are shedding unwanted and often unlucrative divisions, subsidiaries, and product lines in order to concentrate on what they do best and most profitably. When they do buy another company now, it's done to enhance the core business. This is conglomeration in reverse.
>
> (*US News and World Report*, 15 April 1985, p. 69)

Numerous reports in the business press suggest that during the 1980s many American firms refocused their strategic configuration; that is, they reduced their diversification. This phenomenon has received prominent exposure in the press, where it has been heralded as a managerial revolution that is producing "leaner and meaner" companies which are more efficient vehicles for creating and distributing stockholder wealth (see for example, *Business Week*, 1 July 1985, p. 50 and *Fortune*, 2 March 1987, p. 37). The

Strategic Renaissance and Business Transformation. Edited by H. Thomas, D. O'Neal and J. Kelly.
Copyright © 1995 John Wiley & Sons Ltd.

practice has been labeled with different names, such as "de-con-glomerating," "de-diversifying," and "getting back to basics."

If this "de-diversification" drive is indeed taking place, it represents a dramatic change in the evolution of the American corporation, which begs for an explanation. It was only 25 years ago that the elite of corporate America was fully immersed in diversification and conglomeration. In fact, all statistical evidence suggests that throughout the post-war period (1945–1985), American firms were diversifying (see, for example, Dugger, 1985, p. 694; Mariotti and Ricotta, 1987, p. 24; Ravenscraft and Scherer, 1987, pp. 28–32; Rumelt, 1982, p. 361). What has prompted the emergence of refocusing, and what has been its effect on the American corporation? Furthermore, are *all* diversified firms refocusing, and if that is the case, why are they doing it *now*?

Despite the apparent importance of this phenomenon, *systematic* evidence on its extent and effects is scarce. Refocusing has received negligible attention from academics, and especially from business policy academics in whose agenda divestitures and refocusing naturally fall. The only research that emerged from the strategy camp dealt primarily with divestment implementation (Bettauer, 1967; Clarke and Gall, 1987; Duhaime and Patton, 1980; Harrigan, 1980, 1981; Hayes, 1972; Nees, 1978, 1981; Porter, 1976; Wright, 1985). Economists, on the other hand, have emphasized the main motivations for divestment (Duhaime and Grant, 1984; Lewis, 1983; Maupin, 1987; Ravenscraft and Scherer, 1987).

The purpose of this chapter is to begin the process of examining refocusing in more detail. This study tries to provide some systematic evidence on the extent of refocusing and the nature of the firms that are refocusing. Follow-up studies will examine the effect of refocusing on firm profitability and market value.

THEORETICAL CONSIDERATIONS

Corporate diversification has been studied extensively in both the strategy and the economics literatures. Although these two research traditions differ in their theoretical development of hypotheses as well as in their methodologies, they seem to agree on a critical finding: that there is a limit to how much a firm can grow (diversify).

Penrose (1959), for example, emphasized the long-run constraints associated with recruiting, training and assimilating new managers as the firm grows; Williamson (1967) looked at the costs of diversification in terms of information processing. He argued that the loss and/or distortion of information as it passed from one layer of the firm's hierarchy to the next created inefficiencies that put a limit to how much a firm can grow. Calvo and Wellisz (1978) emphasized the control and effort losses that arise from increasing shirking as the firm diversifies; Keren and Levhari (1983) singled out the coordination costs and the intrinsic diseconomies of scale in the expansion of the firm's hierarchical structure; and Prahalad and Bettis (1986) identified the X-inefficiencies created when managers continue to apply their existing "dominant logic" on newly-acquired, strategically dissimilar businesses.

It is therefore generally accepted that every firm has a limit to how much it can diversify. Since this limit is a function of a firm's non-transferable specific assets, every firm has a different limit. But the existence of an optimal diversification level for every firm implies that if a firm diversifies beyond its optimal level, its profitability and market value will suffer. The question is, if a firm is *profit maximizing*, why will it invest beyond its optimal level? At least two reasons have been proposed in the literature to explain why we should expect to find *some* firms *systematically* over-investing in diversification.

Firstly, agency theory in general (Jensen and Meckling, 1976; Williamson, 1964) and Jensen (1986) in particular have proposed that firms will over-invest in diversification (i.e. invest in diversification projects whose NPV is less than zero) when their managers pursue maximization of their own utility function rather than shareholder-value maximization. The conditions for such behavior are ripe for firms in mature industries that generate more earnings than can be profitably re-invested (Mueller, 1972). As a result, managers can use these retained earnings to finance their "wasteful" investments, without resorting to the external capital market, which can monitor and discipline them.

Considerable evidence has been accumulated that lends support to this prediction. For example, studies by Baumol et al. (1970), Brealey, Hodges and Capron (1976), Grabowski and Mueller (1975), Hiller (1978), Kallapur (1990), and McFetridge (1978), all of which looked at the *marginal* returns on capital, found that the rate of return on investments financed by retained earnings is considerably lower than the rate of return on investment financed by new equity or new debt—and often lower than what share-holders could have earned by simply investing in the capital market (Mueller, 1987). This suggests that, given the right conditions, some firms will over-invest in diversification.

Secondly, it has been proposed that during the past 20 years, changes in the product and capital markets have reduced the inherent benefits of diversification while increasing its costs. For example, Bhide (1989) argued that the rising sophistication of the capital market (due to deregulation and increased competition) has eroded one of the major advantages of the diversified firm, that of acting as an "internal capital market" to its divisions (Williamson, 1975). Similarly, Davis (1985), Hill and Hoskisson (1987), Mariotti and Ricotta (1987), Markides (1990), Mueller (1972), and Williams, Paez and Sanders (1988) have all argued that increased environmental uncertainty and volatility, as well as globalization, have increased some of the costs of diversification, such as the information and control loss problems associated with the steep hierarchies of diversified firms. What these changes imply is that the optimal diversification level of firms is now lower, so that even firms that were optimally diversified 20 years ago are now over-diversified.

The existence of over-diversified firms implies that these firms have sub-optimal profitability and market value. (That this is indeed the case is evidenced by the big gap between the market value of many firms and their break-up value; see, for example, *Business Week*, 8 July 1985, p. 80.) Hence, the appropriate remedial action will be for these firms to reduce their diversification (i.e. to refocus).

It is possible that many of the firms refocusing are doing it voluntarily; that is, as organizational learning takes place, managers try to correct past "mistakes." However, in the academic literature, the market for corporate control has been credited for most of the restructuring taking place (Bhide, 1989; Black and Grundfest, 1988; Budd, 1986; Jarrell, Brickley and Netter, 1988; Jensen, 1989). Although for the purposes of this study it is not imperative to determine the major force driving refocusing, results reported by Markides (1990) are indicative: from a questionnaire survey of 149 firms, he found that of those firms that *felt* they were a possible takeover target in 1981–1987, 76% restructured and 24% did not. Of those firms that did not feel a real threat of takeover, only 35% restructured and 65% did not.

The above theoretical considerations suggest several propositions that can be tested empirically. Specifically:

Proposition 1: Compared to the 1960s, there will be a significantly larger number of firms refocusing in the 1980s.

The rationale for this derives directly from the notion of the existence of an optimal limit to diversification: most firms set out on their diversification programs in the early 1950s (Rumelt, 1974). It is therefore likely that at the beginning of this diversification effort, most firms would have been moving towards their optimal region, and very few would have gone over it. Even if a few firms had over-diversified so early in the process, they would be under little pressure to refocus given the state of the market for corporate control in the 1960s. As a result, we should not expect too much refocusing in the 1960s. As time went by, however, firms diversified more and more, and a larger number of firms passed their optimal region. These are the firms that are now under pressure to refocus. We should therefore find more firms refocusing in the 1980s.

This, however, does not mean that all diversified firms are refocusing, or that firms have stopped diversifying altogether. If we think of diversified firms as located along a finite diversification spectrum, it is very likely that in the population of diversified firms (or from a *random* sample of these firms), some will be below their optimal diversification level, while others will be above theirs. Assuming profit-maximizing behavior on the part of these firms, the "under-diversified" firms will be increasing their diversification, while the "over-diversified" firms will be decreasing theirs. Thus, as opposed to the 1960s, when we should observe only diversifying firms, in the 1980s we should see a rather mixed picture, with some firms diversifying and some refocusing. Therefore:

Proposition 2: In the 1980s, some firms will be increasing their diversification and some will be decreasing it.

More specifically:

Proposition 2a: In the 1980s, the *single-business* firms will be increasing their diversification, while the *unrelated* firms will be decreasing their diversification.

In addition, if the distribution of changes in diversification is *symmetric*, we should expect that the aggregate effect of some firms diversifying and some refocusing will be zero (or very small) overall change in industry diversification levels. If, on the other hand, the distribution is not symmetric, then we should observe net changes in aggregate diversification levels. Since we have no *a priori* reasons for expecting a symmetric distribution, we can test this as our null hypothesis:

> *Proposition 3*: Aggregate diversification levels have not changed in the 1980s.

Finally, in a recent paper Williams, Paez and Sanders (1988) have found that *conglomerate* managers were reducing the complexity of the conglomerate enterprise primarily by engaging in related acquisitions and unrelated divestitures. We hypothesize here that the same is true not only for conglomerates but for all diversified firms that are refocusing. Thus:

> *Proposition 4*: In the 1980s, firms refocused by divesting unrelated businesses while acquiring related ones.

DATA AND METHODOLOGY

To test these propositions, a random sample of 250 firms was selected from the 1985 *Fortune 500* list, in the following fashion: 50 firms were drawn from the *Fortune 100*, 50 from the *Fortune 100–200*, 50 from the *Fortune 200–300*, and so on. The population of *Fortune 500* firms was selected for study because it contains many diversified firms. Because of missing information, 31 firms were eventually dropped from the sample.

To measure the refocusing (or diversifying) activity of these firms, their diversification levels were calculated first in 1981 and then again in 1987 using three different measures of diversification (three measures are used to test the hypotheses three times and so ensure that the results are not sensitive to the particular diversification index used). The three measures of diversification employed are the following:

1. Entropy index of diversification: this is an SIC-based index, traditionally used by economists (Jacquemin and Berry, 1979),

which has been imported into the strategy literature by Palepu (1985). It is defined as:

$$DT = \sum_{i=1}^{N} P_i \log(1/p_i)$$

where P_i is the proportion of the firm's total sales contributed by segment i. Palepu (1985) also shows how this index can be decomposed into its related (DR) and unrelated (DU) parts. All three components of the index were constructed for each of the 219 firms in 1981, 1983, 1985, and 1987, using data from the TRINET tapes.

2. Rumelt's categories: the entropy index is a continuous measure of diversification. Another way to measure changes in diversification is through a categorical measure such as Rumelt's (1974) categories. Rumelt's classification exercise was used to assign the 219 sample firms into four diversification classes: single-business, dominant-business, related-business, and unrelated-business. This exercise was carried out for 1981 as well as for 1987. The classification exercise used in this study differs from Rumelt's in one important respect: instead of going through each firm's annual reports to determine the businesses in which it is competing, as Rumelt did, a breakdown of each firm's businesses was obtained from the TRINET tapes in the form of two-digit and four-digit SICs. The classification then proceeded in the same way as Rumelt's.

In order to calculate a firm's specialization ratio (SR) and related ratio (RR), we had to determine whether the different SICs that the firm was competing in, were related in any way. Basically we started out with the assumption that products from different two-digit SIC industry groups were unrelated, and then tried to determine whether they had anything in common in terms of production technology, customer base and marketing/distribution requirements. If they did, then they were reclassified as related. Unavoidably, this exercise required some value judgement on our part, but it proved to be much more straightforward than it sounds on paper. When difficulties were encountered, the firm's annual reports were consulted. Once these two ratios were calculated for each firm, the classification proceeded as follows:

- If $SR > 95\%$ the firm was classified as single-business
- If $70\% < SR < 95\%$ the firm was classified as dominant-business

- If $SR < 70\%$ AND $RR > 70\%$ the firm was classified as related-business
- If $SR < 70\%$ AND $RR < 70\%$ the firm was classified as un-related business

To test the construct validity of this classification, 40 firms were picked at random and were re-classified using information from their annual reports. Of these 40 firms, 34 were placed in the same categories as before; for the other 6, there was disagreement as to whether they were dominant-business or related-business. The problems arose at the stage of determining what the firm's businesses were (and not at the stage of deciding whether they were related or not). If one were to take management's words at face value, all of their businesses belonged to a single, closely-related business! Since the SIC breakdown seems to be a more objective breakdown of a firm's businesses, the original classification was maintained.

3. Number of SICs: a third way to measure a firm's diversification is by simply counting the number of two-digit SICs that the firm is competing in. This is arguably a crude measure, but comparing the 1981 count with that in 1987 can be revealing. This information was obtained from the TRINET tapes.

Finally, to examine the methods used to refocus (Proposition 4), a sample of 100 firms was randomly selected from the 1985 *Fortune 200*: 50 firms from the *Fortune 100* and 50 from the *Fortune 100–200*. An attempt was then made to discover every acquisition and divestiture that these firms made in the period 1981–1987. Several sources were used for this purpose, including: the SDC Database on Mergers and Acquisitions (SDC.MRG and SDC.LTD), the journal *Mergers and Acquisitions*, Predicast's *Index of Corporate Change*, Quality Services Co.'s *Merger and Acquisition Sourcebook*, W.T. Grimm & Co.'s *Mergerstat Review*, and Cambridge Corp's *Merger Yearbook*. For each transaction, its SIC classification and the year it took place were also collected.

Once this list was compiled, each transaction was classified as related or unrelated to the firm's core business in the following manner: each firm's "core" business was defined as the two-digit SIC in which the company had the largest percentage of its sales (information from TRINET). The classification then proceeded in the same manner as the Rumelt classification reported above: any transaction belonging to an SIC different from the firm's core SIC was initially classified as unrelated. We then tried to determine whether the two SICs had anything in common in terms of production technology, customer base, and marketing/distribution requirements. If they did, the transaction was re-classified as related.

RESULTS

To test Proposition 1, Rumelt's original sample was compared with the sample of this study. Since both samples involve *Fortune 500* firms, direct comparisons are possible. Rumelt (1974) lists the diversification classification of every firm in his sample for 1949, 1959, and 1969. It is therefore possible to calculate the number of firms that refocused during 1949–1969 (by moving, for example, from the unrelated-business category to the dominant-business category), versus those that have diversified (by moving, for example, from the single-business category to the related-business category).

Specifically, firms were classified as diversified when they changed from single-business to dominant-business (2 firms in the sample); from single to related (0); from single to unrelated (0); from dominant to related (6); from dominant to unrelated (6); and from related to unrelated (4). On the other hand, firms were classified as refocused when they changed from unrelated to single (0); from unrelated to dominant (6); from unrelated to related (11); from dominant to single (14); from related to dominant (10); and from related to single (2). The same exercise was carried out on the sample of this study for the period 1981–1987.

Overall, we found that in the period 1949–1959, about 22% of the sample firms were diversifying while only 1% were refocusing (TABLE 18.1). Similar percentages apply for the period 1959–1969. By contrast, in the period 1981–1987, only 8% of the sample firms were diversifying while more than 20% were refocusing. This means that whereas in the 1950s and the 1960s there was a negligible number of firms refocusing, the number has increased dramatically in the 1980s—a strong confirmation of Proposition 1. The exact opposite occurred with diversification: many firms were diversifying in the early period 1949–1969, but the number declined substantially in the 1980s.

TABLE 18.1   Refocusing and diversification, 1949–1987

	1949–1959	1959–1969	1981–1987
Firms refocusing (%)	1.3	1.1	20.4
Firms diversifying (%)	21.7	25.0	8.5

TABLE 18.2   Distribution of firms by strategic category, 1949–1987

	From Rumelt (1974)			This study	
Category	1949	1959	1974	1981	1987
Single-business	42.0	22.8	14.4	23.8	30.4
Dominant-business	28.2	31.3	22.6	31.9	28.1
Related-business	25.7	38.6	42.3	21.9	22.4
Unrelated-business	4.1	7.3	20.7	22.4	19.0

Note: The figures are the percentage in each category, $N = 210$.

The dramatic effect of these changes can be seen clearly in TABLE 18.2, which shows the distribution of firms by strategic category. It appears that in the 1980s, the trend towards unrelated diversification that so dominated the past 30 years was arrested. Its place was taken by a healthy increase in the single-business firms. Overall, in the period 1981–1987 there were 43 firms in our sample that changed their classification to a less-diversified category, 18 firms that increased their diversification, and 149 firms that stayed in the same category over the period. Given the short time period under study, and the broadness of the Rumelt categories, these are quite dramatic changes.

Evidence in support of these findings has been reported in a recent study by Lichtenberg (1990). Using a sample of more than 6500 firms, he found that in the period 1985–1989 there was a substantial reduction in the degree of industrial diversification: the mean number of industries in which firms operated declined by 14%; the proportion of companies that were highly diversified declined by 37%; and the proportion of single-industry companies increased by 54% during the five-year period.

It is often assumed that it is only the conglomerates that are engaged in refocusing (Lee and Cooperman, 1989; Lichtenberg, 1990; Williams, Paez and Sanders, 1988). Although the theory pre-

TABLE 18.3   Distribution of refocused firms by size, 1981–1987

Category	Number of firms with higher:			Number of firms with lower:		
	DT	DR	DU	DT	DR	DU
Fortune 100 (45)	23	29	22	22	16	23
Fortune 100–200 (36)	14	14	14	22	22	22
Fortune 200–300 (44)	22	26	23	22	18	21
Fortune 300–400 (41)	24	23	21	17	18	20
Fortune 400–500 (43)	22	28	19	21	15	24
All firms (209)	105	120	99	104	89	110

Note: The number of firms in each Fortune group are in parentheses.

sented above predicts that the conglomerates will indeed engage in refocusing—since they are the most likely firms to be over-diversified—the theory also predicts that they should not be alone in doing so: every over-diversified firm should be refocusing. Our data allows us to test this proposition directly. As shown in TABLE 18.3, the refocusing firms are distributed quite evenly among the Fortune 500 groups: for example, there are 22 refocused firms in the Fortune 100 versus 21 refocused firms in the Fortune 400–500. In fact, it appears that most of the refocusing occurred in the Fortune 100–200 group. Furthermore, of the 104 firms that refocused, only about one-third of them were classified as conglomerates by Forbes in its annual survey of American business. These results suggest that, along with the conglomerates, other over-diversified firms were also refocusing.

The findings reported in TABLE 18.1 also provide support for Proposition 2: in the 1960s we observed only diversifying activity by firms, whereas in the 1980s, both diversification and refocusing were taking place. A more detailed look at what was happening in the 1980s is provided in TABLE 18.4, which shows the distribution of changes in the entropy index of total diversification (DT) in the period. According to this index, 105 firms increased their diversification while 104 firms decreased it. The distribution of changes in DT looks normal and the two groups (refocusers and diversifiers) appear to have changed their diversification by similar degrees. For example, 55% of the refocusers decreased their diversification by less than 0.3. The corresponding number for diversifiers is 48%.

TABLE 18.4   Distribution of changes in *DT*, 1981–1987

DT 1987–DT 1981	Number of firms
−1.25− −∞	0
−1.00− −1.25	5
−0.9− −0.99	1
−0.5− −0.89	12
−0.4− −0.49	12
−0.3− −0.39	16
−0.2− −0.29	11
−0.1− −0.19	22
0.0− −0.09	25
Total refocused	104
0−0.09	17
0.10−0.19	18
0.2−0.29	16
0.3−0.39	10
0.4−0.49	10
0.5−0.89	26
0.9−1.00	3
1.0−1.26	2
1.3−1.4	2
1.4−1.77	0
1.78−+∞	1
Total diversified	105
Total number of firms	209

Note: Ten firms were lost from the base sample of 219 firms because of missing information in the 1987 TRINET tape.

How do we know that it is the over-diversified firms that are refocusing and the under-diversified firms that are increasing their diversification (Proposition 2a)? To test this proposition we have to account for the "regression to the mean" problem: simple convergence of the diversification index towards a middle value may signify simple regression to the mean rather than proof of the hypothesis. We tried to remove this bias by using two different indices of diversification: we compared the 1981 entropy index (*DT*) of the single-business and unrelated-business firms with their corresponding index in 1987.

The results, presented in TABLE 18.5, provide tentative support for the proposition: the entropy index of total diversification (*DT*)

TABLE 18.5   Movement towards the optimum

	1981 (N = 209)				1987 (N = 209)			
	S	D	R	U	S*	D*	R*	U*
Average number of SICs	6.48	12.95	11.74	16.78	6.18	11.64	11.31	15.15
Average DT	1.211†	1.980	2.249	2.603‡	1.420†	2.051	2.268	2.479‡
Average DU	0.545	1.116	1.470	1.828	0.637	1.155	1.413	1.705
Average DR	0.666	0.862	0.779	0.775	0.783	0.896	0.855	0.774

Note: S, single-business firms; D, dominant-business firms; R, related-business firms; U, unrelated-business firms.
*As classified in 1981.
†Increase in the diversification of single-business firms is statistically significant at the 1% level ($t = 2.45$).
‡Decrease in the diversification of unrelated-business firms is not statistically significant ($t = 1.02$).

for the single-business firms increased from 1.211 in 1981 to 1.42 in 1987; by contrast, the entropy index for the unrelated-business firms decreased from 2.603 in 1981 to 2.479 in 1987. This implies that the low-diversity firms are increasing their diversification, while the high-diversity firms are decreasing their diversification, which is exactly what the hypothesis predicts. The same pattern emerges when the related (DR) and unrelated (DU) components of the total diversification index are examined.

If some firms are increasing their diversification while others are decreasing it, then on average we should not expect a big change in overall diversification. This is especially the case in a symmetric distribution such as the one that emerges in TABLE 18.4, where about 50% of the firms are diversifying and 50% are refocusing. Aggregate diversification levels are shown in TABLE 18.6. The most prominent result to emerge is the fact that overall diversification levels have not changed much. What appears to be happening is that in each *Fortune* group (with the possible exception of *Fortune 100–200*), the refocusing activities of some firms are counterbalanced by the diversifying moves of other firms, so that on average there is no change in overall diversification.

These results suggest that there exists no massive refocusing trend in the overall American industry, as several reports in the business press have proclaimed. Individual firms are refocusing, but the effect is cancelled by the diversifying activities of other firms.

TABLE 18.6 Entropy index of diversification, 1981–1987

	1981			1983			1985			1987*			1987–1981		
	DU	DR	DT	DU	DR	DT	DU	DR	DT	DU	DR	DT	DU	DR	DT
All firms (219)†	1.214	0.790	2.004	1.199	0.800	1.999	1.213	0.766	1.979	1.209	0.833	2.042	-0.005	0.043	0.038
Fortune 100 (45)	1.386	0.950	2.336	1.398	0.989	2.387	1.357	0.956	2.313	1.409	1.043	2.452	0.023	0.093	0.116
Fortune 100–200 (39)	1.346	0.939	2.285	1.301	0.924	2.226	1.312	0.887	2.199	1.264	0.894	2.158	-0.082	-0.045	-0.127
Fortune 200–300 (45)	1.262	0.736	1.999	1.257	0.764	2.021	1.294	0.745	2.039	1.259	0.752	2.012	-0.003	0.016	0.013
Fortune 300–400 (44)	1.106	0.677	1.783	1.067	0.658	1.725	1.135	0.603	1.738	1.154	0.720	1.874	0.048	0.043	0.091
Fortune 400–500 (46)	0.989	0.669	1.658	0.987	0.682	1.669	0.985	0.653	1.638	0.955	0.753	1.708	-0.034	0.084	0.05
Conglomerates‡ (18)	1.904	0.927	2.831	1.927	0.955	2.882	1.815	0.936	2.751	1.772	0.927	2.699	-0.132	0.000	-0.132
Multicompanies§ (13)	1.738	1.104	2.843	1.672	1.084	2.756	1.693	1.000	2.693	1.471	0.955	2.427	-0.267	-0.149	-0.416
Diversified** (31)	1.834	1.001	2.836	1.820	1.009	2.829	1.764	0.962	2.726	1.637	0.939	2.577	-0.197	-0.062	-0.259

*For 1987, N = 209.
†Number of firms in parentheses (except in 1987 when the numbers in parentheses are 209, 45, 36, 44, 41, 43, 16, 13, 29, respectively).
‡A group of 18 firms classified as conglomerates by *Forbes* in its 1981 survey of American business.
§A group of 13 firms classified as multi-industry by *Forbes* in its 1981 survey.
**The sum of conglomerates and multicompanies.

TABLE 18.7   Methods of refocusing, 1981–1987

	Acquisitions		Divestitures		Refocusing Index
	Related	Unrelated	Related	Unrelated	
All firms (100)	393	306	207	315	195
Fortune 100	249	207	136	218	124
Fortune 100–200	144	99	71	97	71
Conglomerates (19)	67	98	50	85	4
Multicompanies (10)	47	57	30	55	15
All others (71)	279	152	127	175	175

Note: The number of firms are in parentheses.

The final exercise for this study is to determine how firms are refocusing (Proposition 4). TABLE 18.7 provides a breakdown of the acquisition and divestiture activity of 100 firms during the study period. A total of 1221 transactions were identified, 699 of which were acquisitions and 522 divestitures; 56% of the acquisitions were related in nature, while 60% of the divestitures were unrelated.

Following Williams, Paez and Sanders (1988), we define as our refocusing index the sum of related acquisitions and unrelated divestitures (both of which increase net business-relatedness), minus the sum of unrelated acquisitions and related divestitures (both of which decrease business-relatedness). A positive index suggests that firms are refocusing by acquiring related businesses while divesting unrelated ones. As shown in the table, the index is positive throughout, and especially for the group of firms labeled "All others," which includes all those firms in the *Fortune* 200 that are *not* conglomerates or multi-companies. This is strong confirmation of Proposition 4, which argues that it is not only the conglomerates that are refocusing by acquiring related businesses and divesting unrelated ones, but all over-diversified firms.

SUMMARY AND MANAGERIAL IMPLICATIONS

This study examined corporate refocusing in some detail and provided a rationale for this phenomenon, as well as evidence on its extent. This is the first study to provide *systematic* evidence on refocusing, and the results presented are generally consistent with the following "story" of diversification. At any given point in time, every firm has a limit to how much it can diversify. This limit is a function of the firm's resources and its external environment. For a variety of reasons, many firms have diversified beyond this limit. As a result, their profitability and market value have suffered. Primarily because of a stronger market for corporate control, but also because of organizational learning, the over-diversified firms are now reducing their diversification to return to equilibrium. At the same time, the under-diversified firms are following a profit-maximizing strategy by diversifying, in an attempt to approach their optimal diversification limit.

The study highlights the importance of looking at competition in a dynamic way: it is only by looking at competition over time, in longitudinal studies such as this one, that we can expect to understand the inherent dynamism of the market-place, and the ever-changing nature of relationships and "accepted wisdoms."

A critical implication of this study is that the relationship between diversification and profitability is not linear, but curvi-linear: at low levels of diversity the relationship is positive, but once a firm diversifies beyond its optimal diversification level, the relationship becomes negative. A future research project could examine whether this prediction is supported by the data.

The most important managerial implication that derives from this study is that refocusing has an underlying strategic logic. Because of external changes over the past 20 years, the diversified corporation has become a less valuable institution than before. This means that many diversified firms will have to rethink their whole diversification strategy. Firms that have—for whatever reasons—diversified beyond their optimal level will need to reduce their diversification. The key question then becomes: how does a firm know that it has diversified beyond its optimal level? Although this is a difficult question to answer, a good indicator of over-diversification is when the break-up value of a firm is bigger than its market value. This implies that firms will need to estimate what their break-up value is and compare it to their current market value. If the two are not approximately equal, then firms will have to reduce their diversification.

Another important implication of this study is that corporate raiders exist (and become wealthy) for a very good reason. It is *not* because the capital market is undervaluing companies that they exist; and it is *not* because they are out to make a quick profit by "destroying" companies. Rather, they exist because many companies—through their over-diversification—allow them to exist. If there were no companies whose break-up value was bigger than their market value, we would not have corporate raiders around. This implies that the surest way for corporate managers to protect their companies from raiders is for them to become "inside-raiders" and take the corrective actions that will improve the market value of their firm before a raider strikes.

It is important to stress that just because so many companies are reducing their diversification, it does not mean that diversification is a mistake for every firm. There are many benefits associated with diversification, and companies can still benefit by diversifying. However, the refocusing phenomenon of the 1980s suggests that: (i) companies cannot and should not diversify to the same extent as in the 1960s; (ii) companies will reap the biggest rewards from diversification if they diversify only in areas related to their core business—in this way they can apply their skills and assets *effectively* in the new areas; and (iii) no matter what route to diversification they choose, they should realize that they cannot diversify for ever, and they should stand ready to stop their diversification when they reach their optimal level.

What if companies have diversified in a lot of unrelated businesses? What can they do then? This study suggests that the era of the conglomerate may be over and these companies will have to refocus. However, it is still possible to manage a conglomerate organization effectively. Even though such a task is extremely difficult, it is not impossible. The corporate center in a conglomerate organization needs to perform two important functions: (i) act as an internal capital market to its divisions; and (ii) act as a disciplinary "shareholder" to its divisions. This basically means that the conglomerate corporate center should decentralize the organization and restrict its activities to (i) setting the overall strategic direction of the firm; and (ii) providing the divisions with the necessary finances. It should *not* get involved in the operating decisions of the divisions or their day to day activities. These tasks should be left to the divisional managers, who know their individual businesses better than the corporate center.

At a more macro-level, the results of this study suggest that the massive restructuring of the past 10 years has been "tonic and not poison" for corporations. Through refocusing, many firms have been able to streamline their operations and improve their competitiveness so that they are now more efficient global competitors.

The results also highlight the endogenous dynamism of the modern corporation and the corporate market-place. Through entirely market forces—and at the expense of no government interference—firms have responded to the challenges of a new environment and positioned themselves for another round of competitive warfare. Just as in any other evolutionary battle, casualties have been incurred and excesses have been committed. But the end result has been the revitalization of the corporation.

The results also highlight the dynamic nature of competition: competitive strengths erode, and new sources of competitive advantage arise as conditions change; people make mistakes, and people learn from their mistakes and adjust their behavior; "sustainable" strengths disappear overnight and new competitors emerge to challenge established dinosaurs. Competitive "renewal" is a continuous process and only managers and companies that make it a way of life than a one-shot affair can expect to be alive in the long run.

REFERENCES

Baumol, W.J., Heim, P., Malkiel, B.G. and Quandt, R.E. (1970). Earnings retention, new capital and the growth of the firm. *Review of Economics and Statistics* **52**, 345–355.

Bettauer, A. (1967). Strategy for divestments. *Harvard Business Review* March/April, 116–124.

Bhide, A. (1989). The causes and consequences of hostile takeovers, unpublished doctoral dissertation, Harvard Business School.

Black, B.S. and Grundfest, J.A. (1988). Shareholder gains from takeovers and restructurings between 1981 and 1986: $162 billion is a lot of money. *Journal of Applied Corporate Finance* **1**, 5–15.

Brealey, R.A., Hodges, S.D. and Capron, D. (1976). The return on alternative sources of finance. *Review of Economics and Statistics* **58**, 469–477.

Budd, F.W. (1986). Hostile acquisitions and restructuring of corporate America. *The Freeman* **36**(5), 166–176.

Calvo, G.A. and Wellisz, S. (1978). Supervision, loss of control, and the optimum size of the firm. *Journal of Political Economy* **86**(5), 943–952.

Clarke, C.J. and Gall, F. (1987). Planned divestment—A five step approach. *Long-Range Planning* **20**(1), 17–24.

Davis, M.S. (1985). Two plus two doesn't equal five. *Fortune* December, 171–179.

Dugger, W.M. (1985). Centralization, diversification, and administrative burden in US enterprises. *Journal of Economic Issues* **XIX**(3), 687–701.

Duhaime, I.M. and Grant, J.H. (1984). Factors influencing divestment decision making: Evidence from a field study. *Strategic Management Journal* **5**, 301–318.

Duhaime, I.M. and Patton, G.R. (1980). Selling off. *The Wharton Magazine* Winter, 43–47.

Grabowski, H.G. and Mueller, D.C. (1975). Life-cycle effect on corporate returns on retentions. *Review of Economics and Statistics* **57**, 400–409.

Harrigan, K.R. (1980). The effect of exit barriers upon strategic flexibility. *Strategic Management Journal* **1**, 165–176.

Harrigan, K.R. (1981). Deterrents to divestiture. *Academy of Management Journal* **24**(2), 306–323.

Hayes, R.H. (1972). New emphasis on divestment opportunities. *Harvard Business Review* July/August, 55–64.

Hill, C.W.L. and Hoskisson, R.E. (1987). Strategy and structure in the multiproduct firm. *Academy of Management Review* **12**(2), 331–341.

Hiller, J.R. (1978). Long-run profit maximization: An empirical test. *Kyklos* **31**, 475–490.

Jacquemin, A.P. and Berry, C.H. (1979). Entropy measure of diversification and corporate growth. *Journal of Industrial Economics* **XXVII**(4), 359–369.

Jarrell, G.A., Brickley, J.A. and Netter, J.M. (1988). The market for corporate control: The empirical evidence since 1980. *Journal of Economic Perspectives* **2**(1), 49–68.

Jensen, M.C. (1986). Agency costs of free cash flow, corporate finance, and takeovers. *American Economic Review* May, 323–329.

Jensen, M.C. (1989). Eclipse of the public corporation. *Harvard Business Review* **67**, 61–74.

Jensen, M.C. and Meckling, W.H. (1976). Theory of the firm: Managerial behavior, agency costs and ownership structure. *Journal of Financial Economics*, October, 305–360.

Kallapur, S. (1990). Estimating the rate of return on retained earnings. Unpublished manuscript, Harvard Business School, February.

Keren, M. and Levhari, D. (1983). The internal organization of the firm and the shape of average costs. *Bell Journal of Economics* **14**(2).

Lee, W.B. and Cooperman, E.S. (1989). Conglomerates in the 1980s: A performance appraisal. *Financial Management* **18**(1), 45–54.

Lewis, T.R. (1983). Preemption, divestiture, and forward contracting in a market dominated by a single firm. *American Economic Review* **73**(5), 1092–1101.

Lichtenberg, F.R. (1990). Want more productivity? Kill that conglomerate. *The Wall Street Journal* 16 January.

Mariotti, S. and Ricotta, E. (1987). Diversification: The European versus the US experience. *Multinational Business* No. 1, 23–32.

Markides, C.C. (1990). Corporate refocusing and economic performance, 1981–87, unpublished doctoral dissertation, Harvard Business School.

Maupin, R.J. (1987). Financial and stock market variables as predictors of management buy-outs. *Strategic Management Journal* **8**, 319–327.

McFetridge, D.G. (1978). The efficiency implications of earnings retentions. *Review of Economics and Statistics* **60**, 218–224.

Mueller, D.C. (1972). A life cycle theory of the firm. *Journal of Industrial Economics* **20**, 199–219.

Mueller, D.C. (1987). *The Corporation: Growth, Diversification and Mergers, Fun-*

damentals of Pure and Applied Economics. London: Harwood Academic Publishers.

Nees, D.B. (1978). The divestment decision process in large- and medium-sized diversified companies: A descriptive model based on clinical studies. *International Studies of Management and Organization* Winter, 67–95.

Nees, D.B. (1981). Increase your divestment effectiveness. *Strategic Management Journal* **2**, 119–130.

Palepu, K. (1985). Diversification strategy, profit performance, and the entropy measure. *Strategic Management Journal* **6**, 239–255.

Penrose, E. (1959). *The Theory of the Growth of the Firm*. Oxford: Blackwell.

Porter, M.E. (1976). Please note location of nearest exit: Exit barriers and planning. *California Management Review* **XIX**(2), 21–33.

Prahalad, C.K. and Bettis, R.A. (1986). The dominant logic: A new linkage between diversity and performance. *Strategic Management Journal* **7**, 485–501.

Ravenscraft, D.J. and Scherer, F.M. (1987). *Mergers, Sell-Offs and Economic Efficiency*. Washington, DC: The Brookings Institution.

Rumelt, R. (1974). *Strategy, Structure and Economic Performance*. Cambridge, MA: Harvard Business School.

Rumelt, R. (1982). Diversification strategy and profitability. *Strategic Management Journal* **3**, 359–369.

Williams, J.R., Paez, B.L. and Sanders, L. (1988). Conglomerate revisited. *Strategic Management Journal* **9**, 403–414.

Williamson, O.E. (1964). *The Economics of Discretionary Behavior: Managerial Objectives in a Theory of the Firm*. Englewood Cliffs, NJ: Prentice Hall.

Williamson, O.E. (1967). Hierarchical control and optimum firm size. *Journal of Political Economy* **75**(2), 123–138.

Williamson, O.E. (1975). *Markets and Hierarchies: Analysis and Antitrust Implications*. New York: Free Press.

Wright, M. (1985). Divestment and organizational adaptation. *European Management Journal* **3**(2), 85–93.

Section V

Research on Top Management: What We Know and What We Need to Know

As we progress through the 1990s, we will more fully develop our understanding of how to achieve successful business transformation. As business leaders wrestle with issues daily, as academics observe and extrapolate the prototypical frameworks to generate a wider understanding from the learning experiences, so will emerge the new models for tomorrow—fluid, flexible, flat organizations involving alliances to deliver the functionality that markets demand and that technology can satisfy. It is fitting, then, to conclude this volume with an overview of the state of research on issues critical to business transformation, and what gaps and needs should drive future research.

Pettigrew reviews, critiques and synthesizes literature on managerial elites. He describes six relevant research streams, examining three in some detail: boards of directors, interlocking directorates and top management teams. He finds that most research in each of these areas is based on second-hand data, and that a general lack of primary data and/or first-hand knowledge limits our knowledge of important processes in all three areas.

Chapter 19   On Studying Managerial Elites
            Andrew M. Pettigrew

Perhaps the most important attribute for any organization will be the ability to live with continuous change and adaptation—the capability for all levels within an organization to work together to achieve a step change to a new level of effectiveness, continue to improve that incrementally, and then achieve another step change to the next level of effectiveness. The process will always be easier to start than to complete, and must involve the mass of the people to ensure continuity and embed a culture of adaptability. It calls for a constant striving to be the best rather than the inflexibility of self-satisfaction.

19

On Studying Managerial Elites

Andrew M. Pettigrew

Introduction

The purpose of this chapter is to synthesize and critically review elements of the research literatures on managerial elites. It assesses a number of intellectual traditions and studies of managerial elites, and then offers a research agenda for future scholarly work in this most important, but difficult, area of social science research.

The phrase "managerial elite" is certainly not neutral, indeed many scholars have articulated the long tradition of value-laden debate around the term "elite" (Field and Higley, 1980; Giddens, 1974). But if the term "elite" is emotive and analytically value-laden for some, it also has the virtue of inclusiveness in the social sciences. This is important for the aims of this chapter, since it is being written partly to draw together aspects of the sociological, organizational and managerial literatures which in the past have not talked to one another. So who are we to embrace in this inclusive term "managerial elites"? Broadly, the interest is in those who occupy formally defined positions of authority, those at the head of or who could be said to be in strategic positions in private and public organizations of various sizes. Institutionally the interest, in the first instance, is in position holders who carry labels such as chairman, president, chief executive officer,

Strategic Renaissance and Business Transformation. Edited by H. Thomas, D. O'Neal and J. Kelly.
Copyright © 1995 John Wiley & Sons Ltd.

managing director, or inside or outside director. However, the focus goes beyond the individual position holder to consider the behaviour of groups of actors as they operate as boards of directors, executive committees or top management teams. No assumption is made by starting with position holders or formal groupings of individuals that power lies with those at the strategic apex of the organization. There is now ample empirical evidence from organizations of many different kinds, in many societies, that the power and influence of senior position holders is constrained by the countervailing influence of others inside and outside their own organizations, as well as by rules, traditions and other institutional arrangements (Herman, 1981; Mechanic, 1964; Pettigrew, 1973). The question of the relative power of managerial elites and others is a crucial empirical issue.

Sociologists and political scientists will quickly remind us that the study of managerial elites has to include not only the leaders of business and political institutions, but also "members of the media, trade unions, educational, cultural, and religious institutions, and voluntary associations" (Mizruchi, 1992, p. 18). Thus, the focus of analysis is not just power and control within the business institution, or indeed within a broader range of institutions, but whether, and to what extent, and under what conditions, there may be an inner circle of business leaders "who define and promote the shared needs of large corporations ... and give coherence and direction to the politics of business" (Useem, 1984, p. 3).

While the purposes and activities of managerial elites are a source of fascination in everyday conversation and in journalistic accounts of the fate of large enterprises (Auletta, 1991), the study of elites within institutions and societies by social scientists remain few and far between. Access difficulties have been and remain a source of constraint on studies of elites. As long ago as 1957, Kahl was arguing, "those who sit amongst the mighty do not invite sociologists to watch them make the decisions about how to control the behaviour of others" (Kahl, 1957, p. 10). Pahl and Winkler (1974), Norburn (1986) and many others have reported the real practical difficulties of getting close to the top of large institutions. But access problems are not insurmountable. The early and clever use of publicly available data by Wilson and Lupton (1959) to reveal the interconnecting networks in the City of London, and the astute use of archival data more recently by Kosnik (1987) and Davis (1991) all show what can be done from public sources. Equally well, the Harvard Business School tradition of work on boards of directors and chief executives (Lorsch and MacIver, 1989; Gabarro, 1987; Mace, 1971; Vancil, 1987) demonstrates that direct access to key figures and important processes is negotiable. The developing tradition of research on top level strategic change processes in the UK by, for example, Pettigrew (1985a), Johnson (1987), Smith, Child and Rowlinson (1991) and Pettigrew and Whipp (1991) should provide further optimistic signals that substantial access to managerial elites is possible even in a society with perhaps even stronger norms of privacy than is customary in the US. I remain sanguine that access difficulties alone need not be an impediment to the extended development of managerial elites as a field of empirical study.

Progress in the study of managerial elites can be characterized under six themes:

1. Interlocking directorates and the study of institutional and societal power.
2. The study of boards and directors.
3. The composition and correlates of top management teams.
4. Studies of strategic leadership, decision making and change.
5. Chief executive compensation.
6. Chief executive selection and succession.

It is beyond the scope of this chapter to review all six of these often quite separated areas of intellectual enquiry. The choice of the first three offers a number of analytical possibilities. First of all, there are strong and distinctive intellectual traditions in two of the three areas. The study of interlocking directorates has a clear focus on the structural analysis of business in its societal context and a distinctive methodological approach in its use of the quantitative techniques of network analysis. Important representative studies in this tradition include Burt (1983), Clawson, Neustadtl and Scott (1992), Galaskiewicz (1985), Mintz and Schwartz (1985), Mizruchi (1992), Palmer (1983), Pfeffer and Salancik (1978), Stokman, Scott and Ziegler (1985), Useem (1984) and Whitt (1982).

Research on top management teams was given a fresh lead in 1984 by the Hambrick and Mason paper setting out a research agenda for the study of the "upper echelons" of business. Since then a noteworthy pattern of work has emerged linking the demographic characteristics of top management teams to a variety of organizational outcomes such as performance, innovativeness and strategic change. Illustrative studies in this tradition include D'Aveni (1990), Finkelstein and Hambrick (1990), Hambrick and D'Aveni (1991), Keck and Tushman (1991), Norburn and Birley (1988), O'Reilly, Snyder and Boothe (1992) and Wiersema and Bantel (1992). With the notable exception of D'Aveni, this research has neither sought nor made any connections with the sociological research on elites and interlocking directorates. Like the interlocks research, the top management team research is held together by a common methodological approach, but this time the use of demographic data and multivariate analysis, rather than network-based multivariate analysis.

Without doubt the weakest of these three areas of research is the work on the composition and operation of boards and the activities of inside and outside directors. A good deal of the literature in this area is "non-academic, even non-analytical, and relies heavily on unquestioned assumptions as a basis of prescription" (Pettigrew, 1992). Nevertheless, there are some scholarly pillars to stand on to develop this intellectual approach exemplified, for example, in the empirical work of Bradshaw, Murray and Wolpin (1992), Goodstein and Boeker (1991), Herman (1981), Kosnik (1987), Lorsch and MacIver (1989), Mace (1971), Norburn (1989), Pahl and Winkler (1974), Pearce and Zahra (1991), Stewart (1991) and Zajac (1990). As yet, this research has developed neither a coherent methodological approach nor a sound set of conceptual categories and findings. Links with research on interlocking directorates and top management teams remain undeveloped. The whole field of research on boards and directors awaits energetic intellectual leadership.

This chapter has four sections. The first three characterize the underlying assumptions and main findings of research on interlocking directorates, boards and top management teams. Each section identifies the strengths and weaknesses of the three areas of research and suggests some profitable themes and questions for future enquiry.

Because three research areas are being considered for critical review, the chapter has had to trade off a certain amount of depth of presentation for breadth. Nevertheless the central tendencies of each research tradition are considered, and in the fourth and final section the beginnings of a new research tradition is articulated for all three areas of research, which combines a contextual and processual analysis of managerial elites (Pettigrew, 1990, 1992).

INTERLOCKING DIRECTORATES AND THE STUDY OF INSTITUTIONAL AND SOCIETAL POWER

Research in this tradition is avowedly sociological. The focus is on the analysis of business power and the corporate elite, rooted in the quantitative techniques of network analysis. The concern is less with the structure of power relations within individual organizations than with the social relations between enterprises. Thus Scott (1991, p. 182) characterizes work in this area as focusing "on the social networks in which enterprises are embedded and the importance of viewing these networks as arenas of power". The deeper sociological assumption in this work picks up on the Granovetter's (1985) embeddedness thesis reinterpreted by Mizruchi (1992, p. X) as "the ability of business to accomplish its goals must ultimately be studied in the context of the actions of other segments of society". United more by method than theory, a strong tradition of work has developed over the past 20 years suggesting that structures of interorganizational relations are consequential for managing resource dependencies (Pfeffer and Salancik, 1978), class action (Zeitlin, 1974), the formation of inner circles of corporate power in society (Useem, 1984), the political activities of business (Clawson, Neustadtl and Scott, 1992; Mizruchi, 1992) and corporate charitable donations in regional (Galaskiewicz, 1985), and national (Useem, 1991) settings. This research has been comprehensively reviewed by Glasberg and Schwartz (1983), Scott (1991), Mizruchi and Schwartz (1987), and Davis and Powell (1992). Although this stream of research has had its descriptive reviewers and commentators, it is only very recently that stronger critical attention has been given to assessing the additive outcomes of such work. Recent notable critical reviewers include Zajac (1988, 1992), Stinchcombe (1990), Davis (1992) and Davis and Powell (1992).

Central to the network approach is the view that interlocking boards of directors represent political and social as well as business ties. An interlocking directorship is said to exist when a particular individual sits on two or more corporate boards. Direct as well as indirect linkages may be included in the analysis. Indirect linkages exist where directors of firms A and B do not sit on each other's board, but are linked through joint membership of a third board. Zajac (1992, p. 13) argues that while the study of indirect links increases the number of ties that can be uncovered, this further aggregation of the network analysis merely adds to the systemic problems of assessing the significance of the wider set.

As Davis and Powell (1992) and others have argued, it is method rather than theory that unites the interlock research. Sonquist and Koenig (1975) describe the developments in graph theory and associated computational algorithms and programmes that have allowed the network researchers to isolate and identify linkages between corporations and other interest groups. Aside from this common methodological approach, one or two data-bases have been crucial in harnessing interest in the study of interlocking directorates. A notable driving force has been the database developed by Schwartz of the State University of New York, Stony Brook. Indeed the Stony Brook group of scholars (Schwartz, Mintz, Glasberg, Mizruchi and Palmer) have them-selves formed a crucial part of the academic network that has launched and perpetuated the interlocking directorates tradition of research.

But what are the consistent empirical findings to evolve from the network researchers? After very careful reading of nearly all of the original studies and personal conversations with a few of the key scholars, this writer finds it remarkably difficult to summarize the key patterns from these studies of interlocking directorates. Part of the reason for the difficulty in identifying unequivocal findings lies in the challenge made to earlier appar-ently conclusive results. For example, Zajac (1988) has used the 1969 Schwartz database to successfully question previous conclu-sions about collusive relationships between competing firms in the chemicals, primary metals and transportation equipment indus-tries. Re-analysing the same data set, but this time using a control group comparison, Zajac (1988, p. 436) is able to query earlier work by Dooley (1969) and Burt (1980), and contend that "inter-locking directorates among competing firms are not significant in number and probably not significant in meaning". However, an even bigger obstacle to pattern recognition in the findings derives from the widely different theoretical interpretations made from the interlock results.

Mizruchi's (1992) successful attempt to describe the natural history of development of the different theoretical interpretations and frameworks used to expose network findings leads him to attempt a synthesis of the inter-organizational and class theorists in what he describes as an inter-organizational model of class cohesion. But this Herculean effort of intellectual synthesis cannot paper over the cracks of the different intellectual traditions, or the inconsistent empirical findings.

The two most easily isolatable theoretical interpretations of interlocks data are the resource dependency and class theorists. Resource dependency approaches, for example, by Pfeffer and Salancik (1978), argue that interlocks are mechanisms designed to reduce the uncertainties created by the dependency relationships that develop between firms. Such links, although widespread, are normally seen as particular instrumental acts by one firm in relation to another, and do not represent class-wide based entities. The purpose of interlocks in this tradition may be to reduce uncertainty, effect cooptation or diffuse information.

Class-based theorists interpret interlocking directorates as evidence of linking between powerful elites into elite class networks (Zeitlin, 1974). Within this approach, bank control and financial hegemony theorists have studied the development of ties between industry and financial institutions, and see the allocation of capital through regional and national networks as evidence of class-based financial hegemony (Mintz and Schwartz, 1985). Useem (1984) takes this argument a stage further and uses a UK–US comparison to propose that the individuals who form the interlocks are an inner circle of the corporate elite who can represent that elite in societal-wide political processes. Later work summarized by Stokman, Scott and Ziegler (1985) and Scott (1991) uses international comparative data to note the striking variations in patterns of interlocks between different countries, and in particular how the centrality of banks differs from country to country. Thus British networks stood out for the low level of interlocking and a much less dense and weakly tied network than, for example, the US. The Stokman, Scott and Ziegler (1985) 10-country comparison also found a positive relationship between the profitability of firms and interlocking with banks, a finding not replicated from the US data. Correspondingly, highly indebted companies in Belgium and the Netherlands seemed less able to attract bankers, or network specialists (Stokman, Scott and Ziegler, 1985, p. 282). Some general tendencies found across all 10 countries were for the largest firms to be most interlocked, for regionally based and foreign owned firms to be less central in national networks, and for family owned companies, generally speaking, to be poorly interlocked compared with publicly owned enterprises.

Mizruchi and Schwartz (1987) conclude their review of resource dependency and class theorists by contending that the empirical predictions made by both approaches are often similar, since the dependency theorists acknowledge the existence of leadership discretion and, to varying degrees, the class theorists admit the possibility of the autonomous dynamics of corporate processes: "As a result much of the dispute between proponents of the two perspectives centres around divergent interpretations of the same data" (Mizruchi and Schwartz, 1987, p. 9).

A more recent stream of work on network ties seeks to go beyond the descriptive codification of interlocks, and tries to link the effects of networks on organizational structure, ideology and action (see Davis and Powell, 1992). Thus, Palmer, Jennings and Zhou (1989) found a link between the adoption of the multi divisional form by firms and their ties with previous adopters. The relationship between ties and innovation was also studied in a quite different domain by Davis (1991). He reports findings that larger firms were quicker to adopt a poison pill takeover defence to the extent that they were tied to prior adopters. These studies, along with research by Galaskiewicz and his colleagues on the impact of networks on charitable giving (Atkinson and Galaskiewicz (1988), and by Clawson, Neustadtl and Scott (1992) on the consequences of business networks for political party contributions, represent attempts to redirect this analysis of interlocking directorates away from the description and interpretation of structural anatomy to examine the more fundamental question of the consequences and effects of network relationships.

INTERLOCKING DIRECTORATES RESEARCH: A BRIEF CRITIQUE

Three broad areas of criticism can be directed towards the interlocking directorates research. The criticisms are themselves interlinked, but they can be disentangled and labelled as:

- The "so what" problem: what do interlocks really mean?
- The methodological problem of aggregation and randomness.
- Problems of inference and proof.

Of these three areas of criticism of interlock research the most fundamentally disabling is "that nobody really knows what they mean" (Mizruchi, 1984, p. 142). As Stinchcombe (1990, p. 380) penetratingly argues, this area of research is driven more by the allure of network methods and the ready availability of data than by substantive issues: "using a method that starts with a dichotomy of presence or absence as a descriptor of a link between corporations condemns us to the sterility of structural theory and irrelevance of the data ... the result is theoretical floundering in tables of data that seem to be mostly random numbers".

This strident criticism is echoed and amplified by Zajac (1992), Davis (1992) and Davis and Powell (1992). In Zajac's (1992) view, the very term "interlocking directorate" prejudges the issue of linkage. He would prefer to use the phrase "multiple-board membership" than interlocking directorate, since the former stops short at describing the phenomenon, while the more customary phrase is already interpreting it. Zajac (1992) wants to start with the basic question: does dual board membership actually serve a linkage function, and if so what function? The related criticism from Davis (1992) and Davis and Powell (1992) starts from the proposition that the network analysts' preoccupation with describing the structural anatomy of networks has not allowed them to adequately explore the consequences and effects of ties. While interlocks research serves a crucial theoretical function in countering atomistic approaches to the corporation, a vexing problem remains: "there is virtually no empirical evidence that particular interlock ties serve any discernible corporate purpose, or that the interlock network has any substantive impact on what corporations do" (Davis, 1992, p. 8).

Of course, doubts about the real purposes of interlocks are very much a function of the highly aggregated data sets used by the network scholars. As Zajac (1988) has argued, there is a need to disaggregate network data to examine precisely who is linked with whom. Adding indirect to direct links merely adds to problems of aggregation and ultimately creates further problems of inference and proof. Hirsch (1982) has been equally scathing of interlock studies iterating around competing models for which critical tests are not provided. The interlocks tradition illustrates "the costs entailed by allowing accessible data to serve as proxies and indicators for theoretical positions whose substantive likelihood and plausibility is increasingly ambiguous and difficult to articulate" (Hirsch, 1982, p. 3). A good example of the shifting and ambiguous character of the interpretation process in empirical research on interlocking directorates is provided by Useem's otherwise notable book, *The Inner Circle*. Thus, Useem (1984) wobbles between the view that the inner circle "can impose a class-wide logic on corporate decisions, and they often do" (1984, p. 116) and the view that "most corporate decisions are, of course, still largely a product of the internal logic of the firm" (1984, p. 146).

The above sharp criticisms invite a corresponding search for positive suggestions to redirect research on interlocking directorates and the structure of corporate power. Clearly, one important way forward is to move away from an exclusive concern with the structural analysis of networks and begin to analyse the purposes of networks and how and why key actors in the networks use links to achieve corporate, political or class-wide interests. In this approach, studies of networks in action, and of links between actions and processes and the achievements of outcomes, would take centre stage in the analysis. So the content of ties, their development and use, would become critical for analysis and not just the structure of ties in the network. As Stinchcombe (1990, p. 391) has so eloquently put it, "we need to know what flows across the links, who decides on those flows in the light of what interests, and what collective or corporate action flows from the organisation of the links, in order to make sense of intercorporate relations".

In a soundly argued paper, Zajac (1992) asserts that the label "interlocking directorates" has itself historically led researchers to assume that multiple board membership is a linkage mechanism. He contends that the study of multiple board membership should begin with the study of individual board membership motives, rather than the study of interlocks. Rather than asking as a lead question, what does multiple board membership represent, the starting questions should be, what does single and then multiple board membership represent? Such an approach might complement inter-organizational and intra-class views of network ties with "a personal advancement perspective" on multiple board representation. In Zajac's view (1992, p. 21), "personal prestige, monetary rewards, and friendship would be posited as significant factors in the decision to accept *and* extend offers of dual board membership".

But any redirection of interlocking directorates research surely needs to go beyond questions of personal motive. Central to any development should be the exploration of how, why and when networks of intercorporate relations affect corporate behaviour and outcomes. How are variations in the structure and conduct of elites decisive for major commercial, political and social outcomes? How are actual relationships of control, co-ordination, and power mobilized around concrete issues and events that are of importance to individual organizations, or sets of organizations in the same or different markets and sectors? It is studies of the actual exercise of corporate and societal power that are needed, and not just distant and highly aggregated analyses of the attribution of power.

Recent reviews of research patterns by Stokman, Scott and Ziegler (1985) and Scott (1991) indicate the analytical and empirical promise of the comparative analysis of intercorporate relations and interlocking directorates. As Scott (1991) argues, much US research has focused on the organization of business activity in relatively homogenous economic, cultural and political terms. However, European and Asian businesses show important differences in the pattern of intercorporate relations. Revealing such empirical differences has now stimulated a search for explanations of those variations. This in turn is drawing scholars to offer more contextualist explanations of the origins and trajectory of development of interlocking directorates across a variety of societies. An important benefit of this process is that historical and cultural factors, the structure of the state, kinship systems and processes of industrialization are now more explicitly being used to explain the fashioning of intercorporate relations both within and between societies (Fligstein, 1990; Hamilton and Biggart, 1988; Stokman, Scott and Ziegler, 1985).

None of the above conceptual and empirical developments is possible, however, without progress in complementing existing network research methods with other styles of research and other forms of data. All of the studies mentioned above on the motives for joining and extending offers to join boards, on the analysis of networks in action, and the varying trajectories of development of corporate relations and elites in different societies, require first-hand data much closer to the phenomenon than was envisaged by the structural analysts of network relations. Perhaps, as Davis and Powell (1992) assert, the primacy of method over substance in the study of interlocking directorates is now nearing its end and the close observation and analysis of actual relationships can begin to inform traditional social science concerns with interlocking directorates and the study of institutional and societal power.

THE STUDY OF BOARDS AND DIRECTORS

While the 1980s has witnessed a burgeoning of popular and scholarly interest in the contribution of top leaders to the fate of organizations (see Bryman, 1992 for a recent review), this preoccupation with charisma, vision, and transformation has not been complemented by equivalent scholarly concern with the study of boards and directors. Policy interest in boards is, of course, now very evident in the UK and the US as boards have been placed at the centre of a number of financial scandals involving major public companies and corporations (see Cadbury Report (1992) and Lorsch and MacIver (1989) for recent policy discussions of corporate governance matters). This policy interest, buttressed by the legal and financial requirements expected of boards, and the assumption that board effectiveness can contribute to corporate performance, has produced a constant stream of prescriptive writing about alternative ways of harnessing the productive potential of boards (Charkham, 1986; Loose and Yelland, 1987). Statements about the importance of boards in the business process are normally underpinned by a list of the critical board functions. Thus Cadbury (1990) summarizes board functions in these terms:

- to define the company's purpose.
- to agree the strategies and plans for achieving that purpose.
- to establish the company's policies.
- to appoint the chief executive and to review his performance and that of the top executives.
- in all this to be the driving force of the company.

Other writers (Pearce and Zahra, 1991) suggest that powerful boards provide useful business contacts, thus strengthening the link between corporations and their environments; that powerful boards are necessary to ensure the protection of shareholder interest; and, finally, that powerful boards play a crucial role in creating corporate identity, especially in the establishment and maintenance of a code of ethics.

Such apparently sensible statements of business intention and practice conceal the dearth of basic descriptive information on the composition, conduct and performance of boards and their directors. Tricker's (1978) observation that "the work of the director, in and out of the boardroom, is rated as the most under-researched management topic" is still ringingly true in 1992. The study of boards and their directors must rank near the top of any management scholar's list of priority areas for the 1990s.

Because research on boards and directors is still in its infancy, there are few theoretical, empirical or methodological guideposts to assist the optimistic yet wary researcher through the prescriptive minefield. What has been written from a descriptive and analytical viewpoint is fragmented and largely non-additive. Methodological difficulties in gaining access for behavioural or interview-based studies, or poor response rates from questionnaire-based studies, have also contributed to the patchy and often inconclusive findings on boards. The interlocks research tradition, reviewed in the previous section, still comprises a large proportion of the scholarly literature on boards.

Perhaps the most clearly stated theme in the prescriptive and descriptive writing about boards has to do with board composition. Typically, boards are composed of a combination of executive (inside) directors (who are also senior managers and include the chief executive) and non-executive (outside) directors, who are external to the day-to-day operation of the firm. From either of these two groups a chairperson of the board will also be chosen. Thus, although a board is composed of individuals, analysis and prescription tends to assume that boards can be subdivided into homogeneous, interest sharing groups. The ready availability of demographic data at least on gender, age, present functional or business responsibility, and, of course, number and proportion of inside to outside directors, has contributed to the range of studies linking board size and composition to variables such as performance (Baysinger and Butler, 1985; Hermalin and Weisbach, 1991; Pfeffer, 1972). However, inherent difficulties in separating out the multitude of endogenous and exogenous factors that influence company performance, make the assumed effects of board demographic characteristics on board effectiveness very difficult indeed to establish. The recently published work by Hermalin and Weisbach (1991), which could find no relationship between board composition and performance, provides a good instance of this general problem.

The issue of CEO duality, where the positions of chairperson and CEO are occupied by the same individual, has also attracted prescriptive and descriptive writing and research. Rechner and Dalton (1991) examined the financial implications of CEO duality (as opposed to the position of an independent chairperson) in terms of investment returns, equity returns and profitability over a six-year period. Their study concluded that firms opting for independent leadership consistently outperformed those relying on CEO duality.

Pearce and Zahra (1991) examine the relative power of CEOs and boards of directors and their association with board performance. Their study suggests that powerful, independent boards were associated with superior corporate financial performance. The study also provided loose support for the author's typology of four board types with different emphases on the power relationship between CEO and board member. One of their most interesting findings was that more powerful board types were viewed by the CEOs as being more progressive and more encouraging and supportive of CEO efforts, which in turn raised a question about the widespread belief that CEOs desire weaker boards that rubber stamp their decisions. Promising as this line of enquiry is, replication of the findings using different populations and measures is certainly necessary to give confidence to the stated results. Behavioural evidence of board processes is also necessary in this kind of study to counter the possible self-reporting biases of CEOs.

Stewart (1991) focuses not on this duality problem but on how a separate chairperson and chief executive interact. Her study of 20 general managers and their chairmen in the National Health Service (NHS) revealed the extent to which such senior roles are open to wide operational interpretation, and how different individuals come to different conclusions about their precise duties, and their relationship with the other. Perhaps because of the particular political and accountability issues in the NHS, the two roles were often seen as interdependent and complementary—indeed, as a partnership. This kind of detailed, longitudinal field-based study, examining from first-hand reports the balance of activities, interdependencies and choices between key figures in and around the board, is a very necessary complement to the more quantitative, correlational and empirically distant studies that suggest board composition, power and performance linkages.

Another tradition of research and writing on boards debates and analyses the Berle and Means (1932) thesis that although shareholders have legal ownership and control of large corporations, they no longer effectively control them. Although this area of research has been bedevilled by conceptual disagreements about the term "control" (Herman, 1981; Mizruchi, 1983) there is now a body of analytical work in this tradition. Mace (1971), in an oft-quoted study, concludes that the powers of control rest with the president, not the board. Herman (1981), in an extended and subtle analysis, argues that management (the CEO and inside directors) control the firm, but always in the context of the varying sets of constraints and latent powers of stakeholders such as the outside members of the board, shareholders and, at certain moments, creditors. Different studies using what Kosnik (1987) describes as the managerial hegemony theory offer different explanations of management's control over the board. The mixture often includes the management's control over the selection of outside board members and the latter's subsequent co-optation; the limited time outsiders have to devote to their duties; the superior expertise, information and advice available to management; and norms of board conduct which restrict the outsiders' abilities to operate as strident independent voices (Herman, 1981; Lorsch and MacIver, 1989; Mace, 1971).

As we have seen, there are a host of difficulties in the research attempting to link board composition to the overall financial performance of the firm. However, recently scholars within the managerial hegemony tradition have been attempting to study the slightly more confined link between board composition and board as distinct from company financial performance. Thus Kosnik (1987), using board decisions to pay greenmail (the repurchasing of its stock at a premium above market price), and Kesner and Johnson (1990), who focused on shareholder suits rather than greenmail as an indicator of board performance, have both attempted to link board composition to board performance.

In the Kosnik (1987) study, greenmail was assumed to be universally defined as against the interests of shareholders and thus indicative of board failure to fulfil its principal function of representing shareholder interests. It was further assumed that greenmail payments allowed poor company management to consolidate its control position when faced with a challenging raider. The study found that the board's effectiveness in preventing greenmail was increased when it was composed of relatively more outside directors, more outside directors with executive experience, and more outside directors with contractual interests in the company. Thus, according to the structure of Kosnik's investigation, board composition did have an effect on board performance.

The Kesner and Johnson (1990) research operated under the assumption that the more times shareholders pressed legal charges against their board, the less effective was the board at reflecting or representing shareholder interests. In this way they hoped to evaluate the effect that a predominance of outside directors had in representing shareholder interest. Their results indicated that boards sued tended to have a greater percentage of inside directors than those not sued, a relationship that was even stronger when the CEO also had the position of chairperson. Crucial also to their findings was the apparent fact that in actual rulings against the boards there was no difference in outcome for the differently composed boards. Thus the proportion of outside to inside director was not related to the company's "guilt" and therefore composition did not affect the degree to which shareholder's interests were represented by the board.

The use of archival data to derive indicators or surrogate measures of board composition and control is also evident in research on CEO "golden parachutes" and board "poison pill" (a form of takeover defence) adoption. Thus, research by Cochran, Wood and Jones (1985) and Singh and Harianto (1989) has found that greater outsider representation on the board is associated with a higher likelihood of having a golden parachute. However contrary to the hypothesis, Davis (1991) found that boards with more insiders were no more likely to adopt a poison pills takeover defence.

Methodologically adroit as the Kosnik (1987), Kesner and Johnson (1990) and Davis (1991) studies are in their clever use of surrogate measure from archival data, they cannot represent the only way forward for studies of boards of directors. All three studies utilize the crisis situations of takeover or litigation to study the performance of boards, when we perhaps also need data on the performance of boards in situations of relative normality. But these studies also suffer from their distance from the phenomenon they are addressing. As a result, great inferential leaps are made from input variables such as board composition to output variables such as board performance, with no direct evidence on the processes and mechanisms that presumably link the inputs to the outputs. The celebrated studies by Donaldson and Lorsch (1983) and Lorsch and MacIver (1989) get much closer to the actual operation of the strategic apex of the enterprise.

The Donaldson and Lorsch (1983) study draws on the analysis of 12 "mature successful industrial companies" from the upper half of the *Fortune 500* list to explore the decision making behaviour of corporate management (defined as the CEO and those who report directly to him). The corporate decision makers are portrayed as pursuers of corporate survival rather than share-holder wealth. The decision making process is characterized as one of great complexity and uncertainty, with beliefs and experi-ence performing crucial roles in filtering out ambiguity in the choice process: "Beliefs serve as uncertainty reducers and to provide continuity and stability when change threatens to under-mine the lessons of experience" (1983, p. 80). Like Herman (1981), Donaldson and Lorsch (1983) capture the constraints on top management choice. There is no pretence of the "senior corporate executive as a man who moves mountains with a memo" (1983, p. 172). Rather, top level decision making is constrained by a com-bination of industry sector pathways and standards, capital market restrictions, the need to attract and retain personnel to achieve rates of growth, and by the implicit belief systems of the executives themselves.

The Donaldson and Lorsch (1983) book provided fresh direct evidence on decision making at the top without dealing specifi-cally with the structure and dynamics of board operation. The study published in 1989 by Lorsch and MacIver responds to that gap. The Lorsch and MacIver research is exceptional not only in terms of the methodology employed, but also in the nature and quality of the empirical findings. The investigation covered the period 1986–1989 and involved a combination of large-scale questionnaire survey, interviewing and case study analysis. Although the response rate from the questionnaire survey of outside directors was a disappointing 32%, the authors claim that the respondents are representative of the underlying population from which they self-selected in terms of age, primary occupation, number of directorships held and the size of companies whose boards they are on.

If this had been the sole aspect of the method employed it would have been open to serious objection from what Mace (1971, p. 3) had earlier described as a director's "self serving and con-science-solving descriptive phrases of his own perception of his role as a responsible director". Consequently the second dimension of the Lorsch and MacIver methodology, the random selection of 100 directors to be interviewed for an hour or more, is significant. In all 80 were actually spoken to (roughly the same number as in the 1971 Mace study). The interviews were conducted throughout the US and in several European countries. The third and final element of the methodology involved interviews with 35 directors and other corporate officers relating to the book's four case studies of boards in crisis.

The Lorsch and MacIver (1989) book confirms the stream of work in the managerial hegemony tradition (exemplified by Herman, 1981 and Mace, 1971) that real power lies with the governed—that is, the top management team—and the success or failure of individual companies normally rests with them. The problem for the outside directors on the board is to translate their legal mandate into effective power over the top managers, especially the CEO. The Lorsch and MacIver case studies illustrate how this can be achievable in crisis situations such as takeover attempts, the death or incapacity or succession of CEOs, or legal, environmental or performance threats, but control relations are quite different in normal times. Lorsch and MacIver argue that gradual declines are a tremendous challenge to directors. Their study also suggests a need for future work on boards to examine processes of problem sensing, choice and change over longish periods of time.

The other strong feature of the Lorsch and MacIver (1989) study is their attempt to characterize directors and boards in operation. Although the Harvard study is still one stage removed from the direct observation of boards in action (for an example of this rare species of work, see Alderfer 1986), the findings of Lorsch and MacIver do add to the little that is known about how and why the norms of conduct on boards influence power relationships between outside and inside directors and the CEO.

THE STUDY OF BOARDS AND DIRECTORS: A BRIEF CRITIQUE

The above brief attempt to characterize existing research on boards and directors has emphasized its limited scale and scope. It is remarkably difficult to offer a thorough-going critique of a body of work that hardly exists. Indeed, one might argue that the issue at present is not one of critical reflection on what exists, but the open, positive encouragement of any serious social science research on the conduct and performance of boards and their directors.

At the early phases of the development of any field of research there is a requirement for certain basic descriptive information. Even given the apparent preoccupation with publicly available demographic data on board composition, and the useful contribution made by surveys conducted by, for example, the Bank of England (1985, 1988) and consultancy firms such as Korn/Ferry International (1992), there is still a need for further surveys of board member characteristics and boards structure, culture and process, linked to theoretical traditions such as managerial hegemony and agency theory (Davis, 1991; Fama and Jensen, 1982; Jensen and Meckling, 1976; Kosnik, 1987).

Studies of the locus of power in and around the boardroom are of crucial importance not only for theorists of intra-organizational power, but also to bridge with the interlocking directorate tradition, with its interest in the structure of elite power in different industrial societies. We still know remarkably little about the behaviour patterns and consequences of the CEO duality situation (where the roles of chairperson and CEO are held by the same person), or of any of the other crucial areas of relational dynamics in and around the board, for example between chairperson and CEO, CEO and outside and inside director, and inside and outside director. Indeed as Stewart (1991) and others have reminded us, we still have limited knowledge of the similarities and differences in what chairpersons, CEOs and directors actually do, and what motivates individuals to be invited, or to join boards.

Recent work by Murray, Bradshaw and Wolpin (1992), trying to establish typologies of patterns of board power and linking those patterns to board and organizational performance, illustrates the analytical value of typologies and classificatory systems at the early development of new research fields. But again, before tenuous links can be made between independent variables and dependent variables, perhaps we need to know more about the substance we are seeking to link with other phenomena. Alongside an interest in different patterns of board power, we need to know much more about the general conduct of board affairs, and how and why board processes impact on empirical patterns and theories of choice and change (Fennell and Alexander, 1989; Goodstein and Boecker, 1991; Pettigrew and Whipp, 1991).

The Pettigrew and Whipp (1991) study reminds us that the examination of choice and change processes cannot stop with the analysis of the strategic apex of the firm. Boardroom and other top influences are shaped not only by the activities of actors at other levels in and outside the firm, but also by a much broader range of contextual forces and processes emanating from economic, political and industry sector conditions. When (if) the ground-breaking work is done on board patterns of behaviour, including questions of control, choice and change, there will be a need in parallel or in sequence to link such analyses to the different settings and contexts in which boards operate, and ultimately to board level and firm level performance.

THE COMPOSITION AND CORRELATES OF TOP MANAGEMENT TEAMS

The social science literature on leadership is immense, as reviews by Stogdill (1974), Bass (1990) and others testifies. However, research on leadership in bureaucratic contexts is much less developed, and still contains a number of controversies, chief among which is whether, and to what extent, leaders make a difference to various kinds of organizational outcomes. Recent writing by, for example, Thomas (1988), Meindl (1990), House, Spangler and Woycke (1991) and Pettigrew and Whipp (1991) illustrates that the leadership impact debate is still very much alive. In 1984, partly as a response to the controversies around leadership studies, Hambrick and Mason published an important research agenda paper arguing that the strategic apex of firms contained more than individual leaders, and was it not time that scholars began to give more attention to top management teams? In so doing, Hambrick and Mason (1984) can justifiably claim to have created a relatively coherent stream of research with its own distinctive set of empirical findings. In this section, the aim is to describe this body of work, its assumptions and findings, and its strengths and weaknesses, then to suggest some complementary research themes and questions on the characteristics, conduct and performance of top management teams.

Hambrick and Mason (1984) describe their approach as the upper echelons perspective in macro-organizational research. The target group for study is the dominant coalition of the firm and their starting general proposition was that "organisational outcomes—both strategies and effectiveness—are viewed as reflections of the values and cognitive bases of powerful actors in the organisation" (1984, p. 193). Eschewing "some important but complex psychological issues", Hambrick and Mason (1984, p. 196) recommend that the primary emphasis be placed on observable managerial characteristics as indicators of the givens that a manager brings to an administrative situation: "These observable managerial givens are demographic factors such as age, tenure in the organisation, functional background, education, socioeconomic roots, and financial position".

Although the 1984 paper by Hambrick and Mason was already sensitive to problems of causality, disentangling intercorrelations and the need for time series data, and there was a special plea for clinical and statistical studies, in fact, the tradition that has emanated from the paper has largely been driven by cross-sectional studies using demographic data. Within this tradition, Hambrick and his students and colleagues have explored links between top team characteristics, managerial discretion and corporate strategies (Finkelstein and Hambrick, 1990; Michel and Hambrick, 1992) and top team characteristics and organizational bankruptcy (D'Aveni, 1990; Hambrick and D'Aveni, 1991). The Hambrick stimulus has also encouraged a stream of research suggesting that the integration and functioning of the top management team is at least partly affected by the demographic composition of the team (O'Reilly, Snyder and Boothe, 1993). This demographic research is now also broadening to include studies linking team characteristics to firm innovation (Bantel and Jackson, 1989), and the nature and extent of corporate strategic change, such as diversification level (Wiersema and Bantel, 1992). Another group of scholars seek to link director and top team characteristics to firm performance (Keck, 1991; Norburn, 1986; Norburn and Birley, 1988). Inconsistent findings, particularly in linking group demography to firm performance, and whether homogeneous or heterogeneous teams contribute to team and organizational success, have forced some rethinking of the theoretical interpretations given to findings, but not yet the wholescale questioning of this style of research.

Faced with inconsistent and contradictory findings about the homogeneity/heterogeneity top team and firm performance link, Priem (1990), in a conceptual paper, argues for a curvilinear relationship between the two. In Priem's view, performance is likely to suffer with extreme levels of homogeneity and heterogeneity. The appropriate degree of homogeneity and heterogeneity is predicted on how much variation exists in the firm's environment. In stable environments, more consensus is productive, while in dynamic conditions, more heterogeneity may be required. This attempt to contextualize theory development has led to a study by Keck (1991), which found that open teams lead to higher performance in turbulent contexts and stable teams lead to higher performance in non-turbulent contexts. More importantly, perhaps, as the former rather acontextual theorizing in this area is discarded, so scholars are beginning to examine the relationships, if any, between executive team context and executive team characteristics. In an important new study, Keck and Tushman (1991) are able to conclude from time series data from the US cement industry from 1900 to 1986, that within the firm, reorientation and CEO succession were both associated with significant changes into and out of the executive team, decreased team tenure and increased executive team heterogeneity. Interestingly, this study was also able to link different kinds of changes, internal and external to the firm, to different forms and degrees of impact on the top team. Thus, for example, technological jolts and non-retirement successions of the CEO were more frequently associated with significant changes in the senior team, decreased executive team tenure and increased team heterogeneity than changes driven by either legal and/or regulatory shifts.

The above brief characterization of the Hambrick-inspired research on top management teams can only give a flavour of what can be achieved by setting out an ambitious research agenda and then following through with a sustained set of empirical enquiries. Progress has been tied to a narrow focus and the rather singular use of demographic data, but the pattern of development has also been to add conceptual and analytical complexity. Control variables are now used more extensively than in the earlier input–output based work. Time series data is helping somewhat with problems of causal attribution. Early universalistic theorizing is being sharpened by the exploration of contextual variation, and notably in D'Aveni's work, there is an explicit attempt to link the top management team tradition both to the interlocking directorates research (D'Aveni, 1990) and to agency theory (D'Aveni and Kesner, 1991). However, if the top management team tradition is not to end up as another triumph of method over substance, new questions and methods need to emerge in order to complement and redirect this research.

TOP MANAGEMENT TEAMS: A BRIEF CRITIQUE AND SOME SUGGESTIONS

So dominated is the upper echelons perspective by demographic analysis that any assessment of its strengths and weaknesses must start there. It is probably no coincidence that a year before the Hambrick and Mason (1984) article appeared, an important review article on organizational demography was published by Pfeffer (1983). In this article Pfeffer defines what he means by organizational demography, and uses a range of examples to explore the largely untested and unfulfilled promise of demographic approaches. Thus "demography refers to the composition, in terms of basic attributes such as age, sex, educational level, length of service or residence, race and so forth of a social entity under study" (Pfeffer, 1983, p. 303). Demographic distributions are described as having a theoretical and empirical reality distinct from the aggregation of responses of individual members, and, crucially, are "readily measured and reasonably objective", certainly as compared with a range of "hypothetical unobservable constructs such as commitment, arousal, conflict, aspiration level, and so forth" (Pfeffer, 1983, p. 352). Demography is portrayed as an important causal variable that affects a number of intervening variables and processes and, through them, a number of organizational outcomes. Pfeffer illustrates the demographic characteristic (independent variable), intervening variable, and outcome variable linear-link by, for example, research on the length of service distribution of an organization, assumed intra-organizational conflict, and rates of turnover.

Pfeffer (1983) suggests that the promise in such an approach will be dependent on resolving a number of empirical and philosophy of science issues. Thus, empirically, to what extent does demography predict and explain variation in either the intervening construct (conflict) or the dependent variable (turnover)? But the bigger issue Pfeffer (1983, p. 351) describes as a matter of taste and philosophy of scientific explanation: "To what extent is it incumbent on the research to trace through a demographic effect on the various intervening constructs; or, to what extent can the postulating effect of demographic effect and a plausible mechanism be examined simply by investigating the empirical relationship between demography and what demography affects?" (Pfeffer, 1983, p. 351). Pfeffer answers his own question: "As soon as you say it is necessary to understand the intervening constructs or process, one inevitably embarks on an infinite regress of reductionism from which there is no logical escape" (Pfeffer, 1983, p. 352). In a carefully researched, and soundly argued article, Lawrence (1991) draws on a good deal of the organizational demography research since the Pfeffer article to present a contrary point of view.

The title of Lawrence's (1991) article, "The black box of organizational demography", makes clear her debate with Pfeffer and also the Achilles' heel of the top management team research. Basically, Lawrence challenges the demographers' assumption that the use of demographic variables as surrogates for intervening processes negates the need to study the intervening process and thereby actually test the links between the independent variable, intervening process and predicted outcome. Lawrence (1991) goes on to put forward a competing case that the black box (between the input and output variable) is populated by weak relationships between dependent variables and intervening constructs, by many intervening social psychological processes besides those assumed, and that perhaps the links between input and output variables are not linear and unidirectional, but dynamic and recursive. Demographic forms of analysis alone "move researchers further and further away, both empirically and theoretically, from the actual mechanisms underlying observed relationships" (Lawrence, 1991, p. 21) and without the direct, concrete analysis of the intervening mechanisms and processes, how indeed can the reasons for any empirical link between input and output variable be explained?

The more damning indictment of the demography-based top management team research is that no one has ever been anywhere near a top team in an organizational setting, either to directly observe a team in action, or to interview the members about the links between their characteristics and structure, processes of communication and decision making and their impact and performance. Recent studies, for example, by O'Reilly, Snyder and Boothe (1993), that have tried to go beyond archival data and demographic analysis have relied upon CEO reports of top team characteristics, structure and dynamics. Thus, enormous interpretative leaps are made from distant demographic surrogates of team characteristics such as homogeneity and heterogeneity, through unobserved and remote intervening processes such as information processing, conflict resolution and problem solving, to outcome variables such as team effectiveness or organizational performance. The result is a series of inconsistent and inconclusive findings, for example, about the relationship between homogeneity and heterogeneity and team effectiveness (see Keck, 1991; O'Reilly, Snyder and Boothe, 1993, for reviews) and continuous problems of disentangling cause and effect. Examples of the reverse causality problem include the question: do long tenure top teams lead to the persistence of business strategies or are the existence of persistent strategies a cause of long tenure teams? (Finkelstein and Hambrick, 1990). And do top teams embark on diversification strategies because of their team composition, or does the pursuit of diversification lead to the creation of certain kinds of top team competences and characteristics? (Michel and Hambrick, 1992).

A further difficulty with the top management team literature is the inconsistency in defining who the top team is. Flatt (1992) is absolutely right in arguing that this issue may be crucially determining the results and in so doing contributing to inconsistency in the empirical findings. Current variants of who is in the top team include those executives on the board (Finkelstein and Hambrick, 1990), the CEO and direct reports, O'Reilly, Snyder and Boothe, 1993) or the two highest executive levels (Wiersema and Bantel, 1992). But this issue cannot be resolved just by the arbitrary choice of titles or levels of management. Keck (1991) has argued that some players without titles may have a role in the team, and others with titles may be marginalized. There is also the deeper issue which warrants investigation: do all executives interact as teams? Such questions can only be answered by some combination of observation and interviewing of top teams in action, as has been demonstrated, for example, by Eisenhardt and Bourgeois (1988), Eisenhardt (1989).

Some of the lines of future research on top management teams have been signalled above. Within the top team demography tradition there is a need to treat team characteristics as a dependent variable: why do teams look the way they do? With this approach can emerge more refined theoretical and empirical work contextualizing the demographic characteristic, intervening process, outcome variable, linkages. But surely the real pay-off in future work will come from a parallel research stream on top teams which examines the structure, process and performance of top teams in action. How and why do teams emerge? How do particular constellations of complementary team assets build up, develop and dissolve in certain firms and industries at certain points in the firm's trajectory of development? What cliques and cabals emerge and how is power won and lost within the team as certain key issues are resolved? How do team interpretations of leadership behaviour match against previous assumptions about the heroic roles of CEOs? How do the task interdependencies within top teams and associated features of intra-team culture and power affect the control relationships between team members, the CEO and the board? Does the character and quality of the group process impact the capacity of the team to learn and change, and if so in what way, and why does team process affect team effectiveness and ultimately the competitive performance of the firm?

CONCLUSION

All three research areas reviewed in this chapter have their strengths and weaknesses. In different ways, using contrasting methods and levels of analysis, they have each contributed to the little we know about managerial elites. The distinctive methodological approach in the interlocks and top management team work has given those traditions greater intellectual coherence and impact than work on boards and directors. The more scattered, limited and prescriptive character of the boards work has produced a less easily identifiable set of theoretical and empirical achievements. By and large, all three areas of research have developed in isolation from one another. A case can certainly be made that incremental developments are possible within the logic and methods of all three areas of research. Progress is also possible, as D'Aveni (1990), Goodstein and Boeker (1991) and others have suggested, by linking some of the questions posed by the three approaches into more broadly based studies.

However, the conclusions of this chapter go beyond suggestions of incremental development within each of the traditions. With a few noteworthy exceptions, all three areas of research share the common limitation of studying managerial elites several paces from the actors, processes and issues facing those elites. Rarely can we see interlocking networks in action. We know little at first hand about why directors form ties across the boundaries of their own organization, to what purposes such ties are put, and what issues are created or resolved through such behaviour. Power relationships are attributed. Control relationships within and between social classes are inferred. The mobilization and use of power to achieve outcomes in line with perceived interests remain unobserved. In the top management team research, easily measurable demographic characteristics are used as surrogates for unobserved intervening processes, and inferential leaps are then made to a range of organizational outcomes. The existence of a top management team is assumed. No one sits close enough to the phenomenon to identify whether and to what extent the top team exists and through what processes the team fashions its impact. Tilting research on managerial elites towards processual studies of interlocking networks, boards and top management teams in action is surely no longer a "nice to have", but an essential.

In making the argument for process studies of managerial elites, there is no concomitant assumption being made that the three traditions reviewed here be replaced by this alternative one. Quite the contrary, the intellectual purpose is to complement, not replace. By tilting the study of managerial elites in a process direction, new answers may be possible to previously baffling questions, new questions will emerge not posed by prevailing approaches, and new forms of knowledge can arise to inform existing empirical patterns. Of course, it is beyond the ambitions of this chapter to specify in detail a range of detailed processual hypotheses on interlocking directorates and networks, boards and top management teams. In conclusion, this chapter suggests some broad areas and questions for empirical enquiry guided by a processual and contextual analysis of managerial elites.

Elsewhere this author has described a range of analytical requirements for studying processes in a contextualist manner (Pettigrew, 1985a,b, 1990, 1992). In summary, six requirements call for attention. These are:

1. Embeddedness: the study of processes across a number of levels of analysis.

2. Temporal interconnectedness: studying the processes in past, present and future time.
3. A role in explanation for context and action.
4. A search for holistic rather than linear explanations of process.
5. A need to link process analysis to the location and explanation of outcomes.
6. A need for the researcher to balance involvement and distance with actors in the research process.

Set against these requirements, existing research in the interlocking directorates and top management team traditions has little to offer the process analyst. Indeed, the logic of both approaches eschews any real concern for process questions. In each case inputs are measured—the structure of interlocking networks or the demographic characteristics of teams—and then inferences are made about the causal role of these independent variables on some dependent or outcome variables. The processes in between the input and outputs have a role in explanation but are not directly analysed or observed. Thus, the interlocks tradition is strong on describing the structural anatomy of director ties, but is largely silent on the observation of the emergence, use and impact of such linkages. It is not surprising that doubts remain about the meaning and significance of interlocking directorates.

Any attempt to redress this imbalance between structural and process analysis would entail the following lines of questioning:

• Why and how do interlocking ties emerge, consolidate and dissolve?
• What mixed motives are behind the offering and acceptance of multi-board membership?
• What flows across the interlinkages, shapes those flows and with what purpose and interests in mind?
• How are influence processes conducted in the network, and is it possible to unravel the place of influence processes from coordination, information giving and control?
• What, indeed, are the purposes of linkages, and do those purposes alter over time in the context of broad changes in the political, social, economic and commercial context of the firm?
• Are there "network stars" in any set of sectoral or national patterns of interlinkage?
• Who are these network stars?

- Do they share any common social class, educational, gender or professional characteristics?
- Are there common threads in the career of network stars, and how and why are they able to exert power in certain kinds of spheres but not others?
- If, as Bauer and Bertin-Mourot (1992) and Hamilton and Biggart (1988) have shown, there are differences in the structure and demographic characteristics of business elites in different societies, what explains these differences and what consequences do they have for the conduct of corporate affairs within and between societies?

Empirical enquiry guided by the above broad questions (and many others capable of development) will rapidly take the interlocks tradition on from the distant description of the structure of networks, to examine the substance, processes, consequences and impact of inter-organizational ties.

The black box in the top management team research contains the assumed but unobserved mediating processes that are purported to link demographic characteristics with organizational outcomes. More fundamentally, however, the black box also contains the essence of enquiry for the process scholar—the emergence, developments, conduct, impact and performance of the team itself. The actual close analysis and observation of the top team will at least help to clear up some of the intractable definitional problems of who the top team is, and whether and to what extent managers operate in groups or teams in processing strategic issues (Jackson, 1992). Rather than assuming titles and positions as indicators of involvement in choice and change processes, the first task for the process scholar is to identify which players are involved, and why. We still know little about why and how top teams and other groupings look the way they do, the processes by which top teams go about their tasks, how CEOs engage with their immediate subordinates, and how, why and when the upper echelons engage in fundamental processes of problem sensing, decision making, learning and change. The pessimists who consider that access is never forthcoming for such research might gain some confidence from progress made in recent studies by Eisenhardt (1989), Eisenhardt and Schoonhoven (1990) and Pettigrew and Whipp (1995).

Progress in our third area of research, the study of boards and their directors, has not been helped by over-ambitious attempts to link independent variables such as board composition to outcome variables such as board and firm performance. The research agenda here need not be guided just by studies testing the relative explanatory power of agency theory or theories of managerial hegemony. The task is perhaps a simpler one—to redress the overwhelmingly prescriptive bias in this literature, and to begin to provide some basic descriptive findings about boards and their directors. We need to know more about the structure and functioning of boards beyond customary preoccupations with size and composition. There are still few surveys of who external directors are, what motivates them to join boards and what they, CEOs and internal directors do. Very little is known of the relational dynamics in and around the boardroom, how relationships are formed and developed between the CEO and a separate chairman if one exists, how CEOs engage with their internal director colleagues on matters of substance, and how and why patterns of relationships between internal directors impact on their relations with external board members.

For the process scholar, however, the real fascination is with the actual operation of the board in and outside the boardroom. What is the extent of the involvement of the board in the strategy process, and how and why are they involved in different kinds of issues at various time periods in the organization's development and with what consequences? The exploration of board functioning and performance needs in the first instance to be linked to the specific concrete issues normally thought to be within the board's sphere of interest and influence. How are boards involved in processes of CEO and director selection and compensation? Who assesses the performance of the CEO, when and how? What board committees are created for what purposes, and how does information flow in and around these committees, the board, the CEO and individual directors? How are complementary assets of human resources on the board defined, created and dissolved around different eras of organization development when crises of performance and succession shake the credibility of cadres of external and internal directors? How does the mobilization and use of power in and around the board impact on the major choices and changes faced by the organization? And how and why are the powerful bolstered by linkages outside the firm and checked by non-elites inside the firm? Sustained attention to these empirical questions, informed by existing theoretical advances in decision making, change and power in and between firms, will advance our knowledge of the conduct of managerial elites in organizations.

ACKNOWLEDGEMENT

I am grateful to Matthew Pettigrew for his assistance in compiling elements of the literature for this chapter.

REFERENCES

Alderfer, C.P. (1986). The invisible director on corporate boards. *Harvard Business Review* November/December, 2–8.

Atkinson, L. and Galaskiewicz, J. (1988). Stock ownership and company contributions to charity. *Administrative Science Quarterly* **30**, 224–241.

Auletta, K. (1991). *Three Blind Mice: How the TV Networks Lost their Way*. New York: Random House.

Bank of England (1985). The boards of quoted companies. *Bank of England Quarterly* June, 233–236.

Bank of England (1988). Composition of company boards. *Bank of England Quarterly Bulletin* May, 242.

Bantel, J.A. and Jackson, S.E. (1989). Top management and innovation in banking: Does the composition of the top team make a difference? *Strategic Management Journal* **10**, 107–124.

Bass, M.M. (1990). *Bass and Stogdill's Handbook of Leadership: Theory, Research and Managerial Applications* (3rd Edn). New York: Free Press.

Bauer, M. and Bertin-Mourot, B. (1992). *Les 200 en France et Allemagne*. Paris: CNRS and Heidrich and Struggles.

Baysinger, B.D. and Butler, H.D. (1985). Corporate governance and the board of directors: Performance effects of changes in board composition. *Journal of Law, Economics and Organisation* **1**, 101–124.

Berle, A.A. and Means, G.C. (1932). *The Modern Corporation and Private Property*. New York: Macmillan.

Bradshaw, P., Murray, V. and Wolpin, J. (1992). Do non-profit boards make a difference? An exploration of the relationship between board structure, process and effectiveness, unpublished paper, Faculty of Administrative Studies, York University, Ontario, April.

Bryman, A. (1992). *Charisma and Leadership in Organisations*. London: Sage.

Burt, R. (1980). Cooptive corporate actor networks: A reconsideration of interlocking directorates involving American manufacturing. *Administrative Science Quarterly* **25**, 557–582.

Burt, R. (1983). *Corporate Profits and Cooptation*. New York: Academic Press.

Cadbury, Sir Adrian (1990). *The Company Chairman*. London: Director Books.

Cadbury Report (1992). Draft report, issued by the committee on the financial aspects of corporate governance, Moorgate, London, July.

Charkham, J.P. (1986). Effective Boards. London: Chartac.

Clawson, D., Neustadtl, A. and Scott, D. (1992). Money Talks: Corporate Pace and Political Influence. New York: Basic Books.

Cochran, P.L., Wood, R.A. and Jones, T.B. (1985). The composition of boards of directors and the incidence of golden parachutes. Academy of Management Journal 28, 664–671.

D'Aveni, R.A. (1990). Top managerial prestige and organisational bankruptcy. Organization Science 1(2), 121–142.

D'Aveni, R.A. and Kesner, I.F. (1991). Top managerial prestige, power and tender offers: A study of elite social networks and target firm cooperation during takeovers, unpublished paper, Amos Tuck School, Dartmouth College, Hanover, NH.

Davis, G.F. (1991). Agents without principles? The spread of the poison pill through the intercorporate network. Administrative Science Quarterly 36, 583–613.

Davis, G.F. (1992). The interlock network as a self-reproducing social structure, unpublished paper, Kellogg Graduate School of Management, Northwestern University.

Davis, G.F. and Powell, W.W. (1992). Organization–environment relations. In M. Dunnette (Ed.), Handbook of Industrial and Organizational Psychology. Palo Alto, CA: Consulting Psychologists Press.

Donaldson, G. and Lorsch, J. (1983). Decision Making at the Top: The Shaping of Strategic Direction. New York: Basic Books.

Dooley, P. (1969). The interlocking directorate. American Economic Review 59, 314–323.

Eisenhardt, K.M. (1989). Making fast strategic decisions in high velocity environments. Academy of Management Journal 33(3), 543–576.

Eisenhardt, K.M. and Bourgeois, L.J. (1988). Politics of strategic decision making in high velocity environments: Toward a midrange theory. Academy of Management Journal 31(4), 737–770.

Eisenhardt, K.M. and Schoonhoven, C.B. (1990). Organisational growth: Linking founding team, strategy, environment and growth and US semi conductor ventures, 1978–88. Administrative Science Quarterly 35, 504–529.

Fama, E.F. and Jensen, M.C. (1982). Separation of ownership and control. Journal of Law and Economics 26, 327–349.

Fennell, M.L. and Alexander, J.A. (1989). Governing boards and profound organizational change in hospitals. Medical Care Review 46(2), 157–187.

Field, G.W. and Higley, J. (1980). Elitism. London: Routledge.

Finkelstein, S. and Hambrick, D. (1990). Top management–team tenure and organizational outcomes: The moderating work of managerial discretion. Administrative Science Quarterly 35, 484–503.

Flatt, S. (1992). A longitudinal study in organisational innovativeness: How top team demography influences organisational innovation, PhD dissertation, University of California, Berkeley.

Fligstein, N. (1990). The Transformation of Corporate Control. Cambridge, MA: Harvard University Press.

Gabarro, J.J. (1987). The Dynamics of Taking Charge. Boston, MA: Harvard Business School Press.

Galaskiewicz, J. (1985). Social Organization of an Urban Grants Economy. Orlando, FL: Academic Press.

Gersick, C.J.G. (1988). Time and transition in work teams: Towards a new model of group development. *Academy of Management Journal* **31**(1), 9–41.

Giddens, A. (1974). Elites in the British class structure. In P. Stanworth and A. Giddens (Eds) *Elites and Power in British Society*. Cambridge: Cambridge University Press.

Glasberg, D.S. and Schwartz, M. (1983). Ownership and control of corporations. *Annual Review of Sociology* **9**, 311–332.

Goodstein, J. and Boeker, W. (1991). Turbulence at the top: A new perspective of governance structure changes and strategic change. *Academy of Management Journal* **34**(2), 306–330.

Granovetter, M. (1985). Economic action and social structure: The problem of embeddedness. *American Journal of Sociology* **91**, 481–510.

Hambrick, D.C. and D'Aveni, P.A. (1991). Top team deterioration as part of the downward spiral of large corporate bankruptcies, unpublished paper, Columbia Business School, September.

Hambrick, D.C. and Mason, P.A. (1984). Upper echelons: The organization as a reflection of its top managers. *Academy of Management Review* **9**(2), 193–206.

Hamilton, G.G. and Biggart, N.W. (1988). Market, culture and authority; A comparative analysis of management and organization. *American Journal of Sociology* **94**, 552–594.

Hermalin, B.E. and Weisbach, M.S. (1991). The effects of board composition and direct incentives on firm performance. *Financial Management* **20**(4), 101–112.

Herman, E.S. (1981). *Corporate Control, Corporate Power*. New York: Cambridge University Press.

Hirsch, P.M. (1982). Network data versus personal accounts: The normative culture of interlocking directorates, unpublished paper, Graduate School of Business, University of Chicago.

House, R.J., Spangler, W.D. and Woycke, J. (1991). Personality and charisma in the US presidency: A psychological theory of leader effectiveness. *Administrative Science Quarterly* **36**, 364–396.

Jackson, S.E. (1992). Consequences of group composition for the interpersonal dynamics of strategic issue processing. In P. Shrivastava, A. Huff and J Dutton (Eds) *Advances in Strategic Management* (Vol. 8). Greenwich, CT: JAI Press.

Jensen, M.C. and Meckling, W.H. (1976). Theory of the firm: Managerial behaviour, agency costs and ownership structure. *Journal of Financial Economics* **3**, 305–360.

Johnson, G. (1987). *Strategic Change and the Management Process*. Oxford: Basil Blackwell.

Kahl, J. (1957). *The American Class Structure*. New York: Rinehart.

Keck, S.L. (1991). Top executive team structure: Does it matter anyway? unpublished paper, School of Business, Texas A&M University.

Keck, S.L. and Tushman, M. (1991). Environmental and organizational context and executive team characteristics, unpublished paper, School of Business, Texas A&M University.

Kesner, I.F. and Johnson, R.B. (1990). An investigation of the relationship between board composition and stockholder suit. *Strategic Management Journal* **11**, 327–336.

Kimberly, J.R. and Zajac, E.J. (1988). The dynamics of CEO/board relations. In D.C. Hambrick (Ed.) *The Executive Effect: Concepts and Methods for Studying Top Managers*. Greenwich, CT: JAI Press.

Korn/Ferry International (1992). *Boards of Directors Study UK 1992*. London: Korn Ferry.

Kosnik, R.D. (1987). Greenmail: A study of board performance in corporate governance. *Administrative Science Quarterly* 32, 163–185.

Lawrence, B.S. (1991). The black box of organizational demography, unpublished paper, Anderson Graduate School of Management, UCLA, April.

Loose, P. and Yelland, J. (1987). *The Company Director: His Functions, Powers and Duties*. Bristol: Jordan & Sons.

Lorsch, J.W. and MacIver, E. (1989). *Pawns and Potentates: The Reality of America's Corporate Boards*. Boston, MA: Harvard Business School Press.

Mace, M. (1971). *Directors: Myth and Reality*. Cambridge, MA: Harvard University Press.

Mechanic, D. (1964). Sources of power of lower participants in complex organizations. *Administrative Science Quarterly* 7(3), 349–364.

Meindl, R.R. (1990). On leadership: An alternative to the conventional wisdom. In B. Staw and L. Cummings (Eds) *Research in Organizational Behaviour* (Vol. 12, pp. 159–203). Greenwich, CT: JAI Press.

Michel, J.G. and Hambrick, D.C. (1992). Diversification posture and top management team characteristics. *Academy of Management Journal* 35(1), 9–37.

Mintz, B. and Schwartz, M. (1985). *The Power Structure of American Business*. Chicago, IL: Chicago University Press.

Mizruchi, M.S. (1984). Who controls whom? An examination of the relations between management and board directors in large American corporations. *Academy of Management Review* 8, 426–435.

Mizruchi, M.S. (1992).*The Structure of Corporate Political Action: Interfirm Relations and their Consequences*. Boston, MA: Harvard University Press.

Mizruchi, M.S. and Schwartz, M. (Eds) (1987). *Intercorporate Relations: The Structural Analysis of Business*. New York: Cambridge University Press.

Murray, V., Bradshaw, P. and Wolpin, J. (1992). Power in and around non-profit boards, unpublished paper, Faculty of Administrative Studies, York University, Ontario.

Norburn, D. (1986). GoGo's, YoYo's and Dodo's: Company directors and industry performance. *Strategic Management Journal* 7, 101–117.

Norburn, D. (1989). The chief executive: A breed apart? *Strategic Management Journal* 10, 1–15.

Norburn, D. and Birley, S. (1988). The top management team and corporate performance. *Strategic Management Journal* 9, 225–237.

O'Reilly, C.A. III, Snyder, R.C. and Boothe, J.N. (1993). Executive team demography and organizational change. In G. Huber and W. Glick (Eds) *Organizational Design and Change*. New York: Oxford University Press.

Pahl, R.E. and Winkler, J.T. (1974). The economic elite: Theory and practice. In P.J. Stanworth and A. Giddens (Eds) *Elites and Power in British Society*. Cambridge: Cambridge University Press.

Palmer, D. (1983). Broken ties: Interlocking directorates and intercorporate co-ordination. *Administrative Science Quarterly* 28, 40–55.

Palmer, D., Jennings, P.D. and Zhou, X. (1989). Growth strategies and institutional prescriptions: Adoption of the multi-divisional form by large US corporations, 1963–1968, Paper presented to the American Sociological Association, annual meeting.

Pearce, J.A. and Zahra, S.A. (1991). The relative power of CEOs and boards of directors: Association with corporate performance. *Strategic Management Journal* 12(2), 135–153.

Pettigrew, A.M. (1973). *The Politics of Organisational Decision Making*. London: Tavistock.

Pettigrew, A.M. (1985a). *The Awakening Giant: Continuity and Change in ICI*. Oxford: Basil Blackwell.

Pettigrew, A.M. (1985b). Contextualist research: A natural way to link theory and practice. In E.E. Lawler (Ed.) *Doing Research that is Useful in Theory and Practice*. San Francisco, CA: Jossey Bass.

Pettigrew, A.M. (1990). Longitudinal field research on change: Theory and practice. *Organizational Science* 1(3), 267–292.

Pettigrew, A.M. (1992). The character and significance of strategy process research. *Strategic Management Journal* 13. Special edition, Winter.

Pettigrew, A.M. and Whipp, R. (1995). *Managing Change for Competitive Success*. Oxford: Basil Blackwell.

Pettigrew, A.M. and McNulty, T. (1995). Power and influence in and around the boardroom. *Human Relations*, 48, special edition on corporate governance, July–September.

Pettigrew, M.A. (1992). Boards of directors: A review of recent research, working paper, Centre for Corporate Strategy and Change, University of Warwick, July.

Pfeffer, J. (1972). Size and composition of corporate boards of directors: The organization and its environment. *Administrative Science Quarterly* 17, 218–228.

Pfeffer, J. (1983). Organizational demography. In B. Staw and L. Cummings (Eds) *Research in Organizational Behaviour* (Vol. 5, pp. 299–357). Greenwich, CT: JAI Press.

Pfeffer, J. and Salancik, G. (1978). *The External Control of Organizations: A Resource Dependence Perspective*. New York: Harper & Row.

Priem, R.L. (1990). Top management team group factors, consensus, and firm performance. *Strategic Management Journal* 11(6), 469–478.

Rechner, P.L. and Dalton, D.R. (1991). CEO duality and organizational performance: A longitudinal analysis. *Strategic Management Journal* 12, 155–165.

Scott, J. (1991). Networks of corporate power: A comparative assessment. *Annual Review of Sociology* 17, 181–203.

Singh, H. and Harianto, F. (1989). Management–board relationships, takeover risk, and the adoption of golden parachutes. *Academy of Management Journal* 32, 7–24.

Smith, C., Child, J. and Rowlinson, M. (1991). *Reshaping Work: The Cadbury Experience*. Cambridge: Cambridge University Press.

Sonquist, J.A. and Koenig, T. (1975). Interlocking directorates in the top USA corporations: A graph theory approach. *The Insurgent Sociologist* 5, 196–229.

Stewart, R. (1991). Chairmen and chief executives: An exploration of their relationship. *Journal of Management Studies* 28(5), 511–527.

Stinchcombe, A.L. (1990). Weak structural data, a review of intercorporate relations, by M.S. Mizrucki and M. Schwartz (Eds). *Contemporary Sociology* **19**, 380–382.

Stogdill, R.M. (1974). *Handbook of Leadership: A Survey and Research*. New York: Free Press.

Stokman, F.N., Scott, J.P. and Ziegler, R. (Eds) (1985). *Networks of Corporate Power*. Cambridge, MA: Polity Press.

Thomas, A.B. (1988). Does leadership make a difference to organizational performance? *Administrative Science Quarterly* **33**, 388–400.

Tricker, R.I. (1978). *The Independent Director: A Study of the Non-Executive Director and of the Audit Committee*. Croydon: Tolley.

Useem, M. (1984). *The Inner Circle*. New York: Oxford University Press.

Useem, M. (1991). Organisational and managerial factors in the shaping of corporate social and political action. In *Research in Corporate Social Performance and Policy* (Vol. 12, pp. 63–92). Greenwich, CT: JAI Press.

Vancil, R.F. (1987). *Passing the Baton: Managing the Process of CEO Succession*. Boston, MA: Harvard Business School Press.

Whitt, J.A. (1982). *Urban Elites and Mass Transportation*. Princeton, NJ: Princeton University Press.

Wiersema, M.F. and Bantel, K.A. (1992). Top management team demography and corporate strategy change. *Academy of Management Journal* **35**(1), 91–121.

Wilson, C.S. and Lupton, T. (1959). The bank rate tribunal: The social background and connections of top decision makers. *Manchester School of Social and Economic Studies* **27**, 30–51.

Zajac, E.J. (1988). Interlocking directorates as an interorganizational strategy: A test of critical assumptions. *Academy of Management Journal* **31**, 428–438.

Zajac, E.J. (1990). CEO selection, succession, compensation and firm performance: A theoretical synthesis and empirical analysis. *Strategic Management Journal* **11**, 217–230.

Zajac, E.J. (1992). Interlocking directorates research and the study of boards of directors, unpublished paper, Kellogg School of Management, Northwestern University, Evanston.

Zeitlin, M. (1974). Corporate ownership and control: The large corporation and the capitalist class. *American Journal of Sociology* **79**, 1073–1119.

Index

Note: Page references in *italics* refer to Figures; those in **bold** refer to **Tables**

Index compiled by Annette Musker